The Politics of Judicial Independence

The Politics of Judicial Independence

Courts, Politics, and the Public

EDITED BY **Bruce Peabody**

The Johns Hopkins University Press | *Baltimore*

© 2011 The Johns Hopkins University Press.
© Scott E. Gant, chapter 9, "Self-Regulation and an Independent Judiciary"
All rights reserved. Published 2011
Printed in the United States of America on acid-free paper

9 8 7 6 5 4 3 2 1

The Johns Hopkins University Press
2715 North Charles Street
Baltimore, Maryland 21218-4363
www.press.jhu.edu

Library of Congress Cataloging-in-Publication Data

The politics of judicial independence : courts, politics, and the public /
edited by Bruce Peabody.
    p. cm.
   Includes bibliographical references and index.
   ISBN-13: 978-0-8018-9771-9 (hardcover : alk. paper)
   ISBN-10: 0-8018-9771-8 (hardcover : alk. paper)
   ISBN-13: 978-0-8018-9772-6 (pbk. : alk. paper)
   ISBN-10: 0-8018-9772-6 (pbk. : alk. paper)
   1. Judges—United States. 2. Judicial independence—United States.
3. Judicial process—United States. 4. Judicial power—United States.
I. Peabody, Bruce Garen, 1969–
   KF8775.P655 2010
   347.73'14—dc22   2010013269

A catalog record for this book is available from the British Library.

*Special discounts are available for bulk purchases of this book. For more informa-
tion, please contact Special Sales at 410-516-6936 or specialsales@press.jhu.edu.*

The Johns Hopkins University Press uses environmentally friendly book ma-
terials, including recycled text paper that is composed of at least 30 percent
post-consumer waste, whenever possible. All of our book papers are acid-free,
and our jackets and covers are printed on paper with recycled content.

Contents

Foreword, by H. Thomas Wells Jr.   vii

Acknowledgments   ix

Introduction
Bruce Peabody   1

1   The Choreography of Courts-Congress Conflicts
    Charles Geyh   19

2   Congress and Judicial Supremacy
    Neal Devins   45

3   Presidential Manipulations of Judicial Power
    Stephen M. Engel   68

4   Institutional Interdependence and the Separation of Powers
    J. Mitchell Pickerill   100

5   The Public and Judicial Independence
    Tom S. Clark   123

6   Judicial Elections and Public Perception of the Courts
    Matthew J. Streb   147

7   Conflicts with Courts in Common Law Nations
    Jason Pierce   168

8   The Siege on the Israeli Supreme Court
    Maya Sabatello   192

9   Self-Regulation and an Independent Judiciary
    Scott E. Gant   213

10   Judicial Credibility
     Louis Fisher   227

     Conclusion
     Bruce Peabody   249

     Appendix: Timeline of Important Events, 1968–2010   255
     List of Contributors   259
     Notes   261
     Index   321

Foreword

Because of my strong and long-held belief that the American judicial system was in danger of losing some of its institutional and decisional independence from a variety of threats, "judicial independence" became a centerpiece of my tenure as president of the American Bar Association from 2008–2009. Indeed, during my run-up year as president-elect of the ABA, I conducted what was essentially a listening tour of the United States legal community. During that time, bar associations and bar leaders, lawyers, judges, and litigants from all across the country spoke to me about their concerns with their own court systems. What they said struck me initially as disparate and unconnected, but as I reflected further, their concerns coalesced into a conviction that, in one way or another, judicial independence was being threatened.

These perceived threats included some well-known ones, such as the high-dollar, highly politicized electoral races for seats in those states that elect judges, including my own home state of Alabama. But other threats were more insidious and subtle. These ranged from ballot initiative attempts in Colorado to impose severe term limits on judges to "national rankings" of court systems that seemed primarily based on disagreement with the results of judicial rulings to inadequate funding of the third, supposedly co-equal branch of government.

The Politics of Judicial Independence recognizes what was related to me by many sources during my years as president-elect and president of the ABA —that we are at an important era for American judicial systems, in which courts and judges face an extraordinarily hostile political situation. It also recognizes what some defenders of judicial independence deny—that politics always plays a role in judicial systems. In many speeches as ABA president, I often utilized the imagery of a boiling pot as an analogy for thinking about critiques of our courts. So long as the heat is controlled, the pot will not boil over; however, if the heat is too high, the contents may well be lost to the atmosphere. So it is with politics and judicial independence. We must ensure that the heat, which is always present, does not boil off the important contents of our legal system. After all, what we aspire to is a judiciary that is perceived as fair and impartial, not unduly influenced by political pressures, campaign contributions, or tightening budgetary purse strings. This book helps us move toward these goals by unflinchingly examining what we really mean by judicial independence and by recognizing that politics inevitably plays a role in both endangering this independence and, ultimately, preserving it.

H. Thomas Wells Jr.

Acknowledgments

One of the truisms about scholarship is that it is often a solitary activity. My research experiences, however, have invariably involved sharing, collaborating, and drawing on the talents of established colleagues while developing new professional relationships. This story has certainly played out in this book. I am grateful to the contributors of this volume for their intellect, insight, selflessness, and openness to my ideas about their work. I thank the authors for their commitment to this project and the excellent work they have shared with me and now share with other readers.

My gratitude also extends to my colleagues in the Department of Social Sciences and History whose good humor, congeniality, and commitment to scholarly pursuits have been reassuringly fixed points of the compass. The Becton College Dean's office awarded me with "grant in aid" funds for this book, facilitating my work with my outstanding and unflappable research assistants: Shavonne Bailey, Diana Davino, Zach Feldman, Kyle Morgan, and Heather Suboleski. The staff at the College at Florham Library and the Ridgewood Public Library provided assistance with a variety of research requests ranging from the banal to the obscure. Henry Tom and Suzanne Flinchbaugh at the Johns Hopkins University Press have been supportive and patient at each stage of the publishing process. Henry's suggestions improved the quality of this book enormously, as did the comments of an anonymous reader in reviewing a draft manuscript and the industry and care of copyeditor Martin Schneider.

Finally, I wish to thank my family and friends for their sustaining mix of encouragement, enthusiasm, and tolerance as this book has unfolded— especially Stephanie, Isaac, Violet, and Mouse.

The Politics of Judicial Independence

Introduction

Bruce Peabody

This is a book about the contemporary politics of judicial independence, that is, the conditions under which our celebrated commitment to autonomous courts and judges might be compromised in today's political environment. In exploring this theme, this introduction and the chapters that follow focus on criticisms of the judiciary over the past forty years and the threats these criticisms pose to judges' distinctive functions and, by extension, our constitutional system as a whole.

Since the ratification of the Constitution, politicians, citizens, and a wide range of scholarly and popular commentators have praised the American court system and its reliance on judges who are free from the direct influence of the "coordinate branches" of government and the vagaries of public passions and opinions. At the same time, these voices have frequently fretted about perceived dangers to American courts, ranging from proposed laws seeking to curtail the judiciary's powers and privileges to popular movements seeking to impeach and remove judges to presidential calls to undo controversial rulings.

This book examines whether prominent recent criticisms of courts pose significant problems for American politics and law, especially by making it harder for courts to fulfill roles and perform functions we have come to rely upon or at least expect. Should we be troubled about contemporary complaints about courts generated by politicians, interest groups, and even judges themselves?

Relevant Scholarship

There is, of course, scholarship and other work pertinent to this question. To begin with, there is a vast, complex, and important literature examining the relationships between courts and elected officials and the conditions under which politicians, interest groups, and the public can direct, influence, temper, and even neutralize judicial authority and judgments. This book draws on and contributes to these debates as part of its exploration of judicial independence and the critiques of courts.

A second, related set of research has focused more directly on various aspects of judicial independence: how we should define it, what its purposes are, and how a judiciary becomes compromised by political and electoral forces. While relevant to this volume, much of the judicial independence literature focuses on nations outside of the United States and is generally courts-centered, that is, it examines the topic using the perspectives and concerns of courts and court advocates. This book attempts to move beyond this emphasis.

A third and final body of pertinent research considers the seriousness, validity, and merits of different criticisms leveled against the contemporary judicial system, like the charge that certain judges are "activist." In general, these writings employ one of two distinctive analytic approaches, sometimes in complementary fashion. Much of this work uses legal arguments, examples, and interpretation to defend, refute, or qualify a variety of critiques brought against the judiciary and to explore the conditions under which sanctions against courts might be legally permissible. Other work in this area is more empirical, probing for the underlying factors likely to induce criticism of courts or spur attempted limitations on judicial power. A subset of these studies evaluates the validity of particular assertions about certain objectionable behaviors, such as judging on ideological rather than legal grounds. But this work tends to focus on the nature, meaning, and accuracy of various criticisms of courts, rather than thinking through their implications for judicial independence and constitutional government generally.

New Orientation Points

An Important Moment?

The Politics of Judicial Independence draws on this literature but also attempts to advance existing scholarship by assuming two distinctive perspectives. First, this book presumes that we are at an important moment for court systems, both in the United States and throughout the world. Since the 1980s, American courts have become more Republican and conservative, especially at the federal level. Today, ten out of the thirteen federal circuits are majority Republican-appointed. Even with President Barack Obama's nomination of two justices to the U.S. Supreme Court, a majority of the Court has been selected by Republican presidents. At the same time, scrutiny of the courts from both the left and the right is intense, especially given the close division of the judiciary on important subjects (such as gay rights, affirmative action, civil rights, civil liberties, and anti-terrorism) and heightened public interest in specific court decisions at all levels.

Internationally, a number of nations striving to build autonomous and effective court systems are experiencing political and sometimes physical battles over these issues. Even in countries with more established traditions of judicial independence, changes in the political priorities and agendas of these nations have frequently induced passionate critiques of judges abroad. While this project primarily considers the U.S. judiciary, many of its arguments and claims pertain to courts overseas.

Our contemporary politics, therefore, are likely to remain preoccupied with the problem of how much power and independence to cede to courts. In turn, this book's investigation of contemporary critiques of courts presumes that these attacks are, at a minimum, politically significant and part of a milieu of heightened judicial scrutiny that is unlikely to disappear.

Revisiting Judicial Independence

A second major orientation point for this book is based on expanding our traditional ways of talking about judicial independence in order to evaluate better whether contemporary critiques of courts and judges are problematic or even historically unusual.

Some of the citizens, judges, and academicians who are most opposed to criticisms of courts make unrealistic assumptions about the judiciary's removal from American politics and depict it as an institution capable of acting in isolation. A countervailing theme running throughout this book is that our conversations and claims about judicial independence need to be placed in political context. More specifically, we cannot identify potentially dangerous political influences on the courts without appreciating the many ways that elected officials, interest groups, and the public already communicate with and shape judicial decisions and policy implementation. On the other side, we should not condemn or dismiss criticisms of judges and courts without trying to understand in a sympathetic way the motivations that undergird the behavior of legislators, presidents, and other officials.

A New Climate of Criticism? Evidence and Initial Discussion

The judiciary has been the target of elected officials, interest groups, and the broader public since before the ratification of the Constitution. The Anti-Federalist Brutus famously warned about the "immense powers" of the Supreme Court and its lack of accountability to "every power under heaven." In the early eighteenth century, Thomas Jefferson and his political allies went after not only Chief Justice John Marshall but also other federal judges, most famously by impeaching (although not successfully removing) Supreme Court Justice Samuel Chase.

Congress, too, has been a recurring, active, and sometimes effective agent in checking the federal courts, regularly proposing constitutional amendments to counter individual decisions of the courts or otherwise seeking to limit judicial power. The Eleventh, Fourteenth, Sixteenth, and Twenty-Sixth amendments to the Constitution all overturned Supreme Court decisions and changed how courts approach significant legal issues. Larry Kramer and Barry Friedman, among other scholars, have also recently offered extended and vivid accounts of the nearly continuous tradition in U.S. politics of "popular constitutionalism" and democratic resistance to individual court judgments and the judiciary's broader impact on policy and politics.

Critiques since 1948: Two Views

Nevertheless, recent decades have seen a significant change in the frequency and intensity of criticisms of American courts. There are a number of indications of this shift: one is the treatment of the judiciary in national party platforms; another is congressional "court-curbing legislation" since World War II. These changes are in line with additional developments distinctive to our more recent political landscape.

National Party Platforms and Judicial Critiques: 1948–2008

While party platform statements are imperfect instruments for capturing party positions and policy goals, they do provide a formal and prominent record of party sentiment for a particular era. Table I.1 lays out what Democratic and Republican platforms have had to say with respect to the judiciary for every four-year cycle from 1948 to 2008.

Up to the 1976 platform, both Democrats and Republicans appear to have been deferential to courts in these official party statements—generally avoiding reference to the judiciary entirely. Interestingly, both the Democratic and Republican platforms of 1956 expressed support for courts in connection with *Brown v. Board of Education* (1954), the then controversial decision ordering desegregation of public schools (Republicans reaffirmed this support four years later). Beginning in 1976, however, we can detect a notable shift in party attitudes, especially for Republicans. As table I.1 shows, Republican platforms became increasingly detailed and negative in discussing courts and judges over this period, while Democrats continued to give the courts a low profile. In responding to *Roe v. Wade* (1973), the Republican platform of 1976 indirectly objected to both the decision and the Court's curtailment of a "public dialogue on abortion." Republicans also expressed support for "enactment of a constitutional amendment to restore protection of the right to life for unborn children."

Save for 1984 (when Republicans had consolidated power, made numerous appointments to federal and state court systems, and President Ronald Reagan's likely reelection raised the prospects of further GOP influence on courts), all Republican platforms from 1976 to 2008 made at least some negative reference to the judiciary. These statements frequently chafed against individual decisions (on such topics as abortion, parental rights, religion, the rights of the accused, and gay marriage) and, at other times, called for specific

Table I.1   References to Courts and Judges in Major Party Platforms, 1948–2008

	Major Party Platforms			Major Party Platforms	
Year	Democrat	Republican	Year	Democrat	Republican
1948	none/neutral	none/neutral	1976	none/neutral	negative
1952	none/neutral	none/neutral	1980	none/neutral	negative
1956	positive	positive	1984	positive	none/neutral
1960	positive	positive	1988	none/neutral	negative
1964	none/neutral	none/neutral	1992	none/neutral	mixed
1968	none/neutral	none/neutral	1996	none/neutral	negative
1972	none/neutral	none/neutral	2000	positive	negative
			2004	none/neutral	negative
			2008	none/neutral	negative
	Totals, 1948–1972			Totals, 1976–2008	
Overall	Democrats	Republicans	Overall	Democrats	Republicans
71% neutral;	71% neutral;	71% neutral;	44% neutral;	78% neutral;	11% neutral;
29% positive	29% positive	29% positive	17% positive;	22% positive	11% positive;
			33% negative		89% negative

moves to counter the judiciary (such as the 1988 pledge supporting "congressional use of Article III, Section 2 of the Constitution to restrict the jurisdiction of federal courts"). Starting with the 1980 platform, Republicans also began calling for the appointment of particular judges whose rulings would be consistent with their policy aims. In sum, the 1976 platform seems to have uncorked a steady flow of tough language from Republicans in their official party statements. Democratic responses, apart from a detailed response in 1984 (warning about the "radical" rights restrictions that would be imposed by a "Supreme Court chosen by Ronald Reagan"), were essentially invisible.

Court-Curbing Legislation, 1948–2008

Examining congressional legislation aimed at limiting the powers of the courts reveals a distinct but complementary pattern of attacks on the U.S. judiciary over the past sixty years. To evaluate the ebb and flow of Congress's interest in such efforts, I use a "court-curbing" data set compiled by political scientist Tom Clark. Clark identified and collected congressional proposals "to restrict, remove or otherwise limit judicial power" from 1789 to 2008. As Clark notes, the "typical Court-curbing bill is what might be characterized as an institutional assault on the Court rather than a case-specific effort to

Table I.2   Court-Curbing Legislation Introduced into Congress by Year, 1948–2008

Year	Court-curbing bills	Year	Court-curbing bills	Year	Court-curbing bills	Year	Court-curbing bills
1948	0	1967	21	1984	1	2003	8
1949	1	1968	34	1985	9	2004	10
1950	1	1969	53	1986	1	2005	25
1951	2	1970	7	1987	8	2006	11
1952	1	1971	34	1988	1	2007	20
1953	4	1972	4	1989	3	2008	5
1954	0	1973	22	1990	4		
1955	6	1974	5	1991	9		
1956	5	1975	25	1992	2		
1957	13	1976	7	1993	8		
1958	3	1977	32	1994	2		
1959	15	1978	3	1995	6		
1960	1	1979	22	1996	2		
1961	6	1980	3	1997	8		
1962	5	1981	26	1998	3		
1963	8	1982	4	1999	10		
1964	4	1983	13	2000	1		
1965	9			2001	3		
1966	5			2002	3		
1948–1966 average: 4.73		1967–1983 average: 18.52		1984–2002 average: 4.42		2003–2008 average: 13.17	

Source: Tom S. Clark (unpublished data set).

reverse a Court decision." Thus, instead of criticizing and singling out, say, an individual First Amendment decision perceived as hostile to religious interests, a members of Congress might propose a bill to eliminate "Supreme Court and Federal district court jurisdiction to review and hear any case arising out of State law relating to voluntary prayer in public buildings and schools."

A review of Clark's data over the past six decades reveals four waves of court-curbing legislation. As table I.2 indicates, from 1948 to 1966, Congress averaged under five court-curbing proposals every year. These numbers are somewhat inflated by the special dynamics of the Congresses of the 1960s, which included southern and conservative lawmakers bitterly opposed to contemporary civil rights and civil liberties decisions, most famously *Brown v. Board*. From 1967 to 1983, Congress entered a period of sustained interest in court-curbing bills that (to date) is without precedent, introducing an average of almost nineteen court-curbing bills every year.

Consistent with the political dynamics surrounding party platforms, this modern enthusiasm for curbing courts and judges seems to have run its course by the second term of the Reagan presidency, presumably reflecting Republican satisfaction with gaining greater purchase on the court system.

From 1984 to 2002, court-curbing proposals dropped back down to a yearly average under five (remarkably close to the 1948–1966 period), climbing again from 2003 to 2007, a five-year surge in court-curbing proposals that was matched only a few times before in our nation's history.

While certainly preliminary, these discussions suggest several general conclusions about critiques of the American judiciary over the past sixty years. First, starting in the late 1960s and continuing into the 1980s, political rhetoric targeting the courts increased in profile and frequency, sometimes accompanied by policy initiatives seeking to impose limits on courts and judges.

In the states, hostility to courts and judges was also stoked over this span, as illustrated by the "Impeach Warren" campaign in the 1960s and, later, by the popular removal of California Supreme Court Chief Justice Rose Bird. Bird, the first woman to serve on her state's highest court, came under fire in the 1970s and 1980s for her rulings and views, especially her opposition to the death penalty. After an organized, high-profile campaign by social conservatives and business groups, Bird and two other justices were voted off the California Supreme Court by the state's voters in 1986. The Bird episode suggested the emerging importance of organized interests in shaping state and national debates about the composition and ideological tenor of courts.

Beginning around 2003, criticisms of courts, and proposals channeling this animus, seem to have gained renewed force. As figure I.1 depicts, the 109th Congress (2005–2006) ushered in a span of heightened legislative interest in checking the judiciary. This conclusion is reinforced by research showing a rise in the use of the term "legislating from the bench" (almost invariably as a criticism) by members of Congress starting in 2003.

Moreover, it is notable in this regard that while the State of the Union addresses since 1948 have sounded generally supportive or neutral themes when discussing the judiciary, in four out of George W. Bush's final five State of the Union speeches, he criticized judicial behavior. In 2006, for example, the president warned that "judges must be servants of the law and not legislate from the bench." In his 2010 State of the Union message, President Obama took the somewhat unusual step of criticizing a recent Supreme Court decision with six justices in attendance. Obama charged that the ruling, *Citizens*

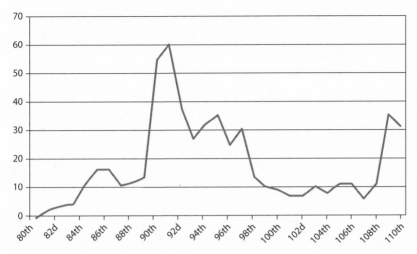

Figure I.1. Number of Court-curbing bills introduced from the 80th to 110th Congresses (1947–2008)

United v. FEC, had "reversed a century of law" and would "open the floodgates for special interests . . . to spend without limit in our elections."

Today's Trends

In addition to these initial measures indicating a surge in criticism of the U.S. judiciary over the past forty years, additional observations suggest that courts face an unusual and hostile political climate in the twenty-first century specifically.

Bipartisan Interest in Reform and Critique

First, while Republicans and conservatives are still the prevailing force behind today's attacks on courts, Democrats and liberals have also contributed to recent rebukes of the judiciary. Some Democratic members of Congress, for example, have identified the "Supreme Court's current conservative majority" as "highly activist," while others have accused conservative justices of "legislating from the bench." In addition, a number of contemporary legislative reforms and amendments targeting changes to the judiciary's powers and autonomy have received bipartisan sponsorship, sometimes by prominent figures in the two major parties. In 2005, thirty-nine Democrats joined over two hundred Republicans in approving the Pledge Protection Act, a bill that would have limited the Supreme Court's jurisdiction to hear cases, on appeal, related to the Pledge of Allegiance; the bill was not approved by the Senate and did not become law. These developments are somewhat striking, given the success of Republicans in naming judges to the federal courts and the modern association of federal courts with liberal causes and interests.

At the same time that today's courts have drawn the fire of conservatives and even some liberals in Congress, prominent scholars in law schools and political science have called for a reevaluation of judicial powers and prerogatives. In recent years, academicians from a range of ideological orientations have made sustained arguments for reforming courts, advancing proposals to allow Congress to override judicial review (the power of courts to invalidate unconstitutional government action) or eliminate it entirely, eradicate lifetime tenure for federal judges in favor of a fixed term, and impose mandatory judicial retirements.

Interest Group Activity and the Courts

The role of organized interests in vigorously contributing to (and opposing) criticisms of the judiciary suggests a second broad way in which we may now be in a different milieu of opposition to courts. While interest group activity focused on (and critical of) the judiciary is as old as the republic, today this behavior seems especially coordinated and ubiquitous. Interest groups are more active than ever in sponsoring cases, submitting amicus briefs, and generally participating in litigation and the judicial process. Ideological and issue groups have used critiques of the courts (or the rallying cry of judicial independence) as the basis for sustained fundraising and mobilization campaigns.

As Steven Teles has powerfully chronicled, the past few decades have witnessed a struggle between legal elites and organizations "outside" of government, as resurgent conservatives have challenged the prevailing liberal legal orthodoxy. Unlike in the past, these partisan groups are now engaged in a pitched battle over the "social institutions that feed the courts with ideas, personnel, and cases." The effect of all this has been to mobilize and concentrate ideological attacks on the judiciary, raise awareness of the stakes of the battle, and expand the contexts in which targeting the courts is considered "fair game." Organized interests have played an active part in developing this environment.

Exchanges between Judges and Critics

Today's political scene is marked by a third dynamic that is arguably distinct from other eras—a more overt public exchange between judges and their critics. At times, this has been a response to targeted and personalized attacks based on perceived individual failings or character flaws of specific judges or justices. Former House majority leader Tom DeLay, for example, famously excoriated Justice Anthony Kennedy in 2005 for his "incredibly outrageous" behavior, including "writing decisions based upon international law" and doing "research on the Internet."

Judges and justices have sometimes answered back, warning Congress to stay out of the judiciary's business and chastising "basic attacks" on the independence of judges (an alarm Chief Justice William Rehnquist sounded in his 2005 report on the state of the judiciary). At times, judges have even sought to engage their critics in direct dialogue, such as when Justices Kennedy and Clarence Thomas testified, for the first time in modern history, before the Senate Judiciary Committee—asking for increased pay for federal judges and urging Congress to abandon legislation that would compel the Court to televise its public sessions. During President Obama's 2010 State of the Union critique of *Citizens United*, Associate Justice Samuel Alito shook his head and appeared to mouth his disagreement with the president's characterization of the case, and Chief Justice John Roberts subsequently stated that he found the president's remarks "very troubling." Judges have also been increasingly active in criticizing and even disciplining their own brethren. On the whole, exchanges between judges and their critics appear to be more fluid and unguarded than in the past. At a minimum, this dialogue raises the profile of today's debates about judicial independence and the courts' role.

Criticism in the States

At least one other element marks the early twenty-first century as an important moment for considering criticisms of courts and their potential impact on judicial independence. State courts and judges have increasingly come under scrutiny and admonishment, as scholars, legal elites, and media figures challenge both the decisions coming out of state judiciaries and the capacity of state judges to rule in impartial ways. Indeed, some of the most prominent national criticisms of court decisions (such as those sparked by the *Goodridge* "gay marriage" decision and the judicial rulings removing life support for Terri Schiavo) have targeted state judges. Animosity toward and disapproval of state courts and judges is frequently underscored in judicial elections, as sitting judges, aspiring candidates, organized interests, and the media provide, at various turns, condemnation of specific decisions and judicial behavior generally. While there is scholarly debate about their actual impact on judicial behavior, contemporary judicial elections have often taken on a harsh and internecine character, as opposing candidates and organized interests question the integrity and fitness of both sitting judges and those vying to assume the bench. At the same time, voters have considered laws through both the initiative and referendum process to impose term limits on state judges (Colorado), ease procedures for removing judges who make controversial decisions (Montana), and eliminate judges' immunity from lawsuits arising from their official duties (South Dakota).

Paradigms for Analyzing Criticism of Courts

There is, then, some intriguing, and perhaps disturbing, preliminary evidence to suggest that from the late 1960s until the early 1980s and then again in the first decade of the twenty-first century, there has been a shift in the quantity and quality of criticisms of courts and judges. These observations underscore the point that we are at an important moment for weighing these critiques, for assessing whether they are politically healthful or deleterious.

"Judicial independence" is the traditional reference point for evaluating whether the coordinate branches of government or political figures have overstepped their bounds and threatened the powers and operations of courts. There has certainly been a great deal of open fretting about the courts' independence in recent years from former and sitting judges, scholars, and representatives of organized interests. How are we to understand and assess these concerns? Stated differently, how can we know whether to be concerned with increased scrutiny and chiding of judges and courts unless we know what judicial independence is, and what it is good for?

A Traditional Understanding of Judicial Independence

Federalist 78 is a helpful starting point because it has become a widely referenced account of the meaning and purposes of judicial independence. In the essay, Alexander Hamilton, writing as Publius, defends the Constitution's provision of federal judges who serve "during good behavior" and whose continued service in office is not (unlike the other branches) dependent on periodic elections or ongoing selection by political officials. This insulation is intended to keep the courts separate from the influence and power of the federal legislative and executive branches as well as the "occasional ill humors in the society," that is, our popular impulses to oppress "the minor party in the community." Keeping judges separated from the ambitions, agendas, and priorities of the legislative and executive branches will leave the judges free to enforce a limited Constitution and ensure "a steady, upright, and impartial administration of the laws." The alternative is to allow the other branches to place the courts under their thumbs, threatening an imbalance in power and encroachments on "the rights of citizens."

For the purposes of this introduction, let me identify these core claims about and in defense of judicial independence as the "traditional understanding" of judicial independence. Direct extensions as well as basic variants of these arguments have recurred frequently in historical and contemporary debates about the judicial role and whether it is threatened by criticisms or proposed reforms.

The traditional understanding rests upon three underlying beliefs. First, it sets the judiciary apart from the other branches of government. The need for "independence" seems to be a peculiar concern for courts and judges. Neither *The Federalist Papers* nor our contemporary debates are as preoccupied with legislative independence or executive independence, presumably because we expect and even insist that these branches will be openly influenced by one another as well as by other electoral, popular, and political forces.

Fragility and Power

The traditional approach also assumes that the courts are institutionally fragile. They lack the formal authority and the "electoral connection" that furnishes the other branches with their power base. Moreover, courts have limited capacity to influence the other branches or take up an active policy agenda. Again, as Hamilton famously put it, the judiciary "has no influence over either the sword or the purse; no direction either of the strength or of the wealth of the society; and can take no active resolution whatever. . . . [It] is beyond comparison the weakest of the three departments." These claims about the weakness and contingency of the judiciary's power highlight the importance of keeping the courts free from the influence and pressure of the other branches.

Finally, the traditional defense of judicial independence rests on a judgment that the court's distinctiveness and institutional weakness is important to defend because of the special functions it provides for our legal and political order. These traits would be compromised if judges worked too closely with elected officials or otherwise succumbed to their influence. *The Federalist Papers* are explicit in suggesting that these distinctive institutional functions include enforcing a limited Constitution of enumerated powers, facilitating the fair interpretation of laws, and protecting rights. Other accounts have also emphasized independence as a prerequisite in allowing courts to serve as umpires or referees between the three branches of government or between the federal government and the states.

New Ways of Thinking about Independence

Questioning Political Independence

The Politics of Judicial Independence supplements, tests, and challenges this traditional view of judicial independence, questioning or expanding on each of the model's basic presumptions. To begin with, we take issue with the contention that "independence" is uniquely important for defending courts and their prerogatives, because the judiciary is the only branch that is "apolitical" and largely free from electoral and popular forces. This book presumes, instead, that courts are a proper object of political study and that they are arguably more alike than different from the other branches, at least with respect to their place in the constitutional system and interactions with other branches. The American system of separation of powers anticipates vigorous disagreement and even contestation among the different branches of government (at both the state and federal level), both to check the actions of coordinate branches of government and to improve policy and governing by adding each branch's distinctive concerns and perspectives. This model of vibrant, dynamic institutional interaction requires not only that each branch should have formal tools for superintending and interfering with the others but also that "each department should have a will of its own." At the state level, the "political connection" is perhaps even more obvious, given the proliferation of judicial elections (some of them openly partisan) and the general importance of elected officials and interest groups in helping to select judges and fill judicial vacancies.

There are several consequences of this outlook for assessing critiques of courts. One observation is simply to note that if we assume a high level of *interdependence* between the branches as a normal part of the separation of powers, we should not be surprised by finding periods of criticism and rebuke —such institutional chafing is inherent to our political system of divided institutions sharing powers. In this environment, more serious dangers to the judiciary (or any branch) will depend not just on the weapons (and defenses) available to each branch but also on the role that perceived threats may have in altering the exercise of judicial power or even compromising the special institutional concerns and functions we associate with each branch (such as the court's ability to articulate and defend individual rights).

Similarly, our inquiry into whether the judiciary and its institutional role are being imperiled must look beyond the "traditional" threat of encroachment by elected officials to the broader context that can compromise the courts' work and ability to secure its most important ends. For example, the judiciary's ability to articulate and defend rights, resolve disputes between adversarial parties (including the various branches of government), and promote the rule of law are buffeted by such forces as public opinion, the courts' broader relationship to national (and more local) policy agendas, party politics, and many other factors. Not the least of these concerns is the question of whether the judiciary retains a "will of its own," that is, whether it possesses sufficient ambition or interest in scrutinizing the work of the coordinate branches or the states. Stated differently, judicial independence has both an institutional quality based on courts' ability to perform its core functions in the thicket of competing departments and powers and a motivational and subjective element involving their willingness to do so. The traditional model's emphasis on the formal "independence" of courts from elected officials and political forces does not guarantee that judges will be indifferent to the agendas of legislators, the executive branch, and the public or that they will always be vigorous in their performance of judicial roles.

Dynamic Strengths

A second element of the traditional understanding and defense of judicial independence is the assumption that we must be especially vigilant in protecting the courts' powers because they are, invariably, the weakest branch. But while the formal powers of the federal judiciary are sparse and seem almost to invite congressional superintendence—Congress can, for example, regulate the appellate jurisdiction of the Supreme Court and control the structure and even the existence of lower courts—in practice the judiciary is not quite as toothless as Hamilton depicted over two centuries ago. Most famously, the courts have themselves added powers through such innovations as judicial review and judge-made legal rules. In addition, at both the state and federal levels, the number and variety of court cases has risen dramatically over time, providing appellate courts with greater choice over which cases to review and casting doubt on the claim in *The Federalist Papers* that courts "can take no active resolution" of legal and policy measures.

Furthermore, legislatures have often added to the powers of courts, giving them, for example, greater discretion over their docket of cases and providing "fast-track" authority to review certain classes of cases. Arguably, courts also often operate from a position of relative strength compared to their coordinate branches with respect to public opinion, since their popular "diffuse" or institutional support is consistently greater than that of the other branches. Moreover, as a number of scholars have shown, the judiciary's authority can be increased or decreased by the comparative powers of the institutions around it, an additional argument for assessing threats to judicial independence against a somewhat dynamic baseline.

The Hamiltonian conclusion that courts have "no influence over either the sword or the purse; no direction either of the strength or of the wealth of the society" seems a trifle overstated. While courts are certainly imperfect agents of change and affect policy in often unpredictable ways, they are hardly shadow players in state and national politics. Our evaluation of the politics of judicial independence needs to take seriously the judiciary's status as a coordinate institution of government, at times equipped with the formal powers and informal authority to confront other institutions.

Judicial Functions: A Broader Approach

A third aspect of conventional debates about judicial independence is the presumption that courts provide special functions for our constitutional system, underscoring the importance of maintaining independence. As noted, these sorts of arguments often point to the judiciary's role in protecting rights and in maintaining stability and fairness in law.

But while this book presumes that our concern with the politics of independence is closely tethered to our beliefs about what distinctive jobs the judiciary performs in our political and legal system, it strives to transcend some of the more familiar ways we talk about these roles. As Mark Graber has suggested, courts may be useful in helping to reconcile (even if temporarily) divisive, cross-cutting political issues. Also, the judiciary may lend stability not just to the legal system but also to the political system as a whole. Courts may give expression to democratic impulses and popular interests in ways that the other parts of our constitutional order do not. In assessing "the politics of judicial independence," this book will be expansive in considering the range of contributions of courts.

That said, it also makes sense, as a corollary claim, to scrutinize how well courts are actually achieving their purported institutional goals. For example, an important body of scholarly literature has questioned the degree to which courts can protect individual liberties in the face of sustained and organized popular opposition. Other work questions the judiciary's capacity to resolve simmering disputes between Congress and the president, casting doubt on its ability to serve as an effective separation of powers referee. To the degree our vigorous defense of the independence of courts turns on their actual delivery of special functions and objectives, we need to cast a sober eye on whether this promise is vindicated.

In sum, our analysis of judicial independence requires moving beyond the presumptions that courts work best in political isolation, that they necessarily operate from a position of institutional weakness, and that their independence is primarily justified by strictly legal objectives.

One might roughly summarize the revised account sketched here by stating that an independent court is one that can fulfill the judicial role without improper political influence from external or internal forces. Such an account concedes that the courts regularly face political pressures and agendas but denies that this exposure automatically imperils judicial functions.

Conclusion

The Politics of Judicial Independence strives to probe, apply, and extend this revised approach to thinking about judicial independence against the backdrop of the past forty years and, in particular, the first decade of the twenty-first century. How does the current era of court criticism help us to understand the circumstances under which judicial independence can be compromised by "improper" political influences? Answering this question requires moving back and forth between theoretical arguments about the capacities and purposes of courts and the separation of powers and close study of the actual behavior and performance of the different institutions of government.

As indicated, this volume presumes first that we are at an important moment for courts both domestically and abroad and, second, that we must assess threats to courts with a somewhat novel paradigm of political institutions— one that pays attention to the different goals and working parts of our entire system of separated powers. In this light, understanding and assessing the "politics of judicial independence" requires us to study and sympathetically engage the perspectives, motivations, and rationales of organizations and individuals making the most frequent and important attacks on courts today. While committed to a scholarly, analytic, evidence-based approach, this book takes seriously the concerns of those seeking to protect judicial independence as well as those who charge that contemporary courts have strayed from their proper functions and roles. Moreover, by underscoring the courts' own role as a "coordinate" institution of government, this volume considers how judges themselves contribute to (or undermine) their own autonomy and powers.

More broadly, this book's focus on recent surges in attacks on courts is designed to teach us about the nature of our system of separated powers, the special functions of courts, and those occasions when the two come into conflict. Stated somewhat differently, this volume is premised on the idea that examining attacks and criticisms of courts will help us understand more vividly what is at stake in worries about judicial independence: the benefits provided by a strong judiciary and the circumstances under which these contributions can be compromised.

The chapters in this volume should equip readers with the analytic tools, relevant background, and research findings needed to evaluate whether the current waves of criticism are continuous with or distinctive from our long line of challenges to American courts, and whether these swells carry with them reasonable concerns or misguided fears about today's judiciary. The authors assembled in the pages that follow probe the sources of antijudicial attacks, help us understand the political and legal implications of these criticisms, and, ultimately, allow readers to make their own judgments about whether judicial independence is threatened in the twenty-first century and, if so, whether this development is troubling and capable of redress.

chapter 1

The Choreography of Courts-Congress Conflicts

Charles Geyh

Our investigation of contemporary efforts to curb or limit judicial power and independence begins with an overview of why and how Congress and the courts come into conflict. Charles Geyh examines these interactions using two main analytic lenses. First, he argues that the most intense battles between the federal legislature and judiciary have followed a similar pattern or cycle over our history, arising from a common source. The seven periods of sustained anti-court sentiment we have experienced to date have each been fueled by a "political realignment," a term political scientists use to refer to significant shifts in the pattern of popular support for political parties. Second, Geyh catalogues the wide array of instruments both Congress and the federal courts have for communicating and resolving their conflicts. He identifies three "tiers" of techniques these branches have for regulating their disagreements, from relatively mundane warnings to serious attacks that threaten to undermine longstanding norms about their respective powers and roles. Geyh's analysis helps us understand that sustained criticisms of courts are an unsurprising result of our party and electoral system, that the nature and threat posed by congressional court-curbing efforts vary widely, and, finally, that the future of judicial independence requires a more realistic view about the mix of law and politics that influence how courts make decisions.

This chapter looks at how disputes between Congress and the courts arise and resolve themselves, with a particular focus on the ways in which Congress lets its displeasure be known to judges and the judiciary. While the criticism of judges and their decisions is to some extent a perennial drumbeat accompanying the administration of justice, there are periodic crescendos spanning several years and sometimes decades. At the federal level, there have been seven such periods of anti-court sentiment in our history, and they follow a predictable pattern, akin to a four-step dance: first comes political realignment; then attacks against holdover judges; counter-attacks against court critics; and, finally, normalization.

Each dance begins with a major political realignment, in which a new regime replaces its predecessor. With the new regime comes a new ideology intolerant of the old. The first realignment occurred in 1802, when Thomas Jefferson and his Republican Party wrested power from the hitherto entrenched Federalists. The second major political realignment took place in 1828, when Andrew Jackson and his Democratic Party defeated the Whigs and brought with them a new brand of populism. In 1865, the nation reunited after the Civil War under the aggressive rule of "Radical Republicans" in Congress, signaling the third realignment. Fourth, in the 1880s and 1890s, Populists and Progressives concerned for the plight of the industrial laborer gained control of state and national legislatures. Fifth, in the 1930s, Franklin Delano Roosevelt ushered in the New Deal and its unprecedented expansion of the national government. A generation later, in the 1950s and 1960s, a sixth realignment occurred when Chief Justice Earl Warren and his U.S. Supreme Court found themselves at the epicenter of an intense period of social unrest over civil rights, civil liberties, and the war in Vietnam. And in 1994, the Republican Party—armed with an ambitious conservative agenda—took control of Congress after more than thirty years of Democratic rule in the House of Representatives, giving rise to a seventh realignment.

Presidents almost invariably nominate judges from their own political party, and they typically seek to identify nominees who are ideologically compatible. When the party in power is swept from office in a major political realignment, friction between the new regime and holdover judges appointed for life by the old regime is virtually inevitable. And so, the second step in the dance is the attack on holdover judges. Judges of the old regime make decisions unpopular with leaders of the new—both before and after the realignment. Leaders of the new regime respond with a campaign against judges of the old regime whose ideology is incompatible with the new world order.

These attacks include harsh criticism, usually accompanied by threats. The Jeffersonians proposed to disestablish courts occupied by Federalist-appointed judges and to impeach others whose views offended them. Jacksonian Democrats at the state and federal levels denied the supremacy of the Marshall Supreme Court on questions of constitutional interpretation and proposed to defy Court rulings. In the aftermath of the Civil War, Radical Republicans threatened to "annihilate" the Supreme Court if it impeded the

Reconstruction agenda, and Congress manipulated Court jurisdiction to limit the justices' policy reach. At the turn of the twentieth century, Populists and Progressives lobbied to end life tenure for judges, to establish mechanisms enabling the public to recall judges, and to eliminate the judiciary's power to declare government action unconstitutional. During the New Deal, Franklin Roosevelt proposed to pack the Supreme Court and lower courts with additional judges to ensure a decision-making majority in his favor. A generation thereafter, the Warren Court came under siege in a unique cycle of anti-Court sentiment that featured an unexpectedly liberal Court deviating from the more conservative regime that appointed it, in which political realignment (with the election of Richard Nixon) did not occur until after attacks on the Court had begun in earnest. There, critics of the Warren Court angled to impeach members of the Court and introduced legislation to eliminate federal court jurisdiction over school prayer and other controversial issues. Most recently, conservative congressional leaders of the Republican Party, invigorated by electoral success in the 1990s, threatened to impeach "activist" judges, limit their jurisdiction, disestablish their courts, and cut court budgets.[1]

In response to the attack on holdover judges comes a third step: the defense of those judges and of the judiciary in general. Court defenders—public officials (including members of Congress), editorial writers, good-government organizations, academicians, judges, and others—rise up to counter the criticism and blunt the attacks. Some may step up because they approve of the targeted judges and their decisions; others intervene because they support the general independence of the judges to rule without intimidation.

Then begins the fourth and final step: normalization. The new regime appoints judges whose decisions are less likely to anger those in power. Holdover judges gradually become outnumbered and in some cases rethink and soften their positions in response to the attacks. Court defenders gain traction, and the new regime loses momentum. Public interest subsides, and the cycle winds down.

At least as striking as the cyclical nature of anti-court sentiment is the extent to which those cycles have culminated in the imposition of fewer concrete controls on the courts over time. Of the seven cycles enumerated above, the first three yielded concrete, sometimes extreme results: during Jefferson's presidency, sixteen judgeships were disestablished—that is, the offices that the judges occupied were eliminated—and two judges were impeached by the House of Representatives (one was acquitted by the Senate and the other was removed for reasons unrelated to the unpopularity of his rulings). In Jackson's time, Georgia openly defied the Supreme Court by executing a prisoner contrary to Court order. In the aftermath of the Civil War, Congress stripped the Supreme Court of jurisdiction to rule on the constitutionality of Reconstruction legislation in a pending case.

In the four most recent cycles, however, nothing comparably dramatic occurred. Populist and Progressive attacks on the courts made inroads in some western state systems but yielded no concrete results at the federal level. The need for Roosevelt's Court-packing plan was obviated by Justice Owen Roberts, who switched sides and joined the four justices who consistently voted to uphold New Deal legislation—but prior to Roberts's switch, congressional reaction to Roosevelt's plan was decidedly tepid. During the Warren Court era, the impeachment proposals went nowhere, as did the jurisdiction-stripping bills. And most recently, proposals to impeach judges, disestablish courts, and gut budgets never advanced.

I have argued elsewhere that the declining effectiveness of these cyclical attacks on federal courts and judges is attributable to the development of judicial independence norms (or "customary independence") that emerged over the course of the nineteenth century, became increasingly entrenched with each passing cycle, and gradually enabled court defenders to thwart anti-court campaigns more effectively. The framers of the U.S. Constitution repeatedly professed their desire to create an independent judiciary by giving federal judges life tenure and a guaranteed salary, but they also equipped Congress with powers that could render the judiciary subservient to its will. The question for later generations thus became whether the letter of the Constitution, which appears to authorize significant congressional incursions on judicial autonomy, or its spirit, as embodied in the framers' oft-stated intention to create an independent judiciary, would triumph in practice. The eventual outcome, as reflected in the decreasingly productive cycles of court-directed hostility, was much closer to the latter. The net effect is that the most destructive, overt anti-court weapons in Congress's arsenal for controlling rogue judges—impeachment, budget cuts, the disestablishment of targeted courts, the wholesale stripping of subject matter jurisdiction, or simple defiance of court rulings—became politically unacceptable.

This, however, tells only part of the story. Discussing Congress's efforts to control the courts over time solely in terms of its diminishing resort to the most drastic methods at its disposal is a bit like describing how school children seek to win playground disputes with exclusive reference to the declining incidence of knife fights. If one wants to understand how courts and Congress resolve their differences when they are not in the midst of a crisis—which is the vast majority of the time—it is necessary to dig deeper.

The parallel to playground disputes is worth pursuing a bit further. Some have likened the relationship between courts and Congress to a conversation or dialogue, but such measured and civil exchanges do not capture the rough and tumble of the interaction in its ordinary course the way a schoolyard fracas does. Garden-variety playground dispute resolution techniques are regulated to no small extent by children in the group through informal norms that can be divided into three tiers. At the bottom tier are words and conduct that clearly fall within the scope that the participants would regard as normal and routinely acceptable: arguments, criticism, gesticulations, insults, shouts, and threats to enlist the aid of teachers or older siblings. At the second tier are behaviors that the group may deem acceptable only when undertaken in exceptional circumstances: making good on tier-one threats; initiating a skirmish with shoves, wrestling, or a punch or two; and threats of more severe violence. In the third tier are behaviors that the group simply deems unacceptable, to which disputants resort at the risk of provoking a crisis (for instance, a police call) or shunning: attacking an opponent unprepared, or making good on tier-two threats of more extreme violence by reaching for a brick, a broken bottle, or a knife.

It is useful to employ a similar structure when analyzing courts-Congress disputes by differentiating between (1) forms of interaction that are used regularly or without much controversy; (2) forms of interaction that are used sparingly and only in exceptional circumstances; and (3) forms of interaction that are avoided as antithetical to independence norms and what is presumed to be the appropriate relationship between the two groups. Over time, Congress and the courts have exploited a variety of mechanisms for making their views known, communicating the depth of their disaffection, achieving compromises, enabling face-saving acquiescence, and trumping each other without provoking crises.

The dispute-processing techniques discussed below arise in different settings. Conflicts between judges and legislators typically arise in one of two contexts: disputes over judicial rulings in cases or disputes over judicial administration (including court practice, procedure, budgets, and discipline). With judicial rulings, the event triggering the dispute is obviously the decision itself. In the case of judicial administration, the triggering event may be a controversial action, for instance, when the judiciary promulgates a contentious procedural rule or Congress appropriates less funding for the courts than requested. Or the event may be an inaction, as when the judiciary fails to discipline a judge in a publicized misconduct matter or when Congress fails to approve a judicial pay raise.

Tier One: Forms of Interaction Used Regularly or without Controversy

The cycles of intense, anti-court sentiment described earlier feature resort to more draconian mechanisms of interbranch control, catalogued in my discussion of tiers two and three below. Such courts-Congress crises, however, represent periodic departures from or challenges to the state of dynamic equilibrium that typifies the relationship between courts and Congress much of the time. Even during periods of normal relations, there is a perpetual give and take between the branches as they go about their business, negotiate disagreements, and keep each other in check. Both sides are equipped with tools and sometimes weapons, catalogued below, to assist them in making their positions and preferences known, altering the conduct of the other, and winning or avoiding disputes. What defines and delineates the scope of devices in tier one is both the frequency of their use and the likelihood that they can be employed without provoking serious confrontations between the branches typical of devices in tier two or constitutional crises that tier three can provoke.

First-Tier Methods Available to Congress

Critical commentary. Members of Congress may criticize a judicial decision or the judiciary's administration in congressional hearings, on the House or Senate floor, or in the media. Examples abound: In 1996, Federal District Court Judge Harold Baer reversed a controversial decision in which he had excluded from evidence cocaine seized in a drug arrest. His original decision provoked heavy congressional criticism and even talk of impeachment.[2] More recently, in 2005, House Majority Leader Tom DeLay singled out Supreme Court Justice Anthony Kennedy in a radio interview and called for the House Judiciary Committee to probe the meaning of the constitutional provision allowing judges to sit "as long as they serve with good behavior."[3] In the heat of ongoing disputes, when court defenders object to the tactics of court critics, the critics occasionally accuse the defenders of seeking to place harsh criticism outside the bounds of appropriate interbranch dialogue. The defenders, however, almost invariably respond by distinguishing between criticism—to which they claim no objection (thereby confirming the consensus that harsh criticism belongs in tier one)—and what they perceive as threats or intimidation that they characterize as an unwarranted resort to a tier-two or tier-three dispute resolution technique.[4]

Legislative override of a court's statutory interpretation. When a court issues a ruling on the meaning of a statute with which members of Congress disagree, those members often respond by introducing legislation to amend the statute.[5] Congress may not override the Supreme Court's interpretation of the Constitution through legislation, but it may seek to amend an invalidated statute to correct the constitutional infirmity. Overriding a court's statutory interpretation can be complicated by congressional inertia or competing interests that favor conflicting interpretations, but even when it fails, introduction of the bill and its discussion in legislative hearings can play a relevant role in the interbranch dialogue.

Introduction of constitutional amendments. When the Supreme Court issues a disagreeable interpretation of constitutional law, that interpretation can be trumped by constitutional amendment. Only seventeen amendments have been adopted since 1791, of which only four operated to overturn a Supreme Court decision.[6] Clearly, this option is not ordinarily viable. Indeed, on those infrequent occasions when a proposed amendment gains momentum—by receiving a committee hearing or a floor vote—critics of the amendment can be counted on to argue that the need to preserve constitutional stability in general and the Bill of Rights in particular dictates that amendments to the Constitution be approved sparingly.[7] Nevertheless, over ten thousand constitutional amendments have been introduced over the years, many in direct response to a Supreme Court decision.[8] It seems unlikely that the innumerable members of Congress responsible for introducing so many constitutional amendments have been laboring under a delusion of probable success. On the other hand, introducing a constitutional amendment can serve as an exclamation mark that punctuates the sponsor's dissatisfaction with the Court's ruling. It conveys the depth of the sponsor's feeling to constituents, the media, other members of Congress, and the courts. To that extent, even a doomed amendment adds another voice to courts-Congress disputes.

The judicial confirmation process. The Senate confirmation process for judicial nominees has always been an intensely partisan one, routinely exploited
for political gain. More recently (beginning in the late nineteenth century
for Supreme Court nominees and in the last quarter of the twentieth century
for nominees to the circuit courts), the process has become both a prominent
platform from which senators may air their grievances with judicial decisions
and a dominant method of court control.[9] Senators disenchanted with a perceived liberal or conservative bias in the federal judiciary have employed the
Senate's confirmation machinery to block the appointment of ideologically
unacceptable nominees. Senators have delayed hearings in the Senate Judiciary Committee, prolonged Committee debate, exploited arcane "blue-slip"
procedures enabling home-state senators to halt Committee action on nominees, placed "holds" on floor votes, filibustered nominees on the Senate floor,
and simply voted nominees down.[10] Manipulating the confirmation process
to realign the judiciary's ideology remains a controversial practice—at least
from the perspective of whatever side's ox is being gored. But it has been exploited too often on both sides of the political aisle to argue that the practice
is generally regarded as unacceptable or appropriate only if used sparingly.

Judgeships legislation. The legislative power to create new judgeships aug-
ments the confirmation power: the business of reorienting the ideological
makeup of the federal judiciary is hastened if new positions are established
to supplement vacancies created by retirement or death. Unlike the appointment process, however, where the goal of manipulating court ideology is often
explicit (to block liberal "activists" or conservative "extremists"), judgeships
legislation preserves the appearance—and to some extent the reality—of a
process that is less ideologically result-oriented. The discourse of judgeships
debates typically dwells on the need for new judgeships in specified districts
or circuits. In those debates, data generated by the Judicial Conference of the
United States (the administrative arm of the federal judiciary, comprised of
circuit and district judges under the leadership of the Chief Justice[11]) confirming the need for more judges is virtually indispensible to the passage of a
major judgeships bill—although the judgeships created by the bill may vary
in number and location from those recommended.[12] That said, the politics of
judgeships legislation are such that the prospects for passage are usually slim
unless the White House and Congress are controlled by the same political
party.[13] Thus, the likelihood that the judges appointed to fill newly created

judgeships will be ideologically compatible with the congressional majority is essentially a prerequisite to passage.[14]

Encouraging judicial self-regulation. One often-employed tactic to resolve interbranch disputes in Congress's favor is for congressional committees or subcommittees to hold legislative or oversight hearings. Witnesses on behalf of the judiciary are called in and urged to bring their administrative policies in line with congressional preferences on pain of legislative intervention. Recent examples include hearings to encourage more vigilant self-discipline[15] and hearings to limit judicial attendance at expenses-paid educational seminars on issues before the courts and of economic interest to the organizations that underwrite the seminars.[16] The thrust of this approach is to present the judiciary with the choice of losing a little autonomy now (by regulating itself in ways it might prefer not to) or losing more autonomy later (by relinquishing regulatory control of the matter to Congress), which creates a meaningful incentive for the courts to cooperate. Congress may also pass legislation that facilitates judicial self-regulation in ways that Congress seeks to encourage. For example, when Congress became concerned that judicial misconduct falling short of impeachable offenses was going unregulated, it enacted the Judicial Councils Reform and Judicial Conduct and Disability Act, enabling the judiciary to discipline its own judges. In an arguably similar vein, in 2006, House Judiciary Committee Chair James Sensenbrenner introduced a bill to create an office of the Inspector General within the federal judiciary. Sponsors argued that the bill would centralize and streamline the judiciary's budgetary oversight and disciplinary process.[17]

General regulation of court jurisdiction. Congress's power to regulate lower court jurisdiction derives from its power to establish inferior courts, and it enables Congress to control what cases federal courts hear. For the most part, Congress has exploited this power to expand the bailiwick of the federal courts and, with it, federal power. The original Judiciary Act of 1789 authorized the newly minted federal courts to hear disputes between citizens of different states ("diversity jurisdiction");[18] toward the end of Reconstruction, Congress expanded the circumstances in which defendants could remove actions to federal court that plaintiffs had originally filed in state court ("removal jurisdiction") and authorized the federal district courts to hear any case arising under federal law ("federal question" jurisdiction);[19] and in the latter half of the twentieth century, amid assorted federal campaigns relating to civil rights, civil liberties, drugs, and crime, Congress federalized a range of new causes of action.[20] In the opposite direction, Congress has periodically raised the threshold dollar amount that must be in controversy before plaintiffs may bring a diversity action (as a means to reduce diversity jurisdiction filings and control docket congestion),[21] and it has occasionally considered the elimination of diversity jurisdiction altogether.[22] General regulation of court jurisdiction has more recently given rise to interbranch disputes, with the Judicial Conference objecting to the federalization of certain crimes and civil actions and citing federalism concerns and increased burdens on the federal courts.[23] Congress continues, however, to exploit its control over federal court jurisdiction to further its priorities when it is dissatisfied with how state courts are handling given matters. One recent example is the Class Action Fairness Act of 2005, in which Congress relaxed removal and diversity jurisdiction requirements to create a federal forum for actions that, in its view, had been mishandled by state courts.[24] A second is the special legislation Congress enacted in the peculiar case of Terri Schiavo, which created a one-time federal forum to review orders issued by the Florida state courts in a dispute between a woman's husband and parents to remove her feeding tube after a cardiac event had left her in a persistent vegetative state.[25]

Lesser restrictions on judicial review. While targeted congressional efforts to punish courts for bad decisions by stripping them of subject matter jurisdiction (as distinguished from general regulation of subject matter jurisdiction) may be a tier-two or tier-three undertaking, modest tweaks to judicial review of administrative agency and other actions fall well below the radar of customary independence enforcement and are quite commonplace. For example, the Antarctic Science, Tourism, and Conservation Act of 1996 provided that Environmental Protection Agency assessments of the environmental impact of specified activities in Antarctica are not subject to judicial review.[26] Between 1988 and 2004, Congress restricted judicial review in such ways 166 times.[27] While hardly a confrontational gambit to emasculate the courts, these restrictions on judicial action serve—almost silently—to structure, limit, and thereby control the courts' involvement in a host of contexts.

The budgetary process. The judiciary is acutely aware of who butters its bread and on what side. Judges bemoan inadequate budgets and underscore the perils that will befall the courts if they are not adequately funded,[28] but they are very careful not to speak critically of key legislators who influence the budgetary process.[29] For its part, Congress holds annual hearings on the judiciary's appropriations and pays occasional attention to how the judiciary spends its money. For example: in recent years, members of Congress—animated by a spirit of fiscal austerity—have called the judiciary to account for their courthouse construction plans and the efficiency of their work habits.[30] Congressional manipulation of the judiciary's budget to extort ideologically compatible decisions does not occur, but a subtler dynamic has been documented. A recent study showed that when Congress and the lower courts are ideologically compatible, congressional appropriations for court budgets are more generous.[31] This does not necessarily suggest that Congress sets out to reward judiciaries that make agreeable decisions and punish those that do not. The likelihood that Congress would consciously manipulate judicial appropriations in this way and yet manage (or desire, for that matter) to keep its intentions secret seems remote. But it does reveal how the general receptivity of leading members of Congress to the fiscal needs of the judiciary may be colored by the atmospherics of their relationship, including the ideological distance that separates them. Judges cannot control the partisan affiliation of their appointing presidents, but they know to tread lightly and select their Judicial Conference designees with care to avoid unnecessary friction.

First-Tier Methods Available to the Courts

Commentary critical and not. Just as members of Congress may initiate or perpetuate interbranch disputes by speaking critically of judges and their decisions, the reverse is likewise true. Judges may embed in judicial opinions comments critical of Congress or the legislation Congress drafts. For example, in 1997 Justice David Souter grumbled that "in a world of silk purses and pigs' ears, the [Antiterrorism and Effective Death Penalty Act] is not a silk purse of the art of statutory drafting."[32] Judge Gerald Bard Tjoflat of the Eleventh Circuit complained that the Class Action Fairness Act presented "an opaque, baroque maze of interlocking cross-references that defy easy interpretation, even though they are contained in a single paragraph of the amended diversity statute."[33] And in Oregon, exasperated district judge Owen Panner characterized federal judges as "frogs in a simmering pot," cooked alive by "repeated encroachments by the other two Branches."[34] Judges may also criticize legislative proposals or members of Congress in interviews with reporters, at conferences, or in legislative hearings. In 2002, for example, Judge James Rosenbaum provoked a firestorm when he criticized the federal sentencing guidelines in testimony before the House Judiciary Committee.[35]

Frequently, however, comments embedded in judicial opinions may be calculated to resolve rather than provoke disputes by inviting Congress to review and, if desired, override the court's statutory interpretation. In 1992, Professor Robert Katzmann (he is now a circuit judge) instituted a pilot program, with the cooperation of the D.C. Circuit Court and the House of Representatives, in which court opinions commenting on statutes under review would be automatically referred to the House committee with jurisdiction over the statute at issue.[36]

Judicial Conference policy positions. The Judicial Conference of the United States formulates policy positions on pending legislation affecting the courts and proposes legislation of its own.[37] It then communicates those positions to Congress through its judges and the staff of the Administrative Office of the U.S. Courts in a process closely akin to lobbying.[38] The Judicial Conference, acutely aware of the role Congress plays in setting judicial budgets and raising judicial salaries, is reluctant to criticize Congress too bluntly. Nevertheless, the Judicial Conference, speaking on behalf of the judiciary as a branch, regularly steps in to oppose legislation that it regards as antithetical to the best interests of the courts. In recent years, for example, the Judicial Conference opposed criminal gang legislation that would have brought a large number of juveniles into the federal system;[39] bankruptcy reform that would have, in practical effect, allowed bankruptcy court decisions to be appealed directly to the U.S. courts of appeals;[40] and "overly broad" legislation prohibiting judges from accepting gifts at judicial seminars.[41]

Year-end reports on the Federal Judiciary. In recent years, the Chief Justice has issued annual state of the judiciary messages. These carefully worded statements comment on the judiciary's most pressing needs and concerns— often including budgets and salaries. They likewise weigh in on recent developments in the relationship between courts and Congress. For example, state of the judiciary messages have criticized Congress for enacting legislation limiting the power of federal judges to depart from criminal sentencing guidelines and for failing to confirm judicial nominees.[42] Criticism of Congress embedded in state of the judiciary messages is measured, but because it originates with the Chief Justice of the United States, even mild admonishments attract significant media attention.

Judicial review. The most potent weapon in the courts' arsenal is the power to review legislative enactments and invalidate those it regards as contrary to the U.S. Constitution. It can serve to begin an interbranch dispute by gutting a piece of state or federal legislation (*Roe v. Wade*[43] being an obvious example), or it can perpetuate or sometimes end a dispute by invalidating a legislative override (as in *City of Boerne v. Flores*, where the Supreme Court invalidated the Religious Freedom Restoration Act of 1993, which sought to override the Supreme Court's prior interpretation of the First Amendment's freedom of religion clause).[44] The exercise of judicial review invariably annoys defenders of the invalidated legislation, and some court critics argue that a restrained judiciary should override legislative preferences only in exceptional circumstances (if at all)—implicitly moving judicial review's status from tier one to tier two or three.

The "passive virtues." There is a cluster of doctrines that the judiciary has developed over the course of two centuries—Alexander Bickel called them "the passive virtues"—that enable courts to avoid confrontations with the political branches by deciding not to rule on particular matters.[45] These justiciability doctrines authorize judges to dismiss matters that do not present an adequately defined case or controversy where court involvement could embroil the courts in unwanted controversy. Various federalism-promoting doctrines permit federal courts to dismiss or remand suits within their jurisdiction that involve complicated or sensitive issues of state concern better resolved by state courts. The doctrines allow the federal courts to sidestep political thickets of acute local interest and avoid agitating isolated members of Congress or Congress as a whole. Likewise, for the Supreme Court, the power to hand-pick the eighty cases it hears each year from thousands of petitions for certiorari enables it to pick its fights with care. There is no indication that courts systematically avoid controversy through resort to these "passive virtues."[46] However, they do allow the courts to withdraw strategically in isolated cases where the judges involved deem it advisable to walk away.

Tier Two: Forms of Interaction Reserved for Exceptional Circumstances

The foregoing section surveyed mechanisms more or less routinely exploited by Congress and courts to keep each other in check, make their preferences known, and resolve interbranch disputes. During periods of heightened interbranch tension when the courts come under more sustained attack, Congress locks and loads additional weapons. Deploying these additional weapons is always controversial, because it encroaches more obviously and intentionally on judicial autonomy. The weapon itself is often a threat to take some action against the courts that, if actually taken, would violate long-standing independence norms. Court defenders typically conflate the threats themselves (such as proposing to impeach an "activist" judge) with the fulfillment of those threats (actually impeaching and removing an "activist" judge), and so they argue that the critics are engaging in tier-three conduct that is entirely unacceptable. Alternatively, court defenders may argue that the device at issue should be reserved for circumstances more exceptional than those prompting the court critics to propose its use. Congressional resort to tier-two mechanisms remains highly controversial—to judges, certainly, but within Congress as well; precisely for that reason, such mechanisms are rarely brought into serious play except during the cycles of intense anti-court sentiment described at the beginning of this chapter.

Congress and the Second Tier of Conflict

Threats to impeach errant judges. During the most recent cycle of court-directed animus beginning in the mid-1990s, court critics in Congress—including Senator Robert Dole, Speaker of the House Newt Gingrich, and House Majority Leader Tom DeLay—proposed to impeach one or more "activist" judges for making outrageous judicial decisions in isolated cases.[47] While court defenders decried such proposals as inimical to judicial independence, there is no denying that the impeachment threat has a long-established pedigree. In *The Federalist Papers*, Alexander Hamilton argued that the threat of impeachment would prevent judges from deliberately usurping political power.[48] In succeeding years, the House has initiated impeachment inquiries into the conduct of at least seventy-eight judges, of whom the allegations against seventy-four are known. Thirty-two of those judges were accused (often among other charges) of abusing judicial power by making high-handed rulings from the bench. Indeed, more judges have been targeted with impeachment inquiries for their decision-making than any other grounds (including abuse of administrative authority, favoritism, misappropriation of office funds, accepting or soliciting bribes, misuse of the office for financial advantage, incompetence, and poor demeanor). On the other hand, it bears emphasizing that no judge has been impeached and removed for making unpopular rulings, and serious impeachment inquiries into judicial decision-making ceased in the 1940s.[49] Nevertheless, when a congressional leader proposes to impeach an "activist" judge, the impact of that threat is more forceful than generalized criticism.[50] The prospect of being singled out in a House floor statement as a target for impeachment proceedings (followed by the possibility of an investigation, hearings, and a subpoena to testify before an angry subcommittee) may give a judge pause—even if removal from office is not a realistic possibility. Thus, when in 1996 Judge Baer reversed a ruling that had provoked calls for his impeachment, it was understandably assumed (although he denied it) that he had been intimidated by the threats.[51]

Threats to alter court size, disestablish courts, and cut budgets. Threats to manipulate a court's size, structure, and budget in retaliation for unpopular or outrageous judicial decisions continue to make occasional appearances during periods of intense anti-court feeling, though examples of Congress making good on such threats have receded into the distant past. Roosevelt's Court-packing plan did not become law, but the mere threat of its adoption may have had the desired effect of chastening antagonistic judges.[52] In some of the contemporary rounds of court-bashing, Representatives Tom DeLay and Steve King rattled the sabers again by threatening to disestablish the courts and cut court budgets.[53] As with threats to impeach errant judges, proposals to slash budgets or disestablish courts are greeted with shock and horror by court defenders, who oppose such proposals as antithetical to longstanding judicial independence norms. But—as with impeachment threats—even if there is no realistic possibility that Congress will follow through by cutting budgets or abolishing courts, the threats themselves ratchet up the stakes in the courts-Congress dialogue during periods of heightened interbranch tension; to that extent, they have an important role in the prosecution of disputes between the branches.

Significant manipulation of subject matter jurisdiction and "jurisdiction-stripping" proposals. As discussed earlier, general regulation of the courts' subject matter jurisdiction and minor tweaks to judicial review are commonplace. More targeted efforts to curb a court by depriving it of jurisdiction to hear cases in which Congress is concerned that the judges will decide the underlying issues in unacceptable ways, however, are reserved for truly exceptional circumstances. During the most recent cycle of anti-court sentiment, Congress enacted limited jurisdictional manipulations—doubtless born of mistrust for the courts—that restricted federal court involvement in habeas corpus proceedings, prisoner litigation, and immigration matters.[54] To these, one might add more recent legislation, enacted at the behest of the George W. Bush administration, denying enemy combatants in the "war on terror" recourse to the federal courts and providing for their trials in military tribunals—legislation that the Supreme Court subsequently invalidated.[55] While this legislation reflected political branch distrust of the federal courts and was enacted during a cycle of anti-court sentiment, congressional ac- quiescence to the president's initiative may have had more to do with acute anxiety over the war than with a desire to "score points" in its ongoing dispute with the judiciary. More aggressive efforts to strip the district courts of all jurisdiction to hear cases concerning public displays of the Ten Command- ments and the "under God" clause in the Pledge of Allegiance passed the House of Representatives but stalled in the Senate.[56]

Proposing to reduce a court's jurisdiction in retaliation for an unacceptable decision exerts a less obvious impact on the "independence" of the affected judges than threatening to impeach them or cut their budgets, which has led some scholars to question whether such an impact even exists.[57] Threatening judges with less work if they do not decide a class of cases to the satisfaction of the congressional majority is admittedly a double-edged sword—indeed, one might logically suppose that many judges would welcome a lighter docket. That may partially explain why the Judicial Conference has been less hostile to jurisdiction-stripping measures than other incursions on the judiciary's independence.[58] Even so, the link between threats to diminish subject matter jurisdiction and judicial independence is still clear enough: The prospect of being stripped of the power and prestige to adjudicate a matter if a judge ren- ders an unpopular decision constrains that judge's independence to render that unpopular decision. The federal judiciary is weakened as an independent branch of government if its unwelcome decisions force it to surrender judicial power to the political branches or the state courts. That said, the less intuitive relationship between jurisdiction-stripping initiatives and judicial indepen- dence may help to explain why judicial independence norms hold less sway in this context and why modest jurisdictional manipulations have been enacted and less modest ones have advanced in the legislative process.

The Courts and the Second Tier of Conflict

As noted above, a primary weapon available to the courts in their disputes with Congress is the power to declare acts of the political branches unconsti- tutional. Some have argued that the courts should use that weapon sparingly and only in exceptional circumstances, but—as a descriptive matter—its use has become commonplace. Political scientists have demonstrated that in the

Supreme Court, at least, judicial review is often exploited in a manner consistent with the policy preferences of the individual justices.[59] Less common, however, is the tactic of exploiting the power of judicial review to further the judiciary's institutional self-interest. Beginning in the late 1980s, Chief Justice William Rehnquist issued statements and made speeches, sometimes on behalf of the Judicial Conference, openly criticizing congressional proposals to federalize various crimes and civil offenses, including violence against women, on the grounds that such measures would overburden the federal courts and that the underlying issues were more appropriate for the states to regulate. After Congress enacted this legislation over the Chief Justice's objections, the Supreme Court—with Chief Justice Rehnquist writing the majority opinion—invalidated the Gun-Free School Zones Act of 1990, which federalized the crime of handgun possession in school zones,[60] and the Violence Against Women Act of 1994,[61] on the grounds that only the states and not Congress had the authority to regulate such matters. More recently, the Judicial Conference has opposed other proposed legislation on seemingly constitutional grounds, arguing, for example, that a bill to prohibit judges from attending expenses-paid educational seminars would interfere with the judges' freedom of association, which suggested the possibility that, if enacted, the law would be invalidated.[62]

This strategy of lobbying against legislation for reasons later resurrected in the context of judicial review is so new that the frequency of its future use remains difficult to predict. It is, however, a high-stakes gambit that could easily provoke congressional retaliation if its use is not confined to exceptional circumstances. From the judiciary's standpoint, the circumstances culminating in its resort to this "one-two punch" strategy may have been exceptional, in that they arose amid a cycle of anti-court sentiment and collectively constituted what the Judicial Conference regarded as an alarming series of impositions on federal court dockets and operations. If, on the other hand, the judiciary resorts to such hardball tactics routinely, when tradition dictates that tier-one strategies should dominate dispute processing between the branches, it may threaten to disrupt the dynamic equilibrium that has preserved independence norms for generations. If the courts do not want Congress to jettison independence norms and exploit the greatest powers at its disposal to manipulate judicial decision-making, then judges must think twice about using such powers to manipulate congressional decision-making.

Tier Three: Methods of Interaction that are Unacceptable

In this final category are methods of interaction that may be within the constitutional authority of courts and Congress to use against each other but that longstanding institutional norms governing the interbranch relationship have deemed unacceptable. This is not to suggest that these methods serve no useful purpose. Like the theory of mutually assured destruction advanced during the Cold War, which posited that neither the United States nor the Soviet Union would launch a nuclear strike against the other as long as each knew that the other could retaliate in kind, access to "weapons" enabling courts and Congress to precipitate interbranch Armageddon may ensure that neither provokes their deployment and that each side abides by accepted norms.

Congressional Responses in Tier-Three Disputes

Making good on tier-two threats. It is one thing to threaten a judge with impeachment, disestablishment, court-packing, budget cuts, or loss of jurisdiction if her decisions do not comport with congressional preferences; it is another thing altogether to make good on those threats.

Impeachment. In our history, seven federal judges have been impeached and removed for offenses ranging from corruption and criminal behavior to desertion. In that time, no judge has ever been removed for abusing judicial power by making outrageous decisions. Four judges—Thomas Pickering, Samuel Chase, James Peck, and Charles Swayne—were impeached by the House on charges including abuse of judicial power. The first case, that of Thomas Pickering, was unique because his conviction in the Senate turned not on the high-handed behavior described in the articles of impeachment but on the judge's insanity and alcoholism, which was the precipitating cause of his high-handedness.[63] Each of the other three judges argued at their Senate trials that the conduct of which they stood accused was at worst innocent error and that judicial independence principles counseled against the removal of any judge for less than demonstrably willful misconduct. Each was acquitted by increasingly lopsided margins. Over the years, the House investigated an additional twenty-eight judges for abuse of judicial power, the last in 1933, none of whom were impeached.[64] When called upon in the 1980s to investigate three circuit judges for reversing a conviction in a capital case, the House Judiciary Committee's Subcommittee on Courts issued a report that explained its decision not to pursue the matter in light of judicial independence principles:

> Federal judges should not and cannot be impeached for judicial decision-making, even if a decision is an erroneous one. The conduct complained about—entering a judgment and order—is an act that judges are required to do under the Constitution. It would be a great irony if the protections found in the Judiciary's constitutional charter—Article III—did not shield judges in their decisionmaking role.[65]

Disestablishment. In 1802, the Republican majority in Congress effectively removed sixteen recently appointed Federalist judges by abolishing their stations. In 1913, it abolished the unpopular and short-lived Commerce Court (under circumstances too unusual and situation-specific to serve as meaningful precedent) but then retained the court's judges, citing judicial independence concerns.[66] Congress has made no comparable moves in the century since. A more recent effort to manipulate court structure concerns the efforts of conservative members of Congress in western states to split the United States Court of Appeals for the Ninth Circuit, so as to marginalize the regional influence of liberal California judges.[67] Out of deference to entrenched independence norms, however, sponsors typically avoid such explanations when agitating for the split (even though they may rail against "activist" judges in other contexts) and confine their arguments to good-government justifications, for instance, that the Ninth Circuit is too large and would operate more effectively if it were divided.[68]

Court-packing. Similarly, Congress has never openly packed the Supreme Court for partisan purposes. It periodically adjusted the size of the Supreme Court in the nineteenth century, almost always so that the number of justices (each of whom traveled within or "rode" one of the regional circuits each year, sitting as a circuit judge) corresponded to the increasing number of regional circuits. Some have speculated that the Radical Republican Congress reduced the size of the Court during Reconstruction to deny President Andrew Johnson, a Democrat, an appointment, but if so, no member of Congress acknowledged as much; indeed, one colloquy on the House floor suggested that the move was made out of deference to the Supreme Court, which wanted to trade a reduction in size for an increase in salary.[69] And while the need for Roosevelt's Court-packing plan may have been obviated by a change in the voting patterns of the existing Supreme Court, the plan received a chilly reception in Congress and was never adopted. As to the lower courts, new judgeships have never been created absent a showing of administrative need. Moreover, as to the precise timing, number, and location of new judgeships (which is undeniably driven by partisan considerations), such legislation is best understood as ancillary to the appointments process, in that legislation that creates additional openings to fill and the process by which those openings are filled together enable the political branches to staff the judicial branch with like-minded officials. And the appointments process, which applies to executive and judicial branch officials alike, has always been subject to the political rough and tumble and has never been constrained by independence norms to a meaningful extent.

Court budgets. There is no clear precedent for Congress ever holding the judiciary's budget hostage in exchange for favorable decisions or retaliating against the judiciary for rendering unfavorable decisions. It is useful to compare the experience in many state systems, where the political culture can be quite different. Whereas Congress has not openly sought to manipulate the federal judiciary's decision-making by holding its budget hostage, it has been comparatively common for state legislatures to retaliate against state courts in the budgetary process.[70]

Subject matter jurisdiction. A special word is in order with respect to legislation that deprives the federal courts of subject matter jurisdiction over specified issues in order to avert unwelcome decisions. Until very recently, the lines of demarcation seemed relatively stable and clear: Congress routinely exercised general oversight of the courts' subject matter jurisdiction and frequently tweaked judicial review in minor ways to serve the needs of legislation on a case-by-case basis (tier one). During periods of heightened tension between the branches, members of Congress introduced bills to deprive the courts of jurisdiction to adjudicate matters about which they had recently issued unpopular interpretations of the Constitution, and these bills occasionally advanced through the legislative process (tier two). But since Reconstruction, Congress has never enacted legislation stripping a federal court of all jurisdiction for the explicit purpose of circumventing adverse judicial rulings on the specified subject—effectively making the enactment of such legislation a tier-three mechanism. In the latest cycle of court-directed hostility beginning in the mid-1990s, however, Congress has gone further than it has in the past. As noted earlier, it has enacted legislation imposing significant restrictions on the jurisdiction of federal courts to hear habeas, immigration, and prison condition cases, for the explicit purpose of averting "liberal" decisions. Proposals to deprive the federal courts of all jurisdiction to adjudicate several hot-button issues passed the House of Representatives.[71] Even more recently, Congress enacted legislation, at the behest of President George W. Bush, denying all access to federal courts for "enemy combatants" indefinitely detained in the "war on terror" out of concern that such courts would afford prisoners procedural rights that could undermine the war effort.[72] On the one hand, the Supreme Court invalidated these latter enactments, leading one to doubt whether they have cowed the courts in any meaningful way.[73] On the other hand, the willingness of Congress to adopt them in the first place, when combined with its other recent activity in the area, suggests the possibility that institutional norms against the curbing of courts with jurisdiction-stripping legislation may be weakening.

Open defiance of court rulings. It is quite common for representatives of the political branches to complain openly and bitterly when they are irritated by a judicial decision, and it is not unprecedented for them to delay or evade compliance with a court order. But open defiance, in which Congress or the president denies a court's authority and disregards its order is no longer in the repertoire—although exasperated critics sometimes point to centuries-old examples as if it remains an available option.[74] The statement, attributed to Andrew Jackson in the wake of an unpopular decision of the Supreme Court, that "John Marshall has made his decision, now let him enforce it"[75] is apocryphal, but it endures because it so beautifully underscores the fragility of the courts' power and their dependence on the cooperation of the political branches. In our political culture, such cooperation is a given, and commentators often punctuate the point by celebrating moments in constitutional history when presidents and other public figures have peacefully acquiesced to judicial authority, whether by ceding control of the nation's steel mills, relinquishing incriminating tapes to a special prosecutor, or conceding defeat in a presidential election.

Court Responses in Tier-Three Disputes

This category is more speculative because the devices at issue are unused to such an extent that their very existence is doubtful. Suffice to say that if they do exist, norms against their use are so strong as to place them off limits.

Inherent powers over court budgets. Courts in the state and federal systems have deemed themselves to possess certain "inherent" powers—powers that are not enumerated in the Constitution but that are essential to preserving the judicial function. The authority of the judge to maintain control of her courtroom through the exercise of the contempt power is one generally accepted form of inherent power. Some state supreme courts, frustrated by the failure of state and local governments to fund court systems adequately, have resorted to a much more controversial form of inherent power that they have exploited to order intransigent governmental units to provide the judiciary with sufficient resources to function. Such an argument is aided by state constitutions that establish independent and unified judicial systems, where the judiciary's authority to preserve its institutional integrity may inhere in the constitutional structure. In the federal system, the argument that the judiciary has the inherent power to preserve itself by demanding adequate resources from Congress is weakened by the Constitution, which delegates to Congress not only the power of the purse but also the discretionary power to establish the inferior courts—and, by negative implication, the power to disestablish them altogether. A besieged judiciary, however, might nonetheless conclude that as long as Congress chooses to establish such courts and vest them with the judicial power to adjudicate cases and controversies under Article III, the courts possess the inherent power to ensure that they have the minimum resources necessary to exercise the judicial power delegated to them by the Constitution.

Alternatively, a federal court that deemed itself too underfunded could conceivably sidestep the inherent powers issue by finding that the due process rights of litigants are violated when court systems are funded below a minimum level.[76] The point is that there are ways in which the judiciary could attempt to force the hand of a stingy or punitive Congress. Such a gambit could create a constitutional crisis and invite congressional defiance. That such a crisis has never occurred at the federal level—as it has in several state systems—is a testament to the effectiveness of tiers one and two in resolving interbranch disputes. The net effect is that inherent powers and related arguments have remained a tier-three shotgun behind the door.

Removal of judges. Some scholars have noted that under English common law, the judiciary possessed a means to remove judges on its own initiative. These scholars have argued that nothing in the U.S. Constitution deprived the federal judiciary of this preexisting power, and therefore that the power remains available.[77] Given this backdrop, it is at least conceivable to suppose that the judiciary could defuse impeachment showdowns with Congress over "lightning-rod" judges by removing them from office.

Inferring the continued existence of so significant a power from an empty record at the Constitutional Convention by intuiting what the delegates would have thought about it, had they thought about it, is inherently risky business.[78] More to the point, even if the existence of a common law self-removal power is conceded for the sake of argument, over two centuries of complete non-use is powerful precedent for the proposition that longstanding institutional norms argue against its resurrection.[79] In short, if such a power exists, resort to it is politically unacceptable.

The better option is a less extreme one. Scott Gant's chapter in this book discusses how the Judicial Conduct and Disability Act has served as a source of "self-regulation" of the federal judiciary and a means of temporarily suspending and otherwise disciplining district and circuit court judges. Such an approach employs a less exotic means to less extreme ends, and it does so in cooperation with Congress, which enacted the legislation in 1980—a step more in keeping with the familiar choreography of the courts-Congress dance described here.

Where to from Here?

The intricacies of courts-Congress quarrels are considerable. Media and scholarly attention has focused on flashier means for the judicial and legislative branches to keep the other in check, such as impeachment, jurisdiction-stripping, or judicial review, to the virtual exclusion of other, more mundane mechanisms that enable the two to engage each other constructively, resolve disputes, and move on. This chapter has sought to fill that void.

Although it is too early to be certain, the results of the congressional midterm elections of 2006 appeared to signal an end to the most recent cycle of anti-court sentiment that began twelve years earlier. When Republicans lost control of the House of Representatives that year, the leaders of the most recent anti-court campaign lost their power and, in some cases, their jobs. Between then and 2010, publicized conservative attacks on federal judges and courts fell off precipitously.

In the short term, the question naturally arises as to when the next cycle of anti-court sentiment can be anticipated. The 2008 election of Barack Obama constituted a political realignment of sorts, and it is likely that there will be some friction between the Obama administration and a conservative Supreme Court that resulted from appointments by Obama's Republican predecessors. The Obama election by itself, however, does not represent a realignment of the same order of magnitude as that which provoked a backlash against hold-over judges in generations past. While the issue of judicial appointments was not altogether absent from the presidential campaign, the election turned on the economy and the Iraq War—matters with respect to which holdover judges were not deemed complicitous. For that reason, a new, full-blown cycle of court-bashing is unlikely, unless and until the Court becomes emboldened to interfere with the Obama administration's agenda more directly.

Of greater interest, perhaps, is the long term. The reason that cyclical at-tacks on judges have not culminated in the imposition of more draconian controls on the courts has less to do with constitutional law than with insti-tutional norms. While the question is not free of controversy (in part because it arises so rarely), Congress may well have the constitutional authority to dis-establish unpopular courts, impeach unpopular judges, or slash an unpopular judiciary's budget in explicitly punitive ways. But time and again, Congress has declined to exercise that authority because it is thought to be a bad idea, antithetical to the role that an independent judiciary is supposed to play in American government. The role of judicial independence, the argument goes, is to insulate judges from threats or intimidation that could compromise their capacity to uphold the rule of law. The animating assumption underlying in-dependence norms, then, is that independent judges follow the law.

For generations now, an influential segment of the political science com-munity, steeped in the tradition of legal realism, has devoted itself to demon-strating that independent judges are less influenced by the law than their own ideological predilections. And in a series of recent, well-publicized events, the public has received a steady stream of information that corroborates the po-litical science hypothesis: The well-publicized conservative campaign against liberal judicial activism has been devoted to the proposition that too many judges disregard the law and substitute their political preferences; in nation-ally televised confirmation hearings, Senate Republicans and Democrats alike have accused federal judicial nominees of being ideological zealots; and across the states, heavily advertised state supreme court election campaigns have become referenda on the candidates' policy positions on such issues as tort reform, abortion, gay marriage, and the death penalty.

Polling data suggest that the public has, to some degree, internalized the lessons of legal realism. On the one hand, surveys reveal that substantial majorities still think that judges are committed to the facts and the law and should be sheltered from outside pressure and congressional interference. On the other hand, a comparable majority still regards judges as "political" decision-makers, while smaller majorities agree with the propositions that judges may say that they follow the law but often act on their personal beliefs and that judges who repeatedly ignore voter values should be impeached.[80]

If voters and their congressional representatives reach the point of concluding that independent judges are unaccountable policy-makers who disregard the law and do as they please, then the rule of law justification for judicial independence collapses and, with it, the norms that have protected the judiciary for generations. But predictions of apocalypse are decidedly premature. As the preceding paragraph reveals, the public is at worst ambivalent about judges and their independence, and its views on what judges do and how they should be regulated are in some ways contradictory. Such results may be explained in terms of defects in survey instruments or public ignorance or indifference, but they are also consonant with recent social science learning, which has found that judicial decision-making is subject to a range of influences, including but not limited to law, ideological preferences, strategic choices, cognitive biases, and various forms of self-interest.

The long-term future of judicial independence may thus turn on reorienting cyclical defenses of independence norms to accommodate the multivariate influences on judicial decision-making that social scientists and the public increasingly accept. Without abandoning the rule of law as a partial justification for judicial independence (in "easy" cases, to be sure, and as a meaningful constraint in hard cases too, particularly in circuit and district courts, where the influence of law remains strong), there is another defense worthy of exploration. To concede that judges make decisions with reference to more than just the "law" narrowly defined is not to concede the desirability of Congress, the president, or the electorate controlling the decisions judges make. The judicial process ensures that judges do not make decisions until the litigants have had a meaningful opportunity to acquaint the judge with circumstances unique to their particular case—the parties, the facts, the law, the policy implications, and so on. In hard cases, where the law yields no clear answers, it is fatuous to suppose that we want judges to do the impossible and "just" follow the law. Rather, we are asking judges for their best judgment, knowing what they know about the case at hand—and thanks to the judicial process, what they know far exceeds what Congress, the president, or the electorate could possibly know. To ensure that we get their best judgment, we must insulate judges from external interference and intimidation. That judgment will inevitably be influenced by the qualities that make them human: their experiences, ideologies, educations, common sense, and so on. The electorate and its elected representatives are within their rights to pick judges carefully, to ensure that they are women and men with the kind of judgment the public deems acceptable. But there is a difference between selecting judges initially with an eye to whether they are likely to exercise their judgment in a manner that the public regards as sound and seeking to manipulate that judgment once those judges are in office, with threats to their jurisdiction, budgets, or tenure. In short, one can concede that something beyond the facts and the law are in play when judges decide cases without concluding that Congress should abandon the independence norms it has nurtured for generations.

chapter 2

Congress and Judicial Supremacy

Neal Devins

The previous chapter took a broad, historical, and diagnostic view of relations between Congress and the judiciary as a whole. This chapter focuses on a somewhat narrower topic by evaluating whether, in the twenty-first century, the U.S. Supreme Court should be concerned about congressional threats to curb judicial power—especially calls to limit the Court's appellate jurisdiction, that is, the kinds of cases it can hear from lower courts. By drawing on research from political science, case studies of congressional threats to prior Supreme Courts, and examinations of the partisan balance and institutional incentives of recent Congresses, Neal Devins sketches the factors that influence the likelihood and nature of congressional reprisals against today's Supreme Court.

Congress possesses awesome formal powers to set the Court's agenda and to check the Court. As outlined in chapter 1, the Constitution empowers Congress, among other things, to impeach judges, to make exceptions to the jurisdiction of federal courts, to confirm judicial nominations, and to amend the Constitution. Congress also plays a defining role in setting much of the Court's agenda—by enacting the very legislation that is the subject of judicial review and by controlling, to a considerable extent, the terms under which litigants reach the Court.[1] More than that, the Court cannot implement its own decisions and, as such, is dependent on Congress and other elected officials. But should the Supreme Court fear Congress? It may be, for example, that the Court and Congress rarely have divergent policy preferences (so that Congress would have little reason to challenge the Court). Also, if the Court is confident that Congress will adhere to judicial rulings, the justices may feel empowered to strike down acts of Congress with little fear of legislative non-acquiescence.

This chapter will seek to solve the following puzzle: Why is today's Congress so willing to criticize judicial decision-making but so reticent to use court-stripping and other formal powers to check the courts? I will divide my comments into four parts. The first section explains why the Supreme Court is often sensitive to the dominant political forces in Congress. In particular, by providing a quick snapshot of the dominant models that political scientists employ to describe Supreme Court decision-making, I will argue that Congress need not challenge the Court because the Court is often sensitive to congressional preferences. The second section continues to answer this question by looking at congressional efforts to limit Court jurisdiction in the mid-1950s (during the Warren Court) and from 1979 to 1982 (during the Burger Court)—arguing that the Warren Court had good reason to take political backlash into account and that the Burger Court was right to ignore court-curbing proposals. In so doing, I will comment more generally on whether and when the Supreme Court should calibrate its decision-making to avoid political reprisals from Congress. The third section discusses recent congressional efforts to slap down state and federal judges by expanding or restricting federal court jurisdiction. I will argue that, unlike in the Warren Court era, there is no dominant coalition in the modern Congress that is truly upset with the Supreme Court. Instead, reflecting the tendency of today's lawmakers to strengthen their electoral base by staking out positions on politically charged issues, modern-day court-stripping proposals are largely empty threats. Indeed, unlike the Warren Court era, today's lawmakers are largely uninterested in interpreting the Constitution and, as such, seem unusually deferential to the Supreme Court's power to speak the final word on the Constitution's meaning. The final part comments more generally on the future of judicial independence and provides another answer to the question of why today's Congress is unlikely to turn to court-stripping. By highlighting both public support for judicial independence and Congress's power to respond to disfavored Supreme Court rulings through less draconian means, I will argue that Congress has little to gain and much to lose by direct legislative attacks on the Court.

The Political Science Models

Supreme Court justices typically pursue policy initiatives consistent with the policy preferences of Congress. This phenomenon is detailed in the leading political science models of Supreme Court decision-making. While assuming that Supreme Court justices are principally interested in pursuing favored policies, these models underscore the tremendous influence that Congress has in shaping Supreme Court decision-making. The attitudinal model assumes that "judges vote reflexively in each case; that is, they cast their votes based solely on their individual reactions to the facts and legal issues presented, rather than by considering, in addition, how judges or institutions are likely to react to the decision."[2] A second model, the strategic model, posits that judges take the reaction of others into account when advancing their policy and legal preferences. A Supreme Court justice, for example, might take implementation concerns into account and, with it, potential resistance from either elected officials or the American people.[3]

Congress-Court relations figure prominently in both the attitudinal and strategic models. The attitudinal model emphasizes the role that political actors play in shaping Court decision-making through the appointments and confirmation process. Specifically, "[b]ecause presidents usually nominate justices with philosophies similar to their own and the Senate generally confirms only nominees who have views consistent with the contemporary political mainstream, regular turnover results in a Court majority rarely holding significantly divergent policy preferences from those held by the president and Congress."[4] In particular, by confirming justices who will either overrule disfavored doctrine or affirm favored doctrine, Congress helps steer the path that the Supreme Court will follow. For attitudinalists, these ex ante influences on judicial decision-making are profoundly important. Justices may vote their policy preferences, but the appointments and confirmation process ensures that those policy preferences are palatable to elected officials.

Unlike the attitudinal model, the strategic model emphasizes the ex post influences of Congress and other actors. According to the strategic account of judicial decision-making, justices will bargain or retreat in the face of a challenge or will adopt insincere positions on the merits in order to avoid a conflict with powerholders who are in a position to thwart the will of the Court.[5] By taking elected officials' desires into account, a strategic justice may seek to advance his or her preferred positions, whether those positions are simply an expression of personal policy preferences or, instead, reflect "distinct professional roles, [a] sense of obligation, and salient institutional perspectives."[6] These justices are concerned about both the refusal of elected officials to implement Court edicts and the prospects of elected officials negating or limiting an unpopular ruling by statute, constitutional amendment, or some other court-curbing action.

That a Court lacking the powers of the purse and sword would take implementation concerns into account is hardly surprising. Likewise, it is to be expected that some justices take into account lawmaker efforts to punish the Court for politically unpopular decisions. Justices with weak policy preferences do not want to precipitate an imbroglio with Congress; justices with strong policy preferences want Congress to acquiesce to, not nullify, Court rulings.

For these very reasons, the Court sometimes backs away from long-established doctrine in order to embrace doctrinal formulas supported by Congress. In the wake of Congress's approval of a proposed Equal Rights Amendment, the Court—making explicit reference to the Equal Rights Amendment—began to retool its gender decision-making so that Court doctrine would largely conform to the proposed Equal Rights Amendment.[7] Likewise, after Franklin Delano Roosevelt's landslide victory in 1936 (but before Roosevelt and the Congress seized control of the Court through the appointment and confirmation of New Deal justices), Justice Owen Roberts began to supply key votes to sustain New Deal measures. After leaving the Court, he explained the force of majoritarian pressures facing the Court: "Looking back, it is difficult to see how the Court could have resisted the popular urge for uniform standards through the country for what in effect was a unified economy."[8]

That Supreme Court decision-making is responsive both to the appointments process and to the efforts of elected officials cannot be denied. The question remains: When should the Supreme Court fear Congress, so that a justice should "live to fight another day" by moderating favored legal policy positions in the short run in order to advance those very positions in the future? The next section tackles this question by focusing on jurisdiction-stripping proposals introduced during the Warren and Burger Courts. These two examples point to different outcomes when Congress and the Court clash on policy, suggesting some preliminary lessons about the Court's calculus of fear.

The Court versus Congress: Two Case Studies in Fear

Article III of the Constitution recognizes a direct link between judicial power and politics. Under Section I, the power to ordain and establish lower federal courts rests with Congress. Moreover, Section 2 makes the Supreme Court's appellate jurisdiction subject to "such exceptions, and under such regulations as the Congress shall make." Unlike judicial review, which the

Court uses to expand its own power, court stripping concerns external political forces curtailing judicial power.

Before 1953, Congress rarely looked to its jurisdictional power as a mechanism to statutorily undermine undesired Supreme Court rulings. When jurisdiction was limited, such as in the Reconstruction Era, it was typically a preemptive strike to protect legislative priorities by foreclosing judicial action. That said, the period before 1953 is replete with examples of Congress seeking to influence Supreme Court decision-making by either enacting or considering legislative proposals dictating the timing of decisions, the size of the Court, and other Court-curbing measures. Examples include Congress's legislation in 1802 abolishing the circuit courts of appeal and preventing the Supreme Court from meeting (for fourteen months) to review Congress's handiwork; Congress's 1868 repeal of a statute (granting the Supreme Court jurisdiction to review habeas corpus actions) in order to stave off a Court decision on the constitutionality of the Reconstruction military government in the South; Congress's consideration of legislative proposals requiring a supermajority of justices to invalidate state or federal legislation; and Congress's 1937 rejection of Court-packing legislation allowing the president to appoint one additional justice for each justice over the age of 70 (so that the votes of elderly justices against New Deal reforms would be neutralized by the votes of younger justices who supported Congress's power to enact such reforms).[9]

The volume of Court-curbing measures, the intensity of congressional opprobrium toward the Court, and the willingness of Congress to strike at individual Court decisions (by removing federal court jurisdiction) underwent a sea change during the Warren Court. By striking down scores of politically popular laws, the Warren Court seemed quite willing to overturn the legislative apple cart and open itself to political reprisals. From 1953 to 1968, over sixty bills were introduced in Congress to limit the jurisdiction of the federal courts over school desegregation, national security, criminal confessions, and other areas of dispute. More than that, Congress considered a slew of constitutional amendment and legislative proposals that were intended to override unpopular Warren Court rulings.

The Warren Court calibrated its decision-making in response to a threatened backlash by Congress. In the 1950s, the Court retreated from a series of "pro-Communist" free speech rulings. In the late 1960s, the Court scaled back its efforts to limit police prerogatives by constitutionalizing criminal procedure. As we will see in exploring both of these areas of constitutional law, the Warren Court had good reason to moderate its decision-making in the face of congressional attacks.

The Rise and Fall of Free Speech Rights for Communists

During its 1956–1957 term, the Court decided twelve cases involving Communists, ruling against the government in every case. Congress responded with a vengeance, coming—as Chief Justice Warren put it—"dangerously close" to enacting legislation that would have stripped the Supreme Court of appellate jurisdiction in five domestic security areas.[10] The Court relented, issuing decisions that limited the scope of earlier rulings and otherwise permitting the government to prosecute subversive cases. As *The New York Times* editorialized in early 1960, "What Senator Jenner [the principal sponsor of court-stripping legislation] was unable to achieve [in Congress] the Supreme Court has now virtually accomplished on its own."[11]

The question remains: Should the 1957 Warren Court have feared Congress? I think that the answer to this question is a qualified yes. First, the Court could not take comfort in Congress's longstanding tradition of defending judicial independence. In 1937, FDR's infamous Court-packing proposal had almost been enacted. Twenty years later, the received wisdom about Court-packing was that the Court had saved itself by executing an "astonishing about-face" by approving state and federal reform efforts in the midst of congressional consideration of the Court-packing bill. Second, the Warren Court's "pro-Communist" free speech decisions were profoundly upsetting to significant factions within Congress. Fears about Communism and its threat to domestic security resonated with both lawmakers and the American people. Even though the crisis atmosphere of the early 1950s had eased, Congress continued to beat the anti-Communist drum. More than that, judicial credibility in Congress was strained for another reason. Southern lawmakers strongly disapproved of *Brown* and, with it, the Court. One hundred and one of the 128 Southerners in Congress signed a manifesto pledging "to use all lawful means to bring about a reversal of" the decision.[12] With Southern lawmakers joining forces with anti-Communist lawmakers, the Court understood that it could ill afford to agitate this potent coalition. Third (and relatedly), a substantial number of lawmakers in the late 1950s thought that courts should give great weight to congressional interpretations of the Constitution. These lawmakers embraced an "independent constitutionalist" perspective, emphasizing the distinctive constitutional responsibilities of the legislature and pointing to drawbacks associated with leaving interpretation strictly to judges. In particular, 40 percent of lawmakers thought that courts should give "controlling weight" to congressional interpretations of the Constitution.[13] For these lawmakers, Congress had reason to assert itself in the face of Court decisions undermining lawmaker interpretations of the Constitution.

That Congress was poised to act, of course, does not necessarily mean that Congress would have acted. After all, Congress did not enact jurisdiction-stripping legislation in 1957. Indeed, even with a number of factors in the 1957–58 Congress making Congress disposed to oppose the Court, the actual Jenner bill failed to pass and was almost completely tempered during the legislative process.[14] Congress, moreover, had signaled some support for an independent Court through word and deed. Roosevelt's Court-packing plan had been rebuked, and a subsequent "uninterrupted expansion of federal court jurisdiction . . . revealed a high degree of congressional respect for and reliance on the federal courts that a few unpopular decisions simply could not erode."[15]

On balance, however, the Court's moderates in 1957—Felix Frankfurter and John Marshall Harlan—had good reason to reverse course. By approving government regulation of subversives, the Court "helped sap the vigor of the Court attacks" and "provided a ready means by which Court foes could execute a face-saving retreat of their own." Assuming that Frankfurter and Harlan were ambivalent about the Court's Communist rulings, the benefits of this retreat certainly outweighed the risks of jurisdiction-stripping legislation and strained relations with Congress. As Walter Murphy concluded in his study of this episode: "The retreat of the Warren Court was a tactical withdrawal, not a rout."[16] No constitutional rulings were overturned, and the Court held firm to its rejection of Jim Crow.

Miranda and Its Aftermath

Before 1962, the Warren Court was sharply split, so much so that the divided and besieged set of justices avoided the sharpest confrontations with each other by agreeing to issue indeterminate opinions.[17] "History's Warren Court," the Court that "virtually rewrote the corpus of our constitutional law," was ushered in only after the 1962 appointment of Arthur Goldberg.[18] In sharp contrast to Felix Frankfurter (the justice whose seat Goldberg filled), Goldberg was a self-defined liberal and activist. Together with Warren, Douglas, Black, and Brennan, Goldberg gave the Court five secure votes for liberal outcomes.[19]

Ideological cohesion in the post-1962 Warren Court played out in many ways, including the Court's willingness to go as far as it could in advancing its vision of legal policy-making. Put another way: Without needing to appease centrist justices like Felix Frankfurter and John Marshall Harlan, the post-1962 Warren Court was willing to risk elected-branch disapproval in order to advance their legal policy agenda. Indeed, as the Warren Court's criminal procedure revolution makes clear, the post-1962 Warren Court had strong legal policy preferences and was only willing to back away from those preferences when there was good reason to fear retaliation.

Miranda v Arizona is the quintessential example of the post-1962 Warren Court's willingness to take political risks to pursue its vision of legal policy making. Notwithstanding public opinion polls showing significant opposition to Warren Court criminal procedure decisions and the calls by twenty-seven states (in an amicus brief) for the Court to slow down its criminal procedure revolution, *Miranda* mandated a specific set of warnings that police must read to criminal suspects.[20] In so doing, the Court required every state to change its interrogation practices.[21]

The post-1962 Warren Court's willingness to constitutionalize criminal law tested the limits of what elected government and the American people would tolerate. Indeed, Richard Nixon and George Wallace both took aim at Supreme Court liberalism in their 1968 presidential bids. At the same time, the post-1962 Warren Court was sensitive to potential congressional backlash and, after Congress enacted legislation seeking to override *Miranda* statutorily, the Court sought to diffuse political attacks by scaling back their criminal procedure revolution.[22] Unlike the Court's earlier retreat from its pro-Communist rulings, the post-1962 Court responded to the actual enactment of anti-Court legislation.

The Burger Court and Beyond

The Warren Court had good reason to respond to threats of congressional retaliation. The pre-1962 Court, controlled by centrist justices who were more interested in preserving political capital with lawmakers than in pushing the boundaries of judicial authority, had moderated its decision-making in the face of threatened (and nearly enacted) court-curbing proposals. More to the point: Not only was the pre-1962 Court less unified and ideological than the post-1962 Court, the pre-1962 Congress was also primed for a knock-down, drag-out fight with the justices. Centrist justices simply could not ignore the confluence of anti-Communist sentiment in Congress and Southern lawmaker opposition to *Brown*. The post-1962 Court likewise acted soundly in slowing down its criminal procedure revolution in the face of actual anti-Court legislation enacted by the Congress. In particular, even though these ideologically simpatico justices were willing to push the envelope of what Congress was willing to tolerate, the Court nonetheless had much to lose and little to gain by thumbing its nose at a Congress that signaled its disapproval with the Court through the enactment of anti-Court legislation.

The sensitivity of the Warren Court calibrating its decision-making in the face of a hostile Congress does not mean that the Supreme Court should ipso facto moderate its decision-making when faced with criticism by Congress or other elected officials. Unlike the Warren Court, for example, the Burger Court had no reason to fear the enactment of anti-Court legislation of Carter- and Reagan-era proposals to strip the courts of jurisdiction over abortion, school busing, and school prayer.[23] Not only did the Democrat-controlled House refuse to act on these proposals, the Reagan administration did not back Court-stripping proposals.

The Burger Court experience is revealing for another reason. Even though the Court did not retool its doctrine on abortion, school prayer, and busing, it did not block Congress from expressing disagreement with these decisions. Congress, for example, was able to use its appropriations powers to signal its disapproval of abortion rights and busing remedies.[24] Through the Equal Access Act (mandating that public schools allow religious organizations equal access to school facilities), moreover, Congress was able to facilitate religious expression in public schools. By providing elected officials with an opportunity to register their policy preferences, the Court helped avoid a head-on confrontation with Congress and the White House.

The lesson here is simple: the Supreme Court can pursue its favored policies *so long as* Congress can pursue *its* favored policies.[25] Congress's rejection of Court-packing in the 1930s and its failure to enact jurisdiction-stripping legislation in the 1950s and the 1980s suggests that lawmakers are reluctant to challenge the premises of an independent judiciary. Nevertheless, if Court decision-making cuts at the core of lawmaker preferences, Congress may act and may act boldly. Congress's enactment of legislation to nullify *Miranda* statutorily is an example of this phenomenon.

What, then, of today's Court? As the next section will detail, Congress considered a slew of court-stripping measures from 2003 to 2006 and actually enacted three different bills that impacted federal court jurisdiction over divisive questions involving enemy combatants and abortion rights. Against this backdrop, should the Rehnquist Court have moderated its decision-making in response to these measures? Likewise, should the Roberts Court see ongoing attacks on judicial independence as a harbinger of things to come? In short, in the face of recent attacks, should today's Court view itself as a vulnerable Warren Court or a secure Burger Court? In the next section of this chapter, I will argue that, due to changes in the ideological composition of Congress, neither of these referents is wholly applicable. Congress-Court relations during the past decade signal a congressional lack of interest in the Constitution and the Supreme Court. For these and other reasons, the Roberts Court should not fear Congress.

Making Sense of Recent Legislative Challenges to Judicial Independence

As the introduction to this volume suggests (see, for example, table I.2), Congress, from 2003 to 2006, took aim at the federal courts, including the U.S. Supreme Court. Lawmakers considered proposals to strip federal courts of jurisdiction over same-sex marriage, the Pledge of Allegiance, judicial invocations of international law, and the public display of the Ten Commandments. And while none of these proposals were enacted, the House of Representatives (but not the Senate) approved proposals to strip the federal courts of jurisdiction in cases involving same-sex marriage and the Pledge of Allegiance.[26] More striking, Congress enacted legislation limiting federal court review of legal challenges involving "enemy combatants."[27] Finally, Congress expressed its disapproval of state court decision-making in the Terri Schiavo case by expanding federal court jurisdiction. Specifically, rather than accept state court findings that Terri Schiavo, then in a persistent vegetative state, would rather die than be kept alive artificially, Congress asked the federal courts to sort out whether the removal of a feeding tube violated Ms. Schiavo's constitutional rights.[28]

Against this backdrop, the specter of lawmakers expressing their disapproval of court decision-making through retaliatory legislation seemed more real during 2005 and 2006 than at any time since the Warren Court. In addition to jurisdiction-altering proposals and legislation, Congress enacted legislation requiring that records be kept of judges who made downward departures of Sentencing Commission guidelines and debated the creation of an officer of "inspector general" to monitor federal court decision-making. Commenting on how this dramatic increase in the criticism of judges has exacerbated "the strained relationship between the Congress and the federal Judiciary," Chief Justice William Rehnquist spoke, in January 2005, of his "hope that the Supreme Court and all of our courts will continue to command sufficient public respect to enable them to survive basic attacks on the[ir] judicial independence."[29] Three months later, Justice Antonin Scalia sounded a more ominous message. Responding to Justice Stephen Breyer's claim that "the treasure" of this country is that people who criticize the Court will still follow its rulings, Scalia suggested that the Supreme Court "has become a very political institution. And when that happens, the people in a democracy will try to seize control of it."[30]

Despite this seemingly threatening backdrop, I argue that today's Court need not moderate its decision-making in anticipation of a political backlash by Congress. To make this point, I will highlight differences between today's Congress and the Congress that the Warren Court confronted. In particular, the Warren-era Congress truly wanted to undo what the Court had done and had very strong feelings about Congress's power to interpret the Constitution independently. The Congress of recent years is both polarized along ideological lines and (before the 2008 elections, at least) pretty closely divided in terms of members. Recent proposals to expand or limit federal court jurisdiction exemplify this ideological divide. In the balance of this section, I will explain how it is that these proposals, more than anything, speak both to Congress's interest in making symbolic statements on divisive social issues and its lack of interest in challenging judicial authority by independently interpreting the Constitution.

Congress and the Constitution

Dramatic differences between today's Congress and the Warren- and Burger-era Congresses explain why lawmakers now have incentive to launch rhetorical attacks against the courts through jurisdiction-stripping and related proposals. The defining feature of today's Congress is political polarization along ideological lines. Liberal "Rockefeller Republicans" and conservative "Southern Democrats" no longer ensure ideological diversity within the parties. In the South, conservative Democrats were replaced with Republicans—so that the remaining Southern Democrats are far more liberal. Correspondingly, moderate Republicans were replaced by cadres from the Reagan Revolution. Studies published in 2004 and 2005, for example, documented that, with the single exception of Zell Miller, every Republican member of the House and Senate is more conservative than the most conservative Democratic member of Congress.[31]

This ideological divide now seems a permanent feature of Congress. Outside of presidential elections, Democrats and Republicans have little reason to appeal to median voters. With only one-half of eligible voters actually voting in most races, candidates and party leaders increasingly look to the party's partisan base for support. For this very reason, President Bush targeted religious conservatives in his 2004 reelection campaign.[32]

Equally significant, competitive races in the House of Representatives have declined drastically. District lines are drawn in ways that guarantee certain seats to Democrats and other seats to Republicans.[33] As a result, the party primary controls who will win most elections, so candidates focus their energies on the partisans who vote in these primaries.

Against this backdrop, it is not surprising that Democratic and Republican lawmakers increasingly see themselves as members of a party, not as independent power brokers. Correspondingly, Democrats and Republicans look to party leaders to formulate a message that will resonate with their increasingly partisan bases.[34] Constitutional values certainly figure into this message: Democrats emphasize that they are the party of civil rights and individual liberties. During the Roberts and Alito confirmation hearings, for example, Democratic senators spoke at length about abortion, voting rights, the use of torture in fighting the war on terror, and federalism-based limits on Congress's power to enact antidiscrimination legislation.[35] Republicans, especially House Republicans, sent a message that resonated with social conservatives. Republican-led efforts to countermand state and federal court decisions on same-sex marriage, abortion, the Pledge of Allegiance, and the Ten Commandments exemplify this practice.

The consequences of this shift to "message politics" are profound. First, lawmakers are less interested in what happens to legislation after it is enacted—including court decisions striking down legislation.[36] As compared to earlier Congresses (including the Warren-era Congress), "[t]he electoral requirement [for today's lawmaker] is not that he make pleasing things happen but that he make pleasing judgmental statements."[37] In so doing, lawmakers reach out to the very partisans who are likely to vote for them in ideologically charged primary elections.

Second, the contemporary Congress's disinclination to enact actual court-curbing legislation or other reforms is compounded by another development: today's lawmakers do not place a high value on their power to interpret the Constitution independently. Consider, for example, congressional committee consideration of constitutional questions. As compared to the Warren and Burger Court eras (where regional divides and ideological diversity reduced the power of party leaders), today's lawmakers are committed to their party's policy agenda. The question of whether the Supreme Court will find that agenda constitutional matters less to today's lawmakers. Consider, for example, the Rehnquist Court's federalism revival. Even though the Court invalidated all or part of twenty-three statutes from 1995 to 2000, Congress held as many hearings about federalism in the 1970s as it did in the 1990s. More than that, the hearings that it did hold in the 1990s did not focus on the Court; instead, they were mainly concerned with the federalism implications of the 1994 Republican takeover of Congress.[38]

When today's Congress considers constitutional questions, moreover, lawmakers steer clear of nonpartisan witnesses, preferring instead to hear from witnesses that will back up the preexisting views of the party that selects that witness.[39] An increasingly ideological, increasingly polarized Congress sees hearings as staged events in which each side can call witnesses who will explain their views to the public.[40] In sharp contrast, committee hearings during the Warren and Burger Court eras reflected ideological diversity within the Democratic and Republican parties. Most notably, several Senate committees made use of unified staffs and generally operated in a bipartisan way—so that hearings considering constitutional questions often featured nonpartisan academic experts.[41]

Another measure of how today's Congress differs from the earlier Congresses is lawmaker attitudes toward congressional interpretation of the Constitution. In 1959, when lawmakers cared intensely about Warren Court decisions on school desegregation and subversives, 40 percent of lawmakers thought that courts should give controlling weight to congressional interpretations of the Constitution.[42] In 1999 and 2000 (during the height of the Rehnquist Court federalism revival), only 13.8 percent of lawmakers thought that the courts should give controlling weight to congressional interpretations of the Constitution. Correspondingly, 71 percent of today's lawmakers adhere to a "joint constitutionalist" perspective whereby courts should give either "limited" or "no" weight to congressional assessments of the constitutionality of legislation.[43]

Third, lawmakers have an incentive to launch rhetorical attacks against the courts. As noted above, today's Congress is both more accepting of Supreme Court decisions invalidating federal statutes and less constrained by its responsibility to interpret the Constitution independently. By placing significant emphasis on the message they deliver to their bases, lawmakers see court rulings as opportunities to make judgmental statements that resonate with their parties and their constituents (voters and interest groups).[44]

The 2003–2006 Attacks on the Courts: Social Issues

Unlike attacks against the Warren and Burger Courts, the Rehnquist Court issued very few decisions that were terribly upsetting to lawmakers. Even though the Rehnquist Court invalidated more federal statutes than any other Court, these decisions largely resonated with the Republican majority in Congress.[45] Correspondingly, rather than express disapproval of Rehnquist Court decision-making, the 2003–2006 attacks against the courts seem much more a reflection of fundamental changes in Congress than anything else. On social issues, for example, the only Rehnquist Court decisions that Congress took issue with were decisions that invoked foreign law in cases involving the death penalty and same-sex sodomy.

The most striking feature of the 2003–2006 attacks on the courts is the peripheral role that the Supreme Court played in spurring on the lawmakers' opprobrium.[46] Rather than focus on the Supreme Court, lawmakers targeted *any* judicial rulings that were upsetting to its constituents. Some of these rulings came from state courts (the Massachusetts Supreme Court's gay marriage decision and decisions of the Florida courts in the Terri Schiavo case); others came from lower federal courts (the Ninth Circuit's invalidation of the Pledge of Allegiance and a district court order requiring Alabama Chief Justice Roy Moore to remove the Ten Commandments from the state Supreme Court rotunda). It did not matter that some of these rulings involved issues that were not subject to federal court review (the Massachusetts gay marriage decision) and that others are about issues that the Supreme Court had signaled its likely agreement with Congress (the Pledge of Allegiance). Proponents of these measures wanted to send a message: Congress will advance its policymaking agenda by striking back at the courts. This message, however, is a symbolic one. More to the point, the message is not directed at the courts; it is directed at interest groups and voters.

Consider, for example, legislation expanding federal court jurisdiction in the Terri Schiavo case.[47] The National Right to Life Committee drafted the original bill. More significantly, House Majority Leader Tom DeLay and Senate Majority Leader Bill Frist both pushed for legislation in order to strengthen their ties to Christian conservatives. Frist spoke of the bill as affirming "our nation's commitment to preserving the sanctity of life" to shore up support from right-to-life interests in his burgeoning 2008 run for the presidency.[48] DeLay used the Schiavo issue to rally social conservatives behind him in the face of charges and attacks over alleged ethics violations. In a speech to the Family Research Council, DeLay linked the negative response to the Schiavo legislation from media elites to coordinated attacks on American conservatism and his own ethics battles. For DeLay, "[t]hat whole syndicate that they have going on right now is for one purpose and one purpose only, and that is to destroy the conservative movement."[49]

Recent court-stripping proposals were cut from the same cloth.[50] The Constitution Restoration Act of 2004, for example, sought to strengthen ties between the Republican Party and religious conservatives by denying federal courts the power to review a government official's "acknowledgment of God as the sovereign source of law, liberty, or government."[51] The bill responded to a longstanding grievance between the religious right and the courts, namely, that "since the famous prayer in school cases [in 1963], our Federal courts have showed increased hostility toward the acknowledgment of God in the public square."[52] More immediately, the bill expressed disapproval of a federal court decision ordering Alabama Chief Justice Roy Moore to remove a granite monument of the Ten Commandments from the state Supreme Court rotunda. That Moore had been removed from office for failing to comply with this federal court ruling did not deter bill sponsors; if anything, Moore's willingness to stand on conviction encouraged sponsors to strengthen their ties to religious conservatives by celebrating Moore's faith-based campaign against the courts.

Republicans also used jurisdiction-stripping proposals on same-sex marriage, the Pledge of Allegiance, and judicial invocations of international law to reaffirm their commitment to the social conservative agenda. In so doing, Republican leaders hoped that religious and other social conservatives would back the GOP in congressional and presidential elections. For example, the House debated and voted on the Pledge and same-sex marriage bills immediately before the 2004 elections. At that time, Republican strategists thought that President Bush's reelection might hinge on the willingness of religious conservatives to vote in the 2004 elections. More generally, Republican leaders sought to detract attention from the war in Iraq by turning the 2004 election into a referendum on moral values.

In pursuing these objectives, it did not matter whether jurisdiction-stripping proposals were enacted, let alone found constitutional. Indeed, since Americans have historically supported judicial independence,[53] Republican leaders had little to gain by pushing for the enactment of these bills. Perhaps for this reason, two of the 2003/2004 jurisdiction-stripping bills never made it out of committee (official acknowledgments of God, invocations of international law); the other two were approved, but the vote was so late in the 2004 session that the bills were never considered in the Senate (same-sex marriage, Pledge of Allegiance). In the 2005–2006 session, the House voted on only one such measure, addressing the Pledge of Allegiance. As was true in 2004, that vote took place too late in the legislative session (August 2006) for the Senate to consider the measure.

Following the Democratic takeover of Congress in the November 2006 elections, social conservative attacks on the courts abated. Democratic lawmakers had no incentive to launch such rhetorical attacks on the courts in order to score points with their partisan base. Instead, reflecting the ideological polarization of the parties, Democratic lawmakers were principally concerned with the court's failure to advance the Democratic Party agenda. In particular, Democrats, ever since the Supreme Court intervened in the 2000 Florida recount dispute between George W. Bush and Al Gore, complained about what they characterized as conservative judicial activism.[54] This complaint principally manifested itself in the judicial confirmation process— where Democrats cloaked opposition to George W. Bush's judicial nominees in high-minded rhetoric about the need for ideological balance on the courts. Unlike the Warren Court era, however, there was no broad-based coalition to reflect heartfelt and widely shared disappointment with the Supreme Court. Congressional Republicans and Democrats were at loggerheads, and neither side would join the other in attacking the Court. For this very reason, congressional consideration of court-curbing measures on the Pledge, same-sex

marriage, and other social issues during the 2003–2006 period did not mean-
ingfully threaten judicial independence.

Enemy Combatants

In 2005 and 2006, Congress enacted legislation limiting federal court review of enemy combatant challenges to their detention at Guantanamo Bay.[55]
The 2005 statute, the Detainee Treatment Act (DTA), provided that "No court,
justice, or judge shall have jurisdiction to hear or consider" any action filed
by Guantanamo detainees.[56] Instead, enemy combatants were directed first
to pursue their cases before military tribunals. Appeals of tribunal sentences
exceeding ten years could subsequently be appealed to the D.C. Circuit Court
of Appeals and presumably the Supreme Court. In its June 2006 *Hamdan v.
Rumsfeld* decision, the Court concluded that the DTA did not provide the
Bush administration with statutory authority to pursue its military commission policy. In the immediate aftermath of this decision, Congress enacted
legislation, the Military Commission Act (MCA), which both authorized
military commission trials of enemy combatants and prohibited federal court
consideration of habeas petitions filed by detainees.[57] At the same time, the
MCA authorized federal court review of all military commission sentences.

At first blush, the DTA and MCA appear to be direct rebukes to the Court.
The DTA was enacted in anticipation of *Hamdan,* and the MCA seemed to
signal congressional disapproval of *Hamdan.* On closer inspection, however,
these two statutes signal legislative acquiescence both to Supreme Court authority to settle the enemy combatant issue and to the need for federal courts
to play an important supervisory role in enemy combatant disputes. Put another way: the DTA and MCA are the exceptions that prove the rule—statutes
that explicitly limit judicial review but do so in ways that signal congressional
support of judicial authority.

To start with, Congress did not intend the DTA to strip the Supreme Court
of jurisdiction in *Hamdan.* Even though congressional debates began three
days after the grant of certiorari, the bill had been filed before the Court's decision to hear the case. On top of this, Congress ultimately deleted language
in the original bill precluding federal court review of pending cases. Beyond
removing language governing the retroactive application of the bill, Congress
modified the DTA in ways that make it clear that it did not see the bill as a
rebuke to the courts. For example, by providing for D.C. Circuit and Supreme

Court review of military commission sentences exceeding ten years, lawmakers intended to preserve independent judicial review of significant military commission verdicts. Correspondingly, lawmakers depicted the bill as both recognizing the need for "federal court oversight" of military operations and advancing military effectiveness by allowing the military to prosecute the war on terror without being unduly burdened by frivolous lawsuits.[58]

In other significant ways, lawmakers made it clear that they did not see the DTA as an attack on either the Court or an independent judiciary. Several lawmakers suggested that the Supreme Court had been "shouting to us in Congress: Get involved, to tell us whether Congress intend[s] for . . . enemy combatants . . . to challenge their detention [in federal courts] as if they were American citizens?" Lawmakers also spoke of detainee habeas petitions as an "abuse" of the federal courts and warned that such petitions might unduly "clog the courts," thus "swamping the system" with complaints.[59] Under this view, the DTA's confining of federal court jurisdiction "respects" the Court's independence and its role in the detainee process.

Congress's response to *Hamdan* backs up these claims, even though the MCA eliminates the federal courts' jurisdiction over enemy combatants' habeas corpus petitions. Lawmakers did not challenge the Court's ruling in *Hamdan*. Republicans who were instrumental in passing the DTA depicted *Hamdan* as a rallying call for Congress "to do our job, to clarify the law."[60] Representative Duncan Hunter, who introduced the legislation on the House floor, said during the debates that the bill was a response to the "mandate of the Supreme Court that Congress involve itself in producing this new structure to prosecute terrorists."[61] And DTA sponsor Lindsey Graham stated: "The Supreme Court has set the rules of the road and the Congress and the president can drive to the destination together."[62] Even lawmakers who expressed disappointment in the Court's ruling did not criticize the Court. Senator John Cornyn, for example, blamed Hamdan's lawyers for misleading the Court about the legislative history of the DTA.

In eliminating habeas filings, Congress did not intend to pick a fight with the courts. Just as the DTA recognized an important judicial role while eliminating habeas filings, the MCA likewise was premised on the view that habeas filings both clogged the courts and "hampered the war effort."[63] Debates over the MCA habeas provision, moreover, reveal that lawmakers thought that the Supreme Court was responsible for determining the meaning of habeas protections. Specifically, lawmakers argued that they were operating within parameters set by the Court and, if not, that the Court could eviscerate the MCA's habeas provision.[64]

In summary, legislation that strips the courts of habeas jurisdiction in enemy combatant cases was anything but a rebuke to the Court's rulings in *Hamdan*. Lawmakers did not criticize the Court for these rulings. Rather, when enacting the MCA, lawmakers claimed that they were following Court interpretations of the Constitution by codifying the provisions of the *Hamdan* decision while respecting to the Court's habeas corpus jurisprudence. Lawmakers likewise recognized that the Court would pass judgment on their handiwork and that they would support a Court ruling that nullified the habeas corpus provision of the MCA, just as they backed the Court's interpretation of the DTA in *Hamdan*.

The 2003–2006 period stands in sharp relief to both the Warren and Burger Court eras. On social issues, lawmakers were not upset with the Supreme Court. The principal targets of the 2003–2006 legislative attacks were state and lower federal courts; Rehnquist Court decisions overturning federal statutes never prompted legislative opprobrium. At bottom, Republican lawmakers, who controlled the legislative agenda during this period, simply wanted to stake out a position on these socially divisive issues—solidifying support among their base and, in so doing, contrasting their agenda to the Democratic Party agenda. In sharp contrast, Congress was not polarized along ideological lines during either the Warren or Burger Court eras. During the Warren era, attacks on the Court brought together a broad coalition of Democrats and Republicans. For just this reason, the Court had reason to fear Congress. This was especially true of centrist justices who were not strongly committed to the Warren Court's progressive agenda. During the Burger Court era, the Court diffused congressional opposition to divisive rulings on abortion and busing by approving congressional efforts to enact funding and other restrictions in which lawmakers signaled their disagreement with the Court.

Legislative consideration of the DTA and the MCA likewise reveals that the 2003–2006 Congress accepted the Court's power to define the Constitution's meaning and invalidate or limit federal statutes. That these bills restricted federal court jurisdiction over Guantanamo detainee filings reflected Congress's policy preferences, not Congress's attitudes about the Supreme Court. Specifically, lawmakers look to the courts to settle constitutional questions. Indeed, the legislative debates surrounding jurisdiction-limiting bills—like the DTA and the MCA—demonstrate lawmaker acquiescence to the court's power to say what the law is. For all these reasons, it is not at all surprising that Congress took no action in response to the Court's 2008 invalidation of the MCA.[65] More to the point, Republican legislators may not have liked the *outcome,* but they never questioned the Court's authority to arrive at that outcome.

Conclusion: The Future of Judicial Independence

The Supreme Court need not fear today's Congress. Republicans and Democrats are sharply divided along ideological lines, and it is extremely unlikely for a dominant coalition to coalesce around an anti-Court agenda. Indeed, the 2003–2006 attacks on the courts were not really attacks on the Supreme Court at all. When lawmakers did advocate jurisdiction-stripping proposals on social issues, their primary targets were state courts and lower federal courts. More striking, notwithstanding fiery speeches about "activist" judges and the need for Congress to assert its supremacy on these social issues,[66] lawmakers never seriously pursued enactment of these measures.[67] In stark contrast, legislative consideration of a jurisdiction-limiting proposal on enemy combatants was extremely deferential to the courts and the supremacy of Supreme Court interpretations of federal statutes and the Constitution. This mismatch between rhetoric and reality suggests that Congress has little desire to pressure the Court into adhering to Congress's preferred vision of constitutional truth. The rhetorical attacks on the Court were addressed not to the Court but to social conservatives. When Congress did address the Court, such as through legislation restricting court jurisdiction on Guantanamo appeals, Congress left it to the Court to sort out whether to give effect to this legislation.

That Republican lawmakers, during a period when they controlled both the Congress and the White House, did not aggressively pursue the social conservative agenda through jurisdiction-stripping measures is revealing for other reasons. In particular, lawmakers have little to gain and much to lose by launching a frontal assault on the federal judiciary. First, median voters have historically backed judicial independence. For example, although most Americans are disappointed with individual Supreme Court decisions, there is a "reservoir of support" for the power of the Court to interpret the Constitution independently.[68] Consequently, even though some Supreme Court decisions trigger a backlash by those who disagree with the Court's rulings, the American people nonetheless support judicial review and an independent judiciary. Indeed, even President George W. Bush and Senate Majority Leader Bill Frist backed "judicial independence" after the federal courts refused to challenge state court fact-finding in the Terri Schiavo case.[69]

Second, there is an additional cost to lawmakers who want to countermand the courts through coercive court-curbing measures. Specifically, powerful interest groups sometimes see an independent judiciary as a way to protect the legislative deals they make. In particular, interest groups who invest in the legislative process by securing legislation that favors their preferences may be at odds with the future legislature or executive, who may prefer judicial interpretations that undermine the original intent of the law. Court-curbing measures that "impair the functioning of the judiciary" are therefore disfavored because they "impose costs on all who use the courts, including various politically effective groups and indeed the beneficiaries of whatever legislation the current legislature has enacted."[70]

Third, and correspondingly, lawmakers who disapprove of court decision-making can usually express that disapproval without pursuing court-curbing legislation, a point certainly supported by Charles Geyh's thorough catalogue in chapter 1 of the mechanisms available to Congress in this regard. This is especially true of federalism rulings. Rather than foreclose democratic outlets, federalism rulings can be circumvented by both Congress and the states. Congress can advance the same legislative agenda by making use of another source of federal power or enacting a scaled-down version of the bill. Interest groups, moreover, need not rely exclusively on Congress. They can also turn to the states to enact state versions of the very law that Congress could not enact. Rights-based rulings, in contrast, severely limit lawmaker responses.[71] Consider, for example, abortion rights. After *Roe v. Wade,* neither federal nor state lawmakers could regulate abortion in the first trimester. Likewise, Supreme Court decisions on school busing and school prayer could not be nullified through legislation. At the same time, rights-based rulings do not completely foreclose democratic outlets. Congress can eliminate federal funding and otherwise express its disapproval of the Supreme Court.

Fourth, jurisdiction-stripping measures do not nullify Supreme Court rulings—or any court ruling, for that matter. And since proponents of court-stripping also cannot count on state courts to back their policy agenda, these bills may not accomplish all that much. Accordingly, interest groups may be better off pursuing their substantive agendas through funding bans, constitutional amendments, the enactment of related legislation, and the appointments of judges and justices. Court-curbing measures, in contrast, seem more a rhetorical rallying call than a road map for change.

That the Roberts Court need not worry about jurisdiction-stripping legislation is important, but it ultimately does not answer the question of whether the Court should fear Congress. Congress, after all, can slap the courts down in other ways. Nevertheless, changes in Congress over the past twenty years suggest that the Roberts Court has less reason to fear Congress than did the Warren or Burger Courts. As detailed above, today's lawmakers are less engaged in constitutional matters and less interested in asserting their prerogative to interpret the Constitution independently. Correspondingly, lawmakers place comparatively more emphasis on expressing their opinions than on advancing their policy preferences. For example, even though the Rehnquist Court invalidated more federal statutes than any other Supreme Court, Congress did not see the Court's federalism revival as a fundamental challenge to congressional power. Lawmakers instead preferred to appeal to their bases by speaking out on divisive social issues—launching rhetorical attacks against lower federal courts and state courts.

Let me close on a cautionary note: the past may not be prologue. Widespread accusations of judicial activism may chip away at the Court's "reservoir of support."[72] A September 2005 poll, for example, suggests that a majority of Americans think that " 'judicial activism' has reached the crisis stage, and that judges who ignore voters' values should be impeached."[73] And while recent polling data suggests that the American people still back judicial independence, time will tell whether the American people are open to political attacks on the Court. Time will also tell whether Supreme Court decision-making will frustrate the policy preferences of a dominant coalition of lawmakers as well as the president. Against the backdrop of increasing party polarization, Republicans and Democrats are not likely to join forces, so major challenges to the judiciary would seem to require a filibuster-proof majority of one or the other party. More than that, the Supreme Court would need to stymie lawmaker preferences in ways that lawmakers could not find alternative means to advance their policy agenda.

All of this seems plausible—but quite unlikely. It would require the perfect storm of one dominant political party, a Court that frustrates the policy preferences of that political party (the electoral checks of the appointments and confirmation process notwithstanding), an electorate that would countenance court-stripping, and the inability of lawmakers to advance their policy agenda through means other than court-stripping. Apart from these roadblocks, court-stripping requires that Congress be willing to assert its prerogatives as an independent interpreter of the Constitution. Unlike the Warren Court era, when party polarization did not stand in the way of a dominant coalition coming together to countermand the Court, today's Congress seems more interested in scoring rhetorical points than in engaging the Court on constitutional questions. Indeed, today's Congress, for reasons detailed in this chapter, seems quite accepting of judicial control of constitutional questions.

chapter 3

Presidential Manipulations of Judicial Power

Stephen M. Engel

As we have seen in the past two chapters, many prominent criticisms of courts and proposals to curb judicial power come from Congress. But, as Stephen M. Engel points out, presidents also have tools at their disposal for influencing and using judicial power—including the appointments process and resisting or ignoring court decisions. Engel helps us see that presidents' attitudes toward judicial independence and their responses to court decisions with which they disagree are evolutionary and highly contextual. When executive branch officials respond to objectionable exercises of judicial power, they do not simply label courts as antidemocratic and dismiss their judgments. Instead, their response depends upon a variable strategic stance that reflects historical and partisan conditions, administration attitudes toward constitutional interpretation, and the president's acceptance (or rejection) of the judiciary (and especially the U.S. Supreme Court) as a divergent, but still politically useful, author of policy and constitutional law. Among other implications, this chapter helps us understand the nature and purposes behind today's presidential opposition to courts as well as the conditions under which we might regard this opposition as signaling a genuine threat to court independence.

On March 3, 2009, former justice of the Supreme Court, Sandra Day O'Connor, appeared on Comedy Central's *The Daily Show with Jon Stewart*.[1] She told Stewart: "What I became aware of increasingly in those last years [since my retirement] was all the criticism of judges across America. We heard a lot from Congress and in state legislatures, we heard a lot about activist judges, didn't we—secular godless humanists trying to tell us all what to do—I mean that was what we were hearing. And I just didn't see it that way. And I thought perhaps a lot of Americans had stopped understanding about the three branches of government." O'Connor was not recognizing a new state of affairs; as the introduction to this book testifies, there has been growing concern among legal scholars and advocates about public anger toward courts and judges since at least the early 1980s.[2]

As O'Connor's comment makes clear, a great deal of attention has focused on political attacks on the courts by members of Congress. This chapter, however, examines presidential manipulation of the federal judiciary, specifically how different presidents understand and have reacted to the federal judiciary's power to interpret the U.S. Constitution. Historically, most presidents seem to defer to the judiciary as the ultimate interpreter—a position termed judicial supremacist.[3] But a select few presidents assert a strong claim to interpret the Constitution independently—a position termed "departmentalist"—which can trigger a constitutional crisis. Recent scholarship has focused on Thomas Jefferson, Andrew Jackson, Abraham Lincoln, Franklin D. Roosevelt, and Ronald Reagan as presidents who definitively exerted their own authority to say what the Constitution means. As Lincoln claimed, "[t]he candid citizen must confess that if the policy of the Government upon vital questions affecting the whole people is to be irrevocably fixed by decisions of the Supreme Court . . . the people will have ceased to be their own rulers."[4]

These challenges have recurred at regular, almost generational, intervals in American history.[5] Some scholars have argued that these episodic assertions of the president's power to interpret the Constitution independently are products of particularly rare circumstances, of men leading insurgent parties newly ensconced in power and confronting entrenched judges of an older and increasingly discredited regime.[6] Seen in this light, "departmentalist" presidents are elected when the political and policy assumptions underlying the status quo are acutely vulnerable, presenting the opportunity to make new moves—including confronting judges appointed by repudiated presidents but entrenched in their positions through lifetime appointment.[7]

Scholars have offered explanations for both the recurrence of conflict and the decreasing effectiveness of direct presidential challenges to the judiciary's "supreme" authority to interpret the Constitution. First, they have pointed out that the structural juxtaposition between the unelected federal judiciary and the elected presidency creates the recurring possibility of interbranch conflict. Federal judges operate under a specific vulnerability: since they are unelected, judicial review can seem illegitimately countermajoritarian.[8] The Constitution establishes a judiciary with a profound democratic deficit. Legal scholar Alexander Bickel referred to this as the court's "countermajoritarian difficulty."[9] Second, scholars have argued that today's presidents are simply less able to challenge the federal courts' interpretative authority due to the development of judicial supremacy, or the idea that once the Supreme Court has issued its ruling, "whether legitimately or not, as to that issue *the democratic process is at an end.*"[10] As we shall see in the next section, scholars disagree over whether judicial supremacy constitutes an ingrained and accepted norm or whether it is more instrumentally exploited to serve politicians' interests.

In this chapter, I challenge the widespread characterization of presidential relations with judicial power as a manifestation only of the nondemocratic structure and countermajoritarian potential of courts. Additionally, rather than considering prior departmentalist presidents as all of a particular type, I highlight and explain variations in their relations with judicial authority.

Once we begin to examine the differences within the group of five presidents identified above, we cannot help but notice that earlier departmentalist presidents seem more successful in challenging the federal judiciary's authority. Jefferson's supporters eliminated a layer of federal courts, limited the Supreme Court's ability to convene more than once per year, and oversaw the only impeachment of an associate justice of the Supreme Court. Lincoln's assertions of executive power steamrolled Chief Justice Roger B. Taney's objections.[11] By contrast, Roosevelt's plan to pack the Supreme Court with as many as six more justices and to restructure the lower federal judiciary to secure his New Deal policies went down to ignoble defeat.[12] Reagan proved unable to increase significantly the number of judicial appointments to balance increases authorized during the Democratic administration of Jimmy Carter, which preceded his own, and he watched his most conservative Supreme Court nominee fall to extraordinarily divisive public Senate disapproval.[13]

Thus, rather than categorize presidents as either judicial supremacists or departmentalist, it would be a useful exercise to interrogate variation within the latter category. We should assess how our departmentalist presidents have manipulated federal judicial power differently from one another and review possible explanations for this variation. That is the motivating aim of this chapter. And, as we move through the brief case studies of individual presidents, we shall see that presidential manipulations gradually changed over time, from aggressive attacks to passive-aggressive ignoring of court rulings to harnessing judicial power for partisan aims to, ultimately, soliciting that power.

I argue that at stake in explaining this variation is not presidential acceptance of judicial supremacy but presidents' gradual acceptance of a notion of "loyal opposition" and, with it, the gradual acceptance that dissenting views of the Constitution are nonetheless legitimate and nonthreatening to the stability of the republic. Such acceptance of the plausibility of multiple interpretations as part of the constitutional culture ultimately alters how presidents (and, indeed, other politicians) view the court as a tool to achieve partisan aims. By the term *opposition*, I refer to formed, stable, and permanent interests not holding the reins of power and representing a vision of constitutional meaning that is different from that of the president and his supporters. As such, politicians' views toward opposition are observable in how they articulate the use and threat posed by political parties.[14]

Put differently, explaining variation in presidential manipulations of federal judicial power—from attacking to ignoring to harnessing to soliciting—requires a more thorough accounting of how presidents' views of the legitimacy of a loyal opposition changed over time. Today's presidents do not exactly relinquish their power to examine constitutional questions independently and challenge Court interpretation of our supreme law, but they have demonstrated a new readiness to accept and work with the judiciary's opposing viewpoints and constitutional vision. I examine four cases of presidential relations with federal judicial power, all focusing on the Supreme Court, to illustrate how a shift in perspective on the threat posed by opposition influences how manipulations of judicial authority take shape.

My main point is that as presidents' perceptions of opposition shifted, their attitude toward the judiciary—where opposition may become entrenched under rules of lifetime appointment—changed in tandem. Once politicians in general, but presidents in particular, understood that opposition did not undermine the Constitution and that multiple interpretations could be considered plausible and legitimate, judicial power could be construed less as the seat of an illegitimate and threatening antidemocratic minority and more as an instrument to achieve political ends. So, once presidents granted that no single interpretation of the Constitution would hold absolute authority and that different interpretations would contend as a matter of course, their strategic repertoire expanded. They could challenge the finality of judicial power *and* try to use that power as effectively as possible.

I concentrate my analysis in this chapter on the years prior to Reconstruction, although I do present a brief discussion of Reagan's administration to offer thoughts on how presidential relations with judicial authority look once multiple visions of constitutional meaning are considered less threatening. This focus on the Antebellum Era calls attention to developmental connections between two of the early republic's critical political institutions: courts and parties. Early nineteenth-century American politics was, to a large extent, defined by antijudiciary and antiparty sentiment. And yet, by the mid-nineteenth century, the polity could plausibly be characterized as a state of "courts and parties" in contrast to the emerging bureaucracies of Western Europe.[15] The parallel legitimization of these institutions is intriguing not only for how each occurred but also for how they affected each other. Grappling with these institutions' connections—particularly to the extent that changing viewpoints on parties indicate changing perspectives on opposition—can help us understand the source and contemporary nature of popular and elite-level criticism of judicial authority and teach us about the strategic use of courts by presidents (as political party leaders) today.

Connecting Views about Opposition and Tactics toward Judicial Power

Scholarship in law and political science offers a variety of answers to the question of why judicial authority persists (and may even grow stronger over time) despite nearly continuous criticism. Each explanation frames hostilities toward courts and judges as a recurring theme of American politics, as the manifestation of an ingrained constitutional tension, the effects of which have diminished due to the recognition of strategic interest in (or the development of normative deference to) a strong judiciary. Where each of these theories, reviewed briefly below, rests on a static structural problem, I point instead to a developmental process that brings to the fore presidents' direct engagement in altering the terms of politics in which they find themselves leading.

One theory, associated mostly with the early work of Robert Dahl, positions the Court as an essentially majoritarian institution; its rulings are out of line with majority interests only for brief moments. Anti-Court hostilities may flare up, but they subside once the president secures new judicial appointments. Dahl argues, "Presidents are not famous for appointing justices hostile to their own views on public policy nor could they expect to secure confirmation of a man whose stance on key questions was flagrantly at odds with that of the dominant majority in the Senate."[16] In other words, if the countermajoritarian potential exists, it will not last for long if we can plausibly assume a steady rate of judicial retirement.

A second explanation for the persistence of judicial authority dismisses the countermajoritarian potential to the extent that strong judicial power, regardless of this potential, often serves politicians' interests. Those interests include avoiding electoral accountability on contentious issues such as slavery, abortion, or same-sex marriage. By passing responsibility to judges, politicians—presidents and members of Congress alike—avoid taking stands on issues that may divide their constituents, and they maintain judges as a rhetorical foil, which may mobilize voters. In other words, they can pass on accountability and blame judges as undemocratic activists to rally voters.[17] But this model cannot easily explain why hostile actions in the early 1800s—which included eliminating federal courts and impeaching federal judges for politically motivated purposes—and in the 1860s—which included tampering with bench size, transferring jurisdiction, and eliminating jurisdiction—were, in fact, carried out. Why would attacks on courts during the early republic appear to have so much depth and breadth, while those since Reconstruction have failed? What changed?

A third theory answers this question of change over time by positing the development of a pervasive norm of deference to judicial authority or acceptance of judicial supremacy among politicians and the people alike. The attacks during Jefferson's presidency and the late 1860s occurred *before* the norm was adopted.[18] Yet, problematically, the empirical data supporting public acceptance of judicial supremacy is weak; opinion polling has yet to substantiate any such norm.[19] And if, as Justice O'Connor claims, contemporary politicians frequently inveigh against judicial authority, that observation alone would call into question a judicial supremacy norm.[20] If such a norm were truly popular, why would politicians continue to attack independent judicial authority? Such antagonism would potentially fall flat among the wider public. Also, this norms-based theory forces questionable interpretations of relevant history. For example, it compels the assumption that Roosevelt's court-packing plan was doomed to fail, when there is evidence that if Roosevelt had agreed to add two or three justices to the Supreme Court instead of holding out for six, Congress would have secured the increase.[21] Furthermore, it cannot easily explain the passage of Court-curbing legislation in the 1910s, the 1930s, and as recently as 2005 and 2006, all times when this norm should have been operative.[22]

This chapter builds on the useful insights of each of these theories while developing an alternate strategic and historical explanation for patterns of executive branch relations with the judiciary. The alternative I put forth ties presidents' strategies of contesting judicial authority to their perceptions of the loyalty of the opposition and the legitimacy of party competition. The relevant normative change, I suggest, did not entail wide popular or elite-level acceptance of judicial supremacy; instead, it entailed the gradual recognition among political leaders that no one group holds a monopoly on legitimate claims to rule, including assertions of authority through judicial review and constitutional interpretation. Thus, public and stable opposition to the president's interests was not, on its face, illegitimate, disloyal, or portending of civil strife.

Put differently, political leaders over two hundred years of American history have understood the threat opposition (and its institutional manifestation as a stable and permanent party) poses to civic stability and to the sanctity of the Constitution in different ways, leading to consonant shifts in how these leaders view their relations with the judiciary, which potentially represents an entrenched opposition protected by rules of lifetime tenure. As a result, we might expect variation in views toward party and toward opposition to track their views toward judicial power.

The connection between changing views toward opposition and changing tactics toward the judiciary is not altogether intuitive. To make it clearer, consider that the founding generation, taking as their point of reference the English Civil War of the seventeenth century, assumed that stable political opposition could lead to civil unrest and ultimately to civil war.[23] Therefore, if such a factional opposition were to occupy the judiciary, stable governance would require extrajudicial constitutional interpretation by the executive, Congress, political parties, or the people themselves, measures that would remove judges from power altogether or at least severely undercut judges' ability to rule, such as the imposition of supermajority decision-rules on the bench. If, however, opposition is considered loyal and thus not threatening to the Constitution or civic stability more generally, then each opposing party can lay claim to the constitutionality of its policy aims. Squashing the opposition outright is no longer necessary or even acceptable. In this circumstance, *harnessing* the judiciary to promote policy aims rather than *undercutting* its legitimacy may be more rational from a strategic perspective. And even if hostile actions seem to be nonetheless taken, politicians would likely seek to narrow the effect of their own Court-curbing.[24] So, hostile rhetoric may remain and a Court-curbing statute may pass, but that law may do little more than take action where Court decisions have already trended, making the gesture more symbolic in nature. Alternatively, politicians may narrow jurisdiction or transfer jurisdiction from a state court to a federal court, depending on which is considered friendlier to the partisan interest. Additionally, politicians may deliberately introduce ambiguity into statutory language to invite judicial review from a Court they view as ideologically aligned or open to such alignment.[25] In other words, as this last tactic makes most clear, politicians will attempt to *exploit* judicial legitimacy, not undermine it.

The distinction I propose between politicians' perceptions of the threat of opposition, while useful in introducing observable actions, is blunt. And it would be implausible to suggest that there existed a definitive point in the history of ideas after which politicians suddenly shifted their perspective on political opposition. Instead, it is more plausible to contend that ideas and rhetoric about the threat posed by opposition changed more gradually.[26] One aim of this chapter is to trace that gradual shift from an aggressive attack against judicial power to decisions to ignore that power to presidential attempts to harness that power. We can get some sense of it by investigating how political leaders—here presidents—changed the terms by which they characterized opposition and its institutional shape as a political party.[27]

Thomas Jefferson: Eliminating Courts and Impeaching Judges

Traditionally, scholars have suggested that Jeffersonian animus toward courts and judges (occurring primarily between 1801 and 1805) can be traced to (1) public perceptions of colonial judges as lackeys of a corrupt king; (2) a protestant agency culture that viewed unelected judges as illegitimate intermediaries between the people and their Constitution; and (3) anti-Federalist concerns centering on the unelected and thus undemocratic status of federal judges.[28] Yet, Jefferson's hostility to judicial power was more nuanced than outright opposition to courts because of judges' unelected status. Indeed, he drafted provisions in the Virginia constitution for judicial appointment, mandating life tenure for judges under conditions of good behavior, that were similar to those of the Constitution itself. And in a letter to James Madison, Jefferson noted the benefits of independent judicial review to the extent that it could guard against majority tyranny: "In the arguments in favor of a declaration of rights, you omit one which has great weight with me, the legal check which it puts into the hands of the judiciary. This is a body, which if rendered independent, and kept strictly to their own department merits great confidence for their learning and integrity."[29] Thus, it is not true that Jefferson was hostile to courts or judicial review because unelected judges embodied a democratic deficit. Furthermore, Jefferson drew his support, in part, from those who identified as anti-Federalists in the debate over constitutional ratification, including Brutus, who conceded the necessity of unelected judges and judicial review.[30] Therefore, to understand the rationale behind Jefferson's attack on the Marshall Court, it is necessary to look elsewhere.

That search begins by noting that the Jeffersonian assault on judicial authority occurred in a larger political milieu that considered stable, formed, and public expressions of opposition to government and leaders in power as portending civil conflict and as inimical to civic health. Several scholars have already shown that stable opposition in the form of a political party was not a legitimate idea until at least 1815. The assumptions of early American politicians were structured by eighteenth-century fears of opposition and factionalism as underlying causes of civil war inherited from English political thought.[31] Far less scholarship has examined the implications of these assumptions and this context for presidential relations with the judiciary.

Notwithstanding images of separate powers checked and balanced, the founding generation tended to expect the judiciary to be part of a *unified* governing regime. They could not conceive of a legitimate federal government in which different branches would act on different meanings of the Constitution. The meaning of the Constitution was "immutably fixed" and approved by the people themselves.[32] By the same token, however, the Jeffersonian experience of Federalist rule—particularly after the passage of the Sedition Act of 1798—pushed another concern to the fore: that the federal branches working in concert might be animated by the *wrong* principles and operate together to swallow up the authority of the separate states.

Jefferson's early antijudicial rhetoric flared over how federal judges were ruling in cases involving the Sedition Act, not over the illegitimacy of judicial authority per se, and it would reach its height in response to Chief Justice John Marshall's ruling in *Marbury v. Madison*. The Sedition Act banned organized and assembled opposition to any passed legislative measure and criminalized any utterance or publication about Congress or the president considered false or malicious. Jefferson's disgust with the Sedition Act compelled him to anonymously pen the Kentucky Resolution, which stipulated that each branch of government, and perhaps even the state governments, have equal right and responsibility to declare constitutional meaning rather than defer to the judiciary as the supreme interpreter. In a letter to Abigail Adams, Jefferson aptly summarized his constitutional interpretative authority as based in the power of the presidency as a separate but equal branch: "You seem to think it devolved on the judges to decide on the validity of the sedition law. But nothing in the Constitution has given them a right to decide for the Executive, more than the Executive to decide for them. Both magistrates are equally independent in the sphere of action assigned to them."[33] The problem of institutional reconstruction in 1801 in the wake of Jefferson's election to the presidency, then, was to reestablish *unity* in the national government and to do so based on what they considered to be the *proper* constitutional principles.

Jefferson interpreted his victory as a fundamental expression of popular sovereignty, as a full repudiation of Federalist beliefs. Federalists disagreed. Federalist judges, Supreme Court Justice Samuel Chase foremost among them, took it as their responsibility to speak out against Jefferson and his supporters, as they saw his leadership as undermining the Constitution itself. For example, in a grand jury charge at Baltimore in 1803, which would ultimately provide the basis of one of the eight articles of Chase's impeachment, Chase contended that Jefferson's election signaled "our republican constitution will sink into a *mobocracy*, the worst of all possible governments."[34] Commenting on the charge, Jefferson wrote to a representative in the House: "You must have heard of the extraordinary charge of Chace [*sic*] to the Grand Jury at Baltimore. Ought this seditious and official attack on the principles of our Constitution, and on the proceedings of a State, to go unpunished? And to whom so pointedly as yourself will the public look for the necessary measure?"[35] The letter reveals not only Jefferson's prodding to begin impeachment proceedings against Chase but also his willingness to invoke the charge of sedition against political opposition when it served his purposes.

Jeffersonians viewed rulings in sedition cases as an indication of federal judges' refusal to recognize popular repudiation of Federalism in 1800. Chase was at the forefront of such rulings; for example, he maintained sedition charges against popular Jeffersonian pamphleteer James Callender.[36] Such rulings provided evidence of the federal judiciary's independence from the elected branches' aims, but was that the framers' notion of judicial independence, much less Jefferson's own?

Federalists and Jeffersonians alike agreed that judges should be indepen-dent of corrupt executives and legislators. But, for Jefferson, if his presiden-tial election were taken as an expression of popular sovereignty, judges such as Chase, through their rulings, had shown an independence from the people themselves. Such a role was intolerable in a democratic republic insofar as it indicated that one branch of government would actively contradict the ex-pressed popular sovereignty. Put differently, when Chief Justice John Marshall articulated the principle of horizontal judicial review in *Marbury v. Madison* or the idea the Supreme Court could nullify an act of Congress as inconsistent with the Constitution, he demonstrated that the governing regime was not unified.[37] It was splintered by the open opposition of a recalcitrant judiciary unwilling to bend to the people's choice as reflected in overwhelming sup-port for Jeffersonian politicians in the elections of 1800 and 1802. Stable and expressed opposition, the key danger to civic stability, was now entrenched in the judicial branch of the federal government. From the Jeffersonian perspec-tive, it was not Marshall's finding that Section 13 of the Judiciary Act of 1789 was unconstitutional that was illegitimate; he acted illegitimately because he represented an aristocratic and electorally deposed minority faction out to repudiate the people's expressed choice.

Since Federalists and Jeffersonians alike viewed stable opposition (includ-ing party politics) as a threat to civic stability, each side was unwilling to con-cede the legitimacy of the other, leaving Federalists to fret about the collapse of the Constitution that Jefferson's victory portended and to consider seces-sion. Such consideration of exit is a manifestation of the notion that opposing viewpoints are not granted legitimacy.[38] A letter from Senator John Quincy Adams reflects this feeling: "The acquisition of Louisiana, although the im-mediate occasion of this project of disunion, was not its only, nor even its most operative, cause. The election of Mr. Jefferson to the presidency was. . . . The party overthrown was the whole Federal party,—the disciples of Wash-ington, the framers and supporters of the Constitution of the United States."[39] Adams was not alone. Quite a few Federalists considered secession even as there was little agreement on how it should be pursued. As one Federalist politician wrote, "On the question of separation . . . we all agree there can be no doubt of its being desirable."[40]

Beyond considerations by some New England Federalists to secede, there were other aspects of this interbranch conflict that suggested politicians' con-cerns with stable opposition. For example, even though the Court acquiesced to the congressional repeal of the 1801 expansion of the federal judiciary, which eliminated federal judgeships even though there had been no violations of the good behavior standard, and thus the Court seemingly retreated from a showdown with Jefferson and the Congress, the Jeffersonians did not stop their assault.[41] By the terms of the repeal of the 1801 Judiciary Act, the Congress eliminated more than ten federal judgeships, and the constitutionality of this action was never addressed. Congress also sent the Supreme Court justices on the move once more to ride their respective circuits. But even though Congress had won the statutory game and the Marshall Court had retreated from the aggressive policy of judicial review that might have followed from *Marbury,* the logic of illegitimate opposition compelled Jeffersonians to consider that what was at stake was not simply policy victories but the security and stability of the Constitution. So Jeffersonians turned to impeachment to remove factional opposition from government and to restore civic tranquility under a unitary Jeffersonian regime.[42]

The Jeffersonian-dominated Congress pursued a strategy of impeaching federal judges. It first tested impeachment on a federal district judge.[43] The House then brought charges against and impeached the most outspoken of the Supreme Court justices, Samuel Chase. Chase narrowly escaped conviction in the Senate. The failure to convict Chase saved Chief Justice Marshall from an impeachment attempt, but the Chase trial had the critical effect of removing the judiciary not only from partisanship but also from politics altogether; in other words, it helped to construct a wall between law and politics, setting the standard of judicial "good behavior" as political neutrality.

That is to say, even as Federalists and Jeffersonians agreed that judges must be kept independent from corrupt politicians, Jeffersonians contended that the Marshall Court strayed beyond its acceptable institutional role by refusing to acknowledge the popular will. For Jefferson, judges, as much as actors in the elected branches, were representatives of the people. As such, "any claims of judicial independence must be tempered by [that] recognition," and impeachment should be used "for holding judges accountable to the people."[44] Instead of representing the people, the justices appeared to be protecting the views of a repudiated aristocratic minority that was seeking to undermine the Constitution.

And yet, Federalists, operating from a similar premise, construed Jeffersonians as party-driven and politically corrupt and thus as intent on undermining the republic. As such, the assertion of independent judicial will was necessary to protect the Constitution. When one looks at the assumptions unique to this period, which characterized stable opposition as a harbinger of civil war, then the Jeffersonian attacks on the judiciary reveal themselves to be driven by concerns about the illegitimacy of opposition rather than the structural legitimacy of judicial review.

Therefore, in the face of the Jeffersonians' inability to achieve unification of all federal branches, the meaning of judicial independence was transformed. It came to signify not merely independence from the influence of potentially corrupt executives or legislators, but also independence from politics altogether.[45] Judicial independence and political neutrality were conflated. This construction was a second-best outcome to achieving the elusive goal of regime unity. Instead of seeking improbable unity among the three federal branches, politicians were now directed to clamor for politically neutral judges who might operate as umpires. In this regard, Jeffersonians laid the foundation for what we might consider the modern concept of judicial neutrality, a tradition that informed John Roberts's widely noted comparison of judges to baseball umpires in his 2005 Senate confirmation hearings. In doing so, they opened the possibility of masking future attacks on the judiciary via the language and rhetoric of reestablishing that branch's neutrality. In other words, the impeachments—although the Chase episode failed in its most direct objective—served to reconstruct the judiciary's place among the three federal branches, that is, to move from the Federalist notion of a unified governing elite toward the vague ideal of judicial neutrality, which ironically leaves the judiciary perpetually vulnerable to hostile criticism.[46] But, the dream of unity did not die. As we shall see in the next section, Martin Van Buren contended that the very institution that so agitated the Founders, namely political party, was the very means to create the regime unity that eluded the Jeffersonians.

Andrew Jackson and Martin Van Buren: Ignoring Courts and the Struggle for Regime Unity

Andrew Jackson's hostility toward the judiciary is often summarized by the legend of his baiting of Chief Justice Marshall: "John Marshall has made his decision, now let him enforce it."[47] That statement, which is of dubious historical accuracy, followed the Cherokee removal case of *Worcester v. Georgia* and is said to connect Jacksonians to their Jeffersonian fathers. While Jackson's moves were more passive-aggressive than those of the Jeffersonians—he generally ignored the Court rather than attempting to dismantle it—they nonetheless created a sense among legal and political scholars that Jacksonians were "vigorous critics of the federal judiciary."[48] Therefore, Jackson's relationship with the Court has been understood either as hostile and thereby following the Jeffersonian tradition or as simply opportunistic, ignoring rulings if they undermined executive power but enforcing them when doing so served presidential interests.[49]

Yet, Jackson, like Jefferson, was no obvious foe of judicial review. He defended the principle before and during his presidency. In 1822, Jackson wrote to his nephew, "the constitution is worth nothing and a mere buble [sic] except guaranteed to them by an independent and virtuous judiciary."[50] That statement echoes the themes of Jefferson's letter to Madison discussing the importance of courts to a constitutional democracy. Furthermore, no evidence exists of Jackson supporting the Court-curbing congressional legislation proposed while he was president, which included measures to limit judicial tenure and to alter decision rules to require unanimity on constitutional questions.[51] Nor did he support repeal of Section 25 of the 1789 Judiciary Act. Section 25 authorized the Supreme Court to review state court rulings that upheld state laws against federal prosecution, declared federal laws unconstitutional, or rejected rights claims grounded in the federal Constitution. It was therefore anathema to advocates of states' rights.[52] Jackson also supported judicial review against South Carolina's doctrine of nullification. At the same time, Jackson did ignore *Worcester v. Georgia* and actively opposed the Court's upholding of the constitutionality of the national bank.[53] This varied track record reveals a pattern of pragmatic opportunism, supporting the Court's authority to interpret the Constitution when it served his interests and ignoring that authority when it did not. However, when we consider the changing assumptions about the legitimacy of a loyal opposition, something beyond sheer opportunism comes into focus.

The writings of Martin Van Buren offer a sense of this changing context of political ideas about the legitimacy of stable opposition. Van Buren's writings are relevant to the extent that he was Jackson's key political lieutenant, and he was recognized in his own time and by subsequent generations of historians as the primary founder of the Democratic Party.[54] Indeed, Van Buren is often considered the inventor of our contemporary system of stable two-party competitive politics.[55] However, his writings suggest something else. They suggest that he understood all politics to be a recurring battle between an eternal aristocratic minority and an eternal democratic majority.[56] This characterization led him to describe opposition to his party, what he referred simply to as "the Democracy," as opposition to the Constitution itself. Van Buren may not have been as ardent as Jefferson, who revealed his fear of opposition and civil strive when he once stated that he sought "to consolidate the nation once more into a single mass, in sentiment & in object."[57] Nevertheless, while Van Buren understood that dissent and factionalism could not be suppressed, he still contended that rule by the necessarily minority faction of Hamiltonians, whether they be called Federalists, Whigs, or Republicans, epitomized constitutional collapse.

When discussing the reemergence of factionalized politics in the wake of the "Era of Good Feelings" of the late 1810s and early 1820s, Van Buren characterized the Quincy Adams administration as attempting "to revive the heresies of former times."[58] He criticized the "old Federal party and its successors for their persevering efforts to destroy the balances of the Constitution." And he lamented how the Hamiltonian faction—in which he included National Republicans and Whigs—was aiming to disrupt civic tranquility. He noted the possibility that "if the Constitution had been upheld in good faith on both sides partisan contests must of necessity have been limited to local or temporary measures and to popular excitements." But unfortunately, in Van Buren's view, Hamilton and his followers were instead driven by an "attempt to make the Government which had been established . . . a delusion, and the Constitution a shame, to pave the way for its overthrow."[59] Thus, while Jefferson held out hope that the national community might be consolidated in common interest, Van Buren concluded that the opposition could not be eliminated. And, to ensure that the Constitution did not fall prey to the Hamiltonian aristocratic minority, Van Buren sought to create a stable permanent political party to protect it.

While Van Buren strove to construct a political party, he did not conceptualize a stable system of party competition that would concede loyal opposition. Van Buren's acknowledgement of the perpetual nature of opposition did not correspond to an intention to establish a competitive two-party system. A party was not, for him, what our modern functionalist notion suggests, namely an electorally and policy-driven federated organization.[60] Rather, Van Buren saw his party as the embodiment and protector of the Constitution —and his opponents' party as a threat to the same.

As legal historian Gerald Leonard has argued, "Politicians could not just state the obvious: that organization of party was an effective way to advance an agenda. Everyone knew that; yet, party remained out of bounds as ultimately inconsistent with popular sovereignty and confederated government."[61] The earlier negative connotation of parties as a threat to civic stability had to be abandoned and its meaning transformed given a new reality on the ground. That reality was the continued existence of political corruption despite Madison's innovative institutional architecture. The 1824 presidential election, in which Jackson won the popular vote but Quincy Adams gained the presidency through action taken in the House of Representatives, was, for Van Buren, an indication of that corruption. To combat it, Van Buren restructured the political party to be the institutional embodiment of the Constitution, meant to guard against corruption and abuse; the party would be the sole source of proper constitutional interpretation and meaning.[62] Following Adams's selection by the House, permanent political party was no longer the cause of civil strife—as the Founders considered it to be—but rather the means to civic stability. Furthermore, if political history really was only a repetitive story of a permanent democratic majority rarely losing to an aristocratic permanent minority—as Van Buren maintained and as he claimed the victories of Jefferson, Madison, and Monroe indicated—then Quincy Adams's victory in 1824 was all the more an aberration, a sign of a "corrupt bargain" among political elites.[63]

How does this account help us understand executive-judicial relations in the early nineteenth century? With Van Buren's party vision, his justification of Jackson's veto of the Second Bank of the United States, which essentially reversed the Court's ruling in *McCulloch v. Maryland* that a national bank was constitutional, can be understood as neither opportunistic nor simply motivated to assert executive supremacy. Rather, for Van Buren, the veto followed from (1) Jackson's unique role as the leader of the permanent constitutional majority, that is, as the leader of the Democratic Party; (2) a characterization of supporters of the Second Bank as the minority aristocratic opposition; and (3) a desire to reestablish the regime unity, Jefferson's elusive goal as well. In his veto of the Second Bank, Jackson reiterated the Jeffersonian notion that "each public officer" held the responsibility of constitutional interpretation. Supporters of the Second Bank latched on to this phrase and its chaotic implications to undermine the veto's legitimacy. Van Buren, somewhat surprisingly, agreed with Jackson's critics to some extent, but he also contended that their interpretation of the veto entailed "gross perversions of his message."

Van Buren argued that this statement could not mean that actors at *all* levels of government could freely engage in independent constitutional interpretation. These were, for Van Buren, merely "unguarded words." So while he defended the veto by noting that the three federal branches "each have the right, and it is the duty of each to judge for themselves in respect to the authority and requirements of the Constitution, without being controlled or interfered with by their co-departments," he also repudiated any Jeffersonian implications (mentioned in the Kentucky Resolution) that would undermine federal supremacy and provide more power to the several states. For Van Buren, that implication was "too preposterous for credulity itself to swallow."[64] Judicial review was appropriate to maintain federal supremacy over the states.

Van Buren's restricted reading of the Second Bank veto, Jackson's antipathy toward nullification, and Jackson's refusal to support repealing Section 25 of the 1789 Judiciary Act are all premised on maintaining federal supremacy. The nullification doctrine would curtail not only federal judicial power but more generally limit the federal government's ability to maintain a semblance of legal uniformity among the states. More pointedly, the nullification doctrine and the repeal effort laid bare the idea that political opposition was intent on undermining the Constitution; those measures would, to some degree, return federal-state relations to a design to something more like the system outlined in the failed Articles of Confederation. Thus, Jackson's support of judicial review against both nullification and the repeal effort and his seemingly paradoxical resistance to the Court's legitimacy by ignoring its authority on the national bank question and on Cherokee removal were actually linked by a single idea. That idea was the necessity to protect the Constitution from a dangerous aristocratic opposition, a minority that often supported upending the precarious balance between federal and state power.

Van Buren held that the Democratic Party was the perpetual majority and that the majority, by definition, sought to uphold the Constitution. So the majority, being on the side of the Constitution, was likewise never wrong.[65] This logic of a single constitutional party was entirely tautological. According to Van Buren, presidential constitutional interpretation was legitimate when it was superior to judicial interpretation, and that superiority could be gauged by whether the interpretation aligned with the principles of the Democratic Party. Van Buren grounded his logic in Jackson's leadership of the single constitutional party and the idea of a perpetual democratic majority and a permanent aristocratic minority. Within the framework of Van Buren's party theory, if the Supreme Court ruled in ways that undermined Democratic Party principles, it necessarily undermined constitutional commitments.

Van Buren criticized Chief Justice Taney's *Dred Scott* ruling on these grounds. Van Buren was troubled not because Taney claimed that African Americans could never be citizens but because the Court had invalidated the Kansas-Nebraska Act. That legislation enabled residents of the individual states themselves to decide whether their states would be free or slave. Thus, the ruling invalidated the constitutional and Democratic Party commitment to popular sovereignty. Van Buren could only account for this outcome by arguing that Taney, appointed Chief Justice by Jackson, as well as Democratic president James Buchanan, who openly sought the Court's ruling as a means to resolve the growing sectional rift, were both actually Federalists bent on undermining the Constitution: "For the first time since [the Democratic Party's] ascent to power in the Federal Government, two of the three great departments, the Executive and the Judicial, are presided over by gentleman who . . . had not been bred in its ranks but joined them at comparatively advanced periods in their lives, and with opinions formed in an antagonistic school."[66]

Taney and Buchanan identified as Federalists in the early years of the nineteenth century. However, Van Buren's claim that they remained members of that faction despite their respective service to the republic and membership in the Democratic Party borders on the delusional. Van Buren's absurd characterization of Buchanan and Taney is the consequence of being boxed into a corner by the parameters of his own distrust of factional politics and competing views of the constitutional order. Taney and Buchanan could be nothing other than a threatening opposition. So, in Van Buren's reading, the increasing sectional crisis was brought about by members of the minority faction, which had always been intent on undermining the Constitution.

Abraham Lincoln: Harnessing Courts

Lincoln adopted the mantle of Jackson to justify his attempts to limit the precedent-setting effect of the *Dred Scott* ruling. In debates with Stephen Douglas, Lincoln belittled his opponent's reverence for the Court as not holding true to Jacksonian roots:

The sacredness that Judge Douglas throws around this [*Dred Scott*] decision is a degree of sacredness that has never been thrown around any other decisions. . . . I ask, if somebody does not remember that a National Bank was declared to be constitutional? . . . That recharter was laid before General Jackson. It was urged upon him, when he denied the constitutionality of the Bank, that the Supreme Court had decided that it was constitutional; and General Jackson then said that the Supreme Court had no right to lay down a rule to govern a coordinate branch of Government, the members of which had sworn to support the Constitution as he understood it. I will venture here to say that I have heard Judge Douglas say that he approved of General Jackson for that act. What has now become of all his tirade about "resistance of the Supreme Court"?[67]

Paralleling this criticism of his Democratic opponent's position on the judiciary, Lincoln's first inaugural address, particularly its discussion of the *Dred Scott* ruling, seems to rehash Jeffersonian and Jacksonian hostilities toward the Supreme Court and efforts to curtail its authority:

I do not forget the position assumed by some that constitutional questions are to be decided by the Supreme Court, nor do *I deny that such decisions must be binding in any case upon the parties to a suit* . . . while they are also entitled to very high respect and consideration in all parallel cases by all other departments of the Government. . . . At the same time, the candid citizen must confess that if the policy of the Government upon vital questions affecting the whole people is to be irrevocably fixed by decisions of the Supreme Court. . . . the people will have ceased to be their own rulers, having to that extent practically resigned their Government into the hands of that eminent tribunal.[68]

Lincoln's assertions that the Court could not be the final arbiter of constitutional meaning, that constitutional interpretive authority extended beyond the judiciary, and that constitutionalism is grounded in popular sovereignty all carry a Jeffersonian valence. Indeed, similarities among Lincoln, Jefferson, and Jackson were noted at the time of the inaugural. The *Louisville Democrat* remarked on Lincoln's inaugural: "Some may censure the general remarks about the decisions of the Supreme Court; but the intelligent reader will see that it is but the old Democratic doctrine of Jefferson and Jackson. If it be a heresy, it is not Lincoln's."[69]

Yet, this perspective skims over clear differences among Jefferson, Jackson, and Lincoln's arguments, particularly Lincoln's *acceptance* of the authority of the *Dred Scott* ruling, at least for the parties involved. As he put it, "I do not propose to disturb or resist the decision."[70] His position thereby stands in marked contrast to Jefferson's rejection of *Marbury* and Jackson's repudiation of *McCulloch* and *Worcester*. But if Lincoln's assertion of presidential interpretive authority was not as extreme as that of his predecessors, neither was it a concession to judicial supremacy. Lincoln situated himself between these polar views on judicial authority, unwilling to undermine judicial authority and yet seeking leverage to place limits on some judicial rulings.

The differences between Jackson and Lincoln's positions on judicial power are evident when we attend to Lincoln's contention that law is settled over time. In summarizing Republican reaction to *Dred Scott,* Lincoln stated, "We believe . . . in obedience to, and respect for the judicial department of government. We think its decisions on Constitutional questions, when fully settled, should control, not only the particular cases decided, but the general policy of the country, subject to be disturbed only by amendments of the Constitution."[71] This passage highlights a key distinction between Lincoln and his presidential predecessors who had sought to confront, ignore, and deny the validity of judicial rulings they opposed. Lincoln would not *actively* oppose Taney's ruling. He would restrict its implications by claiming that while the decision would stand for the parties to the case, the mater of law at issue was not as yet fully settled. Legal meaning could only be settled over some length of time.

And time afforded opportunity. It afforded the opportunity to persuade the electorate to elect leaders who could appoint judges who might overturn the ruling. Lincoln conceded such an instrumental use of judges when he explained how the *Dred Scott* ruling came to pass in the first place. According to Lincoln, *Dred Scott* was only possible through electoral politics: "[I]t is my opinion that the Dred Scott decision, as it is, never would have been made in its present form if the party that made it had not been sustained previously by the elections. My own opinion is, that the new Dred Scott decision, deciding against the right of the people of the States to exclude slavery, will never be made if that party is not sustained by the elections. I believe, further, that it is just as sure to be made as to-morrow is to come, if that party shall be sustained."[72] In other words, for Lincoln, the *Dred Scott* ruling was predicated on Democratic electoral success in 1852 and 1856. This claim implied that elections could embody the root of constitutional meaning. If judicial decisions contradicted the principles of the political party most recently victorious at the polls, then presidents could legitimately not enforce the decision beyond the particular case until the ruling became more settled. In short, not only were judicial decisions political, as judges may "hold the same passions for party" as Jefferson once claimed and as Lincoln often quoted, but enforcement of those decisions could be likewise political. The extent of enforcement could be warranted by a party's electoral success.[73]

Lincoln's focus on *time* as a factor in presidential interpretive authority was fundamentally distinct from Jackson's claim. Jackson held that he always had the authority, as president, to come to a different constitutional interpretation than Congress or the Court. Lincoln held that law only became stable over time and that the President would become eventually bound by that meaning. Indeed, Lincoln's construction undermines the logic of Jackson's Bank veto since the question of the Second Bank's constitutionally *had* been settled over a long stretch of time going back to the Washington administration by presidential action, repeated congressional action, and a Supreme Court ruling.[74] According to this logic, Lincoln's attempt to restrict the implications of the *Dred Scott* ruling are fully reconcilable with his earlier support for a National Bank and opposition to Jackson's veto.[75] For the question of slavery's extension to the territories was not comparably settled. For Lincoln, Taney's ruling was not "the unanimous concurrence of the judges, without any apparent partisan bias, and in accordance with legal public expectation, and with the steady practice of the departments through our history." If it had been, disobeying it would amount to "factious, nay, even revolutionary" action; but, given division on the bench, "it is not resistance, it is not factious, it is not even disrespectful, to treat it as not having yet quite established a settled doctrine for the country."[76]

So, for Lincoln, the more people elected leaders who would uphold a ruling, the more the law would become settled. For this conception of "congealing" law to be nonthreatening to southern slavery interests that might claim the Constitution had an alternate construction, Lincoln would have to claim that the Constitution did not necessarily hold answers to contemporary questions. In essence, he had to claim that there were multiple plausible renderings of constitutional meaning. He did so in two ways: first, by focusing on the document's silences and, second, by reconfiguring the meaning of majority itself.

First, in his First Inaugural Lincoln made special note of the legitimacy of disagreement on constitutional meaning precisely because the Constitution was silent on so many questions: "No organic law can ever be framed with a provision specifically applicable to every question. . . . No foresight can anticipate nor any document of reasonable length contain express provisions for all possible questions. Shall fugitives from labor be surrendered by national or by State authority? The Constitution does not expressly say. May Congress prohibit slavery in the Territories? The Constitution does not expressly say. . . . From questions of this class spring all our constitutional controversies, and we divide upon them into majorities and minorities." This framing would not only legitimize the actions a Republican administration might undertake as simply implementing its own interpretation of those silences, but it would also be a means to stem the secession crisis. If constitutional meaning were ultimately grounded in popular sovereignty, then the law would only come to be settled if reaffirmed continuously by the majority. From Lincoln's pre–Civil War perspective, if southern slavery interests prevailed in the election of 1864 and Lincoln and the Republicans were rebuked, then the constitutional status of slavery would continue to remain unsettled just as his own 1860 election kept the issue unsettled. In other words, if the people continued to vacillate in their convictions toward slavery by electing presidents from parties with different views on its constitutionality, then the constitutionality of slavery would remain unsettled until a consistent electoral pattern emerged. On the other hand, if the people reelected Lincoln or supported an even stauncher advocate of abolition in the future, then the legitimacy of overruling *Dred Scott* would be on even surer footing.

Second, Lincoln's characterization of majoritarian politics appears to be similar to Van Buren and Jefferson's assertions—with one critical caveat, namely that Lincoln did not view the majority as static. Instead, he stipulated the dynamic nature of the majority in his First Inaugural and, more important, that this very dynamism was legitimate. To deny it would spell the end of liberty: "A majority held in restraint by constitutional checks and limitations, and *always changing easily with deliberate changes of popular opinions and sentiments,* is the only true sovereign of a free people. Whoever rejects it does of necessity fly to anarchy or to despotism."[77] If constitutionalism was an expression of popular sovereignty, and popular sovereignty was dynamic, then constitutionalism itself was dynamic. The Constitution's meaning was not a settled affair.

Through this reconfiguration of the meaning of majority, Lincoln held open the possibility that an interpretation of the Constitution explicitly protecting slave-property rights could be implemented if that interest acquired the requisite votes.[78] Instead of seeking those votes through the normal election cycle, six states—South Carolina, Mississippi, Florida, Alabama, Georgia, and Louisiana—seceded from the Union in the wake of Lincoln's election. By the time of Lincoln's inaugural, five others—North Carolina, Arkansas, Virginia, Missouri, and Tennessee—held elections for a convention to consider secession. Desperate to hold the union together, Lincoln used his inaugural speech to legitimate his own rule and to calm anxieties about the effect of his leadership on slavery interests. He restricted his aim: "I have no purpose, directly or indirectly, to interfere with the institution of slavery in the States where it exists. I believe I have no lawful right to do so, and I have no inclination to do so."[79] He also cited the Republican platform, which paid homage to state sovereignty: "The right of each state to order and control its own domestic institutions according to its own judgment exclusively, is essential to that balance of powers on which the perfection and endurance of our political fabric depends."[80]

Providing opposition with a sense of security was crucial to the maintenance of civic stability. Lincoln was compelled to claim that disagreement was not only inevitable and natural given constitutional silences but also *nonthreatening* as long as secession did not follow. If exit were an option, then a polity would necessarily dissolve into anarchy. To prevent secession, Lincoln built on the foundation laid by Van Buren when he emphasized majority rule as the only procedural mechanism that could confer legitimacy to rule. Yet he abandoned the notion of opposition as a minority threat, which Van Buren relied on to frame his Democratic Party as a mechanism of civic stability and as a perpetual majority. Instead, Lincoln offered a narrower meaning of majority, one that focused on numerical superiority granting only temporary authority to lead.[81] Once Lincoln moved to a dynamic conception of majority, he no longer cast the minority as a static aristocratic threat or the majority as perpetual and right. And, indeed, Lincoln admitted that the majority could be wrong. Given this possibility, Lincoln contended that simply trying again for electoral victory made more sense than secession: "I do not deny the possibility that the people may err in an election, but if they do, the true cure is in the next election."[82] To another audience, he argued, "Though the majority may be wrong . . . yet we must adhere to the principle that the majority shall rule. By your Constitution you have another chance in four years. . . . elect a better man next time. There are plenty of them."[83] As these statements made just before his inauguration demonstrate, Lincoln admitted that the Southern cause could win the next time around. He granted that the majority might be wrong and that its legitimacy to rule was fundamentally temporary. These were propositions Van Buren would not grant.

In summary, this redefinition of majority as granting only *temporary* authority to lead would not only be a means to lower the stakes of politics—which ultimately failed—but also allow Lincoln to cast the *Dred Scott* ruling as fundamentally unsettled. He had, after all, won the election. If legal status was settled by repeated affirmation and grounded in popular sovereignty, then Lincoln's victory, by definition, seemed to suggest that Taney's ruling was not popularly accepted.

Ironically, the secession crisis compelled Lincoln to validate, to an extent, the opposition's cause and to suggest that while its constitutional vision was different, it was not "anti-constitutional" in and of itself.[84] Put differently, if the opposition were merely another political party and not considered an a priori threat to the Constitution, then multiple parties could coexist. And, if multiple parties could coexist and each party represented a constitutional vision, then multiple constitutional visions could likewise exist. So, just as Van Buren would reformulate the meaning of political party as promoting civic health, Lincoln, by stipulating that the majority was a temporary entity, that it was persuadable about the meaning and implications of the Constitution, would try to assure the opposition of its full voice. He would thereby cast that opposition's participation in normal election procedures as securing the Union's longevity, not as destructive of it.

So, for Lincoln, just as for Van Buren, party remained the source of constitutional vision. But Lincoln, unlike Van Buren, granted that multiple parties could legitimately exist. It followed, then, that multiple equally legitimate constitutional visions could exist and that judges could represent one or another particular constitutional vision. The necessary implication is that judges were a means to implement the parties' respective constitutional visions. Lincoln's attorney general, Edward Bates, gave this ideal full vent: "The Supreme Court is to be a mere party machine, to be manipulated, built up, and torn down, as party exigencies require."[85] Thus, for Lincoln, any party that wins as long as it plays by the rules can implement its particular constitutional vision, suggesting that constitutional visions vary—unlike Van Buren's vision of his Democratic Party as synonymous with the Constitution's proper commitments, unmistakably leading to the conclusion that judicial decisions opposed to this agenda threatened the Constitution itself. And, while Jackson and Van Buren construed judicial outcomes supporting opposition as threats to civic stability, Lincoln gave them legitimacy and conceded that they were subject to future electoral affirmation.

In short, this reliance on a dynamic majority created flexibility to ignore and to *harness* judicial power. It maintained judicial authority while providing the rationale to use the judiciary for the instrumental purpose of promoting a particular constitutional vision, which had been allegedly validated by the people in the most recent election. Lincoln's notion of a dynamic majority would enable him to frame his victory in two ways. First, it was unthreatening to Southern interests because he had won only this most recent election. Other interests may prevail at a later date. Second, it sufficed to confer legitimacy on Lincoln's rule and to provide him with leverage to minimize the impact of the Court's *Dred Scott* ruling. By linking judicial authority and electoral politics, Lincoln found a way to maintain judicial authority without deferring to it as supreme. He could deny that national governing policy could be "irrevocably fixed by decisions of the Supreme Court." However, if a given issue had "been before the Court more than once" and had "been affirmed and reaffirmed through a course of years," then it would be "even revolutionary, to not acquiesce in its precedent."[86] As such, Lincoln could occupy the quixotic position of placing limits on judicial authority while also ascribing to it legitimate authority, which could be harnessed to serve his political ends.

Ronald Reagan: Soliciting Courts

Rather than a simple recurrence of the Jeffersonian demand that judges should be kept apart from politics, such that judicial independence becomes synonymous with neutrality, we can now see that Lincoln's model for judicial behavior was quite different. He understood, like Jefferson, that judges could be political. Yet he also recognized that their political leanings could be harnessed to achieve policy ends, and, more importantly, that doing so was *legitimate*. For Lincoln—as for Van Buren—judges were tools of the political party. The difference was that for Lincoln, multiple parties could loyally exist and for Van Buren they could not. In short, Lincoln exposed the Court as political— his interpretation of *Dred Scott* relied on this claim—and justified its usage as a political instrument; his desire to see that ruling overturned demanded this idea. This conception of the Court as a tool of partisan interests, such that the stability of law and the process of democratic election became increasingly intertwined, competed with the earlier, and thus more entrenched, Jeffersonian conflation of judicial independence and political neutrality.

We see these rhetorical themes compete today in the now more familiar language of "originalism," which has been associated with neutrality versus the notion of a "living constitution," or legal realism.[87] Any tendency to see conservative rhetorical aspirations toward judicial neutrality as not an inherently political strategy ultimately only serves to misguide our fuller characterization of presidential-judicial relations, leaving unexplored the very variation over time we seek to uncover in these relations.[88] To take a more recent example, the Reagan administration has too often been characterized as hostile to judicial authority, as attempting to reign it in just like Jefferson. Yet, in sharp contrast to the Jeffersonians, the Reagan administration engaged in a thorough strategy of harnessing judicial power—not delegitimizing it—by adapting patterns developed by liberals in the 1960s.[89]

The Reagan administration, particularly Attorney General Edwin Meese III, was preoccupied with utilizing judicial power to "institutionalize the Reagan Revolution so that it can't be set aside no matter what happens in future presidential elections."[90] A number of strategies were developed to achieve this goal, including appointing federal judges who were ideologically aligned with Reagan administration policy aims, creating and expanding an intellectual network of conservative lawyers such that the bureaucracy of the Justice Department could be transformed and could support the development of future young conservative lawyers, and utilizing the presidential signing statement in previously unexplored ways.[91] The last strategy is examined in this section. It was developed by young lawyers in the Justice Department during Reagan's first term, in part because the president did not have the immediate opportunity to counterbalance the expansion of federal judgeships passed under the Democratic Carter administration.[92]

The signing statement has historically served a ceremonial role akin to a press release. However, lawyers in the Reagan-era Office of Legal Council (OLC) explored ways to enhance executive power, which had been curtailed in the wake of the Watergate scandal.[93] The signing statement was a means to that end. OLC lawyers sought to reframe the signing statement as a tool to *guide* judicial interpretation of statutory meaning. The statement could signal that the president preferred a particular constitutional interpretation; doing so, however, did not guarantee that judges would agree, but it did serve as another way to achieve a particular constitutional interpretive result. By opening another path of interpretation, the statement attempts to bring the judiciary to the president's side, to utilize judicial authority for executive policy and institutional aims rather than ignore, counter, or otherwise undermine it.

To integrate the signing statement into the broader theoretical connection between changing views toward the legitimacy of opposition and manipulations of judicial power, we can recall that earlier in this chapter, I suggested that when opposition is considered legitimate and loyal, politicians may deliberately introduce ambiguity into statutes to solicit judicial review from a court they consider ideologically affiliated. Presidential signing statements, as conceptualized by lawyers in the Reagan administration, attempt this very thing. They offer an interpretation of a statute that the president signs into law that may differ from that indicated by the legislative record. Obviously, the signing statement strategy may not work, since many levels of the federal judiciary are multi-judge panels, and a given judge, much less a majority of judges, may not be convinced by the presidential signing statement. But, my point is not to show that the strategy always works but rather to point out that it was simply created as a means to circumvent Congress and exploit a potentially affiliated Court.

One of the earliest memos outlining the use of signing statements to guide judicial decision-making was authored by Yale Law School graduates and Federalist Society founders, Steven Calabresi and John Harrison. It begins, "The abuse of legislative history is a major way in which legislative power is usurped by activist courts, ideologically motivated congressional staffers and lobbying groups." It outlines how judges have no written record alternative to legislative history to serve as "a guide to the interpretation of statutory language." The remedy, Calabresi and Harrison suggested, was "a potentially powerful, if so far unused tool: presidential signing statements." The immediate challenge was that signing statements were not considered part of legislative history even if, in the young lawyers' words, they were better than congressional committee reports as guides to statutory meaning since the former "represents an *entire* branch's view of the matter."[94] By contrast, committee reports represent only the majority of a committee, not the entire Congress. Given that the statement were used rarely and that statements were not published and thus not immediately accessible to lawyers and judges, Calabresi and Harrison recommended that Meese take the following actions: (1) publish the statements; (2) give speeches to spread awareness about them; (3) ask the Litigation Strategy Working Group, which has been called "a brain trust of about fifteen political appointees drawn from throughout the Justice Department," to consider how to disseminate existing statements to staff attorneys to familiarize themselves with the document; and (4) have the OLC draft law review articles on behalf of Meese encouraging the use of signing statements by judges to interpret statutory meaning.[95]

In February 1986, Samuel Alito Jr., deputy assistant attorney general in the Office of Legal Council, summarized the main goal of the Litigation Strategy Working Group: "Our primary objective is to ensure that Presidential signing statements assume their rightful place in the interpretation of legislation." For Alito, the problem was that "in interpreting statutes, both courts and litigants (including lawyers in the Executive branch) invariably speak of 'legislative' or 'congressional' intent. Rarely if ever do courts or litigants inquire into the President's intent." Alito repeated ideas outlined by Calabresi and Harrison, namely that although the signing statement had been "often little more than a press release," an "interpretive signing statement" would "increase the power of the Executive to shape the law and "by forcing some rethinking by courts, scholars, and litigants, it may help to curb some of the prevalent abuses of legislative history."[96] In short, these Reagan administration officials offered judges an alternate route to interpret statutes in line with presidential interests. They sought to harness judicial authority rather than to counter it directly.

This "interpretive" signing statement has been utilized by presidents since Reagan, but it was increasingly scrutinized during the administration of President George W. Bush.[97] This tactic is perhaps more innovative than the presidential veto—as we examined in the Jackson case—to the degree that it manipulates the construction of law without directly confronting congressional or judicial authority. Traditional presidential vetoes initiate a constitutionally mandated dialogue between the legislative and executive branch.[98] With signing statements, by executing a law but nevertheless holding out the possibility it may not be enforced at the president's discretion, the president reduces the likelihood of a congressional response. Recognizing this problem, members of Congress have called for legislation to curb the influence of these statements, either by refusing to allocate funds for their publication, thereby preventing their citation because they will be less accessible or by directly preventing citation altogether.[99] But since the statements tend to posit *possible* rather than *definitive* presidential action, it is far more difficult to counter; since the action is only hypothesized and not taken, there is no action to oppose.[100]

This form of extrajudicial interpretation is less blunt than either Jackson's Second Bank veto or Lincoln's containment of *Dred Scott*. It may be more insidious precisely because it is less pointed. Through the statement, the president articulates a constitutional interpretation and ensures that, if the law is challenged, judges will have recourse to multiple options to gauge statutory intent. Thus, the underlying logic of the interpretive signing statement assumes that multiple interpretations are plausible and legitimate as a matter of course. The strategy of using them for judicial guidance purposes does not assure a presidentially preferred judicial outcome; it merely points in that direction. As such, this Reagan-era invention relies on judicial authority rather than undermining it. Considering Reagan simply to be a departmentalist recurrence of the Jefferson model misses too much variation and fundamentally leaves unexplored crucial developments in presidential-judicial relations.

It is important to note that the Reagan-era intention behind the interpretative signing statement as guiding judges has not yet come to fruition. The Supreme Court has refused thus far to use signing statements even as Reagan-era machinations to include them as part of the legislative record opened up that possibility. Even so, recent judicial moves point toward that possibility. For example, Justice Antonin Scalia scolded his colleagues for not treating the statement as an indication of a statute's intent. In his dissent in *Hamdan v. Rumsfeld*, Scalia noted, "In its discussion of legislative history the court wholly ignores the president's signing statement, which explicitly set forth his understanding that the [Detainee Treatment Act] ousted jurisdiction over pending cases."[101] Justices Clarence Thomas and Alito (who had since become a Supreme Court justice) joined in this dissent. Even if the original aim of signing statements represents only a minority view on the Court, minority views can become majority views over time. As one scholar characterized the aim of using presidential signing statements as statutory history, it "may be of more importance in the long term than any other impact of the signing statements."[102]

Conclusions, Implications, and Extensions

This chapter advances two main contentions. First, the categorical distinction between departmentalist presidents, who believe in independent constitutional interpretation by the executive branch, and judicial supremacist presidents, who defer to judicial review, is too blunt. It ignores variation within type and thereby ignores crucial political developments over time that may affect the nature of presidential-judicial relations. Jefferson, Jackson, and Lincoln did make claims that seemed very similar, but they were grounded in different logics and their corresponding actions toward judicial power reflected these changing logics. My second contention identifies that underlying logic, which is to say that the changing tactics employed by presidents do not illustrate a growing acceptance of judicial supremacy, but they do correlate with an increasing awareness of the legitimacy of multiple plausible constitutional meanings—and thus acceptance of formed and stable opposition as politically loyal to the republic.

As the brief case studies in this chapter have shown, where Jefferson eliminated courts and impeached judges, Jackson more passively ignored courts, and Lincoln outwardly respected rulings even as he acknowledged the legitimacy of using courts to achieve partisan aims. This shift in tactics toward judicial power represents changing responses to a judiciary that presidents, over time, have taken to represent not so much an illegitimate minority but a means to enunciate a particular plausible constitutional vision.

By paying more attention to the shifts in politicians' perceptions of and ideas about the threat posed by formed and stable opposition, we reorient our understanding of presidential relations with the judiciary. This reorientation leads to numerous conclusions and possible extensions for further research. First, by focusing on the politics of opposition rather than on the structural form of the judiciary and its potential for countermajoritarian judicial review, we can better specify the nature of concern about judicial power at different historical moments. Thus, during the early republic federal courts were often depicted as threatening regime unity in a way that seems harder to imagine in our contemporary era of recurring "divided government."

Second, the arguments laid out in this chapter help us understand not just the nature of opposition to courts but also the manner in which elected officials respond to the perceived threats (and opportunities) presented by judges acting at odds with an administration's constitutional vision. We should pay

closer attention to how politicians understand opposition and political parties in their own time, how these ideas change over time, and how those ideas
structure politicians' range of legitimate actions against courts. This orientation helps us grapple with how strategic rationality is historically situated.

Third, while my argument may imply that the shift toward viewing opposition as legitimate and loyal (and possessing a consequent right to rule) developed over time and has seemingly held since Lincoln's presidency, there is
no immediate reason to believe this result is fixed. Opposition could be once
again considered illegitimate or disloyal. We have witnessed such rhetoric at
the heights of McCarthyism in the early 1950s, it has characterized some aspects of the 2008 presidential campaign, and it has marked the public debate
over the recently passed health insurance reform legislation. The notion of
illegitimate opposition has existed since the Founding, and there are differing
views as to whether and why it resurfaces in political rhetoric. Nevertheless,
it certainly remains a potentially potent rhetorical trope.[103]

But, as we take note of a possible recurrence of rhetoric about illegitimate or dangerous political opposition, we also should notice who is articu-
lating these ideas and to whom are they speaking. In other words, normative
acceptance of the opposition's right to rule may be more apparent at the level
of political elites than among the voting public. For example, in the presidential campaign of 2008, John McCain's explicit statements that his party's
opponent, Barack Obama, was a "good man" from whom Republicans had
nothing to fear and Obama's statements that McCain was similarly honorable indicate that the norm of loyalty of opposition still holds among political
elites even if it may not be as diffuse among the wider citizenry.[104] Put differently, while presidents and other politicians may tend to recognize a general
norm of loyal and legitimate political opposition, this norm may not be held
as strongly by the larger public.[105] Indeed, politicians may strategically rely
on its absence to mobilize a base and gain election. And we do see some
examples of this rhetoric of disloyal opposition characterizing contemporary
popular discourse about judicial power. For example, a recent *New York Times*
bestseller characterized some judges—judges who offered an interpretation
of the Constitution clearly disagreeable to the author—in terms that are strik-
ingly reminiscent of Jeffersonian-era fears of opposition undermining the
Constitution's stability and longevity: "Judicial activists are nothing short of
radicals in robes—contemptuous of the rule of law, subverting the Constitution at will, and using their public trust to impose their policy preferences

on society. In fact, no radical political movement has been more effective in undermining our system of government than the judiciary."[106]

The potential consequent danger of this statement lies in its hyperbole. Even as the author of this quotation subtitles his book, "How the Supreme Court Is Destroying America," he immediately retreats from that characterization. The first lines of the hardcover jacket's inside flap are "You're right: It's not." But the careless making of such extremist claims has the potential to obfuscate legitimate concerns about the nature and extent of judicial authority in the United States. And, as former justice O'Connor noted—as cited at the beginning of this chapter—most Americans remain relatively uninformed about the courts and a judge's role in American democracy. As such, they remain vulnerable to misinformation and are potentially swayed by such dangerous overstatement and mischaracterization.

Finally, with regard to the changing nature of the president's relationship with the federal judiciary and particularly with the Supreme Court, this chapter has pointed to the need to think beyond judicial appointment to other strategies of presidential influence on the judiciary. Such strategies, like using the signing statement for purposes of interpretive guidance, are not so much about undermining judicial authority as relying on it and seeking to channel it toward particular political ends. That this conception of the "interpretive" signing statement was invented by modern conservatives and is thus paired with a rhetorical emphasis on "originalism" as judicial neutrality only serves to highlight how much the Jeffersonian and Reaganite constructions of legitimate judicial authority in a democracy clash with one another.

Such mismatches between the rhetoric of neutrality and the reality of presidential aims of harnessing judicial authority are evident in the recent strife surrounding the hearings and confirmation of federal judge Sonia Sotomayor to the Supreme Court. President Obama's aspiration to appoint a Justice with "empathy" was taken by his political opponents to mean using the Court for particular political purposes.[107] Conservatives clung to the allegedly neutral analogy of judge as "umpire" articulated by Chief Justice Roberts during his own confirmation hearings.[108] Such superficial dichotomies leave the history of judicial development profoundly misunderstood, mischaracterizing the objectives of presidents like Jefferson, Jackson, Lincoln, and Reagan, and they may only perpetuate the lack of widespread understanding of courts, judges, and the Constitution, which Justice O'Connor has lamented so publicly.

chapter 4

Institutional Interdependence and the Separation of Powers

J. Mitchell Pickerill

While our previous discussions have examined conflicts with Congresses and presidents, this chapter is centered on the idea that we can weigh today's criticisms of courts only with an appreciation of how the federal judiciary is a vital and capable player in our separation of powers system. The relationship between courts and the other branches can best be described as "interdependent," given their continuous legal and policy dialogue and their reliance on one another for a variety of political needs and institutional objectives. In place of a recurring image offered by court defenders (of judges as embattled and vulnerable), J. Mitchell Pickerill offers an account in which the judiciary is able to hold its own in a dynamic environment of mutual deference, conversation, criticism, and adjustment. Our assessment of today's attacks on courts requires rethinking the very nature of judicial independence in light of courts' institutional vibrancy.

As other chapters in this volume suggest, courts in the United States have been the subject of some very visible and very public attacks by politicians, pundits, and opinion leaders of various stripes. These attacks have ranged from court-stripping legislation to impeachment threats and other rhetorical criticisms of judges or their decisions. For many, these attacks give cause for grave concern, especially insofar as elected officials and other critics are seen as trying to politicize the courts and influence judicial outcomes. And, of course, attempts to politicize courts in this way are understood as an affront to the longstanding principle and norm of judicial independence.[1] While there may be some valid reasons to pay attention to the contemporary attacks and heed some of the concerns expressed by the courts' defenders, there are also good reasons for tempering those concerns. In this chapter, I examine these so-called attacks on judicial independence over approximately the past decade as a launching point for assessing the meaning of judicial independence in the U.S. federal government in light of those attacks.

I begin the chapter by reviewing the most highly publicized attacks on the judiciary, especially at the federal level, and how they have given rise to concerns by scholars and commentators that judicial independence in the United States is at risk. Next, I examine how arguments about the nature of judicial independence in the U.S. system of separation of powers are typically overstated and misinformed to the extent that they are premised on the principle that courts are truly independent from politics and are countermajoritarian in nature. That is, many defenders of judicial independence insist that judges must be truly free to interpret law and decide cases as they see fit, serving as a check against the elected branches to protect us against the tyranny of the majority. A growing scholarly literature calls the premises for these arguments into question despite a popular discourse that seems to reinforce them. In short, the U.S. judiciary is inherently connected to politics in many ways, from the basic fact that the laws judges interpret are the product of a political process to the reality that elected officials routinely use court decisions and doctrine for political purposes.

Therefore, I argue that attacks on the Court must be understood in the context of the multi-institutional, "governance as dialogue" political system that constitutes U.S. government, a point made by Louis Fisher both in his contribution to this volume and in his scholarship more generally. I suggest that the most appropriate understanding of judicial independence should take into account the ways in which institutions in the U.S. federal government are separated but share powers with one another. Any serious assessment of attacks on the judiciary must proceed from an accurate empirical understanding of judicial power and judicial independence. As I will review, courts are able to exercise power for a number of reasons, many of which involve the political support of the other branches. It should not be surprising that political actors in other branches watch over an institution to which they have delegated authority and that these conditions have created compromises and conflicts between the branches.

I conclude, against this background of institutional interdependence, comity, and accommodation, that while a number of attacks on the courts may seem ill-advised and impolitic, they do not constitute a serious threat to the U.S. judiciary. What is needed, therefore, is a new vocabulary that moves popular discussion of courts away from debates over securing judicial independence toward a more realistic understanding of the unique role courts play in our inter-institutional system.

Recent Attacks on the Courts: New Threats to Judicial Independence?

In order to assess the extent to which the U.S. judiciary is under attack and its independence is in jeopardy, I begin with a short review of some of the most highly publicized criticisms of courts and, in response to those criticisms, the countervailing calls for protecting the judiciary. The number and intensity of these criticisms during the last part of the twentieth century and the beginning of the twenty-first have raised concerns among scholars, advocates, and legal practitioners about the integrity and independence of the U.S. judiciary. As I argue later in this chapter, however, the focus on the incidents described in this section and the rhetoric that has ensued regarding judicial independence have mischaracterized the interdependent relationship between courts and other governmental institutions and have overstated threats to the judiciary.

The Judiciary Under Attack at the Turn of the Century

The claims that judicial independence is under attack in the United States are based on a number of rhetorical assaults on judges and judicial decisions as well as a smattering of legislative proposals that seem aimed at diminishing judicial authority or forcing judges to act in the service or support the interests of legislative majorities.[2] Concerns along these lines seem to have heightened over the last several decades leading into the beginning of the twenty-first century—and especially during the first decade of the new millennium. An oft-cited example is the Terri Schiavo case in Florida. In 2005, Florida courts ruled that Terri Schiavo's husband had the right under Florida law to discontinue the feeding tube that was keeping her alive in a persistent vegetative state. The U.S. Congress, in a highly publicized debate, passed a bill titled "An Act for the Relief of the Parents of Theresa Marie Schiavo" to give federal courts jurisdiction to hear the case. In the end, however, the U.S. Court of Appeals for the 11th Circuit upheld the decision to remove the feeding tube.[3]

In addition to the widely publicized Terri Schiavo legislation, members of Congress have also proposed other laws to strip courts of their jurisdiction to hear certain types of cases.[4] In 2002, Representative Todd Akin (R-MO) introduced the Pledge Protection Act in the House to strip the federal courts of jurisdiction to hear legal challenges to the constitutionality of the Pledge of Allegiance. Although the bill has not been passed, it has been introduced in subsequent congresses. Similarly, Representative Robert Aderholt (R-AL) and U.S. Senator Richard Shelby (R-AL) introduced the Constitution Restoration Act in 2005 in an effort to strip federal courts of jurisdiction to challenges to public displays of the Ten Commandments or other state efforts to acknowledge "God as the sovereign source of law and liberty." Other bills introduced in Congress in recent years that would strip the federal courts of jurisdiction to hear particular types of cases include the We the People Act, first introduced in 2004, which would preclude federal courts from hearing constitutional challenges to a range of local laws involving "religious liberty, sexual orientation, family relations, education and abortion," and the Marriage Protection Act, which would deny jurisdiction to federal courts to hear challenges to the Defense of Marriage Act of 1996.[5]

In addition to these legislative attempts to influence judicial policymaking, the anti-Court rhetoric of elected officials and other commentators seemed especially incendiary during the first decade of the twenty-first century. The public criticisms, which some characterize as verbal assaults, on courts by religious and social conservatives seem especially troubling to many.[6] According to Bert Brandenburg and Amy Kay of Justice at Stake Campaign, a nonpartisan public interest group that promotes judicial independence: "For those seeking to use the courts to impose their own religious views in violation of the Constitution, any judge who doesn't obey their wishes, even if simply upholding settled law, is a target. Such judges are increasingly finding themselves, and their courts in general, the objects of impeachment threats and venomous speech." They cite several examples of harsh rhetoric, including threats of impeachment against judges whose decisions are unpopular or controversial, such as a comment by Senator Sam Brownback (R-KS) on the floor of the Senate in response to a federal court decision involving partial birth abortion, in which he spoke of the "need to reign in an increasingly reckless judiciary . . . through impeachment, when necessary."[7]

While not every criticism of the judiciary rises to the level of an impeachment threat, there seems to be a sense among scholars, journalists, and practitioners alike that the relationship between the Congress and the courts can be characterized as one of "mutual wariness, suspicion, jealousy and even a bit of spite."[8] In his interviews with members of Congress and congressional staff, Court-Congress scholar Mark Miller reports that the relationship between the two was described using words such as " 'venomous,' 'hostile,' 'tense,' 'deteriorating,' 'contentious,' 'animosity,' and 'strained.' " And, as Miller notes, several former and sitting U.S. Supreme Court justices have described the relationship between the two branches in a similar manner. Miller concludes: "These assaults on the federal courts, however, may result in the loss of judicial independence. Many in the legal and academic communities consider this too high a price to pay."[9] He is not alone in expressing these concerns, as the next section will demonstrate.

Attacks on the Courts and Concerns about Judicial Independence

To some, these recent examples are evidence of a trend of increasing frequency and growing intensity of assaults on the judiciary that should raise grave concerns because they are a challenge to judicial independence. Justice Sandra Day O'Connor has been one of the most vocal defenders of the courts from their contemporary critics. Since she retired from the U.S. Supreme Court, O'Connor has appeared on popular television programs, written op-eds, and given interviews and speeches on the general topic including a 2006 piece in *The Wall Street Journal* entitled "The Threat to Judicial Independence" and a 2008 piece in *Parade Magazine* entitled "How to Save Our Courts." O'Connor has also started the Sandra Day O'Connor Project on the State of the Judiciary, which has sponsored numerous programs around the country designed to illuminate threats to judicial independence, educate the public on the subject, and promote more independence from the other branches of government.[10] In 2006, for instance, the O'Connor Project hosted a conference called "Fair and Independent Courts: A Conference on the State of the Judiciary at Georgetown Law Center," co-chaired by O'Connor and Justice Stephen Breyer and attended by distinguished law faculty, journalists, and even a majority of sitting justices on the Supreme Court, including Chief Justice John Roberts, who gave an address to attendees on the topic.[11] Clearly, this issue has attracted the attention of judges, legal academics, and journalists, whether the concerns expressed comport with reality or not.

As a further sign that concerns over threats to courts are on the rise, in 2008 the incoming president of the American Bar Association, the national professional association representing the interests of lawyers and legal practitioners in the United States, H. Thomas Wells Jr., identified judicial independence as one of the top priorities for the ABA under his leadership.[12] And the American Judicature Society, a self-described "nonpartisan organization with a national membership of judges, lawyers and other citizens interested in the administration of justice," has created the Center for Judicial Independence "to promote understanding of the critical need to have a judicial branch that is free to apply the Constitution and the law, regardless of political and even popular pressure to do otherwise."[13] In sum, the recent jurisdiction-stripping efforts and anti-Court rhetoric of the last decade or so have heightened concern among many that politicians are seeking to compromise the independence and impartiality of courts to achieve their own policy or partisan objectives. It is not clear, however, how accurate these fears are; that is, do these examples, as harsh as they may seem, really amount to threats, or have they just created the perception of a problem? Moreover, the concerns may not be grounded in a meaningful understanding of the concept of judicial independence, to the extent that commentators' understanding of judicial power and the definition of judicial independence are based on an outdated notion that courts actually exercise power in a hermetically sealed world without any connections to the broader political universe. Before we can conclude that rhetorical attacks and court-curbing efforts of the past decade are in fact compromising the independence of our courts, we must be clear about what judicial independence means, not simply as a normative good but also as an empirical matter.

In order to assess the seriousness of this threat critically and to determine the extent to which our judicial independence really is imperiled, the remainder of this chapter carefully considers the role of the judiciary in the U.S. system of government and how it actually functions as part of the separation of powers. In the next section, I review the nature of judicial independence, or rather *interdependence,* in the U.S. system of separation of powers. As I will demonstrate by reviewing the scholarly literature on the topic, clashes between the judiciary and the other branches of government are not uncommon, nor should they be unexpected. As a matter of course, however, the court both influences and is influenced by the other branches of government. As a result, the critics of the court-attackers have framed the issue incorrectly, drawing attention away from many of the substantive issues involved in these examples. As we will see, judicial independence is not an either-or; that is, the question is not whether the judiciary is independent from the other branches or not. Instead, the Court's *relative* independence must be assessed in the context of how it and the other branches *share* powers and participate in inter-institutional decision-making. Independence, or interdependence, is most threatened when the actions of one branch actually shuts out or realistically threatens the ability of another branch to participate in that process. As I will argue in the final section of this chapter, such has not been the case with the attacks on courts over the past decade or so.

The Nature of Judicial Interdependence in a Separated System of Government

In order to assess the real threat to courts, it is necessary to examine what we mean by judicial independence and the nature of judicial power in the U.S. separated system of government. In his recent review of scholarship on judicial independence, Frank Cross observes, "[f]ew cows are more sacred than judicial independence. Yet the concept of an independent judiciary is more commonly apotheosized than analyzed." He continues, "Americans generally and even legal academics often take for granted a belief that our judiciary is independent, at least in the fundamental sense of freedom from interference by the other branches."[14] Yet, a precise definition eludes even those who advocate for judicial independence and express concern that the modern judiciary is under siege. The reason such a precise definition eludes us is that the judiciary is not, nor has it ever been, truly independent from the other branches of government. So before we can assess the extent to which attacks on the judiciary are compromising judicial independence in a normative sense, we must have a more realistic and empirical understanding of the judiciary's role in the U.S. government. Given the true nature of judicial power in the United States, the concept of judicial independence is a complex and nuanced concept.

Interactions and Interconnections among the Branches

In order to understand the nature of judicial independence in the United States, it is essential that we consider the nature of judicial power in a sepa-rated system of government. In the U.S. system of separation of powers, inter-action between and among the different branches is to be expected—it would be simplistic and naive to characterize the three branches as independent from one another. While all three branches of government maintain certain degrees of autonomy from the others, they are also interconnected in fundamental ways that make each branch dependent to some extent on the others. In order to exercise power, actors in one branch may need the cooperation of those in a coordinate branch; in order to justify a decision—or a nondecision— they may choose to blame officials from a coordinate branch; and actors in one branch may engage in a range of behavior in an attempt to force the other branches to comply or help enforce their decisions or to consider their policy preferences in the policy-making process. As this section will examine, it is well understood that presidents and members of Congress routinely interact in cooperative and antagonistic ways as they pursue their preferred policies. What is less understood by many is that the judiciary is also interconnected with the other branches in fundamental ways, and they are all three interdependent on the other two. In short, actions by one branch regarding coordinate branches may not always be what they seem to be when considered in isolation from their counterparts.

Political scientists have long observed the numerous ways that presidents and members of Congress interact. In his classic account of presidential power, for example, Richard Neustadt observed: "The Constitutional Convention of 1787 is supposed to have created a government of 'separated powers.' It did nothing of the sort. Rather, it created a government of separated institutions *sharing* powers."[15] As a consequence, he explains, presidents do not derive their greatest authority from the inherent powers of the office or even the formal powers granted the executive in the Constitution. Rather, Neustadt argues that it is the "power to persuade" others to carry out or comply with the president's policies. Key to Neustadt's understanding of the presidency and the U.S. government is the notion that Congress and presidents must work together to exercise power; Congress needs the president's signature to enact legislation, except in the rare case of a veto override, and to implement policy once legislation is passed. Conversely, presidents need members of Congress to support, enact, and fund their agendas and programs if they are to be successful.[16]

Although there is by now a wealth of research to draw on that illustrate the interactions between presidents and Congress as they "share" powers, to use Neustadt's phrase, one excellent example of how presidents and Congress are interdependent on one another is the role the executive veto plays in the legislative process. Indeed, President Dwight Eisenhower boldly claimed, "I am part of the legislative process," referring to the veto power.[17] In fact, Charles Cameron provides compelling evidence to demonstrate that the executive veto is not simply exercised by presidents to obstruct Congress from legislating by killing legislation. Rather, presidents may use the veto as leverage to encourage Congress to bargain with them.[18] Presidents frequently *threaten* to veto proposed legislation under consideration in Congress to pressure members of Congress to modify the proposed bill in a manner that incorporates their preferences. Additionally, presidents may exercise the veto to force Congress to revise legislation and pass an amended version that incorporates their preferences. Cameron characterizes this special form of bargaining between presidents and Congress as "veto bargaining." For instance, President Bill Clinton vetoed welfare reform bills passed by the Republican Congress in 1996. Each time, Clinton sent a message to Congress that he was willing—indeed wanted—to sign welfare reform legislation, but that he would only do so if certain changes were made. And the Republican leadership in Congress responded by sending Clinton a third bill that satisfied his preferences. The landmark statute, the Personal Responsibility and Work Opportunity Reconciliation Act of 1996, was then signed into law.

There are many other examples of the inter-institutional nature of executive-legislative power, but the main point here is to illustrate as a general matter the ways in which the U.S. political system creates interdependency among the different branches of the federal government.[19] In some ways, the interdependency between the executive and legislative branches is fairly intuitive due to the public nature of the interactions between the two (for example, President Clinton making public statements explaining his veto of welfare reform legislation as well as his desire to sign a modified version of the bill). Nonetheless, similar types of interactions and interdependencies exist between the judiciary and the other two branches.

The Inter-Institutional Nature of Judicial Power

Courts are inherently connected to politics and the other branches of government in basic ways. For instance, the laws judges interpret are the product of politics. They are bargains and compromises by political actors, who, in our system, need to enact laws as the main vehicles for delivering public policy. When judges interpret those laws, they are influenced by past political factors (the policy and other intentions of the legislature when the law was passed), present ones (the facts before them and their current understanding of the law), and future political considerations (such as how their decisions will be implemented by other governmental actors across all three branches of government). And judges attain office through political processes, whether by election or by appointment, and they bring with them their own personal policy preferences or ideologies that to some extent influence their decisions.[20]

Moreover, by design "the executive and legislative branches of the U.S. federal government have considerable power to constrain or influence the federal judiciary."[21] Because the president and the Senate appoint most federal judges, they have the power to shape the membership of the judiciary, and they also retain control over which judges, if any, are promoted to a higher office (a higher court). Congress has the authority under the Constitution to impeach judges. Moreover, Congress controls the judiciary's budget—and although it may not reduce judicial salaries, it can refuse to allow pay raises or fund staffing or other administrative costs for courts. Congress also has authority over the judiciary's jurisdiction, and it may override the statutory interpretation decisions of judges by amending the legislation in question or passing new laws. And lastly, judicial decisions are not self-executing, which means judges usually have to rely on the other branches of government to enforce or implement their decisions if they are to be effective.

These last points in particular point to the interdependent nature of the judiciary's role in the U.S. system of separation of powers—or what Charles O. Jones refers to as a "separated system."[22] The point that needs to be emphasized is that the U.S. system requires and encourages a certain amount of interaction between and among *all three* branches; as Neustadt observed in his study of the presidency, ours is a system of separated institutions but shared powers. The checks and balances in the polity do not create a system where one branch simply obstructs another but rather a system in which the different institutions are interdependent. Inevitably, then, the relationships among the branches will result in cooperation, compromise, and even conflict. This is the main emphasis of the "Governance as Dialogue Movement"; as Mark Miller writes, "Although *governance as dialogue* is an umbrella term for many different specific approaches to the study of governmental institutions, most works from this movement reject the notion of either total legislative supremacy or total judicial supremacy in favor of a more complicated and nuanced, continuous process of interaction among institutions."[23]

One line of research that has provided insights into the nature of interactions between courts and other branches derives from rational choice theory and separation of powers games (or "SOP games"). In brief, these studies show how the members of each branch of government in our system must make a number of strategic calculations in pursuit of their policy and political objectives.[24] Among the factors that influence those calculations are the numerous ways in which the other branches of government might respond. Thus, justices on the Supreme Court (and judges on lower courts) may need to anticipate the reactions of other political actors in rendering their decisions, in order to avoid attempts by the other branch to reverse or deviate from their decisions, and this process leads to a complicated multiplayer game.[25] This calculation may cause judicial actors to moderate their positions in certain circumstances.[26] And because "lawmaking occurs through stages of development across institutions, and policy ideas change as they pass through these stages . . . this means that neither the judicial decision nor the statute [passed by Congress] is definitive—law is shaped and reshaped at both institutional sites at different points in time."[27] Therefore, the Court's exercise of judicial review can be an important source of information for members of Congress during the legislative process—as a signal of the judiciary's assessment of its policy capacities and its expectations regarding the reactions of lawmakers.[28]

A different research tradition yields similar insights. Writing about the Constitution outside courts, an increasing number of scholars make both normative and empirical claims regarding the elaboration of constitutional meaning by political officials. Leading scholars in this tradition include Walter Murphy, who argued for a theory of "departmentalism," which requires, out of necessity and practicality, that actors in all three branches of government be involved in constitutional interpretation.[29] Similarly, Louis Fisher has claimed that constitutional interpretation takes places as part of "constitutional dialogues," in which constitutional meaning is constantly changing and being shaped in different institutional venues, oftentimes in response to the actions or interpretations of the other branches.[30] Moreover, some work emphasizes differences in the approach or substance of constitutional elaboration in the different branches; for example, Keith Whittington makes an important distinction between "constitutional construction" as a political activity and "constitutional interpretation" as a narrower and primarily legalistic exercise.[31] This work does not attempt to account for the effects of the separation of powers on strategic decision-making within institutions, as does the rational choice and SOP research already mentioned. Instead, it shows how constitutional meaning is debated and shaped in an incremental fashion across various governmental institutions—not just courts. Hence, legal developments are inherently connected to political debates and political development.

A good example of the inter-institutional context in which constitutional meaning is shaped involves abortion rights. Although *Roe v. Wade* (1973) is applauded by those who are pro-choice and is vilified by those who are pro-life for establishing and protecting a woman's right to have an abortion, the decision has hardly been the last word on the topic. As Neal Devins has chronicled in some detail, the constitutional status of abortion rights has evolved since *Roe* was handed down in 1973 through continuous debates and actions among interest groups, state legislatures, and governors, as well as different Congresses, presidents, and courts.[32] Thus, U.S. abortion policy and law serves as an example of how institutions outside the courts engage in constitutional dialogues with the judicial system and each other. Such dialogues should be viewed as natural in our system because "[a]s a matter of constitutional design, the United States simply does not feature a hierarchy of lawmakers or compartmentalized niches for each branch of government. Instead, the U.S. Constitution creates a system of overlapping and diversely representative branches of government, which share and compete for power."[33]

One important mechanism that creates the conditions for the elected branches to share and compete for power with the judiciary is judicial review. The power to "strike down" the acts of the other branches is commonly understood as one of the judiciary's key checks on the other branches; however, judicial review cannot simply be characterized as an obstacle to lawmaking by the other branches. In fact, judicial review is a veto—a judicial veto—distinct from but not altogether unlike the executive veto. Like its executive counterpart, the use of the judicial veto does not always amount to the permanent termination of legislation. Congress frequently revives legislation by modifying invalidated legislation in ways that accommodate the Court's constitutional preferences but preserve some portion of the policy. Moreover, the threat and anticipation of judicial review can pressure Congress to accommodate and incorporate constitutional doctrine into legislation while also pursuing the majority's policy preferences. This interaction between the Court and Congress is analogous to Cameron's theory of "veto bargaining," in which a "president may use actual vetoes not only to block legislation but to shape it."[34]

The choice facing Congress after it has seen legislation vetoed by a president or the Court is *not* a dichotomous one. When enough members of Congress are committed to the underlying policy, they may try to find ways to overcome a veto short of an override or reversal of the veto. In these situations, presidents may veto a bill to force Congress to include provisions he favors, and "in most cases Congress and the President find their way to an agreement that reflects the preferences of both parties."[35] Likewise, the judicial veto leaves Congress the opportunity to modify legislation to accommodate the Court's constitutional preferences after it has "struck down" a federal statute. If enough members of Congress are committed to a policy, they may find ways of revising the judicially vetoed statute to revive it and keep the policy intact and also to satisfy the Court's constitutional holding.

In *Constitutional Deliberation in Congress*, I identified seventy-four distinct statutes or statutory provisions struck down by the Supreme Court from 1954 through 1997.[36] Congress modified and revived thirty-five of the seventy-four invalidated laws (47%). It only formally overrode the Court with a constitutional amendment once; it repealed ten of those statutes and did not respond at all in twenty-eight of the cases. A careful reading of the thirty-five congressional revivals reveals that nearly every one of them modified the relevant legislation in a manner that complied with and accommodated the Court's constitutional holding and apparent preferences. Much of the time, then, even when confronted with the Court's most overt exercises of power in the form of a "judicial veto," Congress is able to pursue its basic policy goals, although it has to adapt the means for achieving those goals to satisfy the Court's constitutional preferences.

In addition to reacting to the actual exercise of a judicial veto, members of Congress may also anticipate the potential that a proposed bill might be vetoed. Certainly this is the case with the executive veto. Presidents routinely threaten the veto to force Congress to draft legislation that incorporates their preference. As already discussed, because presidents are not formally part of the legislative process, the threat of the veto is an important source of leverage for them to influence the content of legislation. Similarly, courts cannot be part of the legislative process, but the threat that a statute might be struck down can encourage members in Congress to consider the constitutional dimension of a bill in anticipation of judicial review. Of course, the justices cannot communicate with members of Congress in as direct a manner as presidents. It is the current state of the Court's constitutional doctrine in a given area that provides the information available for members of Congress to assess the degree of a judicial veto threat. Therefore, constitutional issues are more likely to be debated in Congress when there is a perception that courts might strike down legislation. Under these conditions, members of Congress frequently draft legislation in a manner that incorporates judicial doctrine—especially the Supreme Court's constitutional jurisprudence. When Congress considered and passed the Child Labor Act in 1916, the Civil Rights Act in 1964, and hate crimes legislation in 2009, members of Congress debated whether these statutes fell within the scope of the interstate commerce clause in Article I, Section 8 of the Constitution; the bills were all drafted in an attempt to satisfy the Court's commerce power jurisprudence as it existed at that time.[37] Similarly, whenever Congress considers reforms on campaign finance for election campaigns, debates often center round the Supreme Court's *Buckley v. Valeo* (1976) decision and its successors, which hold that election campaign contributions and expenditures are part of political speech protected by the First Amendment; for instance, when Congress passed the Bipartisan Campaign Reform Act in 2000 (BCRA), it was carefully drafted to incorporate and satisfy the Court's free speech doctrine.[38] The Supreme Court initially upheld the constitutionality of BCRA in *McConnell v. Federal Election Commission* (2003) but later struck down some provisions of BCRA in *Citizens United v. Federal Election Commission* (2010).[39] Whether the remaining provisions of BCRA will survive further judicial scrutiny is uncertain, but the back and forth between the judiciary and Congress over the issue illustrates the nature of governance as dialogue. This judicial veto bargaining that takes place between the Court and Congress is meant to show how judicial review frequently compels a dynamic interaction between the Court and Congress in which they both contribute to the content of legislation and the development of constitutional interpretation.

Since interaction between the courts and the other branches of government is a natural occurrence, it is difficult to characterize the federal judiciary as being entirely independent from the elected branches. In fact, law and courts research has shown that elected political elites often support judicial power for strategic or other purposes. In 1957, Robert Dahl published a seminal article arguing that because of various institutional features of the Court and, most importantly, because it is composed of justices who are appointed by presidents through a political process, the U.S. Supreme Court is inevitably part of a national policymaking coalition in which it usually acts to further the policy goals of majority electoral coalitions.[40] The Court is not simply an independent institution that stands in the way of the policy preferences of democratically elected majorities. While there are limitations to the extent to which the Court is simply an agent of a national majority electoral coalition, Dahl's insights have provided the foundation for a contemporary scholarship that has identified ways in which the Court's purported antimajoritarian nature is less than meets the eye, with much of its power ultimately contingent on the cooperation and sanction of these other departments of government.

For example, Mark Graber has shown how the Court's exercise of judicial review can reflect the preferences and choices of elected officials who might prefer to leave, or even delegate, policymaking for the courts in order to avoid responsibility for making controversial policy choices.[41] In his book *Legislative Deferrals*, George Lovell chronicles how members of Congress had indeed left a number of important policy choices to the courts in a series of labor statutes passed in the earlier part of the twentieth century. According to Lovell, the Court's decisions against labor interests during that period have been improperly characterized as countermajoritarian—not because the Court was clearly acting to support a legislative or electoral majority but rather because in the first instance members of Congress had not expressed a clear majority position on the issues before the Court. In fact, Lovell's detailed legislative histories demonstrate mixed motives on the part of members who voted for labor legislation. He also explains how legislative compromises that were part of the drafting and political process left a number of issues ambiguous; Congress essentially deferred policy-making to the judiciary. For example, when the Supreme Court invalidated anti–yellow dog contract provisions (contracts in which employees agree not to engage in union activities) of the Erdman Act in *Adair v. United States* (1908), it was accused by some of acting counter to pro-labor majorities in Congress. However, Lovell's evidence indicates that members of Congress bowed to a range of political interests and pressures, accepting many compromises in the bill while under consideration that led to highly ambiguous statutory language and ambivalence among members of Congress. Indeed, it was viewed by many legislators and commentators alike as "symbolic" and "harmless as an infant." Thus, Lovell successfully challenges the conventional wisdom that "judges shaped the labor movement by thwarting important legislative victories that labor organizations thought they had won through democratic processes in the legislative branch."[42] Instead, he shows that legislators essentially empowered courts to make policy-making decisions that they were unwilling or unable to make for political reasons.

In addition, elected officials might support judicial power, and judicial review in particular, as a way to overcome entrenched interests or legislative obstructions. Keith Whittington has demonstrated how numerous judicial decisions in the area of federalism have helped "to bring states into line with the nationally dominant constitutional vision" when elected officials were unable to do so themselves due to the fragmented nature of the U.S. system of federalism.[43] Similarly, oftentimes there are entrenched minority interests in Congress that are able to obstruct majority preferences, and the Court can aid majority interests by "dislodg[ing] those "entrenched political actors and interests."[44] Michael Klarman refers to this as "majoritarian judicial review" in explaining how the Supreme Court in *Brown v. Board of Education* (1954) helped a national majority overcome the Southern Democrats in Congress.[45] Similarly, the Court may serve to help manage divisions or cleavages within a dominant political coalition, such as when Democratic presidents between 1940 and 1970 encouraged the Court to reform American race relations in cases such as *Brown* as a way of circumventing opposition from the powerful Southern Democrats who controlled Congress.[46] In these ways, then, the judiciary does not act as an agent of elected officials (as Dahl initially theorized), nor is it entirely accurate to say that courts simply act as independent checks on the elected branches to prevent tyranny. Courts often enjoy the support of elected officials even when it *appears* they might be acting against those officials.

Finally, elected officials might also want to empower courts as a way of entrenching policies and programs that they believe are becoming vulnerable to new or emerging electoral majorities.[47] Through their judicial appointments, presidents do attempt to entrench their policy agendas by appointing judges who are sympathetic to that agenda and who hold judicial philosophies that are consistent with that agenda. In fact, scholars have also shown how elected officials in other countries and political systems also empower judiciaries and seek to entrench policy preferences in courts in similar ways.[48] Judges should not be expected to follow in "lock-step" as agents of the majority, but in general, we should expect trends on the court to reflect majoritarian values in society and politics.[49] However, as the Court extends the values of old electoral coalitions, it may bring a controversial topic to the fore that can evolve into a cleavage issue among the parties, as minority parties attempt to redefine coalitions for political and electoral gains. For instance, Republicans were able to use pre–1980 Court decisions on abortion and prayer in school to develop the "values" agenda and attract religious conservatives and other voters who identified with the religious right and conservative social values; this agenda helped Republicans build electoral majorities from the Reagan administration in the 1980s through the Bush administration in the early 2000s.[50]

As this somewhat limited review of this literature indicates, judicial power in the United States must be understood as something more than a countermajoritarian power that independently thwarts the will of elected officials and national governing coalitions.[51] While the Court might occasionally act in a manner inconsistent with an identifiable majority, the relationship between the Court and democratic politics is more complex and nuanced than is often appreciated or portrayed. Judicial power is just as often employed as a mechanism for repealing outdated legislation, to extend the values of the current political regime to recalcitrant local jurisdictions, to protect the policy commitments of a current majority that are becoming democratically vulnerable, to overcome obstacles such as federalism or entrenched minority interests, to manage cross-cutting pressures within the dominant governing coalition, and to advance the policy agendas of the dominant political coalition in many other ways. The important point for our discussion here is that not only does the judiciary serve a multitude of functions vis-à-vis electoral majorities, but the nature of judicial power vis-à-vis the other branches of government is also likely to change over time, depending on strength of the electoral majority.[52] And the extent to which courts enjoy independence from the other branches may have its roots in the political choices of the actors in those other branches.

What should be clear from this section is that in the context of the American separated system, judicial power, in theory and in practice, cannot be said to possess an inherently independent check on the other branches in the manner typically depicted by those claiming to support judicial independence. Rather, the judiciary is interconnected and interdependent with the elected branches in many ways. Therefore, those who criticize the courts on the basis of this notion of judicial independence may be focusing on a shibboleth,[53] just as those who criticize courts for being antimajoritarian and having too much power do so based on an inaccurate understanding of the reality of judicial power in our separated system. It is not that recent criticisms of the court are not important or lack meaning but rather that concerns over their impact on judicial independence are likely to be misplaced without a meaningful understanding of the full context.

There are at least three implications of the research chronicled in this section for the purposes of this chapter. First, interactions among the branches of the U.S. government—and specifically between the judiciary and the other branches—are common and inevitable. Second, no theory of what judicial independence is or how it can be preserved is plausible if it is premised on an inaccurate view that courts and other institutions exercise power separate from the others. The relative independence of courts must account for the interdependence that exists within our system of government. In effect, judicial independence may be as much an empirical puzzle as anything else. Finally, the meaning of specific interactions between courts and other political actors, whether friendly or antagonistic in nature, are likely to be complex and nuanced. And thus, our assessments of how attacks on the judiciary affect the independence of the judiciary should be deliberate and nuanced, not rash and reactionary.

Rethinking Judicial Independence in a Separated System

The most common understanding of judicial independence is rooted in a separation of powers rationale.[54] Americans are taught at an early age that the separation of powers creates independent branches of government exercising separate powers from the others. In particular, judicial independence places the court outside of electoral politics and all that goes with it, providing a crucial check against tyranny.[55] Therefore, judges should decide cases according to law, and not public opinion polls or in compliance with the demands of other political actors. And, as some argue, judicial independence fosters the protection of individual and minority rights. These points have been reinforced by numerous commentators, practitioners, and scholars,[56] and it is this rather simplistic take on judicial independence that seems to be the basis for many commentaries decrying the so-called attackers.[57]

Yet there are any number of reasons to question this simplistic account. To begin with, the extent to which judges mechanically apply law without influence of political or personal preferences is a dubious one; reasonable judges often disagree over the proper "legal interpretation" in cases they decide, and those disagreements frequently correlate to ideological predispositions.[58] And there is little reason to think that courts are always better suited to protect individual or minority rights than other government institutions. Indeed, research indicates that in many instances, elected branches have protected or even expanded rights and liberties when courts have refused to do so.[59] After all, as Judge Richard Posner has observed, excessively insulating judges could easily result in "exchanging one set of tyrants for another."[60] And as noted earlier in this chapter, the political branches enjoy a number of formal powers to check the judiciary explicitly provided for in the U.S. Constitution, such as impeachment, power over budgeting, and so on.

This is not to say that courts do not enjoy any independence at all. But theories of judicial independence cannot disregard the wealth of evidence regarding the limitations on that independence and the interdependent na-ture of institutions in the U.S. separated system. To the extent that courts are "independent" from the other branches, that independence occurs in an inter-institutional context of shared powers. So at any given moment, courts are anticipating and reacting to decisions of other branches, and conversely, the other branches are anticipating and reacting to judicial decisions. How independent the judiciary is in this context is largely an empirical question. As Frank Cross observes, "Judicial independence is not a binary condition but exists on a continuum of relative independence and accountability."[61]

In order to assess purported threats to judicial independence, we need a more accurate, thick, and empirically grounded description of the conditions under which courts are likely to generate critiques, including charges that they have overstepped their institutional roles. To be sure, some scholars have offered more thoughtful and careful considerations of judicial independence that understands judges as "an independent voice in the inter-institutional constitutional dialogue,"[62] judges as independent voices who are not mere policy agents of elected officials,[63] and judges as actors who can act with-out brute manipulation by political actors outside the judiciary.[64] Courts and judges must be understood as contributing to lawmaking and policymaking by adding their unique perspective—one that is autonomous and is rooted in law and legal reasoning; but at the same time, it must be equally understood that there are political foundations for judicial power.[65] And much of what we understand as judicial independence may be customary in nature, dependent to some extent on the other branches choosing to honor that customary prac-tice.[66] This is a particularly important point, because insofar as the judiciary enjoys a certain degree of power, it is likely that the other branches have either granted that power or acquiesced to it. This being the case, it should not at all be surprising that the actors in those branches would remain vigi-lant over the courts, with which they *share* power. They may be expected to respect a degree of judicial independence, even when they disagree with par-ticular court decisions, so long as other political objectives are being served and power is being shared between the branches. As previous discussion has demonstrated, this is the reality of how the U.S. separated system works, and it reflects the ways in which responsibility and accountability are "diffused" throughout the system.[67]

In the U.S. system of separation of powers, there are inherent limits to the true independence of courts. Judges are engaged in a complicated process of lawmaking and policymaking in which the distribution of power ebbs and flows in a continuous manner over time. Courts may at times take the lead in policymaking, they may sometimes ratify the choices of others, or they may find themselves at odds with other political institutions. As a consequence, not every attack by an elected official on the judiciary, nor every attempt to curb the power of the courts, is necessarily an assault on judicial independence in any meaningful sense of that phrase. Instead, it is important to inquire what the actual effects of those assaults are. This inquiry is necessarily an empirical and contextual one. To begin, some baseline of judicial power needs to be established. What magnitude of authority and autonomy in decision-making did the courts enjoy before the criticisms or anti-court activities began? And importantly, how was that authority and autonomy established—was it granted by the political branches, is the authority explicitly inherent in the Constitution, did the Court attempt to expand its own authority? Second, can we observe a measurable decrease of authority, and, if so, to what levels? Finally, what is the political context and motivation behind the attacks? Is there a sincere attempt to deny the Court not simply authority in some matter but also the opportunity to engage in shared inter-institutional decision-making? In assessing the actual impact of attacks on the judiciary, it is thus necessary to distinguish those that actually deny courts the opportunity to participate with the other branches in the exercise of power or those that have no measureable impact on the level of decision-making authority and autonomy of the judiciary.

Reconsidering "Attacks" On the Judiciary

Nothing in this chapter is intended to challenge the claims set out in the introduction of this book that court-curbing legislation, threats of impeachment, and other rhetorical attacks do seem to have increased and intensified in the 2000s. Nonetheless, when we consider the actual impact of these so-called attacks on the courts, the role of the courts in the U.S. political system, and the true nature of judicial independence, the siege on the courts would appear to be more hyperbole than reality. That is, we seem to end up in a situation in which each side claims the sky is falling because of the actions of the other—first politicians, who claim in exaggerated language that judges are abusing their powers by engaging in "judicial activism" and "legislating from the bench," and, in the next instance, judges, political activists, and court scholars who, in a spiraling war of words, become critics of the critics. And yet, it is highly debatable that judicial independence has been compromised in the sense that the ability of federal courts and judges to participate in the exercise of shared powers had been significantly damaged.

In this concluding section, I argue first that the magnitude of judicial authority has been on the rise for a long time. There is very little evidence that the recent attacks have diminished the judiciary's ability to participate in inter-institutional decision-making. At the micro level, the specific actions by those outside the courts that have given rise to criticisms have had de minimus effects in reaching the results sought by those supposedly attacking the courts. At the macro level, too, the attacks do not seem to have diminished judicial power. Next, I examine the political context and motivations of the anti-court movement and conclude that the efforts by those "attacking" the courts are more symbolic than real, more likely rooted in electoral politics than sincere or sustained efforts to reduce judicial power in significant ways.

So what effects have the recent efforts had on judicial power? Not much. Of all the prominent court-curbing bills that have raised concerns by watch-dogs, only the Terri Schiavo bill passed, a measure that apparently was intended to encourage federal courts to overrule state court orders preventing Ms. Schiavo's feeding tubes from being removed. Yet the federal courts refused to take up this invitation. Indeed, although they were repeatedly introduced in subsequent sessions of Congress, proposed bills described earlier in this chapter, such as the Pledge Protection Act, the Constitution Restoration Act, the We the People Act, and the Marriage Protection Act, have all failed to pass Congress. And even when Congress does pursue court-curbing efforts, the evidence suggests that it does so in ways that are deferential to the courts. While some have claimed that these efforts indicate that political actors on the ideological right are trying to force their religious views in the courts, their ability to do so has been limited. One might also note in this context that impeachment proceedings have also not been initiated against any of our sitting justices.[68]

At a more macro level, the attacks too do not seem to have had much actual impact on curbing judicial power. At some level, common sense tells us that many of the concerns seem unrealistic. As Arthur Hellman argues in response to many of Justice O'Connor's claims, even criticism that consists of "intemperate language" cannot be taken as a serious threat to the judiciary.[69] And there are also plenty of examples of the courts standing their ground against the elected branches.

Perhaps the best examples involve the Supreme Court's enemy combatant cases. During the Bush administration, the war against terrorism and the war efforts in Afghanistan and Iraq resulted in the detention of enemy combatants and suspected terrorists (or those who have aided terrorism efforts against the United States). As these detainees were held for extended periods without criminal charges or hearings of any sort, the detentions were challenged in U.S. federal courts on various grounds. The administration made an array of arguments against the jurisdiction of federal courts to hear many of these cases, supporting continued detention and trying the prisoners in military tribunals with very limited degrees of due process (as opposed to granting them access to the federal court system). Almost across the board, the U.S. Supreme Court ruled against the Bush administration and these arguments, even though seven of the nine justices on the Court were appointed by Republican presidents.

Next, it is important to consider the political context and motivation for these attacks on courts. Although a number of those agitating against courts may be sincere in their pursuit of court-curbing policies, it is almost certainly the case that many of these measures were advocated with other political and electoral calculations in mind. Since Republicans became something like a majority party in 1980, an increasingly important part of their coalition has included religious and social conservatives who favor a "values agenda." This agenda has included a range of proposals to encourage a revival of "traditional" social values, greater government support for religion, elimination of abortion (or at least a reduction in the number of abortions performed in the country and restrictions to access), opposition to expanding rights for gays and lesbians (especially same-sex marriage), and other objectives. While the social-religious bloc has been part of the Republican coalition since at least the 1980s, the turnout of evangelical voters in the 2002 and 2004 elections was seen as pivotal for the success of Republican candidates in those years, including the reelection of George W. Bush.

In light of these observations, there can be no doubt that many of the attacks on courts in the twenty-first century were largely, if not primarily, about signaling to this group of voters that the Republican Party was committed to their concerns. So when Kansas Senator Sam Brownback stated in response to a court decision on partial birth abortion that it might be necessary to "reign in an increasingly reckless judiciary . . . through impeachment, when necessary," his intended audience was not so much federal judges, none of whom have been impeached over this or any other issue but, instead, important segments of the GOP coalition and voters in Brownback's home state of Kansas. I do not suggest here that attacking judges for their decisions is a laudable method for attracting voters; however, the motivations behind much of the anti-court rhetoric and actions of the past decade seem better characterized as symbolic political gestures than real threats to judicial power.

Although it is a slightly different point, one might conjecture that to the extent the attacks were led by a single party and motivated by somewhat narrow political and electoral calculations, they were not successful either. Republicans suffered serious electoral losses in both the 2006 and 2008 elections. Although it would be speculative to assert that the Republican attack on courts caused losses at the polls, it is clear that Republicans were not *rewarded* for their anti-court efforts and rhetoric. And there is no reason to believe at this point that the Democratic majority in Congress or President Barack Obama intends to take up similar or countervailing attacks.[70]

Given the true nature of courts and judicial independence in the U.S. political system, the court-curbing efforts and verbal expressions of disagreement with the courts are not out of the ordinary or unexpected. Courts and judges can no more exist above criticism than any other political institution or actor. In a system of governance as dialogue, governmental institutions will and should assert themselves when they disagree with the decisions of their counterparts. Absent evidence that judges have indeed been coerced into becoming mere agents of elected officials or otherwise obstructed from participating in an inter-institutional system of shared powers, it is far-fetched to claim that independence, autonomy, or institutional parity have been compromised as a result of these "assaults" on the judiciary.

chapter 5

The Public and Judicial Independence

Tom S. Clark

So far, this book has considered potential incursions on judicial independence by focusing on elites, especially the institutions and officials of the U.S. government. But, as Tom Clark makes clear, our exploration of criticisms of courts must understand the "electoral connection" under-girding much of the behavior of our political leaders—their awareness of and sensitivity to the views of the public. In examining the popular and electoral sources of today's opposition to courts, this chapter makes the case that our assessment of court-curbing efforts should look beyond what policies gather substantial political support or are passed into law to what these proposals may indicate about the public's underlying discontent with the judiciary.

This volume is concerned with the causes, consequences, and implications of political criticism of and antagonism and hostility toward the judiciary. Recent trends in political assaults on the courts have raised concerns among scholars doing research on judicial independence and those charged with protecting judicial integrity. In this chapter, I investigate the motivations behind congressional attacks on the U.S. Supreme Court and suggest that they can usually be traced to public discontent with the judiciary. The "electoral connection" between legislators and the public means that legislative behavior, especially public behavior such as the current prominent criticism of the courts, is tied inextricably to constituent opinion. With this argument in hand, I present some very cursory supporting evidence, explore one historical example of Court-Congress interaction to show how the theory works in action, and speculate about the broader implications of current confrontations between courts and elected politicians.

Elite Hostility and the Public

As the other contributions to this volume demonstrate, a significant tradition of research in American politics has been concerned with the determinants of legislative efforts to rein in the judiciary. From Congress's power to remove federal jurisdiction from a set of cases to more extreme measures, such as the failed Court-packing plan of 1937, we have often seen over the course of American history attempts to use the constitutional legislative powers to exercise some political muscle on the courts. However, confrontations between the elected branches of government—Congress in particular—and the courts have also entailed other types of hostility—hostility that may not easily be explained by reference to legislative muscle. That is, these confrontations are not driven by a legislative desire to *enact* policy change; instead they seek to gain electoral support by demonstrating their opposition to the Court.

A body of scholarly research has focused on the introduction of "Court-curbing" bills.[1] Court-curbing bills may be thought of as legislation whose primary stated purpose is to restrict, remove, or otherwise limit judicial power, specifically the Supreme Court's power. In a seminal study, Stuart Nagel combed the legislative record to identify every such bill that had been introduced in Congress; in doing so, he identified seven distinct periods of heightened Court-curbing. Later, Gerald Rosenberg extended Nagel's study and identified two additional periods of heightened Court-curbing. In his analysis, Rosenberg asked whether there was evidence that the Court was constrained by the threat of Court-curbing. He concludes that during six of the nine periods of Court-curbing, the Supreme Court either exhibited "subservience" to Congress or at least exercised some degree of deference. That is, during the majority of eras in which Court-curbing is introduced in larger volume, the Court seems to defer to legislative policy preferences. The key to this claim, a claim that has largely been accepted or at least not been subjected to significant empirical scrutiny, is that the justices worry about the enactment of Court-curbing, because such legislation, if enacted, would directly affect the Court's institutional capacity.

From a different perspective, I demonstrate elsewhere that Court-curbing can best be interpreted as an example of electoral posturing. Whereas the previous research has largely equated a "successful" Court-curbing bill as one that is enacted (or at least comes close to enactment), I define a successful Court-curbing bill as one that earns an electoral benefit for its sponsor. That is, these bills can be thought of as efforts by members of Congress to position-take or credit-claim, to use Mayhew's terms.[2] Relying on evidence from interviews I conducted with justices of the U.S. Supreme Court, members of

Congress, former law clerks from the Supreme Court, and legislative staffers, I assert that Court-curbing is primarily about congressional responsiveness to constituent interests and opinion. At times, the judiciary has become a politically salient topic—in part, this volume reflects the increasing salience of the Court in contemporary politics. While previous scholarship and the other contributions to this book have focused on confrontations with the Court from the perspective of elite-level interactions, there is much that can be learned about these interactions by considering the "electoral connection" and the role of public opinion in explaining the behavioral motivations of elected officials.

A Theoretical Framework

Public Opinion and Legitimacy Theory

Before considering how public support for the Supreme Court affects legislative criticism of the Court, a preliminary question needs to be addressed: Where does public support for the Court come from, and what causes it to change? To answer this question, we must first be clear about what we mean by "public support." In the scholarly literature, two basic senses of public support dominate. The first, *specific support,* refers to approval of a judicial decision in a particular case. The second, *diffuse support,* refers to a broader support for the Court as an institution, independent of a particular decision. Diffuse support is often what scholars mean when they invoke the term "judicial legitimacy." In a sense, diffuse support for the Court is the "reservoir of good will" that keeps the Court in positive public favor when it does not have specific support for a given decision. It can draw on its diffuse support to induce compliance with a decision that may be unpopular. That is, judicial legitimacy is central to judicial power, because "institutions without a reservoir of good will may be limited in their ability to go against the preferences of the majority, even when it may be necessary or wise to do so."[3] These two types of support have been analyzed and evaluated in a large body of research on legitimacy. The overriding lesson from this literature is that courts generally benefit from high levels of diffuse support (especially relative to the other branches of government) that enable them to weather the fallout from even exceedingly unpopular individual decisions.

Where does this diffuse support come from? Two views, which are not necessarily in contention with each other, are often proposed. The first view is that people ascribe a mythical role to the courts. They view courts as special institutions whose decisions are based on law and neutral principles, rather than self-interested politicians looking for personal gain above all else. Interestingly, survey research has demonstrated that the more attentive one is to the workings of the courts, the *more* likely she is to ascribe to this mythical view.[4] The second view is that diffuse support—that is, institutional legitimacy—derives from long-term accumulations of specific support. Either through incremental exposure to the courts over the course of one's early life[5] or through accumulated instances of specific support indicating a court will on average be more likely to deliver preferred outcomes,[6] repeated positive interactions with courts accumulate into diffuse support and a "reservoir of good will" for the courts.[7] Indeed, approval of judicial decisions is a strong determinant of support for the courts as institutions.[8] Thus, one way in which judicial legitimacy may be undermined is if the courts move too far out of line with general public opinion for too long.

Public Opinion and Court-curbing

When judicial legitimacy wanes, support for institutional checks on the courts increases.[9] When the public perceives a court as an illegitimate decision-maker, a natural reaction is to support efforts to curtail that court's power. That is, decreases in support for the courts are associated with greater support for political attacks on the courts and the introduction of Court-curbing legislation. One view, the one implicitly adopted by most studies of political attacks on the courts, assumes that these bills are introduced so that Congress may flex its constitutional muscle—that it may intimidate the Court into deferring on salient political issues. The Constitution gives Congress considerable power over the federal judiciary. The Supreme Court's composition, term, budget, and (crucially, it is argued) appellate jurisdiction are all determined by Congress. As a consequence, when these bills are introduced, scholars argue, the Court must assess the likelihood of their enactment. When they are likely to be enacted, we often suppose the Court will be mindful of the institutional harm it would suffer and in some way defer to congressional preferences on the key issues at the heart of the confrontation.[10] This picture of events is largely true. Congress does indeed have these powers over the Court, and the justices would be reckless to ignore this possibility. However, there is an additional motivation for Court-curbing, one that might similarly have consequences for judicial independence.

It is widely accepted that members of Congress care first and foremost about winning reelection.[11] While they may have other goals such as enacting good policy and accumulating power,[12] without first securing reelection, members of Congress cannot possibly pursue any of their political objectives. In pursuit of their goal of reelection, Mayhew famously argued, legislators engage in three specific activities: position-taking, credit-claiming, and advertising.[13]

Court-curbing can easily be regarded as a position-taking or credit-claiming undertaking. When a member's constituents become displeased with the courts, one thing they can and will do is contact the member. The member may then respond by proposing a Court-curbing bill in Congress—a relatively cost-free action—and then point out to the constituent that he or she also opposes the Court and has taken action to rein in the runaway courts. In doing so, the member is able to take a position on the Court (opposing the "activist" judges or some such) and claim credit for taking action to rein them in. While this bill may never make it to a committee hearing, it need not. Members of the public generally see their own representatives in a more favorable light than Congress as an institution,[14] and any member can blame institutional resistance or inefficiency for the stalled bill.[15] Thus, the member can earn a considerable benefit with her constituents by pointing to something specific—the sponsoring of a Court-curbing bill—while avoiding blame for its failure to be enacted by citing the institution's unwillingness to act.[16] Constituents who are particularly interested in Court-curbing may be frustrated by the failure to enact the legislation, but the mechanics of legislating in Congress give any representative who may be just placating her constituents sufficient political cover to avoid blame for the proposed legislation's failure.

This relationship illustrates the "electoral connection"—the idea that congressional behavior is intrinsically linked to public (constituent) opinion. Indeed, we generally assume that because House members face reelection every other year, while senators face reelection every six years, the electoral connection should be stronger in the House than in the Senate. (As Madison points out in *Federalist* 57, this was intentional in the design of the Constitution.) On this point, then, it is instructive that 78 percent of the Court-curbing bills introduced since Reconstruction have been introduced in the House.[17] Members of the House, more so than their counterparts in the Senate, are sensitive to short-term fluctuations in constituent opinion. Their shorter electoral cycle creates an incentive for them to reflect their constituents' views more closely, whereas senators' longer electoral cycle gives them the capacity to ignore momentary passions in their state.

This general sentiment is confirmed by interviews I conducted with members of Congress and legislative staffers. As part of these, I spoke with a number of Supreme Court justices, members of Congress, former law clerks, and legislative staffers, to whom I refer anonymously.[18]

Congressman A offered perhaps the most insightful discussion of Court-curbing and the legislative motivation for such legislation. Having introduced a number of these bills over the course of his legislative career, Congressman A observed that there were two distinct strategies for a legislator who wants to confront the courts. The first strategy he referred to as the "scalpel." The scalpel strategy is one where a legislator develops a carefully constructed piece of legislation that will reverse a court decision or remove jurisdiction from some particular type of case. The consequences of the legislation would certainly be narrow, but this type of bill would have a great chance of success in the legislative process. These bills are often drafted by legislators who actually want the legislation passed; however, owing to their narrow and arguably minor policy implications, the bills rarely attract much public attention. Congressman A then described a second strategy, which he called the "B-2 bomber." The B-2 bomber strategy is one where a legislator crafts some broad piece of legislation that seeks to "level" the courts. These bills, perhaps more familiar to the casual observer, seek to "pack" the courts, amend the Constitution, reverse salient constitutional decisions, limit judicial tenure, or impeach a justice. Bills introduced in the B-2 bomber strategy have very little chance of being enacted and are often of dubious constitutionality.[19] Congressman A then observed that the B-2 bomber strategy was much more common than the scalpel strategy among Court-curbers. Why? The reason is simple: no one pays attention to the scalpel; the B-2 bomber gets a lot of attention. What Congressman A was trying to convey is that the broader, flashier bills, while not likely to accomplish their goals in a formal institutional sense, attract considerable public attention and provide their sponsors with some electoral benefit. Their constituents are pleased with the proposals, even if they are not enacted.

An example of a "B-2 bomber" is the Congressional Accountability for Judicial Activism Act of 2005,[20] which was introduced by Ron Lewis of Kentucky and cosponsored by seventeen members of the House. This bill provided,

The Congress may, if two thirds of each House agree, reverse a judgment of the United States Supreme Court—

(1) if that judgment is handed down after the date of the enactment of this Act; and

(2) to the extent that judgment concerns the constitutionality of an Act of Congress.

The legislation was referred to the Judiciary Committee and the Rules Committee, from which it never emerged.

Indeed, many other congressional insiders echoed this sentiment. Staffer 1 commented, "these bills rally the base every other year." Staffer 2 noted, "Flag burning—a lot of people care about that. The Pledge [of Allegiance] too; constituents called up a lot and asked, What kind of an atheist country do we live in?" Congressman B observed, "on the [*deleted*] issue, most of my constituents would be interested in that. . . . Obscenity is [also] very important to my constituents."[21] In fact, the Court itself acknowledges the electoral connection. Justice C commented, for example, "The Court is pretty good at knowing how far it can go. . . . Congress is better than we are, especially the House. They really have their finger on the pulse of the public." Taken together, these insights from legislators and judges alike demonstrate that one, if not the primary, determinant of congressional attacks on the Court is public discontent with the judiciary.

The electoral connection motivating congressional attacks on the Court is evident in congressional actions other than Court-curbing as well. For example, the justices receive direct communication from the public and Congress. Justice Blackmun famously read all of his mail and kept it—it is still in his personal papers at the Library of Congress.[22] One example is a letter from Representative Carroll Hubbard, from the 1st District of Kentucky, to the justices, written on October 20, 1975, advising them of a planned demonstration the following Saturday by her constituents against school busing and inviting them to attend the demonstration. School busing was, at the time, one of the most hotly debated political topics and directly implicated the Supreme Court as a consequence of its decision to allow race-based busing programs.[23] The letter read, in part,

Dear Member of the U.S. Supreme Court:

On this Saturday, October 25, there will be thousands of Kentuckians in Washington to urge the President, the Members of the U.S. Supreme Court and the Members of the 94th Congress to work toward bringing about an end to forced court-ordered busing in Louisville (and Jefferson County), Boston and other parts of our country.

Constituents of mine have asked me to urge you to witness this rally of Kentuckians at approximately 12 noon at the U.S. Capitol.[24]

This letter and other examples of direct communication from members of Congress to the Court evince a direct connection between public discontent with the judiciary and elite criticism of the courts.[25]

Of course, a question arises concerning whether members of Congress respond only to the opinion of a select, attentive constituency—one that is concerned with the Court. It may be that initial discontent with the Court begins in a segment of the constituency that is particularly concerned with the Court. It is nevertheless the case, though, that the attacks are fueled by public discontent. To be sure, the significance of these attacks as larger institutional indicators of waning judicial legitimacy hinges on the idea that as the attacks grow, so too does the depth and breadth of public discontent with the Court. Two points are particularly instructive here. First, the justices are keenly sensitive to the growth of anti-Court sentiment. For example, in a memorandum circulated by Chief Justice Burger to the other justices, he mentions a Court-curbing bill that had been introduced in Congress. In the memorandum, he notes that it was a bill comparable to one introduced several years previous, which had not attracted "much attention." Nevertheless, Burger thought the issue sufficiently important to discuss. Burger's memorandum indicates that the justices do indeed worry about issues "snowballing" from specialized complaints to larger public discontent with the Court. Second, the Court may very well be concerned with its standing among specialized interests. The Court has several audiences, some of which are specialized groups concerned with the bench, such as legal professionals and interest groups.[26] Thus, even if a particular complaint against the Court starts with a specialized interest and does *not* snowball into a larger discontent with the Court, waning judicial legitimacy within a specialized group may nevertheless be important to the Court.

Beyond Court-curbing and Court-Congress interactions, there are other, often more direct, ways in which the Court interacts with the public. For example, briefs filed in Supreme Court cases, especially briefs filed amicus curiae, often make reference to the larger political climate in which a case has arisen; these briefs are often quick to note public opinion about particular issues. Moreover, the justices and their clerks live and work in Washington, D.C. They are often "plugged in" to the political scene and at the very least are as aware of the public mood as most other informed citizens. Their awareness of the larger political context is evidenced in their internal deliberations. For example, in a memorandum concerning a petition for certiorari in two cases about school busing in the early 1980s, one of Justice Blackmun's clerks advised against certiorari, in part due to the ongoing heated public debate about the issue. While members of Congress are certainly more directly tuned in to day-to-day fluctuations in public opinion, my interviews with the justices, combined with public statements by members of the Court, make clear that the Court is keenly aware of its level of public support.

Public Opinion and Judicial Politics

The bottom line is that public discontent with the courts fuels much of the elite confrontations with the judiciary. The consequence of waning pubic support for the Court in the current context remains to be seen and is beyond the scope of this chapter. Nevertheless, legitimacy theory, as described above, and analyses of the power of judicial institutions both suggest that diffuse public support for the courts is critical for their capacity to be efficacious policy-makers. Thus, one may speculate that instances of confrontation between elected elites and courts are correlates of periods during which the courts must exercise greater self-restraint in the interest of preserving their institutional strength. These periods of conflict can serve to inform courts that their standing with the public is on the wane. That is, during crises of judicial legitimacy, the courts may be aware of their weakened institutional position. As William Lasser has noted, one of the reasons that the Court has been able to weather political crises and make bold decisions in part is due to the Court's strategic timing of those decisions.[27] Major decisions have tended to come at times when the Court has a maximum of political capital and when its political opponents are at their weakest. Of course, any number of institutional signals may serve as indicators of waning public support for the Court. The justices themselves may be aware of direct measures of public opinion and may learn about their standing with the public through other avenues. I do not deal with this question here.[28] I simply note that given an assumption that members of Congress are better informed about public opinion than are the justices (an assumption I believe is not hard to accept) and an assumption that members of Congress have an electoral interest in accurately reflecting constituent opinion (even though they may sometimes disregard constituent opinion), congressional criticism of the Court can be informative to the Court.

Some Empirical Evidence

In support of the claim that the Court often comes under siege from the public and that congressional criticism of the Court can often be explained as a mechanism by which public discontent is communicated to the Court, I present a few pieces of empirical evidence. First, I present some simple and cursory statistical evidence. While far from a critical test of causality, these data are intended to demonstrate a general, systematic pattern consistent with the argument proposed above. Second, I describe a notable historical example; in particular, I provide a brief account of the relationships among the Congress, the Court, and the public during the constitutional crisis of 1937.[29] Taken together, these two pieces of evidence help establish the role of the public in political assaults on the courts.

Aggregate Patterns

I begin by examining the relationship between public confidence in the Supreme Court and the introduction of Court-curbing bills. To do so, I identify whether each member of Congress sponsored or cosponsored any Court-curbing bill during each of the 108th and 109th Houses of Representatives (in session from 2003 through 2006). These two Congresses witnessed a dramatic increase in the numbers of Court-curbing bills and sponsors relative to the previous twenty years. In fact, about 57 percent of the members of Congress during these four years sponsored or cosponsored at least one Court-curbing bill. This represents a significant increase from the average of about 15 percent during the 1990s.

Next, I collect every Gallup poll between 2003 and 2006 that asked respondents how much confidence they have the in U.S. Supreme Court for which individual-level responses are available.[30] With these data in hand, I estimate state-level confidence in the Supreme Court.[31] I then divide all members into those whose states had above-average confidence in the Court and those whose states had below-average confidence in the Court. Among those members whose states had above-average confidence in the Court, 52 percent sponsored or cosponsored at least one Court-curbing bill. Among those whose states had below-average confidence in the Supreme Court, 69 percent sponsored or cosponsored at least one Court-curbing bill. This is a substantial difference and is in fact statistically significant.[32]

To be sure, the correlation between public opinion and (co)sponsorship of Court-curbing is readily apparent in the raw data. Figure 5.1 shows individual-level sponsorship or cosponsorship of Court-curbing bills against estimated state-level confidence in the Supreme Court.[33] The downward slope on this line indicates that as public confidence in the Supreme Court grows, members of Congress become less likely to introduce Court-curbing. Indeed, at the lowest observed level of confidence, a member is about 80 percent likely to introduce a bill. By contrast, at the highest observed level of confidence, a member is about 40 percent likely to introduce a bill. This is a 50 percent reduction in the predicted probability of introducing a Court-curbing bill.

To assess the statistical significance of this relationship and control for the other key theoretical predictor of Court-curbing, I estimate an empirical model.[34] Here, the dependent variable is whether a member sponsors or cosponsors a Court-curbing bill in either of the two Congresses included in these data. As key explanatory variables, I include estimated state-level confidence in the Supreme Court and the ideological distance between the member of the Court median.[35]

The results of this empirical model are striking. Ideological distance between the member and the Court median is indeed a strong predictor of whether a member will sponsor Court-curbing. The empirical model predicts that an increase in ideological divergence between a member and the Court equal to the average distance between a Democrat and a Republican increases the predicted probability of sponsoring a Court-curbing bill by about 73 percentage points. To be sure, this is a considerable effect and suggests that ideological divergence from the Court is a powerful determinant of a member's decision to (co)sponsor a Court-curbing bill.[36]

At the same time, the data provide additional evidence that public confidence in the Court affects the sponsorship of Court-curbing. Figure 5.2 shows the estimated relationship graphically.[37] Here, the lines show the predicted probability of introducing Court-curbing bills for two different types of federal legislators—one who is ideologically proximate to the Court and one who is ideologically distant from the Court. As the figure makes clear, there is a

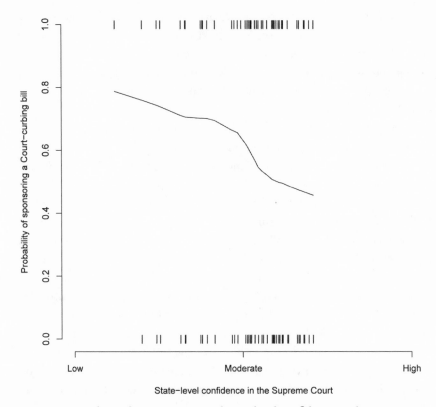

Figure 5.1. Correlation between estimated state-level confidence in the Supreme Court and the (co)sponsorship of Court-curbing bills

considerable inverse relationship between public confidence and the probability of sponsoring a bill. At low levels of confidence, the predicted probability that a member who is the Court's ideological ally will introduce a Court-curbing bill is about 50 percent; at high levels, the predicted probability that member will sponsor a bill is about 10 percent. By contrast, at low levels of confidence, the Court's ideological opponents are about 90 percent likely to introduce a Court-curbing bill; at high levels, they are about 40 percent likely to introduce a bill.

In sum, there is a strong and substantively considerable correlation between public opinion about the Court and the introduction of Court-curbing bills. Members of Congress from states with lower confidence in the Supreme Court are much more likely to sponsor or cosponsor Court-curbing bills than are members from states with high levels of confidence in the Supreme

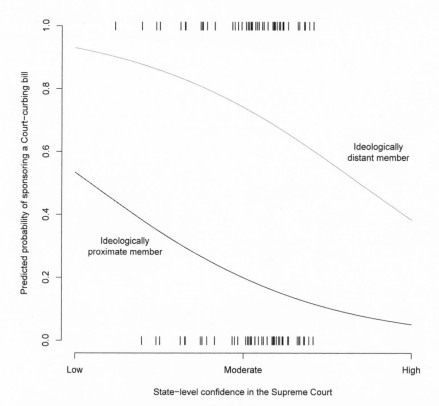

Figure 5.2. Predicted probability of introducing a Court-curbing bill as a function of estimated state-level confidence in the Supreme Court

Court. This relationship holds even while controlling for an individual member's ideological alignment with (or divergence from) the Supreme Court. Of course, the analysis here treats only two Congresses, during which we have seen a considerable increase in the introduction of Court-curbing.

A secondary question that follows, though, is whether the ideological orientation of the sponsors of Court-curbing legislation is driven by the Court's decisions or public mood more generally. We saw above that the Court's ideological opponents are more likely to sponsor Court-curbing than its allies. But, are those sponsors responding to the Court's decisions or their constituents' policy views? While I cannot treat this question here fully, some cursory evidence suggests that it is the latter.

I begin by noting the correlation between public opinion and congressional attacks on the Court. If Court-curbing is truly motivated by congressional

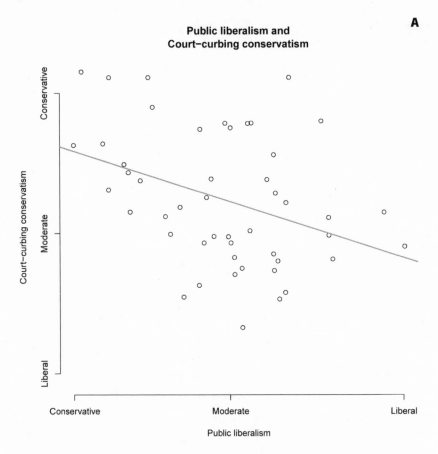

Figure 5.3. Correlation between Court-curbing sponsors' conservatism and each of (A) public liberalism and (B) the Supreme Court's decisional liberalism

displeasure with Court decisions, then one would expect that more liberal Court decision-making should lead to more conservative Court-curbing, and vice versa. By contrast, if, as I have argued here, Court-curbing is instead a position-taking method through which public opinion is translated into elite posturing, then we should instead expect to find that when the public becomes more liberal, more liberal members of Congress will engage in Court-curbing. To assess these two possibilities, I present some basic descriptive data. First, I identify the ideologically median Court-curbing sponsor for each year since 1953.[38] I then identify the liberalism of both the public mood and the Supreme Court's decisions.[39] With these data in hand, I simply compare the median Court-curbing sponsor's conservatism (using the Poole Common

B

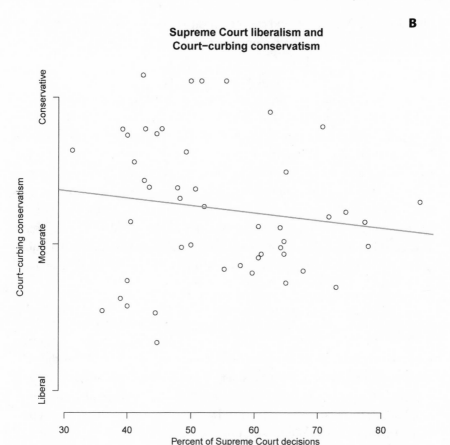

Space scores[40]) with public liberalism and Supreme Court liberalism. The results are shown in figure 5.3.

We see in the left-hand panel the relationship between how conservative the median Court-curbing sponsor is and how liberal the public is each year. The grey line shows the linear best fit line. There is a strong negative relationship. As the public becomes more liberal, so too does the median Court-curbing sponsor. Indeed, this single variable alone can explain a good deal of the variation in Court-curbing ideology. By contrast, we see in the right-hand panel the correlation between Court-curbing conservatism and the proportion of the Court's decisions coded as "liberal." As these data make clear, there is virtually no relationship between Court-curbing conservatism and judicial liberalism. In fact, one would expect a positive relationship here—more liberal decisions associated with more conservative Court-curbing—but the correlation is slightly negative.[41]

Taken together, these two plots strongly suggest that the ideological orientation of those introducing Court-curbing is strongly influenced by public opinion, while it does not appear to be influenced directly by the Court's decision-making. Such a pattern can easily be seen in the recent period of Court-curbing. Of course, one might imagine many other, more extensive ways of assessing the determinants of Court-curbing, but this is not my goal here. My aim is not to demonstrate that waning judicial legitimacy *causes* Court-curbing; it may very well be that Court-curbing and public support for the Court have a sybmiotic relationship, simultaneously driving each other. Rather, these data serve simply to highlight the correlation between public opinion and Court-curbing; congressional attacks on the Court are associated with a decline in diffuse support for the judiciary.

An Example: Packing the Court

The correlations shown in figures 5.1 through 5.3 are instructive, but they only take us so far. To gain a deeper contextual understanding of how this relationship works in practice, we consider here one notable historical example of the role of the public in Court-Congress conflicts. Perhaps the most notable example of conflict between the Court and the elected branches of government—at least during the twentieth century—is the constitutional crisis of 1937 and Franklin D. Roosevelt's "Court-packing" plan. I argue here that because of its elite-level focus, the conventional account of the Court-packing plan misses the importance of public opinion as the driver, both *before* the bill's introduction and *during* the political debate that ultimately led to its demise.

During Roosevelt's first term in the White House, his New Deal legislative program was frustrated on several occasions by the Supreme Court. The "Four Horsemen," as they were known—Justices Pierce Butler, James McReynolds, George Sutherland, and Willis Van Devanter—voted to invalidate several key pieces of the New Deal program in the spring of 1936, joined often by Justice Owen Roberts and sometimes by Chief Justice Charles Evans Hughes. Among these invalidated laws were the Agricultural Adjustment Act, the Federal Farm Bankruptcy Act, and a New York State minimum wage law. Earlier, in May 1935, the Court had unanimously invalidated the National Industrial Recovery Act.

Roosevelt's advisors, including the future Supreme Court Justice Felix Frankfurter, counseled the president that the Court's recalcitrance would only strengthen public sentiment against the Court and provide Roosevelt with political leverage on which he could campaign.[42] In an effort to shore up support for Roosevelt, one of his advisors, Professor Edward Corwin of Princeton University, wrote a piece in the Princeton newspaper against the Court.[43] The intuition behind this counsel follows directly from the logic outlined above. By politicizing the Court, which was at the time unpopular with the public, Roosevelt could gain some electoral benefit. Indeed, an early Gallup public opinion poll indicated that the public strongly supported a change in the Court's jurisprudence,[44] and a strong contingent supported limiting the Court's powers.[45] Throughout the 1936 campaign, however, Roosevelt conspicuously refused to comment on the Supreme Court or his plans in response to its frustration of his legislative agenda. This was not, to be sure, attributable to the Court's lack of political salience; rather, both the Republican and Democratic platforms were critical of the Court.[46] Shortly after his reinauguration in 1937, Roosevelt announced the Court-packing plan, which had been developed and kept secret during the presidential campaign the previous year.

The Judiciary Reorganization Bill of 1937, as it was known, would have essentially allowed Roosevelt to appoint an additional justice to the Court for every justice who was at least 70 and a half years old and had not retired.[47] The thinly veiled intention of this legislation was either to force the Four Horsemen into retirement or else to negate their votes with those of additional justices chosen by Roosevelt. Shortly after the plan was announced, on March 24, 1937, the Court decided *West Coast Hotel v. Parrish*, in which it upheld the constitutionality of a Washington State minimum wage law, reversing its decision in the New York State case. (That same day, which came to be known as "White Monday," the Supreme Court upheld other New Deal legislation in *Wright v. Vinton Branch* and *Virginia Railway v. Federation*.) Less than two months later, Justice Van Devanter announced his retirement, effective at the end of the Court's term. Two weeks later, on May 24, the Supreme Court upheld the constitutionality of the Social Security Act in two cases, *Steward Machine Co. v. Davis* and *Helvering v. Davis*, which came to be known as the Social Security Act cases. The Court's reversal from its position hostile to the New Deal in the White Monday and Social Security cases combined with Van Devanter's retirement to undermine public discontent with the Court.

By May, only a third of Americans supported the Court-packing plan, and a year later less than 30 percent of Americans admitted to having supported the proposal.[48]

While the Court-packing plan has attracted a great deal of historical attention, it is important to place it into the larger context of contemporary events. Beginning two years earlier, after the New Deal Democrats gained seats in the House and Senate in the midterm elections of 1936, there was a considerable Court-curbing movement in Congress. These bills were being introduced just as public outcry about the Supreme Court was growing. Editorials bemoaned the Court's antagonism toward the New Deal program; members of Congress conveyed their constituents' discontent in speeches from the floor. In 1936, two legislative proposals nearly identical to the Court-packing plan—H.R. 10102 and H.R. 10362—were introduced in Congress. While Roosevelt did not confront the Court on the campaign trail, the Court was certainly an issue in the election, and downticket New Deal Democrats, especially House members, explicitly took the Court on. In what can only be interpreted as a referendum on the New Deal legislative program,[49] the New Deal Democrats won a landslide reelection in November 1936. (At the same time, as noted earlier, a Gallup poll showed strong support for curtailing the court's judicial review powers.) When the new Congress came to Washington in January 1937, no fewer than thirteen Court-curbing bills were immediately introduced, ten of which focused specifically on the Court's use of judicial review. It was during this period—before 1937 rather than after the Court-packing plan's announcement—that public opposition to the Court reached its zenith and during which congressional attacks on the Court were also the most fervent.

Thus, while the Court-packing plan may have been a primarily elite-level confrontation—it was designed and hatched by the White House, and ran against public sentiment for most of its legislative journey—the historical focus on this single bill overshadows the larger political story about the New Deal confrontation with the Court. The Court-packing plan came at the end of this confrontation; it was unpopular in part because shortly after it was announced, the Court backed down, rendering moot the need to restrain the Court. However, during the eighteen months or so leading up to the Court-packing plan, there was considerable public animosity toward the Court, which was marked by a concomitant legislative assault on the courts. History has overshadowed the growing tension between Congress and the Court during the mid-1930s by focusing nearly exclusively on the Court-packing plan and the apogee of hostility toward the Court in 1937.

In this abbreviated timeline of events, we see a pattern that highlights the public-Congress-Court relationship. The Court's decisions deviated, in a relatively extreme way, from dominant public preferences during the New Deal's early years. As the Court continued to frustrate the New Deal, public evaluations of the Court fell. In the language of legitimacy theory described above, the stream of decisions lacking specific support continued to an erosion of the Court's diffuse support. As predicted by legitimacy theory, waning diffuse support in turn increased popular support for curtailing judicial power. Members of Congress, especially in the House, were thereby motivated to represent their constituents' views by introducing Court-curbing legislation. Of course, they may have disagreed with the Court simply on policy grounds, but it is likely that constituent opinion contributed to the volume of anti-Court legislation proposed in the 74th Congress (1935–1936). All of this came to a head with the introduction of the Court-packing plan in February 1937. However, subsequent moves by the Court, including its decisions in favor of New Deal legislation and the retirement of Justice Van Devanter, served to bring the Court back into favor with the public. That is, the Court's diffuse support rebounded; as a consequence, support for curtailing judicial power dissipated.

Explaining the Patterns

Patterns in Court-curbing strongly track patterns in public opinion. While I have not demonstrated here that changes in public opinion *cause* changes in Court-curbing, I have shown that when Congress engages in attacks on the courts, we should expect that public support for the courts—what I have called here judicial legitimacy—is on the decline. The evidence presented in figures 1 through 3 above reveals that the introduction of Court-curbing bills is strongly correlated with low public confidence in the Court and that the ideological orientation of Court-curbing is strongly correlated with underlying public ideology. That is, the intensity and ideological sentiment of Court-curbing in Congress serves as an elite-level representation of broader public confidence and ideology. By contrast, there appears to be no evidence of the Court's liberalism affecting who sponsors Court-curbing. Together, these two pieces of evidence suggest that Court-curbing is more closely associated with public opinion than with elite policy-making. The history of events surrounding the Court-packing plan and the conflict between the New Deal Democrats and the Court further suggest that Court-curbing movements have their origins in public discontent with the Court. While history has focused our attention on the Court-packing plan and the confrontation between Roosevelt and the Court, this historical perspective unnecessarily distracts us from understanding the larger period of conflict and the role that public support for the Court played in the elite movement against the Court. From this evidence, then, we can conclude that Court-curbing is at least partly motivated by public opinion and waning public support for the courts.

Judicial Legitimacy and Contemporary Politics

What are the consequences of congressional attacks on the Court that are motivated by the public? One consequence is that they signal and possibly trigger decreased judicial legitimacy, that is, declining public support for the Court as an institution, a development important in and of itself. Scholars of judicial legitimacy have noted that diffuse public support for the courts is critical for their institutional efficacy. To the extent that judicial independence is defined by the ability of courts to make decisions with which elected officials may disagree but nevertheless feel obliged to respect, judicial independence may be lost without diffuse public support. That is, without judicial legitimacy, courts may be compelled to make decisions that comport with the will of the popular majority or risk seeing their decisions ignored. The ability of courts to stand up against popular majorities—to decide cases *independently*—is beneficial for various elements of society, such as economic growth and minority rights. Thus, to the extent that diffuse public support waxes and wanes and Court-curbing reflects and reinforces rises and declines in judicial legitimacy, elite-level attacks on and criticism of the courts may have broad implications for overall systemic stability supported by the courts.

Court-Curbing and Judicial Legitimacy

Legitimacy theory suggests that diffuse support for the courts—institutional support that is not contingent on agreement with specific decisions—is a key source of the courts' institutional efficacy. From Rosenberg's ground-breaking volume[50] to formal and comparative analyses of judicial independence,[51] scholars have recognized that when there does not exist public support for the courts, enforcement of judicial decisions is at risk. Because courts are inherently weak institutions—they generally lack direct enforcement powers—they rely on compliance by other actors, usually elected officials. When both those elected officials and their constituents are aligned against the Court, divergent decisions risk being ignored. By contrast, when the public *is* aligned with the Court, then officials charged with enforcement will be under electoral pressure to comply with the Court's decisions. However, a third condition may hold: the public may be opposed to the Court decisions on policy grounds, but because it views the Court as a legitimate decision-maker, it will believe enforcement of the Court's decisions is required and press elected officials to enforce the decision. Patterns of public support for decisions with which it disagrees have been documented by scholars of legitimacy theory and adopted (explicitly and implicitly) by theorists of judicial independence.[52]

What, then, does Court-curbing have to do with judicial legitimacy? Court-curbing, to the extent that it is driven by public discontent with the Court, is one indicator of waning judicial legitimacy. Moreover, because judicial legitimacy hinges on the perception of the Court as "above politics" and Court-curbing drags the Court into politics by highlighting its role in policy-making, congressional criticism of the Court suggests to the public that the Court is "just another branch." In this way, Court-curbing may be both a reflection of waning diffuse support for the judiciary and a reinforcement of negative public perceptions of the Court. This is the function that Staffer A tried to capture in the comment noted above, that Court-curbing can "rally the base." Of course, one might imagine that the extent to which this dynamic takes place depends to some extent on the type of Court-curbing in which Congress is engaged. In his chapter in this volume, Charles Geyh suggests that the particular type of Court-curbing matters. Insofar as Court-curbing reflects congressional position-taking before constituents, we might imagine the most relevant forms of Court-curbing are those that are designed to attract public attention, rather than those that are less salient (B-2 bomber versus the scalpel).

As I noted above, judicial legitimacy is critical for judicial efficacy. Having "neither purse nor sword," the courts rely on political will to give effect to their decisions. In his classic study, Rosenberg argues that in order for courts to bring about significant social change, there must be popular and political support for the policy.[53] In fact, one can take this claim further. Compliance with judicial decisions is a crucial factor in understanding both judicial independence and judicial power. Comparative scholars, more so than their U.S.-oriented counterparts, have given this concept considerable thought. An important lesson from this research is that courts are often faced with a choice between (a) making a decision that will be enforced but does not "go as far" as it might otherwise, and (b) making a decision that pushes the court's policy goal as far as possible but will likely be ignored by the public and those responsible for carrying out the decision. When faced with this choice, it is usually in a court's interest to make the decision that will be carried out. Thus, we might expect that during periods of Court-curbing, to the extent this indicates waning judicial legitimacy, the Court will find itself in a less efficacious position and be more constrained in its decision-making. While judicial advancement of social change may be constrained, it may be the case that judicial power more generally is constrained by the need to sustain public (and political) support for the courts.

Implications for Contemporary Politics

As I have noted, there is some reason to believe that we are currently entering an era in which the courts are becoming "just another branch." There is some evidence of declining diffuse support for the Court. During the summer of 2008, the Supreme Court's disapproval rating climbed to about 40 percent. A Gallup poll taken in September 2008 found the Supreme Court's disapproval rating to be 39 percent.[54] In July 2008, a Quinnipiac University poll put its disapproval rating at 43 percent.[55] This figure was up from the 33 percent of Americans who disapproved of the Supreme Court's job performance in 2003[56] and the only 29 percent who disapproved of the Court's job performance in 2000 (before its decision in *Bush v. Gore*).[57] Similarly, the Harris Poll found that only 25 percent of Americans claimed to have "a great deal of confidence" in the Supreme Court in February 2008.[58] This figure represents a substantial decline from the 34 percent of Americans who reported a "great deal" of confidence in the Court in early 2000.[59]

Indeed, as we would expect, this period has also seen an increase in the volume and intensity of Court-curbing proposals. Since 1937, on average seventeen Court-curbing bills have been introduced during each Congress. That figure, however, masks the periodicity of the introduction of Court-curbing. Between 1984 and 2004 (99th through 108th Congresses), for example, an average of ten bills were introduced during each congressional session.

Since 2004, however, we have seen a marked increase in the introduction of Court-curbing bills. During the 109th Congress (2005–2006), thirty-six Court-curbing bills were introduced. That number dropped only slightly to twenty-five bills during the 110th Congress (2007–2008). Indeed, when compared with other periods in history, the intensity of Court-curbing during the past few years has looked more like those eras of Court-Congress tension (the mid-1930s, the late 1950s, the late 1960s, the mid-1970s) than those eras of relative harmony between the branches (the 1940s, the early 1990s). To the extent that the sheer number of Court-curbing bills is an indicator of broader anti-Court sentiment, the current, fairly conservative, Supreme Court may find its support among an increasingly liberal public and government to be on the wane.[60]

While I have resisted the temptation to speculate about the judiciary's likely response to a sustained period of hostility toward the courts, the discussion above about legitimacy theory and compliance with judicial decisions is suggestive. As noted, Lasser's study of judicial independence demonstrates that the Supreme Court has been particularly savvy in navigating the political waters. The Court has been willing to use its power aggressively when institutional legitimacy and public support for the Court is strong; by contrast, when the Court finds itself alone in the political wilderness, it has chosen to exercise self-restraint. None of this is to say that the current conflict between politicians and the Court will necessarily lead to a self-restrained judiciary. However, the historical patterns do seem to foreshadow a period of cautious judicial action.

Conclusion

This chapter has attempted to demonstrate that public opinion about the Supreme Court is an important determinant of elite-level attacks on the courts. While policy disagreement between Congress and the Court may be one impetus for sieges on the judiciary, the electoral connection between legislators and their constituents necessarily ties elite-level behavior to public opinion. Evidence in support of this connection is apparent in both aggregate patterns of Court-curbing sponsorship and qualitative accounts of conflict between Congress and the Court. As a consequence, periods of increased hostility toward the judiciary are associated with waning public support for the courts. Legitimacy theory shows that losses of diffuse support lead to decreased judicial efficacy. As a consequence, one implication of elite confrontations driven by public opinion is that, independent of actual institutional changes that might be made, these confrontations can have adverse consequences for judicial independence and judicial power. What the consequence of the current level of public discontent will be remains an open question. Elsewhere, I have argued that when public support for the Court declines and elected representatives respond with Court-curbing, the Court will have an incentive to exercise self-restraint.[61] However, the current Court is different from previous ones in an important way: with the retirement of Sandra Day O'Connor and her replacement with Samuel Alito, for the first time in history not a single justice on the Supreme Court has ever held elective office. How a justice's experience in electoral politics might affect her sensitivity toward public attitudes about the Court is unknown. On the one hand, judges who have electoral experience may be more sensitive to public opinion, as they are more aware of the consequences of sustained divergence from the public mood. On the other hand, career jurists may have a greater appreciation, or reverence, for the judiciary's "special" role in government and the significance of judicial legitimacy. In either event, the contemporary period of hostility toward the judiciary suggests that the early Roberts Court may ultimately be a more constrained Court than its predecessor.

chapter 6

Judicial Elections and Public Perception of the Courts

Matthew J. Streb

Many of today's most intense criticisms of the judiciary target state courts and judges. Prominent recent controversies about legal decisions involving such topics as flag burning, same-sex
marriage, and abortion have come from state judicial systems. At the same time, advocates of
judicial independence have often chastised the states for relying on elections and campaigns
in selecting judges. Matthew J. Streb critically reviews one of the principal arguments against
judicial elections—that they undermine public confidence in courts. Furthermore, Streb argues
that many of the proposed "solutions" to judicial elections are unlikely to be effective and have
generally unreported negative consequences. In looking for purported threats to courts in the
states, we should consider other sources, such as the effects fundraising and campaign expenditures may have on the public's perception of justice and the possibility that "direct democracy" (manifested in state initiatives and referenda) can put courts and the public on a collision
course.

In 2002, the Brennan Center for Justice issued a report documenting a "new
politics of judicial elections" that emerged in the 2000 election cycle.[1] According to the report, judicial races were getting costlier and nastier, and interest groups were taking a more active role. In other words, judicial elections
were mirroring races for other offices. This occurrence was problematic, because it led judges to come increasingly under attack—both based on substantive issues and personal characteristics (integrity, honesty). The authors of
the report feared that these attacks could lead the public to lose confidence
in the integrity of judges and the institution of the judiciary as a whole.

Although scholars had documented these "new style" judicial campaigns
before the Brennan Center report,[2] the conventional wisdom painted judicial
elections as sleepy affairs that were hardly interesting to follow. In fact, one
journalist compared the excitement of judicial elections to playing a game of

checkers by mail.[3] Judicial elections, it was thought, were rarely contested and contested elections were rarely competitive.[4] Candidates virtually never stated their positions on issues (mostly because judicial canons prevented them from doing so) or attacked their opponents. To detractors of judicial elections, these traits were positive since they protected judicial independence and the integrity of the courts. If judges were rarely challenged and those who were challenged were rarely attacked or defeated, then, in theory, they would be free to rule as impartial interpreters of the law and not worry about public backlash to their rulings. Moreover, the public would likely view judges as upholding the law instead of being "politicians in robes." The Brennan Center report, in announcing an emerging new landscape of combative judicial elections, raised red flags among those concerned about the legitimacy of the courts.

After the 2000 election cycle, the Brennan Center issued three subsequent reports corroborating the findings of the first "new politics" study.[5] The overarching conclusion was that judicial independence and the integrity of the courts were increasingly threatened by judicial campaigns that were surprisingly expensive and negative.

A recent example illustrates why organizations like the Brennan Center are worried about the legitimacy of the judiciary. In a 2004 West Virginia Supreme Court election, Don Blankenship, the CEO of Massey Coal, spent roughly $3 million independently in support of the campaign of a little-known attorney, Brent Benjamin, and in opposition to incumbent Justice Warren McGraw.[6] Benjamin defeated McGraw, winning 53 percent of the vote.

Blankenship's independent spending was controversial because it highlighted the increasingly expensive and negative nature of judicial elections. It became all the more contentious, however, once Blankenship and Massey Coal found themselves before the state supreme court on which Benjamin now sat. That court, in a 3–2 decision, overturned a $50 million verdict against Massey Coal. Benjamin failed to recuse himself from the case and cast the deciding vote.[7] He argued that there was "no reasonable basis" for doubting his impartiality, therefore there was no need for recusal.

Not everyone agreed. Numerous groups, including the American Bar Association (ABA) and the Brennan Center, filed briefs encouraging the U.S. Supreme Court to take up the case because of the argument that the legitimacy of the courts was at stake. According to those briefs, not only did the West Virginia example undermine due process because of the conflict of interest that was created, it showed that justice was for sale or, at the very least, gave that impression. "If the public believes that judges can be bought," said Keith R. Fisher of the ABA, "that is really poisonous and undermines public confidence in an independent judiciary."[8] In 2009, the Supreme Court ruled that the due process clause required Benjamin to recuse himself "given the serious risk of actual bias."[9]

In a democracy, for any government institution to survive, the public must view that institution's power as being legitimate. This statement applies to the judiciary even more so than to legislatures or executives because, as Hamilton noted in *Federalist* 78, the courts have the power of neither the purse nor the sword but "merely judgment" and therefore depend upon widespread support to implement rulings.[10] If the public is indeed losing its faith in the impartiality of the courts because of the new politics of judicial elections, that would be cause for concern.

This chapter addresses how the new politics of judicial elections has opened the courts (and judges who sit on those courts) to attack and whether those attacks have affected the public's perceptions of the judiciary. Although there may be many reasons to oppose judicial elections, the argument that they undermine the public's faith in the judiciary is not the most persuasive one. The concern about the effects of the new politics is understandable, but the empirical evidence, at this point anyway, indicates that it has not undermined the public's faith in the judiciary in any serious way, much less created a "crisis," as some have argued.[11] Moreover, as I discuss, attempts to take the politics out of judicial elections, such as implementing public financing or nonpartisan elections, may not work and could have negative consequences. However, before documenting the new politics of judicial elections in more detail and analyzing its effects on public confidence in the courts, it is important to understand how judicial selection in the states works and why some states elect judges.

Judicial Selection in the States

Unlike the straightforward federal model (the president appoints, the Senate confirms), each state has its own rules regarding how judges are selected and how long they serve. Although Maine and New Jersey follow the federal model, and others, such as Hawaii and New Hampshire, use a variation of the federal appointment method, thirty-nine states have some electoral component to their selection process. Because of the nature of the position, many states elect their judges in nonpartisan elections; in other words, a candidate's party affiliation is not listed on the ballot. A smaller number of states, including West Virginia, choose their judges in partisan contests that look no different on the ballot from elections to Congress or the state legislature. Finally, some states employ a method unique to the state judiciary: the retention election. Here, once a judge obtains the bench (either through appointment by the governor or by election), he or she serves a set term. When that term expires, the public then votes to keep the judge or remove him or her from the bench; the judge does not have an opponent. If the judge is not retained, which is rare, then the process starts over. Many states use some combination of nonpartisan, partisan, and retention elections for different levels of courts.[12] The important point here is that an overwhelming percentage of today's state judges face some sort of election.

However, it has not always been this way. Immediately after the ratification of the Constitution, no state elected its judges. In all states at the time, either the governor or legislature appointed judges. After the Supreme Court's ruling in *Marbury v. Madison* granting the courts the power of judicial review, people became more concerned about promoting judicial accountability than protecting judicial independence.[13] Others wanted to promote judicial independence from the state legislatures, although not necessarily from the people. Perhaps more than any other factor, the early interest in bringing courts under popular control was fueled by the era of "Jacksonian Democracy," which was marked by a desire to grant increased power to the people and was dominated by a belief in the accountability of elected officials. In 1832, Mississippi became the first state to amend its constitution to require that all state judges be elected. Several other states followed suit. In fact, every state that entered the Union between 1846 and Alaska's admission in 1959 allowed for the election of some—if not all—of its judges.[14] Since that time, some states have switched selection methods (for instance, Arkansas and North Carolina moved from partisan to nonpartisan elections), but support for an elected judiciary at the state level has remained strong.[15]

The Emergence of a "New Politics of Judicial Elections"

That roughly 80 percent of states require at least some of their judges to stand for election is problematic to those concerned about the integrity of the courts, primarily because of the emergence of a new politics of judicial elections mentioned previously. As noted, the reports issued by the Brennan Center indicated that, in many ways, running for judge was no longer much different than running for Congress. Perhaps the finding in the Brennan Center reports that alarmed organizations committed to protecting judicial independence the most was the increasingly expensive nature of judicial races. Each election cycle in the 2000s seemed to break a record for spending in a state. For example, in 2006, of the ten states that had entirely privately financed elections, five set records for candidate spending in a single court race.[16] The increase in spending was not a result of inflation. Chris Bonneau found that, even when controlling for inflation, total campaign spending in supreme court races grew substantially from 1990 to 2004, especially if the race was partisan.[17] Median candidate spending in 2006 was $243,910 in supreme court races, more in line with what one might expect from a contentious election for the U.S. House of Representatives rather than a "sleepy" judicial contest.[18] Some court races actually rivaled U.S. Senate elections in terms of expenditure. For instance, two candidates combined to spend roughly $10 million in a 2004 Illinois Supreme Court race. That contest was more expensive than nineteen of the thirty-four U.S. Senate races held that year. Furthermore, substantial candidate spending was not limited to races for the high court. In 2002, judicial candidates for six circuit seats in Broward County, Florida, spent more than $2.7 million combined.[19] A candidate for a Georgia intermediate appellate seat donated more than $3 million of his own money to his campaign in 2004.[20] In a 2006 trial court election in Madison County, Illinois, expenditures reached $500,000.[21]

Even more worrisome than the fact that candidates were spending millions of dollars in some judicial races was the issue of who was donating the money. Not surprisingly, given their likelihood of appearing before the court, business interests and trial lawyers are the two largest donors to judicial campaigns. These groups had always contributed to judicial candidates, but they have started to see an even greater opportunity to influence the outcomes of judicial elections. They realized that it was much easier to win a few seats on the bench than to control a state legislature. In the 2005–2006 supreme court election cycle, business groups contributed to judicial candidates more than $15 million and trial lawyers donated $7.3 million (44% and 21%, respectively, of all money raised).[22] The Florida Bar Association calculates that 80 percent of all campaign contributions to state judges come from lawyers.[23]

In the 2004 Illinois Supreme Court race mentioned previously, one group estimated that national tort reform groups contributed more than $1 million to one candidate, while the other received money primarily from trial lawyers.[24]

These figures do not include money the two groups spent independently of candidates. Consider just a few examples. In a 2006 Michigan Supreme Court election, the Chamber of Commerce spent more than $700,000 on independent advertising in favor of Justice Maura Corrigan. The National Association of Manufacturers, through its political action committee American Justice Partnership, independently spent more than $1.7 million backing a candidate challenging a sitting Georgia supreme court justice. Independent groups combined to spend more than $2.7 million in the state of Washington's 2006 supreme court elections.[25]

Both the direct contributions and the independent spending by interest groups raise red flags about conflicts of interest that emerge when these groups appear before the court. Although the results of studies testing whether campaign contributions influence court rulings are murky at best,[26] the public clearly believes that there is a link between campaign expenditures and jeopardized judicial independence. Even though the public supports electing judges, one survey found that 72 percent of respondents reported being concerned that the money raised by judicial candidates would compromise judges' impartiality.[27] This fact is not lost on former Associate Justice of the United States Supreme Court Sandra Day O'Connor, who wrote that interest group spending and the rising costs of judicial elections "threaten the integrity of judicial selection and compromise public perceptions of judicial decisions."[28] Moreover, as I will document, a significant portion of the money that is being spent on judicial elections is used to attack judicial candidates and the courts, which could indirectly affect the public's attitudes toward the judiciary.

The increased role of money is not the only concern regarding the new politics of judicial elections. The weakening of state codes governing judicial behavior and the increased ability of judicial candidates to speak openly about their political views also is viewed as problematic. Unlike candidates for most offices, judicial candidates must abide by canons that are endorsed by the ABA and implemented on a state-by-state basis. For example, judicial canons often limit the political activity of candidates (they cannot act as a party officer, for example) or keep candidates from personally accepting or soliciting campaign funds. One canon, the "announce clause," prohibited candidates from "announcing their views on disputed legal or political issues."[29] This particular canon was controversial, because some people argued that it was needed to protect the impartiality of the judge, while others believed it infringed on the candidates' right to free speech. Greg Wersal, a judicial candidate from Minnesota, and the state's Republican Party filed a suit arguing that Minnesota's "announce clause" was unconstitutional on First Amendment grounds. In *Republican Party of Minnesota v. White,* a divided Supreme Court agreed. Writing for the majority, Justice Antonin Scalia argued that the First Amendment does not permit "leaving the principle of elections in place while preventing candidates from discussing what the elections are about." He continued, "It is simply not the function of government to select which issues are worth discussing or debating in the course of a political campaign. We have never allowed the government to prohibit candidates from communicating relevant information to voters during an election."[30] In other words, judicial elections should be treated like elections for other offices, at least when it came to taking policy positions during the campaign.

The fear of many judicial scholars was that the Court's ruling in *White* would politicize judicial elections even further and lower the public's perception of the courts. As law professor and critic of judicial elections Charles Geyh argued, "[t]o the extent that [the *White* decision] liberates judicial candidates to emulate their counterparts in political branch races by committing themselves to positions on issues they are likely to decide as judges, it will accelerate the downward spiral of politicization that can be arrested only if judicial elections are eliminated."[31]

Although the Court's ruling in *White* applied only to the announce clause, several states started revising or eliminating other judicial canons in anticipation of potential court challenges.[32] These changes concerned some in the legal community because of the fear that judicial elections would revolve around partisan issues more than the qualifications, characteristics, and courtroom demeanor of candidates. Indeed, after the *White* decision, interest groups began sending questionnaires to judicial candidates asking them for their positions on a variety of issues, such as abortion or same-sex marriage. In these surveys, candidates are normally asked to simply respond "yes" or "no" or "agree" or "disagree" to certain statements without the opportunity to provide a narrative on their positions. Although interest groups of various ideological stripes have sent questionnaires to candidates, socially conservative groups have been especially aggressive in their use of questionnaires. For example, in 2006 right to life groups in Kentucky and North Carolina asked judicial candidates whether they agreed or disagreed with the statement "I believe that *Roe v. Wade* was wrongly decided." In an Alabama Supreme Court race, a socially conservative group asked candidates whether they agreed or disagreed with phrases such as "Unborn Child Is Fellow Human Being," "The State Can Acknowledge God," and "Alabama 'Lawsuit Abuse' Harms Economic Development."[33] If candidates fail to complete a questionnaire, then they can likely expect the sponsoring organization to run negative advertisements against the candidate accusing them of not being forthright with their positions. Not surprisingly, these questionnaires are quite controversial in the legal community, especially because they normally force candidates into a simple dichotomous answer without providing them an opportunity to explain the nuances of their positions. "When you send a candidate a questionnaire and say you cannot give a narrative response," says Alabama attorney Mark White, "then I think that's grossly unfair. That demonstrates . . . [that] whoever's asking the question not only wants to frame the question, they want to frame the answer."[34] Some judicial candidates have responded quite strongly to questionnaire requests. In a letter to the president of the Florida Family Policy Council, a group that asked judicial candidates to complete a questionnaire, Judge Peter D. Webster wrote:

> I have spent a good portion of my life thinking about issues related to the judiciary. My experiences lead me to conclude without reservation that questionnaires such as that which I have received from your organization are ill-conceived. Over the long term, their impact cannot be anything but bad—bad for the judiciary as an institution; bad for the rule of law; and bad for the people of Florida. I say this because such questionnaires create the impression in the minds of voters that judges are no different from politicians—that they decide cases based on their personal biases and prejudices. Of course, nothing could be further from the truth.[35]

The "New Politics of Judicial Elections" and Attacks on the Courts

Judicial reform groups like the Brennan Center and Justice at Stake worried that the increase in campaign spending and the Supreme Court's ruling in *White* would make judicial elections similar to elections for other offices.

In other words, judicial elections would be dominated by divisiveness and party politics. Campaigns would become more negative, which would increase attacks on the courts and, in turn, could change the public's perception of judges as being impartial interpreters of the law. Moreover, judicial candidates would have to spend significant time fundraising creating conflicts of interest that also could threaten the courts' standing with the public.

The growth in campaign spending in judicial races, both by candidates and independent groups, resulted in an explosion of advertising, particularly on television. In 2000, voters in only four of the eighteen states that had contested supreme court races saw ads. However, by 2006 television ads ran in ten of eleven states with contested supreme court races.[36] Early analysis indicates that spending on television ads in judicial elections rose again in 2008.[37] On the one hand, the increase in television commercials could be viewed positively, because it means that more voters were exposed to information about the candidates. On the other hand, much of that information is negative, a problem in the eyes of those who want to protect the integrity of the bench. In the 1999–2000 election cycle, 80 percent of interest group ads aired on television were considered to be negative. A majority of television ads (57%) run by political parties contrasted the two candidates, and 27 percent attacked the other party's candidate. Only 16.1 percent of the party ads and 9.6 percent of the interest group ads were positive.[38]

Negative advertising by independent groups and political parties is now a mainstay of judicial elections. What is surprising, however, is that even candidate advertising has become remarkably negative. Less than 20 percent of judicial candidates' television ads were negative in 1999–2000, but by the 2005–2006 cycle more than 60 percent of candidate ads attacked their opponents.[39] Many of today's judicial campaigns are as nasty as campaigns for any other office. They certainly are no longer the civil affairs as they were once portrayed.

This negativity has led state courts to come under attack, both directly in the form of criticisms of the rulings of an entire court and indirectly by attacks on judges who sit on that court. As much as negative advertising appears to be disliked by voters, elections almost inherently have to be negative, especially when they involve an incumbent. Challengers can promote their qualifications and backgrounds only so much; at some point, they have to articulate why they are a better choice than the incumbent. Judicial elections are no different, which is exactly why groups like the ABA oppose such elections. Although negative ads can vary in tone and content, opponents of judicial elections view virtually any negative ad as problematic, especially when those ads turn personal.

The negative ads in judicial elections run the gamut of issues and personal attacks. One study of judicial advertisements found that negative ads portrayed opponents as being "corrupted by campaign contributions, the tools of special interests, and soft on crime."[40] Television ads from recent judicial races highlight the claim that incumbent judges are in the pocket of special interests. Consider the following examples from the 2004 Illinois Supreme Court race between Gordon Maag and Lloyd Karmeier referenced earlier:

> "*Multi-national corporations, HMOs, and the insurance industry* are spending millions to buy Lloyd Karmeier a seat on the Supreme Court. They know Lloyd Karmeier will continue to support them as they outsource jobs and eliminate healthcare for workers and retirees. Law enforcement, teachers, and working families choose Gordon Maag because they know Maag can't be bought."

> "*Trial lawyers* are desperately trying to elect Gordon Maag, but newspapers aren't buying it. They reject Maag because he has his roots in the same sleazy, back-scratching, money grubbing politics that made the Madison County mess. With a record of bad judgment, Maag is scolded for distorting Judge Lloyd Karmeier's record with wads of cash from trial lawyers."[41]

Another example of a race in which the candidates accused each other of being in the pocket of special interests comes from a 2002 Alabama Supreme Court election between James Anderson and Harold See. Unlike the preceding example in which the two advertisements mentioned were sponsored by a political action committee and a political party, these ads were financed directly by the candidates:

> "Harold See was disqualified as a judge for distributing false information about Chief Justice Roy Moore. *He's taken millions funneled from big corporations.* And then he was the only judge to side with these corporations against the rights of Alabama families in more than a dozen cases. . . . [James Anderson] *can't be bought.*"
>
> "James Anderson is making desperate last minute attacks on Justice Harold See. Anderson knows political charges were dismissed long ago. Why

the misleading attacks? Anderson has no judicial experience. And *he's taken thousands of dollars from trial lawyers.*"[42]

Finally, consider this 2004 ad run by an independent group against three Alabama Supreme Court candidates:

"Just when you thought we got *trial lawyer money* out of Alabama politics, it snuck back in. Over the last few days lawyers have pumped nearly a million dollars into the judicial campaigns of Pam Baschab, Jerry Stokes, and Tom Parker. Baschab, Stokes, and Parker waited until the last minute to take their trial lawyer money, hoping you wouldn't find out. Ask Pam Baschab, Jerry Stokes, and Tom Parker: Is trial lawyer money really good for the Alabama Supreme Court?"[43]

If candidates, political parties, or interest groups are not running ads arguing that the opposition is being bought by special interests, then they often highlight a controversial aspect of a judge's record. In some cases, these attacks could be considered the equivalent of the Willie Horton ad (made infamous during the 1988 presidential election) for judicial races. The general approach for this kind of attack involves taking a ruling that appears controversial and exploiting it in a thirty-second spot without providing all of the relevant facts of the case. For example, Chief Justice of the West Virginia Supreme Court Warren McGraw was depicted in a commercial by the group "And for the Sake of the Kids" as a "radical liberal" who let a child rapist out of jail.[44] "And for the Sake of the Kids" was funded primarily by the chief executive officer of Massey Coal, the company referenced at the beginning of this chapter in connection with the *Caperton* case. In another instance, Kentucky Supreme Court Justice Janet Stumbo was attacked by her opponent, Will T. Scott, for siding "with criminal defendants most of the time," including reversing the conviction of a person who murdered a preacher.[45] In both the West Virginia and Kentucky cases, the facts were more complicated than portrayed in the commercials.[46]

Additionally, judges, or the court as a whole, may be depicted as being overly activist and legislating from the bench. In a 2009 Wisconsin Supreme Court race, Circuit Judge Randy Koschnick criticized his opponent, Chief Justice Shirley Abrahamson, for a court ruling that a $450,000 limit on pain and suffering awards in medical malpractice cases was unconstitutional because it violated the equal protection clause of the Wisconsin Constitution. The cap had been set by the state legislature. Koschnick accused the Abrahamson-led court as "taking power from the people."[47]

Finally, judicial candidates are often subjected to outright personal attacks, such as this commercial run by an independent group against a Mississippi Supreme Court candidate:

> "He had spent a lot of time in the bars. When he ran the disco bar and lounge known as Cash McCools, Jess Dickinson was a hands-on manager, hiring the cocktail waitresses and bartenders. And Jess Dickinson had his hands full of law suits against him and Cash McCools. He was even sued for hitting a customer in the face with a whiskey bottle and several times for not paying bills. Jess Dickinson. Is he really who he says he is?"[48]

Although these are only a handful of examples, examining a random sample of state supreme court ads illustrates that such messages are quite common.[49] In short, judicial election advertising is becoming as hard-hitting as advertising for any other office. Even more problematic is that some of the attacks include exaggerations or outright lies.[50] According to an analysis of 2006 judicial commercials by Factcheck.org:

> One ad . . . falsely implied that a candidate for the Kentucky Supreme Court paroled a rapist who 12 hours later raped a 14-year-old and forced her mother to watch. Another portrayed a Georgia candidate as soft on crime, even though independent reviews found that she usually sided with the prosecutor and was tough on defendants in death penalty cases. And a third invited viewers to believe, wrongly, that an Alabama candidate got nearly $1 million from oil companies to run negative ads against his opponent.[51]

The Public's Perception of State Courts

The question that remains, then, is how, if at all, these political, negative judicial campaigns are affecting the public's perception of the courts. At a national level, the public has historically had more confidence in the Supreme Court than Congress or the executive branch, often by large margins. For example, during the 1990s the Supreme Court was rated twice as highly as the executive branch and three times as highly as Congress regarding citizen confidence in the three institutions. Essentially the same trend has held in the 2000s.[52] Even with the Supreme Court's controversial decision in *Bush v. Gore*, views regarding the legitimacy of the Court have not faded.[53] Not only does the American public feel positively about the U.S. Supreme Court, it holds judges in general in high regard. Roughly 53 percent of survey respondents rated the honesty and ethical standards of judges as "high" or "very high." Conversely, only 20 percent rated senators "high" or "very high" and 10 percent said the same about congresspersons.[54] Furthermore, one study of state judges finds that strong majorities believe judges are trustworthy, honest, and fair and that their decisions are based on facts and the law.[55]

Most of the studies regarding the legitimacy and trust of the courts focus on the national level.[56] The interest in the federal courts, primarily the Supreme Court, is not surprising given its visibility and importance. Although there are reasons to believe that the public's positive view of the federal courts might not apply to the state courts (for example, the public is more likely to have contact with state courts and that experience may have been negative), at least one study finds that many similarities exist between public support for federal and state courts.[57]

It appears, then, that the public holds similarly positive views of state courts as they do of federal courts. Because of institutional differences, however, not all state courts may be rated identically by the public. Most federal judges, and certainly those most familiar to the public, are seated in the same manner: the president appoints, the Senate confirms. As noted earlier, state judges obtain the bench in a variety of ways. It is possible that when judges are elected, especially if those elections are partisan, the public may view the court less positively. Partisan elections may magnify the new politics of judicial elections, which could lead to less public confidence in the judiciary. Indeed, Benesh hypothesizes that confidence in courts "is diminished in states were [sic] judges are elected via partisan elections" because judicial independence, something that studies find is quite important to the public, is threatened.[58]

Interestingly, one could hypothesize just the opposite regarding the effects of elections on attitudes toward the court. Wenzel and his colleagues state that it is possible that judicial elections may have the opposite effect on public confidence in courts because they promote accountability to the public.[59] Public opinion polls indicate strong support for the idea of an elected state judiciary, especially if the elections are nonpartisan or retention.[60] It certainly is plausible, then, that the public views courts more positively because of judicial elections precisely because they promote accountability at the expense of independence and regardless of the new politics of judicial elections.

Again, few studies have examined public support and confidence in state courts; even fewer have looked at the effects of selection method on that support or confidence. The results of most of those who have done so, however, provide support for the hypothesis that judicial elections, at least partisan judicial elections, influence public perception of the courts. Using data from a 1999 survey, Benesh found that the public has less confidence in state courts when partisan elections are held compared to other election types or appointive methods.[61] Employing a different 1999 survey, Wenzel et al. uncovered similar results when looking at local courts, although the effects on confidence depend on the respondents' education levels. The most highly educated respondents had less trust or confidence in the courts if their judges were elected in partisan contests. However, the authors did not find any significant effects on attitudes toward the courts for any of the other selection methods.[62] Cann and Yates also examined citizen support for the courts using a 2001 national survey. They, too, found a negative effect on institutional legitimacy in partisan elections but uncovered no relationship for nonpartisan elections or merit selection.[63] Unlike Wenzel et al., however, Cann and Yates found that partisan elections negatively affected the views of the court for those with *less* knowledge of the courts. Making the relationship between elections and legitimacy even more convoluted is that not all research finds that partisan judicial elections undermine confidence in the courts. Kelleher and Wolak uncovered no statistically significant relationship between partisan elections and confidence in the state courts.[64]

The studies in the previous paragraph were conducted before the Supreme Court's ruling in *White* that the announce clause restricting judicial campaign speech was unconstitutional. It is possible, then, that the legitimacy of the courts could be threatened further as a result of the increasingly political nature of judicial campaigns. A 2007 survey conducted by the Annenberg Public Policy Center at the University of Pennsylvania corroborated this conclusion (although the study did not specifically mention the *White* ruling). Controlling for several factors that influence political trust, the study showed that people living in states that hold partisan elections had less positive views of the courts. In particular, they were more likely to agree that "judges are just politicians in robes."[65] The results of these studies seem to corroborate the concerns discussed in the Brennan Center reports.

However, Gibson has provided perhaps the most fascinating analyses to date examining the effects of "new style" judicial campaigns on the legitimacy of the courts; he came to a slightly different conclusion regarding the effect of *White* on legitimacy.[66] Although he found evidence that campaign contributions to judicial candidates can detract from legitimacy, "no support whatsoever is found for the view that the ruling in *White* threatens the legitimacy of elected state courts." He concludes that "policy talk by candidates for judicial office has no negative consequences for the perceived impartiality and legitimacy of state courts of last resort."[67] Although Gibson was unable to test exactly why this finding might be the case, he speculated that it "reflects the sophistication of the American mass public in recognizing that judges do (and perhaps must) make public policy, that on broad policy issues some degree of accountability is desirable, and that the expression of policy views does not prejudice the right of individual litigants to fair and impartial hearings before a court."[68] Moreover, although negative ads are harmful to the legitimacy of legislative institutions, Gibson found that they do not affect court legitimacy.[69] In other words, the concern observers of the judiciary have regarding the detrimental effects of attacks on the court are not supported by Gibson's data.

Possible Reforms to Improve the Public's Perception of the Courts

Even though studies find that people have less trust in courts when partisan elections are held and that there is concern over the conflict of interest created by campaign contributions, the public strongly opposes any efforts to eliminate judicial elections, especially if those elections are nonpartisan or retention.[70] Recently, for example, voters in South Dakota decisively rejected a constitutional amendment (that had passed both houses in the legislature with overwhelming support) that would have eliminated contested elections for trial court elections and implemented retention following a merit screening instead. Similar efforts in Florida, Michigan, and Louisiana have failed as well.

Because judicial elections appear to be here for the long haul, reform organizations such as Justice at Stake and the Brennan Center for Justice have focused on ways that the process can be "improved." Two common proposals advocated frequently by these groups are that judicial elections should be nonpartisan and publicly funded. Indeed, since 2000 Arkansas and North Carolina have jettisoned partisan elections in favor of nonpartisan elections, and North Carolina, New Mexico, West Virginia, and Wisconsin have adopted public funding of judicial elections with several other states considering such a move. It is not clear, however, that either reform will have the intended results.

The argument in favor of implementing nonpartisan elections is that politics (and, hence, partisanship) has no place in a judicial contest. Moreover, it is possible that judges could be removed from office simply for affiliating with a party that is unpopular nationally during an election year. However, there are significant drawbacks to holding nonpartisan elections, even though some studies find that partisan elections lessen the public's confidence in the courts. First, parties remain active in nonpartisan (and even retention) contests.[71] Not listing candidates' party affiliations on the ballot does not dissuade parties from getting involved. Second, and more important, removing partisanship from the process may make it exceedingly difficult for citizens to participate intelligently in the process, something that presumably should be a major goal if elections are to be held. Voter roll-off (when a person votes for the top-of-the-ballot office but skips a down-ballot contest) is significantly higher in nonpartisan elections than in partisan contests.[72] In other words, without party labels, many people desist from voting in judicial contests. Parties provide a relevant cue that helps voters navigate a complex information environment. Expecting voters to cast ballots based on issues such as courtroom demeanor is probably unreasonable. One possible way to avoid partisan elections is to provide information guides to voters, which, in theory, would help voters make decisions. However, information guides do not lessen voter roll-off in judicial elections, at least at the intermediate appellate court level, and may not provide voters with useful background on the candidates.[73] Moreover, although judges are supposed to follow the letter of the law and uphold the states' constitutions, it is hard to argue that Democratic and Republican judges do not interpret those laws or constitutions differently, which means that partisan cues matter when voting.[74] Furthermore, as the Gibson studies referenced earlier indicate, people are not opposed to judicial candidates making policy pronouncements on the campaign trail. These positions likely would mirror the positions of the political parties. In short, reformers need to consider carefully the drawbacks of nonpartisan judicial elections.

Public funding of judicial elections may be a better option because it would eliminate the direct conflict of interest between candidates and interest groups and potentially lessen the negative tone of these races, but even it is not likely to be the panacea that reformers hope. North Carolina's public funding program is considered a model by reform organizations such as the Brennan Center for other states to follow. The program provides funding to candidates who meet certain criteria. Candidates who fulfill these criteria receive a lump-sum payment of public funds equal to 125 times the filing fee for a candidate for the state's court of appeals and 175 times the filing fee for the state's supreme court. The program also has a provision that allocates additional funds to candidates if spending by nonparticipating candidates or independent groups exceeds the spending limit agreed to by the participating candidates; these are known as "rescue funds."

In some ways, the North Carolina program appears to be a success. In 2008, eleven of twelve judicial candidates agreed to accept public funding.[75] That the statute contains a rescue provision encourages candidates to participate. Also, the amount of money donated directly to candidates by business organizations and trial lawyers has declined. Moreover, overall spending declined in the first year after the program's implementation.[76]

However, there are some possible concerns about public financing programs, especially if they do not contain rescue provisions. First, because of the Supreme Court's ruling in *Buckley v. Valeo* in 1976, candidates cannot be forced to accept public funding, as was illustrated by Barack Obama's decision to forego public funding in the 2008 presidential election. Therefore, public financing statues must entice candidates to participate—and forego the thousands or possibly millions they could raise on their own. The problem is that public financing programs can become prohibitively expensive because they are woefully underfunded. In North Carolina's case, funding is generated principally by a $3 check box on individual state income tax forms and supplemented by $50 voluntary contributions from lawyers when they pay their privilege license as well as contributions of any size from individuals, corporations, labor groups, and professional associations. Yet, in 2003 only 7 percent of taxpayers and 12 percent of lawyers contributed to the program.[77] There are possible solutions, such as mandatory $50 contributions from lawyers, but unless changes are made, it is quite possible that the North Carolina program will resemble the presidential public funding system. It will not be able to provide the funding that would make it rational for a candidate to participate. Moreover, in a time of economic uncertainty when states need to cut spending because of ballooning deficits, it is unlikely that they will decide to fund political campaigns at the expense of education, health care, transportation, or other popular programs. From an ideological perspective, conservatives are already skeptical of public financing systems, believing that campaigns should be funded from private sources.

Second, public funding might eliminate the direct conflict of interest that results from campaign contributions, but it cannot prevent indirect effects that result from independent spending. Indeed, the controversy over Massey Coal's involvement in the 2004 West Virginia Supreme Court race would not have been eliminated if the state had relied upon publicly financed judicial elections (and will not be eliminated in the future, even with the state's new public financing law). As Abbe and Herrnson note, "Restricting fundraising activities makes these other forms of campaign support more important and increases the influence of the groups that provide them."[78] It is difficult to believe that judicial candidates will not notice the independent spending on their behalf or against their opponents. Even if the conflict of interest is lessened, the ads are likely to remain negative, something that will continue to upset those concerned about attacks on the judiciary.

Third, the publicly financed grant provided to candidates has to be substantial enough to allow them to get their messages to voters. Judicial elections are generally low-information affairs; they are not heavily covered in the media, which makes candidate spending all the more important.[79] Voters have great difficulty learning valuable information about judicial candidates, especially in those races that are nonpartisan. In most cases, state supreme court candidates must run statewide campaigns that can be quite expensive. An argument could be made that *more* money should be spent in judicial elections, not less money. Again, whether public funding systems can continue to provide appropriate levels of funding to participating candidates remains to be seen.

Fourth, public financing may actually create an undesirable result in the eyes of those concerned with judicial independence. It is possible that public financing will lead to *more* contested, negative, and divisive elections, either because candidates will no longer have to go through the unpleasant process of fundraising in the same way that they would without public money or because candidates who have difficulty raising large sums of money will not have to do so.[80] If anything, reformers want *less* contestation. All of these reasons are not to say that states should not enact public funding of judicial elections, but it must be understood that public funding is not a cure-all for the problem of money in elections and may actually have negative consequences.

The Future of Judicial Elections and Court Legitimacy

It is understandable why reformers, scholars, and practitioners are worried about the potential effects of elections on judicial legitimacy. After all, as noted, no branch depends more on the acceptance of the public for implementing its decisions than the judiciary. The concerns are that the "new politics of judicial elections" are here to stay and that judicial elections will continue to mirror elections for other offices, threatening courts' effectiveness and independence. That the constitutionality of enduring judicial canons remains very much in question is all the more troublesome to many opponents of judicial elections.[81]

However, even for those who oppose judicial elections, it is difficult to argue that the legitimacy of the courts is severely threatened by electing judges. Contrary to the hyperbolic titles of the new politics of judicial elections reports, there is not a crisis in the judiciary (at least in the eyes of the public). Studies do find that partisan elections may lessen public support for the courts, but the magnitude of this relationship is not large and the effect is often only applicable to certain people (for example, the most politically uninformed). Moreover, there does not seem to be any noticeable differences between the judiciaries in partisan and nonpartisan states regarding effectiveness of the courts. If anything, partisan elections promote political participation and provide voters with essential information in otherwise low-information contests. Furthermore, it cannot be said that nonpartisan elections are keeping parties on the sidelines.

Additionally, the ability of judicial candidates to speak more openly on the campaign trail may actually be positive instead of negative. Voters obtain valuable information and do not appear to be turned off by candidates stating their views on political issues. The rise in negative advertising may be more of a concern, especially if the ads are inaccurate, but even negative advertising can give voters important insight. Discussing elections for other offices, Mayer writes, "[w]e need to find out about the candidates' strengths, it is true, but we also need to learn about their weaknesses: the abilities and virtues they don't have; the mistakes they have made."[82] The same holds true for judicial elections. For example, people have the right to know the sources of candidates' contributions, information that is sometimes revealed in negative judicial campaigning.

The biggest concern for the future of judicial legitimacy seems to be the conflict of interest that is created between judges and campaign contributors. Even advocates of judicial elections are likely to oppose such blatant conflicts of interest as the one that existed between Justice Benjamin and Massey Coal. Based on studies such as Gibson's, the public's belief that justice is for sale appears to be far more worrisome than partisan involvement in judicial elections or judicial candidates speaking openly on the campaign trail. Public funding of judicial elections may be a partial solution to this problem. Devising clear recusal standards or disclosure requirements may also help.

However, even examples like the West Virginia case may not be as problematic for judicial legitimacy as one might think. First, elites might be appalled by the relationship between Massey Coal and Justice Benjamin—perhaps rightly so—but it is unclear that the general public, even in West Virginia, is aware of the case. While the average citizen might not like some of the developments that have taken place in recent years regarding judicial elections, it is hardly at the top of their list of concerns. Voters want the right to exercise electoral control over elected government officials, but the particulars of how that control will be exercised does not seem to arouse much passion from the public. Second, although polls show that the public is worried about the influence of campaign contributions on judicial decisionmaking, the public also strongly supports the idea of electing judges and believes that judges are fair and impartial. The new politics of judicial elections has not changed this result. Third, studies of public perceptions of the courts assume that citizens have some understanding of how the courts work and what different selection methods will entail. Yet, citizen knowledge of the courts is not impressive. "To most people, the term 'the courts' conjures up an amorphous image of the judicial branch in which local, State, and Federal jurisdictions merge without distinction," writes David Rottman. "Courts are remote and mysterious. . . . Lack of knowledge about what the courts do—and about what court does what—is pervasive."[83] This is not to imply that scholars, practitioners, and reform organizations are unwarranted in their concerns about elections as a threat to judicial legitimacy but simply to say that the new politics of judicial elections seems to have created, at least so far, a crisis in the eyes of groups like Justice at Stake and the Brennan Center for Justice more than in the eyes of the public.

Finally, while reform organizations such as Justice at Stake and professional organizations like the ABA have spent most of their time worrying about the effects of judicial elections on the legitimacy of the courts, they have virtually ignored another institution that may be even more problematic. The initiative process found in twenty-four states may present a serious threat to judicial legitimacy. State judiciaries are often forced to invalidate initiatives because the measures are unconstitutional. For example, in 1994 citizens of California passed Prop 187, an initiative that denied health care, education, and welfare benefits to illegal immigrants. Roughly 60 percent of voters supported the proposition, but the initiative was declared unconstitutional by a federal district court. This can create great resentment against judges—after all, their ruling goes against the wishes of the majority of the state's voters. As a result, elected judges may be hesitant to hear cases that emerge from a passed initiative, which might keep laws on the books that infringe on minority rights. Although I know of no study that addresses whether citizens in states with the initiative rate their courts more negatively than citizens in states without direct democracy, this issue should be followed closely in the future.

chapter 7

Conflicts with Courts in Common Law Nations

Jason Pierce

The next two contributions to this book make clear that the United States is hardly alone when it comes to significant criticisms of the courts and potential incursions on judicial independence. Jason Pierce considers recent experiences of the high courts in Great Britain and Australia to show both continuity with the American experience (all three nations have experienced a rising tide of critiques of judges, including often highly personalized attacks) and important differences (the distinct causes of the conflicts involving political officials, the public, and the courts). In the end, assuming a comparative perspective deepens our general understanding of judicial independence and our ability to evaluate the specific experiences of the United States and other nations in confronting courts.

The chapters in this volume explore the causes of and consequences to U.S. courts coming under attack from elected officials, organized political interests, and the public. This chapter places these critiques in a broader comparative context. It explores how and why courts in two other countries have come under similar attacks. It gives close attention to the courts of final appeal in Britain and Australia, demonstrating how these sieges are best seen as political and public responses to what scholars describe as the "juridification" of the respective political orders in the last fifteen years.[1] By "juridification, I mean a political system's increased reliance on law and courts for collective decision-making. In these two cases, the courts—particularly the final appellate courts—have assumed new and greater responsibilities protecting civil and political rights. Moreover, the chapter points to political and juridical developments in both countries that suggest the courts are likely to remain under siege. These two case studies offer valuable comparative insights for U.S. court scholars because, while there are some consequential constitutional differences and variations in political practice among these three nations, each is a stable democracy whose legal system draws upon the common law tradition and operates within a political order that has a historic commitment to judicial independence.

A Siege is a Siege? The Broader Global Picture of Attacks on Courts

It bears mentioning at the outset that recent attacks on the courts in Great Britain and Australia are not necessarily representative. Far more politically destabilizing, pernicious, and violent attacks have befallen judiciaries in other parts of the world. In many countries, courts and judges find themselves not metaphorically under siege but quite literally under assault from other political institutions and actors. In fact, Human Rights Watch's 2009 annual report identifies fourteen countries whose judiciaries are plagued by a dearth of institutional independence. Courts in these countries are susceptible to corruption and unable to thwart executive (and, less frequently, legislative) threats to judges, which include ignoring court judgments, manipulating the courts' powers and jurisdictions, and failing to fund the courts' operations adequately. These sieges are different not in degree but in kind to those occurring in the United States, Great Britain, and Australia.[2] Consider Uganda, where in 2007 the government sent armed police officers into the High Court in Kampala for the purpose of re-arresting individuals the courts had set free a few hours earlier. That same year, the Cambodian government replaced the president of the Court of Appeal without consulting or involving the constitutional body charged with nominating and disciplining judges. In 2008, many Liberian judges were unable to hold court for want of security. Mob attacks on courthouses, intended to free or attack suspects, resulted in at least ten deaths.[3]

Since the mid-1990s, three cases have garnered particular attention in international press: Venezuela, Zimbabwe, and Pakistan. Since coming to power in 1998, Hugo Chavez has effectively neutralized the Venezuelan judiciary as an independent branch through legislative reforms, constitutional amendments, abdication of constitutional commitments, and political bullying. In 2004, the Venezuelan legislature passed a law that enabled Chavez to pack the courts with judges sympathetic to the revolution and his policy agenda, remove sitting judges antagonistic toward it, and expand defamation and libel laws to discourage dissent. According to scholars, the courts lack any independence to check the exercise of executive power in ways that undermine property, free speech, and free association rights. By way of example, Venezuela's Criminal Code was amended in 2005 to expand the scope of *desacato* (disrespect) laws, which criminalize speech that defames or libels public officials or state institutions.[4]

Judges in Zimbabwe have endured waves of physical and verbal threats and attacks from President Robert Mugabe's supporters and government-backed militias. In 2001 the Zimbabwean chief justice resigned from his post once it became clear that the government could not guarantee his safety after he received death threats. Fergus Blackie, a High Court judge, was arrested in 2002 and was then paraded through Harare streets in handcuffs by police for sentencing Mugabe's justice minister to three months in jail for contempt of court after the minister criticized another judge for issuing too lenient a criminal sentence. All told, six high-ranking judges have resigned or retired under pressure from the Mugabe government for their unwillingness to toe the party line.[5]

Perhaps one of the most notorious episodes of a judiciary under siege comes from Pakistan. In 2005, the country's chief justice, Iftikhar Muhammad Chaudhry, took up a number of controversial cases about the disappearances of individuals detained by security agencies on suspicion of involvement in terrorism. The cases brought embarrassment to the government, led by President Pervez Musharraf. In March 2007, Musharraf suspended Chaudhry from his judicial post (he was one of sixty sacked judges) on charges of misuse of power, an act that prompted violent protests throughout the country. These protests were orchestrated by a group of lawyers—they became known as the "lawyers' movement"—who thought that Chaudhry was the one hope for checking Musharraf's power and thus sought to challenge the justice's suspension.[6] The protests grew in size and strength during the summer and fall. Musharraf eventually imposed a state of emergency in November 2007, leading to a controversial election in which he sought a second term as president even though the constitution forbade it. Chaudhry and seven other judges were placed under house arrest.

In February 2008, parliamentary elections brought victories to parties that opposed Musharraf. A coalition of these parties drew up impeachment charges, forcing Musharraf to resign from office in August 2008. That next month, the incoming president, Asif Zardari, released several judges detained by Musharraf but initially refused to reinstate Chaudhry because of his own complaints about the chief justice. Continued protests and international pressure eventually prompted the government to reinstate Chaudhry in March 2009.[7]

The threats that these judiciaries experienced fall into an altogether different category than those in the United States, Great Britain, and Australia. Something more than a properly balanced separation of powers system or the judiciary's independence is at stake in places like Venezuela, Zimbabwe, and Pakistan. The rule of law itself—the idea that "public power must be defensible against a set of stable, knowable, and public norms"—is under attack.[8]

If the siege on U.S. courts is modest in comparison to these countries, why dedicate an entire book to a "siege lite"? To begin with, it certainly is valuable to know the spectrum of sieges and to know where the U.S. case, if one can speak in such singular terms, may fall on that spectrum. More important, that government soldiers are not storming U.S. courthouses to rearrest defendants or that U.S. Supreme Court justices are not being placed under house arrest does not negate the attacks that have occurred on U.S. courts. It merely puts the U.S. siege into perspective. Second, what is gained from a closer examination of sieges that have occurred in other common law systems, notably Great Britain and Australia? There are enough constitutional and political similarities between these two countries and the United States for comparisons to have value. Yet there are differences in structure and tradition as well as variations in the causes of and consequences to the judicial sieges. Comparing the U.S. siege, then, to those that have occurred in similarly constituted political systems and in systems that share a common law heritage enables finer distinctions and more precise conclusions to be drawn about the U.S. experience.[9]

Like their U.S. counterparts, judges in Great Britain and Australia have come under heightened scrutiny and criticism in the last fifteen years, and calls for curtailing each judiciary's powers have become politically de rigueur. These criticisms originate from varied quarters—legal elites, politicians, the public, even the judges themselves—but they are animated out of a shared concern: *the juridification of the political order*. In its most basic form, juridification occurs when a political system increasingly relies on courts and court-generated law for collective decision making, and it may also involve the diminution of democratic processes.[10] These two dynamics are not necessarily or uniformly related, but they are related in the British and Australian cases.[11]

Lars Blichner and Anders Molander have identified five different dimensions of juridification that provide a useful conceptual framework for dis-

cussing the British and Australian sieges. First, there is constitutive juridification, whereby "norms constitutive for a political order are established or
changed to the effect of adding to the competencies of the legal system." By
this they mean that a political system's core political values or constitutional
commitments are changed through some action, like a constitutional convention, that vests in courts altered powers and responsibilities. The second
dimension involves law coming to regulate more activities. Third, juridification occurs when people increasingly resolve disputes by referencing law.
The fourth dimension involves the judiciary and the legal profession gaining
power through law becoming increasingly indeterminant or lacking transparency. Finally, juridification occurs when people think of themselves increasingly as legal subjects; that is, when people see themselves belonging first
and foremost to a legal community that promulgates certain laws, rights, and
responsibilities.[12] Recent attacks on courts in Great Britain and Australia are
best seen as responses to perceived and real juridification occurring in each
country.

The British Judiciary under Siege

Tony Blair's Labour Party claimed victory in the 1997 national elections on
promises, in part, for constitutional reforms. These reforms were far-reaching
and significantly altered the country's political and constitutional landscapes.
They included eliminating hereditary peerage and instituting elected and appointed positions in the House of Lords; devolving legislative powers to a
Scottish Parliament, the Northern Ireland Assembly, and the National Assembly in Wales; adoption of a statutory bill of rights, known as the Human
Rights Act 1998; and, although it occurred under Blair's successor, Gordon
Brown, the creation of a new Supreme Court of the United Kingdom wholly
apart from Parliament. All carried constitutional import, but the last two
garnered great attention. Enactment of the Human Rights Act (HRA) and
creation of a new final court of appeal, which began operation in late 2009,
represented profound departures from how rights were historically protected
and how the judiciary was organized. Recent attacks on the British judiciary
may be explained, at least in part, by the constitutive juridification that these
reforms brought.

Juridification through Rights Protection

The Council of Europe was created in 1949 for the purpose of "achieving greater unity between its members" and protecting the common ideals of individual freedom, political liberty, the rule of law, and genuine democracy. To advance these goals, the original ten member states, which included the United Kingdom, signed the Convention for the Protection of Human Rights and Fundamental Freedoms, to give its full title, otherwise known as the European Convention on Human Rights, in November 1950. The ECHR identified fundamental freedoms and rights shared by all member states and provided international institutions to protect those rights. The ECHR was not designed to entrench any new rights but rather to place under international protection a non-exhaustive list of common rights recognized in the domestic laws of member states. Rights include the right to life (article 2), protection from torture or inhuman treatment (article 3), prohibition of slavery (article 4), the right to liberty and security (article 5), the right to a fair and public trial (article 6), prohibition of ex post facto laws (article 7), the right to privacy (article 8), freedom of thought (article 9), freedom of expression (article 10), and the freedom of assembly and association (article 11).

The ECHR is currently enforced by the European Court on Human Rights located in Strasbourg, France. The ECHR allows rights violation claims to be filed in the Strasbourg court after any individual or member state applicant has exhausted all domestic appeals. More claims were lodged and more violations found against Great Britain than any other country from 1959 to 1989.[13] By the 1990s, many politicians and lawyers perceived shortcomings in the Strasbourg system and sought to advance an alternative. Indeed, these shortcomings were a prominent part of Labour's strategy for securing support for the HRA. To begin with, it was expensive and time-consuming for litigants to take cases to the Strasbourg court—attorney fees averaged 30,000 pounds and the disposition of cases averaged five years. ECHR critics also complained that the Strasbourg court, composed of judges from throughout Europe, was not especially familiar with British common law. Some regretted that a group of European jurists was able to dictate the meaning and implications of the ECHR on British law.[14]

The Labour government sought to rectify these deficiencies by providing British litigants with a domestic alternative to the Strasbourg court. To secure this, the government enacted the Human Rights Act 1998, which "incorpo-

rates" the ECHR into domestic law. It requires ministers who introduce legislation to sign off on it, attesting that it does not contravene the ECHR. If
a proposed law is thought to be incompatible, the minister must affirm that
it is incompatible and state the government's intent to proceed nonetheless.
The HRA grants individuals the right to file cases alleging ECHR violations
in domestic courts and to have British judges decide them. British courts are
obligated to interpret legislation in a manner that is consistent with the HRA,
as much as possible. If legislation is at odds with the HRA, certain courts are
given the power to issue "declarations of incompatibility." These declarations
do not affect a law's validity or force, but they put Parliament on notice that
an incompatibility exists. It falls to Parliament to amend the legislation, if it
so chooses, but it is not obligated to amend the offending legislation. If Parliament does not move forward with amending the legislation, the litigant
can file the case in Strasbourg. This obviously constitutes a weaker form of
judicial review than practiced in U.S. federal courts, where courts render legislation at odds with the Constitution null and void.

There was wide agreement when the HRA came into effect in October
2000 that it would fundamentally alter the United Kingdom's constitutional
and political landscapes. Many expected that courts would be flooded with
rights cases filed by lawyers bent on using the new document to its full effect. Others worried that the judiciary would abuse its new power to issue
declarations of incompatibility. Even this weaker type of judicial review was
seen as anathema to the British political culture premised on parliamentary
sovereignty.[15]

Both worries proved illusory. After promulgation of the HRA, courts
were not flooded with human rights cases. In its review of the HRA's first six
years of operation (2000–2006), the Department of Constitutional Affairs
reported that 552 appellate cases (2% of the caseload) concerned HRA matters, with the House of Lords (then the final court of appeal on civil law and,
for some jurisdictions, on criminal law) handling the highest percentage of
those cases. Of those, "The HRA has been substantively considered in about
one-third of the 354 cases which the House decided in this period and could
be said to have substantially affected the result in about one-tenth of those
cases," according to the department report.[16] Scholars point to several factors
to explain why there was no deluge of HRA cases. First, litigants may assert
human rights arguments in lower courts, but the courts often determine that
the HRA is not engaged; that is, that the complaint is better characterized

under a different law or simply does not amount to a rights claim under the HRA. Second, British courts had grappled with ECHR case law and precedents for fifty years before the HRA came into effect, meaning that many rights-related questions already were explored and developed through the Strasbourg system.[17] Third, there is evidence that lawyers in some parts of the country are inadequately trained to raise HRA claims, and many judges have signaled to attorneys their reticence about hearing them. One scholar reports that lawyers and judges, at least in one jurisdiction, perceive HRA claims as last-ditch arguments when everything else fails.[18]

When confronted with HRA claims, courts have not abused their new judicial review powers. A total of twenty-six declarations of incompatibility were issued from 2000 to 2009. That number does not portray a swashbuckling judiciary drunk on its own power. Eight of those twenty-six cases were overturned on appeal. In fourteen cases, the offending legislation was remedied. In the remaining four cases, the government either is considering how to remedy the infringing law or is in public consultation about possible remedies.[19] In sum, the sentiment in most legal circles seems to be that the courts are exercising their new powers with prudence, and Parliament seems relatively responsive to amending laws found to contravene the HRA. The HRA's overall impact on law has been modest, but as a proponent of the HRA points out, its aims were modest to begin with, notwithstanding the fanfare and anticipation from certain quarters.[20] Indeed, the absence of a grander track record has frustrated some.[21]

If "modest aims, limited impact" accurately captures the HRA's first decade, as one observer put it, why then in 2009 did the justice minister and the opposition leader both call for overhauling the HRA because it has proven too potent?[22] In short, a gap has emerged between the public's perception of the HRA (and consequently the politicians' rhetoric about it) and its real effects, driven by the public's fear of the perceived juridification it has brought about. Public support (and therefore political support) for the HRA has eroded. A series of high-profile cases has created a perception that the document coddles eccentrics and criminals at the price of security and community. In its early years, the HRA appeared destined to protect celebrities and the powerful and was seen as irrelevant to average citizens.[23] Two cases illustrate. In 2003, Michael Douglas and Catherine Zeta-Jones successfully sued *Hello!* magazine, alleging their HRA privacy rights had been violated when the magazine published unauthorized photographs of their 2000 wedding. The next year supermodel Naomi Campbell won a similar privacy suit against *The Daily Mirror* for disclosing that she had a drug addiction and was attending Narcotics Anonymous meetings.[24]

While these celebrity trials drew attention to the HRA's privacy protections, its protections for criminal defendants came under intense scrutiny in its early years as well. In 2002, the Law Lords concluded that the practice of the home secretary, an elected member of Parliament, to decide the minimum number of years that "life sentence" prisoners were required to spend in prison violated the HRA.[25] Parliament responded by passing the Criminal Justice Act 2003, which shifted this power from the home secretary to the courts. Any prisoner whose term had been set by the home secretary could appeal that determination. The following year there were several heavily publicized murders committed by individuals released early from their prison sentences and several judge-imposed sentences that the public perceived as overly lenient. A pedophile, in one infamous case, had been sentenced by a jury to life imprisonment for raping a 12-week-old baby, but a judge interpreted that life sentence to mean he could be eligible for parole after only eight years.[26] In another publicized case, a High Court judge concluded in May 2006 that nine hijackers who had spent several years in a British prison and had applied for asylum could not be sent back to their native Afghanistan because it was unsafe and that to deny asylum status would violate their human rights.[27]

These cases and others like them engendered a firestorm of public criticism directed at the judges and the HRA. A tabloid newspaper, *The Sun,* started a "naming and shaming campaign" in which the newspaper published the names and photographs of judges thought to give soft sentences. The judges' photographs appeared in mug-shot format. The newspaper's online edition invited readers to click on the photos to "read their shocking sentencing history." One article from the series concluded with, "Do you know a judge who has gone soft on a crook? Email our campaign team . . . and we'll name and shame them here."[28] Politicians got in on the act as well, blaming the HRA for overemphasizing individual rights. Opposition leader David Cameron criticized the HRA as "practically an invitation for terrorists and would-be terrorists to come to Britain." He called for scrapping it altogether and replacing it with a new bill of rights that would better balance community interests and individual liberty.[29] Home Secretary Jack Straw also announced in late 2008 that it was necessary to "rebalance" the HRA to underscore the importance of responsibilities along with protecting rights. He remarked, "There is a sense that it's a villains' charter or that it stops terrorists being deported or criminals being properly given publicity."[30] The Brown government issued a green paper in March 2009 addressing many of the perceived shortcomings and misconceptions surrounding the HRA. The green paper underscored the importance of economic and social rights, in addition to civil and political rights, but in the end it advocated for the HRA to remain in place.[31] The onset of the credit crisis and the economic downturn that year reshuffled the government's policy priorities, such that as of this writing, no amendments have been made to the HRA.

The political and public backlash against the HRA is attributable to the transfer of power it brings from Parliament to the courts and to the individuals it is perceived to protect. Furthermore, people are concerned about the limitations the Parliament and executive will accept to their powers. Thus the HRA has contributed to attacks on the judiciary because it brings juridification, but not as much as the public and politicians perceive. Additional juridification may come from the HRA. The law also encourages people to think of themselves as legal subjects, or more properly rights-bearers, who can rightfully seek refuge under the HRA's protections. It is not the case that before the HRA British citizens did not think of themselves as rights-bearers. What has changed is that the source for those rights is now enumerated and in a domestic statute. Reactions to the headline-grabbing HRA cases suggest the public and politicians may not like who envisions themselves as rights-bearers—"villains," as the opposition leader put it. That only exposes the courts to additional criticism.

Juridification through Institutional Reform

Another source of juridification within Great Britain came with passage of the Constitutional Reform Act 2005. This Act brought several notable changes, including a new appointment process for British judges and the creation of a new court of final appeal. In its white paper describing the rationale for this Act, the government noted that the program of constitutional reform begun in 1997 was significant and successful but that it "needed to go further" to ensure "the fairest possible distribution of power in our society."[32] Reforms to the appointment system were introduced to reduce the role of the executive branch and hold those who exercise the appointment power more accountable. The creation of a new United Kingdom Supreme

Court was designed to draw a more intentional separation of powers between Parliament and the courts.

Prior to the 2005 Act, the Lord Chancellor, historically the head of the judiciary and a member of the cabinet, played a central role in the appointment process, making recommendations to the Queen or, in the case of senior judicial appointments, making recommendations to the prime minister, who then advised the Queen. At the center of the new appointment system is the Judicial Appointments Commission, created in 2006 and charged with soliciting and reviewing judicial applicants and then making recommendations to the Lord Chancellor, who then makes the appointment, in the case of lower courts, or makes recommendations to the Queen, in the case of higher court appointments. The fifteen-member commission is composed of judges, lawyers, and lay people who serve five-year terms; in practice, their influence over the appointments process appears impressive. The commission reviewed some 2,535 applications for 458 appointments during the 2007–2008 term. The Lord Chancellor accepted all of the commission's recommendations. Rather than providing the Lord Chancellor with a list of acceptable candidates for a vacancy, the commission has adopted the practice of providing a single name for each vacancy.[33]

Creation of the commission was intended to create greater transparency in the appointment process, to ensure that merit drives the selection of judges, and to promote the appointment of judges with different backgrounds and experiences. This reform represents a clear transfer of power from the Lord Chancellor and the government to this nondepartmental public body. By relocating a significant portion of the appointment process outside of the Lord Chancellor's office, it also brings a firmer separation of powers between the judiciary and Parliament.

The 2005 Act also created a new final court of appeal, the United Kingdom Supreme Court. Prior to the Act, two courts resided at the judiciary's apex. The Appellate Committee of the House of Lords heard appeals from courts in England, Wales, and Northern Ireland. The Judicial Committee of the Privy Council heard appeals from overseas jurisdictions and cases that raised questions about devolution. (Devolution refers to the transfer of power away from the Westminster Parliament to administrative governments in Scotland, Wales, and Northern Ireland, a process that began in earnest in the late 1990s.) Both judicial bodies were located within the House of Lords.[34]

The new supreme court, which began its work in October 2009, cuts a more formal institutional separation by removing the appellate court functions from the House of Lords. This new twelve-member court exercises the same jurisdiction as the Appellate Committee, assumes the Privy Council's devolution jurisdiction, and assembles in its own, newly renovated building. The current Law Lords will initially staff the new court and retain their membership in the House of Lords. Future appointments will receive the title "Justices of the Supreme Court" and will be made on the recommendation of a Supreme Court Appointments Commission.[35]

Compared to the political and public reactions that greeted the HRA and many of the controversial decisions concerning it, this institutional reform has not garnered as much attention. It obviously carries great import for how judicial power is exercised, but it is in its infancy and has not generated the sensationalized headlines. So far. The reformed appointment system and newly constituted Supreme Court represent new potential wellsprings for juridification. Just how much juridification occurs depends on how the Supreme Court and the appointment commission exercise their powers. Because these institutional reforms break in significant ways from how British courts previously operated, it is altogether possible that they, in conjunction with the HRA, will usher in what Blichner and Molander call constitutive juridification, where the underlying norms and principles of a political order are fundamentally altered.

In sum, the contemporary British political system is grappling with a number of real, potential, and imagined sources of juridification. The juridification that comes from these constitutional and institutional reforms has begun and will leave open British courts to new levels and forms of attack.

The High Court of Australia under Siege

Over the past fifteen years, the Australian judiciary has come under intense scrutiny and criticism as the political system considers, like its British counterpart, how best to protect civil and political rights. Australia's Commonwealth Constitution came into effect in 1901 without a bill of rights, and no national statutory bill of rights exists to this day. In the absence of a constitutional or statutory statement of rights, the state and federal parliaments, the High Court, and the public have engaged in an intense debate addressing the following questions: Just what rights should the legal system protect? Through what type of legal instrument should rights be identified?

What powers should the judiciary have vis-à-vis the legislature and executive to protect rights? Varying answers have emerged, but operating behind these debates and behind the attacks on the High Court of Australia are larger worries over the aggrandizement of judicial power in a political system steeped in traditions of parliamentary sovereignty.

Some background on the Australian political system is necessary. The federal constitution dates to 1901 and is a hybrid document that borrows heavily from the American and British constitutional traditions. The Australians drafted a written constitution that enumerates the national government's powers and duties, like the American document. Both are built on federalist principles that divide power between state and national governments. The Australian constitution also incorporates separation of powers principles at the national level, such that powers are divided among a legislature, an executive, and a judiciary, although Australia's constitution draws this tripartition of powers in the British tradition, retaining the British monarch as its head of state.

Retaining the British Crown as head of state is just one of many ways in which Australia's political practices exhibit a British heritage. Operating alongside the separation of powers system is the practice of responsible government, whereby executive authority rests in a ministry whose members come from the legislature. The ministry is "responsible" to the legislature in that if the ministry lacks the confidence of at least a majority of the legislature, it is dissolved. The constitution also exhibits its British heritage by containing no statement or bill of rights, although it does contain a few modest enumerated rights such as the right to vote and the right to a jury trial.[36]

Australia's rights-driven juridification is divided into three stages. The first occurred in the mid-1990s when a group of High Court judges attempted to infer unenumerated rights from the constitution's text. Accompanying these "implied rights cases," as they are known, were a number of equally controversial decisions concerning what property rights Australia's indigenous population retains to their native land. This pairing exposed the Court to white-hot criticisms—a siege of sorts—from politicians and the public because of the cases' consequences and the profound power shift they represented from Parliament to the Court. The criticisms directed at the Court and its justices had their intended consequence: the Court flinched at opportunities to develop a more expansive implied rights doctrine as support for it within the judicial ranks fizzled.

The second stage revolves around efforts in the last five years, some successful and others not, to enact bills of rights at the subnational or state level. What one observes in this second stage is how the fear of more robust judicial power, displayed during the first stage, prompted bills of rights that preserved parliamentary sovereignty and vested courts with modest judicial review powers, in line with the British courts under the HRA. The third stage to this rights-driven juridification remains in its infancy, so its outcome is uncertain. The enactment of bills of rights at the state level has prompted the current federal Labor government to investigate the need and support for a national bill or charter of rights. As of this writing, the government was in a consultative phase and had not yet proposed legislation on this front.

Juridification through Implied Rights

The first stage of juridification roughly coincides with Sir Anthony Mason's tenure as Chief Justice from 1987 to 1995. Under his leadership, the High Court reached controversial decisions in numerous areas of law, crafting a new institutional profile for the Court and a new understanding of the Constitution's role in Australian society. Two areas of case law will be addressed here. First, beginning in the early 1990s, the Mason Court, as it is known, held in a series of cases that the Constitution contains certain rights and freedoms that are *implied* in the document and operate as judicially enforceable limits on Parliament's power. That is, the Constitution's text carries certain consequences that are not expressly stated. This broke with a long-established interpretative practice on the Court that recognized the document contained only a few expressed rights and that no others should be inferred.[37] Second, the Court overturned a two-hundred-year-old precedent to establish new land rights for Australia's indigenous people, a right known as native title.

The interpretive debate over implied rights dates back to the 1970s and 1980s, when litigants first introduced the idea. The Court during these years either ignored the argument or dismissed it out of hand.[38] The first real footholds for the doctrine were secured in the early 1990s. In 1992, a majority of the Court concluded in two cases that provisions of the Constitution that call for "representative government" and "representative parliamentary democracy" imply an individual's right to free and open political discussion. One case dealt with whether a newspaper that had published an article challenging the integrity of an industrial relations commission would be penalized under an industrial relations statute. The second case challenged the constitutionality of a law that banned political advertising on radio and television during federal election periods. Media companies argued that both laws violated an implied right to political communication that existed between media outlets and their customers and was protected in the Constitution.[39] A few years later, the Court expanded this implied freedom in *Theophanous v. Herald and Weekly Times Ltd.* (1994) to insulate criticisms of public officials that would otherwise be unlawful under defamation law. This case was noteworthy because it extended the implied freedom to communication between private individuals.[40]

It remained to be seen just how broadly the Court would define political communication and whether it would infer additional rights from the Constitution. The outer boundary of the implied rights doctrine was tested in 1996 with two cases. The first addressed whether the implied right to political communication extended to the act of casting an election ballot, specifically whether someone could purposefully cast and encourage others to cast illegitimate ballots by not following Australia's preferential balloting procedure. This procedure requires voters to rank order their preferences, rather than voting for a single person or party.[41] The second raised the question of whether the Constitution contained an implied right to voter equality; that is, should each member of the federal parliament represent roughly the same number of people?[42] As to the first case, the Court did not extend the implied speech right to the act of casting a ballot. It concluded that the electoral law necessarily rejected ballots that did not properly record a voter's preferences in order to protect the electoral democratic process. In the second, the Court rejected an implied right to equality, concluding that the Constitution tolerates a certain level of inequality in district sizes.

These proved to be watershed cases because they pointed to the limits of the implied rights doctrine. In the late 1990s, the Court further circumscribed this doctrine. An example of this is *Kruger v. Commonwealth* (1997). Here the Court explored the constitutionality of a territory law that sanctioned the removal of Aboriginal children from their families and communities for the primary aim of assimilating them into white Australia.[43] Alec Kruger argued that the law enabling his removal was unconstitutional on the grounds, inter alia, that it violated the Constitution's expressed freedom of religion and its implied constitutional rights to free movement, equality, and association. The Court rejected these arguments and in subsequent cases underscored that the implied rights doctrine extends to political communication but does not countenance other implied rights or freedoms.[44]

A second line of controversial cases emerged in the 1990s concerning indigenous land rights. It began with *Mabo v. Queensland* (1992), which concerned whether an indigenous group retained land rights against a state government's claim of regulatory authority.[45] Eddie Mabo claimed that he and his people possessed "native title" to their land, which included the right to possess, occupy, and use it. The Queensland government objected on the grounds that when the then-British colony of Queensland annexed the land in the late nineteenth century, the land was without owners, or *terra nullius*.[46] The indigenous people, so the Queensland government argued, could not have native title over land owned under international law by no one.

It was nothing less than a legal revolution when the Court rejected Australia's settlement under *terra nullius* and granted native title to Mabo. The decision generated fiery criticism. It was described as "naive adventurism," exhibiting "perverse and politically driven logic" and utilizing the language of the "guilt industry."[47] At a practical level, the decision constructed a mechanism for Australian Aborigines to secure native title rights to land that they use for agricultural, religious, or cultural purposes but do not own. Second, *Mabo* opened a host of unanswered questions concerning how native title rights were to be balanced with other property rights. Third, it engendered fears about the creation of "black states" and excessive native title claims in major metropolitan centers.

Recognizing that uncertainty, expense, and delay were the likely consequences of a purely judicial mechanism for handling native title claims, the Labor government of the day drafted legislation to give statutory force to *Mabo* and provide institutional processes for evaluating native title claims. This preliminary legislative scheme did not end the native title litigation, because *Mabo* left several questions unanswered. In December 1996, the Court affirmed and extended *Mabo* in *The Wik Peoples v. The State of Queensland*.[48] *Wik* addressed whether native title claims to government land could coexist with pastoral leases that a government had granted to the same land. The Court concluded the competing land claims could coexist. This further enraged Australian farmers and miners, who feared that *Wik* would put their livelihoods in still greater jeopardy. Responding to the *Wik* turmoil, the Liberal government enacted in 1998, after much wrangling and the longest debate in Parliament's history, a statute that laid out an amended set of procedures and rules for settling native title claims.[49] Since the 1998 legislation, the High Court has issued several important decisions that have generally narrowed the scope of native title rights and narrowed the scope of people who might successfully claim these rights.[50]

The National Native Title Tribunal is the agency responsible for receiving native title claims and assisting in the negotiation of those claims with other interests. Since 1994, the tribunal has received 1,813 claims. Nearly 85 percent of the claims have been resolved through administrative means and without resort to litigation. The tribunal reports that 128 cases have been resolved through litigation—91 where native title was found to exist and 37 where native title was not found to exist. Indigenous communities also have negotiated over 390 land use agreements. These are agreements between native title groups and others about the use and management of land and resources. Land use agreements currently cover 13 percent of the Australian land mass.[51] Whatever conclusions may be reached about these statistics, it cannot be said that they live up to the post-*Wik* hype. In fact, a growing list of scholars, politicians, and indigenous leaders who heralded the native title decisions and legislation are now questioning its ultimate efficacy. The expansive form of native title that many hoped for or feared from *Mabo* simply has not materialized.[52]

Having explored the implied rights and native title cases, the question arises, why didn't the doctrines advance any further? In previous work, I demonstrate that an interplay of legal, individual, institutional, and political precipitants best explains the denouement of these doctrines and the assertive High Court that promoted them.[53] Among the political precipitants was vitriolic criticism of the Court from the public, members of the judiciary, and politicians in response to these cases. High Court Justice Michael Kirby provided a catalogue of politicians' verbal criticisms of the Court and its judges in a 1998 speech to the American Bar Association. He remarked about how following controversial cases in the 1990s,

[T]he Court and the justices were labelled "bogus," "pusillanimous and evasive," guilty of "plunging Australia into the abyss," a "pathetic . . . self-appointed [group of] Kings and Queens," a group of "basket-weavers," "gripped . . . in a mania for progressivism," purveyors of "intellectual dishonesty," unaware of "its place," "adventurous," needing a "good behaviour bond," needing, on the contrary, a sentence to "life on the streets," an "unfaithful servant of the Constitution," "undermining democracy," a body "packed with feral judges," "a professional labor cartel." There were many more epithets of a like character, many stronger.[54]

It might be expected, if not excusable, for politicians to respond to publicly controversial decisions in such tones, but it is quite another for judges themselves to follow suit. In the wake of the early implied rights cases, various appellate judges described their High Court colleagues as "hyperactive," "adventurous," "incomparably activist," "composed of judicial legislators," and "controlled by Jacobins." The Justices were "under the influence of left-wing theorists," "deciding cases as Marx or Freud would have," "defying common sense," "moving the goal posts instead of just deciding if a goal had been scored," and "overcome with delusions of grandeur."[55]

These critics looked to *Mabo* and *Wik* as examples where the Court usurped parliamentary power and approbated rogue interpretations of the Constitution and common law. Queensland, Western Australia, and the Northern Territory—the three regions most affected by native title—called for Commonwealth legislation to overturn *Mabo* shortly after it was handed down. In 1997, Queensland Premier Bob Borbidge took the lead in attacking the High Court's *Wik* decision. His rhetoric transcended the native title cases and really addressed the High Court's role. For example, he told an audience in February 1997, "If the High Court is going to change its role, and that's what it has signaled, it's going to start to make the laws and not interpret them— then like every other institution in Australia, that comes at a price and the price is accountability." Further, "If the High Court is embarking on a course of judicial activism, the High Court itself has discarded the principle of the doctrine of the separation of powers."[56]

Borbidge and the other premiers coupled their verbal attacks with proposals to alter the High Court radically. Their proposals included a constitutional amendment to enable Australian voters to select and terminate High Court judges; establishing shorter tenure for High Court judges; granting state parliaments the power to veto judicial appointments; giving states the power to fill every second High Court vacancy; establishing a separate appointment apparatus that would enable greater state participation; and creating a new Federal Constitutional Appeals Court, composed of the six state supreme court chief justices and three other state-appointed judges, that would review High Court decisions. These threats never moved beyond rhetoric, but they were clearly animated from a profound sense that the Court was treading where it should not.

The criticisms lodged against the Court in response to the implied rights and native title cases were a turning point because they removed any pretense that Australia's High Court justices were somehow immune from public and political critique because of their institution's status. The historically apolitical court had become politicized, and individual High Court judges became fair game, both for their rulings and for their personal lives. The high level of deference that the Court had enjoyed for much of its history was gone. No episode better illustrates this than a devastating political attack waged against now-retired High Court Justice Michael Kirby in 2002.

Justice Kirby, the first openly gay High Court judge and a member of the *Wik* majority, was accused in 2002 of using a government-provided car and driver to cruise the streets of Sydney for the purpose of picking up boy prostitutes. A close friend of then–Prime Minister John Howard, Senator Bill Heffernan, made these allegations from the Senate chamber using parliamentary privilege, which provided him legal immunity should the allegations prove untrue. Howard stood by Heffernan in the early days of the controversy. Heffernan based these allegations on what proved to be a forged document given to him by one of the drivers. Once the document's inauthenticity was established, Heffernan apologized to Justice Kirby and retired from his cabinet post.[57] Justice Kirby survived the controversy and served on the Court with distinction until his retirement in 2009. The episode illustrates just how far the skepticism of judicial power extended after these controversial cases. It is unlikely that this sort of ad hominem attack on a High Court judge would have been handled as publicly and under the protection of parliamentary privilege in an earlier era.

Juridification through Rights Documents

By the early 2000s it had become clear that native title rights would not upend Australian property law, as some had feared. Those who had hoped for a more thoroughgoing catalogue of implied rights also were disappointed. Even those disposed to favor stronger rights protections recognized the limitations and liabilities associated with the Court finding and protecting rights that have no formal enumeration in the Constitution. With the implied rights doctrine stalled since the late 1990s, proponents of stronger rights protection recently have returned to the question of whether some bill or charter of rights offered a more viable approach.

This is not the first time attention has turned to bills of rights. Twentieth-century Australian history is littered with failed efforts to entrench a national statement of rights. The reasons behind each failed attempt vary, but it often came down to lack of political will, the inability of the Labor and Liberal Parties to reach consensus on the form and content of such an instrument, the presence of an exceptionally high threshold for ratifying constitutional amendments, the sense among many Australians that rights were adequately protected, and a fear that entrenchment of more rights would lead to further juridification, along the lines of the U.S. experience.[58] What dynamism exists on the rights front, at least until recently, was found at the state and territory levels. In the last decade, a number of states have studied the merits of a state-level statement of rights, and in two instances (Victoria and the Australian Capital Territory) these enquiries have led to the adoption of such instruments.

The first inquiry occurred in New South Wales (NSW), where its parliament undertook in 1999 a two-year study into whether the International Covenant on Civil and Political Rights, to which Australia is a signatory, should be incorporated into state law through a state bill of rights, much like incorporation of the ECHR into British law via the HRA. In October 2001, the standing committee that undertook the study rejected the idea that a state bill of rights was warranted. In short, it offered too little gain and would likely cause too much uncertainty. The report expressed strong reservations about how a bill of rights would alter the fundamental relationship between parliament and the courts, diminishing the sovereignty of the former and likely compromising the independence of the latter. Judicial appointments would become politicized, conflicts between parliament and the courts and greater legal uncertainty would arise, and speculative litigation would clog the courts. In place of a bill of rights, the parliament set up a Scrutiny of Legislation Committee in August 2003, charged with reviewing and reporting on the rights implications of all bills introduced into parliament.[59] The parliament has commissioned several studies and briefing papers since, but no legislative proposals have moved forward.[60]

The bill of rights debate next moved to the Australian Capital Territory (ACT). This time, however, the ACT Legislative Assembly concluded from its own investigations in 2002 that the merits of an enumerated statement of rights outweighed possible drawbacks. The result was passage of the Human Rights Act 2004 (ACT), an act comparable to the similarly named British law. The Australian HRA is not a constitutional statement of rights but an ordinary statute amendable through simple legislation. The Act enumerates an extensive list of protected rights including a right to equality, privacy, freedom of movement, thought, conscience, religion, association, and expression. It requires the government to sign off that each piece of proposed legislation comports with the HRA, or when a conflict arises the government must justify why it does not comport. All courts in the territory are required to interpret legislation in a manner consistent with the HRA, and the territory's supreme court is given the power to issue declarations of incompatibility when territory laws contravene the HRA. These declarations put the parliament on notice but do not affect the validity or operation of the law in question. It is for this reason that the HRA models an "institutional dialogue" approach to rights protection—an approach that does not give the judiciary absolute authority in constitutional decision-making and reserves to the legislature the power to derogate from a right when exigencies require it.[61]

The State of Victoria was third to follow suit, initiating in 2005 a community consultation process and investigation into whether a state bill of rights was necessary. The consultative committee recommended the adoption of a state charter of rights. This act, the Charter of Human Rights and Responsibilities, went into operation on January 1, 2007. Like the ACT's HRA, the charter is an ordinary legislative act, susceptible to amendment through normal legislative procedures. It protects those rights identified in the International Covenant on Civil and Political Rights. The government must submit with every new piece of legislation a statement of compatibility or explain why an override of the charter is necessary. The supreme court can issue statements of incompatibility, but it cannot overturn legislation. Parliament must respond to such statements within six months, but as with the HRA, issuance of a statement does not affect the legislation's operation.[62] The State of Tasmania is also grappling with the bill of rights question. Its attorney general charged in February 2006 the Tasmanian Law Reform Institute with the task of investigating and making recommendations on whether it should follow Victoria's path. The institute recommended a non-entrenched charter of rights, and in late 2008 the state premier advised his attorney general to investigate and draw up such a piece of legislation. It has yet to be introduced.

This collage of activity at the state level is not by chance. The literature written by some of the leading advocates for more robust rights protections forthrightly acknowledges the strategy employed. The states are conceived as laboratories for constitutional experimentation. The expectation is that these reforms may be easier to realize at the state or territory level, particularly if the rights-enhancing document is ordinary legislation and not entrenched through constitutional amendment. Furthermore, this bottom-up approach is considered less threatening to political elites. If unintended consequences emerge or if the rights regime runs amok in any single experiment, the effects will be contained rather than permeate the nation. Finally, there is the expectation that once some of the fears are allayed and popularity grows for state or territory bills of rights, the political stage may be set for another attempt at the federal level.

There are other reasons why developments are occurring in states and territories beyond these conceptual strategies for an eventual national statement of rights. Partisan politics is also at play. The Australian Labor Party (ALP) has historically shown greater support for enhancing rights protections through a statutory or constitutional rights document than the Liberal Party. It was Gareth Evans of the ALP who introduced in the House of Representatives in 1985 a national bill of rights that was ultimately withdrawn after facing intense opposition from Liberal Party Senators. The national ALP platform explicitly calls for the introduction at the federal level of a legislative Charter of Citizenship and Aspirations.[63] The Liberal Party platform calls for the protection of rights not through a formal rights document but rather through a system of checks and balances. The Liberal Party platform reads, "The liberties of Australia's people are not, with a few exceptions, specifically protected by the Constitution. The greatest protection of those liberties is the Australian people's understanding of and commitment to them."[64]

Given the parties' divergence on how best to promote political and civil rights, it is little surprise that ACT and Victoria reforms occurred under Labor leadership and that nothing happened on the national front during Liberal Party control from 1996 to 2007. Labor's Jon Stanhope, chief minister of the ACT, was an early and strong proponent of the HRA. Steve Bracks, premier of Victoria and Victorian Labor leader at the time, endorsed the Human Rights Consultative Committee's work and adopted nearly all of its recommendations. The one notable exception to this Labor Party sympathy is NSW's former premier and Labor leader Bob Carr. Carr allowed the Standing Committee on Law and Justice of the NSW Legislative Council to investigate whether a bill of rights was needed in NSW and then sent his own personal submission to the Committee lodging vociferous opposition to a bill of rights.[65] Nonetheless, Labor's recent strength at the state level contributes, in part, to explaining where and why reforms have occurred.

The Labor Party returned to federal power with the November 2007 elections. In December 2008, the federal attorney general created a consultative committee to consider whether a national statement of rights was necessary, and if so, what form it should take. The committee conducted in 2009 a nation-wide consultation, in which expert and lay opinions were sought. Over thirty-five thousand submissions were made, and the committee met with over five thousand individuals. Its report, submitted in August 2009, recommended against a constitutional bill of rights in favor of a national statutory statement of rights that empowers the High Court to issue declarations of incompatibility when a law contravenes the Act. The report also advised that all parliamentary bills include a statement of compatibility. There were early hints that the Labor government in Canberra would draw on the committee's report to introduce a national charter of rights akin to the ACT and Victoria models. In April 2010 the Rudd government rejected the committee's recommendation, responding to division within the Labor Party over a charter, little enthusiasm among voters for it, and a resurging Liberal Party that would use any charter against the Rudd government as a rallying point at the next election.[66]

The connection between the implied rights and native title cases, on the one hand, and the trajectory of the bill of rights debate, on the other hand, should not be overlooked. Through those cases, the High Court ushered in high levels of legal indeterminacy. The implied rights cases showed the Court's propensity, at least in the 1990s, to a modality of constitutional interpretation that left the Court with broad interpretive powers. It had a mechanism, should it be used, to forge an unenumerated list of constitutionally protected rights, denying any role for the state and federal parliaments. The native title cases showed the Court's willingness to take the lead in tackling a politically and legally contentious issue, to risk its institutional legitimacy in the process, and to expose itself to unprecedented criticism. If the Court was willing to tackle native title, what else might it tackle? Both lines of cases encouraged the fourth form of juridification that Blichner and Molander identify, in which courts gain power when the law becomes increasingly indeterminate, which certainly occurs with the reversal of long-established precedents and interpretative traditions.

While the Rudd government passed on introducing charter legislation in 2010, it remains on the national agenda, and any future legislation likely would follow the Victoria and ACT models that enumerate rights but do not leave the last constitutional word to the High Court. This may decrease the level of juridification and the possibilities for sieges on the Court. However, if one lesson appears from Great Britain's experience under the HRA, it is that it takes just a few controversial decisions for the perception of juridification to take hold and for newfangled critiques, attacks, and even sieges to follow.

Conclusions

The aim of this chapter has been to place the siege on U.S. courts in some preliminary comparative perspective. It began with a qualification that not all critiques are alike and then made the case for U.S. scholars to look at attacks on courts in two similarly constituted political systems, Great Britain and Australia.

This chapter advanced the argument that those attacks have occurred largely in response to the juridification that reforms in both countries prompted. Sometimes those reforms were court-initiated, as with the Australian High Court's implied rights cases, and at other times they were prompted by the democratically elected governments, as with the British HRA and creation of the new Supreme Court. It is noteworthy that courts in both systems confronted the most vociferous attacks when the juridification occurred around rights protection, whether it be the implied rights cases in Australia or controversial HRA-inspired cases in Britain. The chapter also pointed to new institutional reforms that, while in their infancy, are likely to generate additional juridification in both systems that will expose the respective courts to ongoing attacks.

chapter 8

The Siege on the Israeli Supreme Court

Maya Sabatello

Like the common law nations discussed in the prior chapter, the Israeli judicial system, and especially its Supreme Court, has been the locus of a great deal of criticism in recent decades. Much of today's controversy can be traced to the 1990s, following the Israeli parliament's approval of two "Basic Laws" protecting individual rights and the subsequent judicial response, developments facilitating what many have called a "constitutional revolution." The Israeli Supreme Court (hereafter, "the Court"), led by the influential judge Aharon Barak, began using the Basic Laws to overturn "ordinary" legislation and to justify its increasing resolution of socially and politically controversial issues—prompting charges that the nation was becoming ruled by a "judicial dictatorship." While Israel has a number of legal and political features that make it difficult to compare to the United States—its absence of a written constitution, its security challenges, and its distinctive political-religious cleavages—it also offers important insights about the possibilities of maintaining judicial independence while implementing dramatic legal change in a diverse, democratic society.

In the past few decades, the Israeli Supreme Court has gained a highly respected status among the legal and judicial professions both inside and outside Israel. In recent years, it has, however, also been accused of practicing judicial "activism," reflected in its ever-increasing involvement with policymaking in all phases of Israel's social, cultural, political, and military life. And while the Court's activism has generally been applauded by the international community, in Israel it is often followed by public outcry and governmental dissent; in this way, the Court's authority is potentially jeopardized from within. It has been charged, at least by some, with promoting its own political agenda and hence also too willing to engage in issues perceived as "sacred" and beyond judicial reach. Certainly, such charges are not unique to the Israeli Court. Other national supreme courts, including the U.S. high court, have faced similar challenges in the past few years. However, the Israeli Court provides a particularly interesting case study for analysis.

The Comparative Value of the Israeli Supreme Court

While institutionally and legally the Court differs from other democratically based judiciaries, as a comparative case study its distinctive characteristics as well as its experiences with political criticism offer insight into the reasons for increasing attacks on court systems and judges in democracies across the globe. Indeed, the Court is an especially promising case for comparative analysis of threats to judicial independence for four central reasons.

First, despite the international trend toward constitutionalism with guaranteed provisions of human rights, no written Israeli constitution exists. Nevertheless, the Court has developed over the years a strong human rights jurisprudence that has fostered international respect. Considering that the human rights agenda is part and parcel of contemporary democracies and that Israel has committed itself to be a democracy,[1] one would expect that the Court would be internally applauded for its human rights protections. As the case of the Israeli Court shows, however, in politically and religiously divided societies the human rights advanced by courts may be controversial as well. Second, and closely related to this point, the Court has had a unique experience dealing with sensitive social, religious, and political cases. Given its function as High Court of Justice (HCJ) with hardly any legal standing barriers blocking access to the Court, litigants from all sects of Israeli society have turned to it for relief, again often raising some of the most divisive policy and legal issues in the state of Israel.[2] Examination of the Israeli Court may thus shed light on the role of the judiciary (as well as questions about access to courts) in rifted democracies. Third, Israel's Court has long grappled with the classic democratic dilemma of how to balance human rights and national security in times of crisis. While certainly not unique to the Israeli court, the country's ongoing existential threat, the occupation of the West Bank, the Gaza Strip, and East Jerusalem in the Six-Day War of 1967, the eruption of the two intifadas (the Palestinian uprising) first in 1987 and then in 2000, and the harsh governmental-military response following the recurring attacks against Israeli civilians have given it plenty of opportunity to examine this dilemma. As residents of the Occupied Territories increasingly challenge the governmental counterterrorism measures in the Court,[3] efforts to balance considerations of human rights and national security have become an integral, ongoing, and inseparable part of the Court's workload. The discussion on the Israeli Court thus illuminates the power—and limitations—of national courts during national emergencies.

A final point suggesting the comparative worth of this examination of attacks on the Israeli Court relates to what scholars have termed the "transnational law dialogue" whereby national judiciaries increasingly cooperate among themselves and refer in their rulings to comparative law and international norms as a means to reach decisions.[4] Under the tenure of Chief Justice Aharon Barak (who was appointed to the Court in 1978, and served as its president from 1995 to 2006), the Israeli Court assumed a leading position in this discourse. Indeed, some of the Court's rulings, particularly with regard to counterterrorism measures, set important international and comparative precedents.[5] Yet this role of the Court also highlighted a contemporary dilemma facing any national court seeking to use and develop legal norms and jurisprudence applicable between nations: is it possible to participate in the "transnational law dialogue" and attempt to entrench universal standards of human rights without losing legitimacy from within? Overall, then, although some stark differences exist between the structure and legal authority of the Israeli Court and other judiciaries, particularly that of the United States, the Court's decisions and the outright hostility it has faced usefully illustrate the growing international quandaries about the role of the judiciaries in the twenty-first century.

This chapter explores the case of the Israeli Supreme Court and the multifaceted social and political challenges it faces today. After a brief overview of the Israeli political and legal systems, this chapter then discusses the reasons for the increasingly dominant role of the Court and for the resentment it has raised. Next, it surveys the resulting wave of attacks against the Israeli judiciary to illustrate the extent of the recent confrontations with the Court and to analyze them in light of Israel's sociocultural and political contexts. The last part of this chapter examines the experience of the Israeli Court within the broader phenomenon of attacks on national supreme courts in other nations, particularly in comparison to the United States. The goal of this concluding discussion is to explore the specific lessons that can be learned from the Israeli experience about the impact of public and political attacks on the court and the role of the judiciary in a democracy.

The argument I ultimately advance is that in contemporary democracies there is a built-in conflict between the political branches and the judiciary, as well as between the judiciary and the public. This is particularly so when courts rule on divisive issues that have broad public policy implications. Consequently, national courts are vulnerable to attacks and also constantly at risk of losing their legitimacy—notwithstanding their international reputation. While avoiding this trap is not always possible, protection of society from tyrannies (whether of a majority or minorities) and mitigating disagreements on the individual case (rather than policy) level should be the Court's primary goals.

Political and Legal Context

Before delving into the details of criticism raised against the Israeli Court, some background on the Israeli political and legal context is in order. To explain the judiciary's vital place in Israeli life, this section considers noteworthy similarities and differences between the American and the Israeli systems.

While Israel's democratic system includes legislative, executive, and judicial branches, as in the United States, its underlying governance is parliamentary. Based on the common law system and remnants of British Mandate rule over Palestine in the period prior to the establishment of the state, Israel has historically been based on the concept of parliamentary supremacy. Accordingly, the legislature (the Knesset) stands "at the head of the pyramid of [the] three authorities, and tilts the center of gravity of power and authority toward [itself]."[6] Although changes over the years have somewhat shifted it away from the original British model, as a structural and legal matter, parliamentary supremacy remained formally intact. In addition, Israel's political form is polyarchal. That is: in light of the large immigration to Israel since its establishment (mainly from nondemocratic states),[7] the Knesset consists of 120 members representing a mixture of social and political sectors, religious and ethnic groups, economic disparities, and other divisions within Israeli society. The government (the executive) reflects this sociopolitical mosaic as well. As no party has thus far received enough seats in the Knesset to form a government by itself, all governments have been comprised of multiparty coalitions. The main parties court the smaller parties, mainly the religious ones, to establish a coalition, hence disproportionately empowering them to demand (and receive) benefits that are of interest only to a minority of the population and are often contrary to the majority's preferences.[8] This reality, combined with tensions produced by Israel's occupation, has produced a fragmented legislature, divisions between the executive and legislative branches, and, overall, great instability.[9]

While, as in the United States, the courts are guaranteed independence by law, are expected to follow the rule of law, and are also based on the British common law system,[10] the two judicial systems differ in some important aspects. First, unlike its American counterpart, the Israeli Court functions without a written constitution or an entrenched bill of rights.[11] Efforts to develop such documents at the inception of the state failed, mainly due to strong orthodox-religious resistance.[12] The Knesset was expected to enact a set of Basic Laws that, while adopted and amendable just as any other legislation by a simple majority, when constituted together, in a subsequent additional governmental resolution, would eventually make up a Constitution. (This proposal was the 1950 Harari Resolution.)[13] The plan hasn't fully materialized, however. Only eleven Basic Laws have been enacted so far, and even among those, the jurisdiction of the Court is stated only vaguely, and not in one comprehensive Basic Law.[14] The main provision from which the Court acquires its power is article 15 of the 1984 Basic Law: The Judiciary, which vests it with the power as the final Court of Appeals for rulings of the District Courts and as a High Court of Justice. In the latter capacity, the Court holds an original jurisdiction to "hear matters in which it deems it necessary to grant relief for the sake of justice, and which are not within the jurisdiction of another court" and to issue orders against governmental entities and officials carrying out public function under law.[15] Second, in contrast to the politically oriented nominations in the United States in which the president appoints preferred candidates, the Israeli selection process is geared toward the forestalling of any political influences and strongly emphasizes technical legal expertise.[16] The political association of justices in Israel is not formally known,[17] and they are nominated after confidential discussions and a vote[18] by an independent and segmented special nine-member Judicial Selection Committee comprised of (1) two governmental representatives (including the minister of justice[19] as the Chair); (2) two Knesset members, selected by secret ballot; (3) three Supreme Court justices (including the Chief Justice); and (4) two practicing lawyers from the Israel Bar Association.[20] Thus, although the customary rule is to include a "sectarian seat" characterized by religious (Jewish-Orthodox), ethnic (Sephardi), gender, and national classification to increase the Court's representation,[21] the Israeli judicial selection system has been often regarded as one of the most apolitical processes in the world.[22]

Third, the Court's workload and panel composition differs. In the American system, the court's decision to grant writs of certiorari is made by a vote of at least four of the nine justices ("rule of four"); if granted, the court hears the cases en banc. The accessibility of the Israeli Court and the simplicity of its procedures, in contrast, have turned it into one of the busiest national courts in the world, hearing thousands of cases per year.[23] The Israeli Court normally hears petitions with a panel of three justices (out of fourteen),[24] and once a petition is filed, one Supreme Court justice alone may rule on interim orders, temporary orders, or petitions for an order nisi.[25] In addition, whenever the Court rules in a manner that is inconsistent with a previous ruling or where the importance, difficulty, or novelty of a ruling made by the Court justifies it, Israeli law authorizes the Chief Justice or the Deputy Chief Justice to hold an additional "further hearing" with an extended panel of five, seven, nine, or eleven justices.[26] Thus, unlike the American counterpart, the Israeli Court has greater flexibility in hearing cases—if the Chief Justice so chooses. Indeed, as will be discussed in the next section, the Court has increasingly utilized these tools, turning it into an active—and controversial—player in Israeli politics.

The Israeli Court as a Political Actor: Reasons for Its Empowerment—and for the Resentment against It

In Israel, much of the Court's transformation into a political player has been attributed to the charismatic leadership of Barak, initially as a justice of the Court (appointed in 1979) and then as Chief Justice (1995 to 2006). In both his judicial rulings as well as his extensive academic writings off the bench, Justice Barak has developed his own philosophy about the judiciary and its role, leaving a significant impact on the Court to a manner and extent that no other Israeli justice has done before. And while in practice the Court has restrained its substantive legal handling of controversial cases,[27] there is no doubt that Barak's activism has also raised considerable social, legal, and political uproar that is not likely to vanish anytime soon. Specifically, three interrelated factors have played a role in this result: (1) Barak's constitutional revolution, especially regarding the Court's assertion of the power of judicial review for itself; (2) the increasing involvement of the Court in core political and public policy questions; and (3) the Court's application of international law. Even if the existence of these factors (or any of them) may be desired in a democracy, the intricacies associated with Israel's political and legal context explain not only the nature of the Court's transformation but also the criticism raised against it.

Barak's Constitutional Revolution and the Power of Judicial Review

Historically, in light of the concept of parliamentary supremacy and of the lack of a written constitution or an entrenched bill of rights, the Court has consistently deferred to the government and legislature.[28] The turning point took place following the adoption in 1992 of the only two Basic Laws addressing certain substantive human rights[29] and Barak's subsequent proclamation of the "constitutional revolution."[30] The groundbreaking decision was delivered by the Court, sitting as a court of civil appeals, in its 1995 ruling in the case of *Mizrahi Bank v. Migdal*. The appellants challenged the legality of a Knesset law dealing with the agriculture sector, arguing that it violated their property rights under the Basic Law guaranteeing human dignity and liberty and was hence void. While each of the nine justices hearing the case issued a separate opinion, the primary approach of the Court was set out in Barak's opinion, establishing that Basic Laws enjoy a constitutional status and higher normative level than regular legislation.[31] Ultimately, the Court did not find the challenged law to be in violation of the Basic Law, hence the implications of the Court's elevation of the two Basic Laws to the status of a "quasi-constitution" were not fully explored. In subsequent rulings, however, the Court expanded the scope of its power of judicial review to all eleven Basic Laws, although they were enacted prior to 1992 and their provisions lack any form of protection, and also determined that any statute that contradicts a Basic Law is void.[32]

To appreciate the Court's revolutionary development in this regard, the unique legal and political landscape in Israel must be taken into account. Naturally, when a court takes for itself powers not explicitly granted to it in the constitution, controversy may ensue as the court appears as acting beyond its legitimate boundaries. This was the case also in the United States, when the U.S. Supreme Court established its power of judicial review in the precedential case of *Marbury v. Madison*. The controversy in Israel has been more acute, however, for two reasons. First, as Rabin and Gutfeld expressed, Justice Barak in fact "created two revolutions—the first is a constitutional revolution, which dealt with the superiority of the basic laws, and the second, which is built upon the first, the judicial review revolution"—even though neither had a formal grounding in Israeli law.[33] Also, the legislation on which the Court relied in its landmark ruling did not even contain proper constitutional elements.[34] Instead, the Court based its decision on the general Limitation

Clauses of the Basic Law, which, while they restrict the power of the political branches[35] do not explicitly provide authorization to deploy judicial review or grant it superiority over other legislation.[36] Thus, while the proclamation of judicial review in both the United States and Israel was controversial, the legal grounding of the latter's decision was far more shaky. The Israeli ruling did not enjoy the stability and solid footing of a constitution with a Supremacy Clause, and it was a judicial creation in its entirety.

The Court's interpretation—and broadening—of its own power has been all the more controversial considering the other circumstances in which the two Basic Laws protecting rights were adopted. Unlike in the American case, where the Constitution's wordings reflect the consensus achieved after intense public discussion, the Israeli public was not involved in the discussion surrounding the adoption of the two Basic Laws.[37] Moreover, there was also nothing remarkable in the manner in which the two Basic Laws were adopted. They were approved "by slim minorities, and without the accompanying celebrations one would expect considering [their] significance,"[38] leading some to argue that even the "legislature did not fully understand the future implications of the enactment of these two laws."[39] Thus, even though over time Barak's constitutional revolution was internalized within Israel's legal community, the tension that arose as a result of the Court's creation of its power of judicial review is understandable. The Court was seen as tilting political power from the legislature to itself.

The Court's Involvement in Core Political and Public Policy Questions

There has been a great deal of discussion in the past few years of the international phenomenon of "judicialization of politics," or "mega-politics," whereby national Supreme Courts have become increasingly relied upon for resolving core political and public policy questions that "define (and often divide) whole polities."[40] Israel is no exception. Particularly since the adoption of the two Basic Laws on human rights and especially Barak's subsequent proclamation of constitutional revolution, the Court has been increasingly involved in this growing tendency to "legalize" various aspects of the national fabric of life.

Accordingly, the Court has heard cases relating to tensions between religious and secular Jews as well as among the various streams of Judaism. In this regard, the Court not only struck down longstanding political arrangements that granted special benefits to the Orthodox stream of Judaism[41] but also delivered a series of rulings helping to define basic questions about the Jewish identity within Israel.[42] The Court has also taken a stance on divisive issues relating to the status of and protections due to minority groups within Israel, including in particular sexual minorities[43] and the social, cultural, and political participation of the Israeli Arab minority.[44] These rulings have often touched at the heart of acute disagreements about Israel's national identity, some of the more entrenched sociocultural and philosophical underpinnings of Israel's legal and political landscape, and the scope and interpretation of Israel's identity as a "Jewish and democratic state."[45] Finally, the Court also increasingly voiced its opinion in one of the most sensitive and volatile issues within Israeli's society: the military and Israel's security. In this context, the Court has been active in petitions dealing with preventive and administrative measures, humanitarian policies both during and after military operations, combat activity, and operational procedures to capture terrorist suspects in a manner and extent that are exceptional among the judiciaries of the world.[46] Indeed, unlike judiciaries in the United States, Great Britain, Canada and others, which have reluctantly heard cases regarding counterterrorism measures, particularly in the first few years following the attacks of September 11, 2001, and subsequent other terrorist attacks in London, Madrid, and elsewhere,[47] the Israeli Court had been involved in such petitions all along.

Israel's political and legal landscape has certainly played a role in this judicial development—and also explains the criticism it has raised. While in theory the Knesset enjoys parliamentary supremacy, in practice the recurring divisions and instability within the Knesset have substantially compromised its effectiveness and ability to supply the public with needed goods and services.[48] In reaction to this political failure, the Court has been increasingly called upon to resolve questions that normally would have had to be determined after proper public debate and by elected representatives.[49] And while many have maintained that in order to uphold a proper separation of powers, and particularly in light of Israel's cleavage society, the Court should resist ruling in such cases,[50] the Court itself has been willing—or as some have seen it, too eager—to entertain precisely these petitions, and yet with only little prospect of political success. Given the frequent fluctuations and cycles of Israeli political life, governing coalitions have also been disinclined to curb the power of the Court: they too recognize the likelihood that they will one day be in the opposition, and therefore in a position in which a strong judiciary may be a desirable ally.[51]

Perhaps the most prominent way for the Court to be involved in controversial cases has been by the relaxing of the rules governing jurisdiction and access to the Court. Beginning in the early 1980s with the Court's president at the time, Justice Meir Shamgar, the Court has substantially liberalized the rules of standing and its internal constraints regarding arguments of non-justiciability (such as the political question doctrine).[52] Contrary to the American "rule of four" and the U.S. justices' politically oriented petition patterns, following Barak's philosophy of the judiciary's role in upholding the democratic spirit, human rights, and natural justice,[53] the Court adopted a policy of hearing almost every petition that raises questions regarding human rights, the legality of governmental activity, and the rule of law. The approach taken by the Court is that there are never legal "black holes," that is, that the legal system is sufficiently broad to provide the framework for evaluating all claims raised about human rights violations. And within the scope of the constitutionally protected rights, it has included not only the rights explicitly enumerated in the two Basic Laws on human rights (such as the rights to life, dignity, property, and the right to pursue an occupation) but also other rights that were not (such as freedom of religious freedom and right to equality),[54] even though politically, the omission of the latter was intentional.

Furthermore, it has taken the view that the protection of human rights under the two Basic Laws includes both human rights during times of peace as well as during times of war. In this way, Barak's Court explicitly rejected Cicero's view that "in times of arms, the laws fall mute" and some elements of the American approach to emergency powers,[55] leading to the consequence that all divisive issues within Israel as well as counterterrorism and emergency measures can be adjudicated. Indeed, the Court's approach that "everything can be adjudicated" has led to a remarkable increase in the number of petitions submitted by individuals, political parties, Knesset members, and NGOs,[56] including petitions submitted by Palestinians and human rights organizations challenging counterterrorism measures.[57]

Another way in which the Court has increased its involvement in controversial cases has been its willingness to reexamine its own rulings with extended panels, as already mentioned. Consequently, while there is no right to appeal on the decisions of the Court, losing parties are not discouraged from resubmitting a petition or from requesting the Court to hold a "further hearing" of the case. In effect, the meaning of this option has been, first, that the Court potentially remains actively involved in controversial issues even after it has issued a seemingly definitive ruling (hence "threatening" the government that its (in)action will be constantly reevaluated); and second, that it may reverse its own rulings in a relatively short period of time, even if only because the panel composition differs. Thus, for example, in 1997, a three-panel Court upheld the administrative detention of Lebanese citizens who, although not accused of wrongdoing nor posing a security threat, were held for possible future prisoner exchanges with Lebanon (this became known as the "Bargaining chips" case). Only three years later, an extended panel of nine justices delivered an opposite opinion, prohibiting the government from holding these individuals as "bargaining chips" and also giving Justice Barak, who wrote the decision in 1997, the opportunity to reflect back and to change his position.[58] Such a change of precedent would have been much harder—if not impossible—to achieve if justices heard the cases en-banc, as in the United States.

Finally, the Court has adopted an interpretive approach that gives it an enormous room to maneuver. In line with Barak's philosophy, in "hard cases," in which the law is uncertain, the Court has a law-making capacity so its interpretation of the law reflects social reality.[59] Accordingly, for the resolution of those religiously and politically controversial cases, Barak has developed the principles of reasonableness and proportionality as cornerstone tenets of the legal system. That is, that for any governmental infringement on human rights to be legal, it has to be reasonable and "properly balanced," taking into account the various interests and rights that are at stake.[60] And while such a balancing act is not unusual for judiciaries, neither of these requirements was stipulated anywhere in Israeli law. Nonetheless, these principles have increasingly taken the center stage in the Court's (mainly Barak's) rulings, seemingly replacing standing and nonjusticiability doctrines. The Court has thus taken for itself tremendous power in the determination of the content and weighting of these principles, and with very little in the way of external restrictions or possible appeals.

The Court's disposition of these matters has been subject to a broad spectrum of criticism, not least of them as a result of Israel's political culture and the ongoing climate of national security crisis, as we shall see. Moreover, as not all interest groups and sectors in Israel support the Court's human rights orientation, particularly on questions related to Palestinian rights, the Court's approach has created a sense among the public that human rights is "a matter of interest only to a narrow, usually elitist, group, with extremely well-defined social features."[61] Thus, ultimately, as Gavison stated, the Court's ongoing interference comes across as materializing the so-called countermajoritarian difficulty, that is, a serious and risky transgression of its legal and institutional role.[62] Beyond that, it has led many to believe that the Court has "taken upon itself the role of an active political player"[63] and that in fact, as Ran Hirschl asserts, the Court epitomizes a "full fledged juristocracy."[64]

The Court's Use of International Law

Another source of tension in the Court's work has been its use of international law in the past few years. This development is not unique to the Israeli Supreme Court: it has been discussed as an international trend, termed by scholars "transnational law dialogue."[65] The Court's increasing reference to international norms has raised controversy, however, both as it seemed to contradict Israel's historical legal culture, and particularly as it has been applied in regard to the status of the Occupied Territories and its residents.

Following the British common law system, the Israeli approach makes a distinction between the two primary sources of international law, that is, customary (or custom-based) international law and treaties (or conventional international law). Whereas the first is enforceable in Israeli courts (unless it is inconsistent with domestic law), the latter requires specific Parliamentary legislation that incorporates the provisions of the treaty into national law. This dualist system is based on the concept of the separation of powers and is aimed at ensuring that the conclusion of international treaties, which is in the hands of the executive, does not overstep the power of the legislature to enact laws. Nevertheless, in the past decade, the Court has actively employed international norms in its rulings—including cases in which the Israeli legislature never enacted incorporating legislation.[66]

The Court's reference to international standards has been all the more apparent with regard to petitions revolving around counterterrorism measures and the Occupied Territories. Although Israel's official position with respect to the Occupied Territories is that the Fourth Geneva Convention does not apply,[67] the Court relied on the fact that the government never contested the applicability of the Hague Regulations to these areas as customary international law and on the government's statement that it would follow the humanitarian provisions of the Fourth Geneva Convention to increasingly incorporate in its rulings references to international norms.[68] Moreover, unlike in earlier cases where the reference to international standards was mostly in obiter, in some of the recent rulings the Court stipulated the controversy about the legality of the governmental military action as a matter of its compatibility with international standards.[69] Finally, the Court has also been willing to entertain itself with questions pertaining to new dilemmas that arise in international law (such as Israel's policy of targeted killing),[70] hence assuming for itself a leadership position in developing international norms.

This additional "mini-revolution" of incorporating international norms as scholar Daphne Barak-Erez termed it,[71] however, faced disapproval of the general (Jewish) public. And while in the United States, opponents of reference to international sources in domestic issues have pointed to the internal strength of the American political and judicial systems or to concern about the countermajoritarian difficulty,[72] in Israel the reasons for dissent lie in international politics: the sense within Israeli society that the international community, and particularly the United Nations and its resolutions, are anti-Israel.[73] Indeed, recent polls on the attitude of the Israeli public further reinforce this point, finding that Israeli human rights organizations that often rely on international norms are criticized for doing so and are also perceived by the public as anti-Israel.[74] Thus, despite Barak's explanation that "Israel is not an isolated island. She is a member of an international system, which has set out standards,"[75]—and even though some have suggested that the Court's shift to international norms should be viewed positively, as the Court's effort to protect Israel's democratic process both internally, by ensuring public debate, as well as externally, by reclaiming national sovereignty in light of and in opposition to the ongoing criticism against it[76]—the Court has been accused of acting for a selfish reason: the justices' (read Barak's) desire to increase their legitimacy in the eyes of other international players.[77]

Responses

The Court's activism has often received considerable interest, both locally and internationally. The evaluations of the decisions have been mixed, oftentimes reflecting the differences in the audience. On the international level, the decisions have certainly contributed to the Court's reputation as an independent and impartial body. They reinforced the Court's status as the protector of the "small citizen" and as an institution that does not fear challenging the government in its pursuit of justice.[78] Human rights organizations often celebrated the Court, praising individual rulings revolving around controversial issues (such as the "Torture case").[79] Moreover, a considerable body of scholarly literature has developed over the years defending the Court's legitimacy and its protection of individual liberties.[80]

As has been indicated throughout this chapter, however, these external enthusiastic responses were often not shared by those within Israeli society. Although the public's trust in the Court is still relatively high and exceeds the trust in the elected and political branches, it has certainly declined in the past decade.[81] Particularly since Barak's "constitutional revolution," the Court has also confronted escalating controversy from various sectors of Israeli society. On the one hand, the Court's "constitutional examination" and overreaching involvement in core political and public policy questions have attracted the wrath of disproportionately powerful minority groups, particularly the ultra-Orthodox group, when it ruled in ways that impact cherished religious values, such as conversion,[82] or political agreements that benefited them, such as the exemption of Yeshiva students from military service. Although the essence of democracy is that the majority's vote prevails, a political culture that allows minority parties to extract privileges in exchange for helping to create a governing coalition develops a sense of entitlement that puts such groups on a frequent collision course with a high court that seeks to protect everyone's equality under the law.[83] For this reason, mass marches and protests in front of the Court's building (mainly by the Jewish Orthodox groups) have taken place more than once when it delivered rulings relating to controversial religious matters. For example, the Court's 1997 ruling that the closure of the Bar-Ilan Street to traffic during prayers on Shabbat and Jewish holidays is illegal[84] was followed by protests of thousands of ultra-Orthodox citizens. The demonstrations often turned into violent confrontations with the police officers on the scene.[85]

Threats to the individual justices are also much more common and have prompted an increase in the Court security.[86] Criticism directed against particular justices, which historically was infrequent, is also increasingly voiced in newspapers and at public events as well as in Knesset hearings concerning key Court judgments or during the pre-judicial selection period.[87] For example, during the ultra-Orthodox demonstrations accompanying the Court's 1999 ruling (at variance with the previous Orthodox policy that the state has an obligation to register non-Orthodox conversions to Judaism carried out abroad[88]), the Court's justices were attacked as "enemies of Judaism" who issue "anti-Semitic" decisions.[89] The spiritual leader of the Sephardic-religious

Shas Party, Rabbi Ovadia Yosef, was also quoted describing the justices as "wicked, stubborn and rebellious," "empty-headed and reckless," and "the cause of all the world's torments."[90]

On the other hand, the Court's intervention in issues pertaining to the Occupied Territories and counterterrorism measures has raised a different democratic challenge, with criticism voiced by a majority of (Jewish) Israelis. Considering that questions of national security fall within the political and institutional responsibilities of the executive and that counterterrorism measures adopted by the government generally receive support by the Israeli public, the Court's activism in these areas make it vulnerable to the charge that it is invading the spheres of proper governmental action as a "lawmaker and an enforcer of public policies" rather than as simply a complementary body that interprets the law.[91] Furthermore, the delays associated with the judicial process leave many with the impression that the ability of the executive to immediately and strongly react to terrorist threats is at risk. It is a short logical step to the conclusion that the Court's rulings are compromising Israel's well-being and security.

The vulnerability of the judiciary in security matters is further exacerbated by the climate of national crisis that prevails as well as a few characteristics of the Israeli (Jewish) public itself. These factors include (1) the historical deference and high regard the public accords the military and its policies;[92] (2) the prevalent perception among Israelis that Palestinians are inherently part of the Arab group, that is, a *political* entity ultimately hoping for Israel's destruction and not just as persons with a distinct cultural identity;[93] (3) the opinion, held by most Israelis, that the conflict over the Occupied Territories is intractable,[94] hence leading the majority of the Israeli (Jewish) public to place a premium on national security and strength over democratic values and civil liberties;[95] and (4) the melting-pot characteristic of the population, leading to acute internal disagreements about the values that the Court should uphold.

In response, political factions dissatisfied with the Court have initiated intensive parliamentary discussions, calling for legislation to overturn the Court's unfavorable rulings. Following the Court's historic ruling in the Torture case,[96] for instance, approximately more than sixty Knesset members introduced a bill authorizing the General Security Service (GSS) to use physical pressure in interrogations (the bill was eventually dropped).[97] In other instances the Knesset's political reaction was more successful. After the Court's controversial decision in the Bargaining chips case, the Knesset enacted a law overruling the decision. Likewise, following the Court's decision about drafting Yeshiva students in 1998, the Knesset passed the Tal Law, which allows their exemption.

Simultaneously, human rights groups and scholars have criticized the Court by claiming that the Court has not gone far enough with its use of judicial review of governmental actions and Knesset legislation. They charge that the Court's guarantee of human rights has been much more limited than its reputation would suggest, pointing out that when overruling legislation was adopted (both for purely internal issues and for national security-counterterrorism measures), the Court has generally refrained from accepting subsequent petitions that challenged it, even if the new law stands in contrast to the very human rights which the Court's original decision aimed to protect.[98] Moreover, while instances of overruling legislation are few, at times the threat of such legislation is enough for the Court to reverse its own decision.[99] In the context of the Occupied Territories and counterterrorism measures, critics also emphasize that the overwhelming number of petitions that the Court decides upon is dismissed, suggesting that the Court's policy of "open doors" hasn't been translated into material resolutions;[100] that the Court's efforts to "adjust" norms to today's reality lead to tests that are too vague to be implemented;[101] and that generally, the Court's interpretation and use of the various international standards has been inaccurate at best and in complete conflict with the interpretation of most authoritative bodies at worst.[102] Overall, human rights organizations and advocates thus argue that the Court is more likely than not to adopt—and hence also legitimize—the governmental stance. As David Kretzmer's comprehensive study of the Court's jurisprudence in cases relating to the Occupied Territories has shown, in substantive matters "the jurisprudence of these decisions is blatantly government-minded," that is, adopting the least restrictive interpretation of state sovereignty (rather than promoting individual rights and freedoms), in effect allowing the authorities to deny human rights of Palestinian residents.[103] Thus, for instance, also when the Court accepted the petition in the *Beit Sourik* case, finding most of the challenged separation barrier route illegal,[104] it has refrained from answering the more basic questions concerning the case: the illegality of settlements under international humanitarian law and the impact of this illegality on the government's authority to construct the barrier in its entirety, although that is the primary cause of the human rights violations involving the Palestinian residents.[105] Given the latter observation, even human rights organizations within Israel increasingly question whether turning to the Court for relief is indeed the best venue to promote human rights.

In some cases, however, the attacks on the Supreme Court have gone beyond objections to individual rulings, scholarly objections, and discord from unsatisfied social sectors and political factions. Former minister of justice[106] Daniel Feldman, for example, has waged a campaign aimed at curtailing the Court's power.[107] Among other changes,[108] he has proposed (1) the creation of a new separate constitutional court with exclusive though limited jurisdiction to hear cases pertaining to the executive actions; (2) a substantial restriction on the Court's power of judicial review of Knesset legislation; (3) a suggestion to add "overriding mechanisms" to allow the Knesset to reenact laws that were deemed as invalid by the Court; and (4) the introduction of a politicized selection process for judges. While Feldman's proposals do not represent the first time such reforms have been introduced[109] and while they are generally unsuccessful so far,[110] these efforts certainly show the volatile dynamic that has developed around the Court's work. In fact, even though much of the intense criticism of the Court was voiced in response to Barak's proclamation of constitutional revolution, it has now become an almost expected and habitual reaction. Indeed, the ongoing attacks on the Court in the past decade have assumed an open, public, and vocal form. Moreover, as the justices themselves have defended the Court and publicly criticized both their detractors and the proposed reforms,[111] the political response has further intensified. Because the multiparty political system makes it very difficult to overrule a Court's decision, the only effective alternative for the political branches to resist the Court's ruling is by simply avoiding enforcement.[112]

Lessons

Drawing lessons from the experience of the Israeli Court to other judiciaries is not easy. As Ruth Gavison points out, the Court's activism is "not a case of 'good guys versus bad guys,' or progressive versus conservatives, or lawyers versus politicians, or judges versus others."[113] It is rather a question of how the normative and political systems in any given country play out, and whether the interaction among the various branches fits the particular society in question. Indeed, although the normative and political frameworks in the United States and Israel share some features (they are both democracies with a common law tradition that have three branches of governance, independent judiciaries with a Supreme Court), there are significant differences as well. The existence of an American written constitution with relatively rigid standards of procedure, the extent of politicization in U.S. judicial selection, and differing procedures for hearing cases in the two nations complicates the comparison. This comparison is rendered more difficult when one considers other dissimilar legal-political factors. Israel's developing legal culture, its polyarchal and dysfunctional political system, the military occupation, the ongoing security threat and, relatedly, the public's faith in the military's might and its distrust in the political institutions[114] have all created an environment that significantly differs from the United States—as well as from Israel's archetype model, the British system.

Nevertheless, there are a few interrelated lessons that can be learned from the experience of the Israeli Court about contemporary attacks on courts in democracies. One observation concerns the dynamics between courts and politics. In the American discourse, the politicization of the courts has often been attributed to the Supreme Court justices themselves, based on the assumption that they are political actors motivated by personal desires and external incentives to advance their preferred political and public policy agendas.[115] But it seems that today strategic political considerations are an inherent part of the judicial decision-making process. As Barak explained, "The dialogue [between the judiciary and its sister branches] seeks to assess the expected response of each governing branch to the act of another—how will the court respond to a challenged legislation, and how will the Parliament react to a constraining interpretation by the court?"[116]

In practice, then, the sources of tension between national courts and the political branches are beyond the justices themselves and their judicial selection process. They are rather the result of a built-in conflict about the meaning of democracy, particularly when the public is not pleased with the political branches. Although basic agreement about the specific democratic structure (parliamentary or presidential) and the principle of checks and balances among the three branches of governance in democracies exist, national courts and the political branches are in a (perhaps natural) clash on the actual content of the democracy. While the political branches argue for a democracy that is based on the public-political vote, the judiciary calls for something beyond the democratic structure. As Barak emphasized, the judiciary calls for the democratic spirit, human rights and natural justice—even when it contradicts the majority's vote.[117] The collision is all the more acute when the political power is not in the hands of a legitimate majority but rather was obtained by political manipulation of an already vulnerable system (as in the case of the religious parties in Israel and, in the eyes of many, also in the United States after the controversial election in 2000).[118] Even if a written constitution may mitigate some of the tensions, as it provides clearer rules for both political and judicial actions, it offers no solutions to governmental dysfunction. The tension between the political and judicial branches is then both initiated and fueled by the very same political system. In Israel, the Court's empowerment and its subsequent politicization would not have been possible had it not been for the government's inaction and paralysis, its tacit consent to the court's activism, and its active referral of political decisions that it could not resolve.[119] More broadly, then, the increase in attacks on judiciaries in democracies is the unavoidable product of the inherently contentious relationship between the judiciary and politics: dissatisfaction with the political branches leads to the empowerment of the courts, which in turn leads to the politicization of courts—and to attacks against them.

Another broad insight offered by this chapter concerns the relationship between national courts and the public and the issue of legitimacy. Although judges are required not to sway their rulings according to public opinion, there can be no doubt that a court's ability to function depends on its legitimacy. Consequently, court rulings commonly do not ignore (and at times openly rely upon) popular values and even call for public support, particularly when invalidating actions of the political branches. The difficulty courts face today, however, is that such legitimacy is hard to obtain—and retain. Part of the reason may be attributed to institutional factors (such as lengthy delays in securing a court ruling, as has been the case in Israel).[120] The more acute reason for the courts' loss of internal legitimacy, however, resides in the pluralist nature of large democracies in our time. States with multicultural social, religious, and political divisions do not always agree on even a shared set of values. Against this diverse and potentially divisive backdrop, when courts become involved in controversial issues of public policy, they are inherently viewed as taking a particular political side. This tension is particularly strong in the context of sustained crises that involve the court's curbing the demands of minorities who have gained political power beyond their actual political strength. While avoiding this hazard may not always be possible, the court's use of its power to pressure the government or to mitigate the clashing parties to reach a "settlement in the Court's shadow," that is, through informal mitigation of the conflict (rather than delivering a judicial decision) is one possible strategy for avoiding recrimination. This approach of avoiding a publicized conflict and its political resolution has worked well in the Israeli context, allowing the Court to evade additional acute attacks against it.[121]

My final observation about the broader implications of the Court's current criticism concerns the rise of transnational judicial dialogue. Scholars studying the phenomenon suggest that the participation of the courts in the development and implementation of international norms would place them in a better position to curb "executive unilateralism," particularly over difficult questions relating to human rights and counterterrorism measures.[122] The implicit assumption has been that the courts' referencing universal standards would pressure national political actors to act in ways that would not jeopardize their international legitimacy and reputation. This may indeed explain the use of transnational law in European countries: the supra-national system of the European Union provides a strong incentive to harmonize domestic standards with international ones to avoid embarrassing clashes among the member states.

Transnational judicial dialogue, however, may also explain judiciaries in Israel and the United States. With so much international criticism raised against Israel, the Court's reference to international norms buttresses its legitimacy. Such a move by the Court emphasizes the political branches' responsibility to uphold international commitments they have taken while also signifying to the world that the (relatively) newly established democracy can deliver justice.[123] Recent references by the U.S. Supreme Court to international norms in prominent cases (*Roper v. Simons*, 2005; *Hamdan v. Rumsfeld*, 2006) can be viewed in this light as well. Heightened international disapproval of U.S. policies, particularly since the 2003 invasion of Iraq, may have played a role in prompting the judiciary to invoke transnational legal standards as a step to regain the international reputation that had been damaged.

In practice, however, the courts' participation in this dialogue has increased their vulnerability to attacks—on all fronts. If they chose to endorse the universal spirit of international norms, they risk their political and public legitimacy from within. The increasing dialogue of judiciaries across the world is part of a larger contemporary international discussion within the legal community, but it is largely unknown and of little interest to the general public, whose values are commonly still nationally and locally oriented. Simultaneously, in many cases courts will not be in a position to partake genuinely in international dialogue. Justices are, after all, part of the society in which they function, and particularly during national crises, their hands are tied. Yet if they attempt to use international norms to support governmental or popular policies unjustly, they risk forfeiting their international legitimacy—and the very essence of the democratic values they are in charge of protecting. The dilemma faced by judiciaries in contemporary democracies is thus that they are inherently positioned at a crossroads, yet whichever path they take is likely to raise an uproar.

chapter 9

Self-Regulation and an Independent Judiciary

Scott E. Gant

As Scott Gant notes, much scholarly and popular discussion of judicial independence focuses on potential "external" threats, such as those posed by elected officials or the public. The next two chapters assume a different stance, considering distinct ways in which courts might contribute to (or possibly jeopardize) their own institutional strength and autonomy. Gant explores "self-regulation" of the courts, that is, how judges monitor and sanction the behavior of their peers, especially through the provisions of the Judicial Conduct and Disability Act. In addition to assessing how the Act has worked in practice, he considers its possible abuses and the conditions under which the Act might run afoul of the Constitution. Overall he praises the Act for providing a check on possible abuses of judicial power while serving the cause of independence as well as important political goals of the executive and legislative branches.

When we discuss an independent judiciary, we typically consider the relationship of the judiciary to others—to legislators, to executive branch officials, and even to the public. The rest of this book focuses on judicial independence from influences, pressures, and threats *outside* the judiciary. This chapter, however, focuses on a significant but rarely examined aspect of the issue of judicial independence: self-regulation of the judiciary.

At first blush, self-regulation of the judiciary may seem to have little to do with judicial independence. Yet consideration of both the descriptive and normative dimensions of judicial independence suggests that any well-developed understanding of the issue requires assessment of the role judges play in investigating—and sometimes punishing—their own colleagues on the bench.

But before turning to the issue of judicial self-regulation, a brief discussion about a particular aspect of judicial independence is warranted. When we consider (and promote) judicial independence, are we discussing the independence of individual judges or only the independence of the judiciary as a whole? For reasons that should be clear by the end of this chapter, examining self-regulation of the judiciary is necessary for any thorough assessment of either conception of judicial independence. But if judicial independence concerns the relationship not only of the judiciary as a whole to external pressures but also of individual judges, then self-regulation becomes even more important.

Like former Supreme Court Justice Sandra Day O'Connor, I embrace the view that judicial independence "has both individual and institutional aspects." As Justice O'Connor recently wrote, "[A]n independent judiciary requires both that individual judges are independent in the exercise of their powers, and that the judiciary as a whole is independent."[1] With that in mind, we turn our attention to the current system by which federal judges monitor and discipline one another.[2]

The Current System of Judicial Self-Regulation

For the past three decades, the centerpiece of self-regulation of the federal judiciary has been a statute called the Judicial Conduct and Disability Act of 1980.[3] The Act establishes procedures for the filing and investigation of complaints against federal judges (other than Supreme Court Justices) for having engaged in conduct "prejudicial to the effective and expeditious administration of the business of the courts."[4] Complaints are reviewed initially by the chief judge of the federal circuit court of appeals in whose jurisdiction the judge in question serves. The chief judge may terminate a complaint or appoint a special committee of judges to investigate the complaint further and then refer it to the circuit's judicial council, comprised of several judges.[5]

Complaints may be dismissed on numerous grounds, including that they lack factual basis or that they relate to the merits of the case from which the complaint arises and therefore can be addressed through the appeals process.[6] Complaints may also be dismissed if appropriate corrective action has been taken, or if action is unnecessary due to intervening events.[7]

When a complaint is deemed to have merit, the Act empowers the judicial councils, as well as the Judicial Conference of the United States,[8] to respond by taking "such action as is appropriate to assure the effective and expeditious administration of the business of the courts."[9] The Act places no express limitation on the nature of those actions, other than providing that "[u]nder no circumstances may the judicial council order removal from office of any [Article III] judge appointed to hold office during good behavior."[10] The Act does, however, describe "possible actions" that might be taken to discipline a judge, including private and public censures and reprimands and orders "on a temporary basis for a time certain, [that] no further cases be assigned to the judge whose conduct is the subject of a complaint."

The Act's complaint procedures are frequently invoked. During the past thirty years, many thousands of complaints against federal judges have been initiated under the statute, with more than eight thousand filed during the ten-year period from October 1, 1999, through September 30, 2009.[11] The subjects of the complaints vary, but most set forth allegations concerning prejudice or bias, abuse of judicial power, corruption, undue delay in rendering decisions, incompetence, conflicts of interest, mental disability, physical disability, or demeanor.

While complaints are frequent, all but a few are dismissed and result in no disciplinary action. For example, during that ten-year period, the more than eight thousand complaints resulted in six public censures, one private censure, and three instances in which some other disciplinary action was undertaken in response to a complaint.

Notwithstanding that few complaints against federal judges have resulted in sanctions, actions involving two judges were vigorously contested by the judges and resulted in lawsuits challenging use of the Act to investigate and punish those judges. The constitutional challenges raised in those lawsuits will be discussed in detail later in this chapter.

The first of those cases involved Alcee Hastings, then a judge on the United States District Court for the Southern District of Florida. In December 1981, Hastings had been indicted by a federal grand jury for conspiring to solicit and accept money in return for taking certain actions as a federal judge. While Hastings was eventually acquitted of the criminal charges, a complaint against him was filed by two fellow judges under the procedures of the Act.[12] The complaint's most serious allegation was that Hastings conspired to obtain a bribe in exchange for an official judicial act, but others alleged he had exploited his judicial position by accepting financial donations from lawyers and others to pay for costs incurred in the criminal case against him and that he had "completely abdicated and delegated" his decisionmaking authority to his law clerk.[13] Upon investigating the allegations, the Judicial Council of the United States Court of Appeals for the Eleventh Circuit determined that

Hastings may have committed impeachable offenses and certified this finding to the Judicial Conference of the United States. The Judicial Conference concurred in this assessment and certified its determination to the House of Representatives, which impeached Hastings on August 3, 1988, on charges of perjury and conspiring to solicit a bribe. Hastings was then convicted by the Senate and removed from office on October 20, 1989.[14] Hastings subsequently ran for Congress and won a seat in the House of Representatives, where he continues to serve.

The second of the cases involved John McBryde, a judge on the United States District Court for the Northern District of Texas. Following a two-year investigation, in 1997 the Judicial Council of the United States Court of Appeals for the Fifth Circuit concluded that McBryde had "engaged for a number of years in a pattern of abusive behavior." As a sanction, the Judicial Council reprimanded McBryde, ordered that no new cases be assigned to him for one year, and disqualified him from participating in cases involving certain attorneys for three years. McBryde filed a lawsuit and otherwise challenged the propriety of those sanctions but did not succeed in having them overturned. He nevertheless remained on the bench and maintains his office as a federal judge.

More recently, three sets of enforcement actions under the Act have garnered considerable public attention. One case involved Judge G. Thomas Porteous of the United States District Court for the Eastern District of Louisiana, who in 2008 was publicly reprimanded and suspended from new case assignments for two years, after the Judicial Council of the United States Court of Appeals for the Fifth Circuit concluded that Porteous had "repeatedly committed perjury" and had "violated several criminal statutes and ethical canons."[15] The House of Representatives impeached Porteous on March 11, 2010, and impeachment proceedings in the Senate were pending at the time this chapter was finalized for publication. Another case involved Judge Samuel B. Kent of the United States District Court for the Southern District of Texas, who pleaded guilty to a charge of obstruction of justice for interfering with the investigation of sexual abuse allegations against him. After Kent was sentenced, on May 27, 2009, the Judicial Council of the United States Court of Appeals for the Fifth Circuit determined that he had "engaged in conduct which constitutes one or more grounds for impeachment under Article II of the Constitution" and certified its determination to the Judicial Conference.[16] The Judicial Conference promptly agreed and referred the matter to the House of Representatives on June 9, 2009, which impeached Kent on June 19, 2009.[17] A third high-profile case involved Judge Manuel Real of the United States District Court for the Central District of California. Real was reprimanded following a finding of several instances of misconduct; during 2006, the House of Representatives held proceedings to consider possible impeachment of Real.[18] Although Real was not removed from office, he continues to be a source of considerable controversy.

The Constitutionality of Judicial Self-Regulation

With the Judicial Conduct and Disability Act, Congress has conferred on the federal judiciary the authority to investigate fellow judges and take "such action as is appropriate to assure the effective and expeditious administration of the business of the courts."[19] While the judges vested with the responsibility for exercising these powers have acted with considerable restraint—too much restraint in the eyes of some—there are legitimate questions about whether the arrangement is constitutional.

Indeed, during the debates over the legislation that led to the Act, some members of Congress voiced concerns about its constitutionality.[20] As one current federal appeals court judge has observed about the Act, it is "highly controversial and viewed by some as an unconstitutional encroachment on Article III independence."[21]

Before we proceed to examine the relationship between judicial self-regulation and judicial independence, we should consider whether the United States Constitution permits federal judges to investigate and punish one another, and whether there are constitutional limits on the nature of the oversight or the sanctions which might be imposed.

Article III of the Constitution provides that U.S. judges "shall hold their Offices during good behavior" and further provides that their compensation "shall not be diminished during their Continuance in Office."[22] These provisions are sometimes referred to as the "Tenure Clause" and the "Compensation Clause," respectively.

The Tenure Clause is generally interpreted to mean that impeachment and conviction is the only method by which a U.S. judge can be removed from office.[23] The Compensation Clause clearly places some limits on the kinds of financial sanctions that can be imposed on a federal judge. Does the Judicial Conduct and Disability Act run afoul of either provision?

The Act describes "possible actions" that might be taken to discipline a judge, including both private and public censures and reprimands. There is nothing about such sanctions that conflicts with either the Tenure Clause or the Compensation Clause of Article III.

Another "possible action" permitted under the Act is ordering "on a temporary basis for a time certain, [that] no further cases be assigned to the judge whose conduct is the subject of a complaint." In theory, if long enough, a suspension of new case assignments might be tantamount to "removal" from office, which arguably can only be achieved through the procedure specified in the Constitution.[24] No suspension thus far imposed under the authority of the Act, however, has come close to effective removal.

As discussed above, in addition to specifically described sanctions the Act also gives judicial councils and the Judicial Conference significant latitude in fashioning sanctions, permitting them to take "such action as is appropriate to assure the effective and expeditious administration of the business of the courts."[25] Seemingly mindful of the Constitution's Tenure Clause, this broad grant of authority is tempered by the Act's mandate that "[u]nder no circumstances may the judicial council order removal from office of any [Article III] judge appointed to hold office during good behavior."[26] Nevertheless, there remains the possibility that actions taken to implement the Act, or the powers conferred by it, may be inconsistent with the Tenure Clause or Compensation Clause.

The Constitution is generally viewed as guaranteeing an independent judiciary through specific provisions (such as the Tenure and Compensation Clauses) as well through is its overall design establishing three coequal braches of government.[27] While part of the rationale for vesting the judiciary with responsibility for regulating itself is to *avoid* concerns about impinging on the independence of the judiciary, the Act and its implementation are subject to challenge as inconsistent with this constitutional requirement on the grounds that they interfere with the independence of individual judges. In fact, the constitutionality of the Act was called into question on precisely such grounds by both Judge Hastings and Judge McBryde in the course of challenging the application of the Act to their conduct.

In response to investigation of his conduct, Judge Hastings asserted numerous constitutional challenges to the Act itself as well as to its specific application to him.[28] Among other things, he argued that the investigatory scheme established by the statute unconstitutionally intrudes on the independence of judges to engage in free and uninhibited decisionmaking, that it violates separation of powers principles established by the Constitution, and that application of the Act to him violated the Constitution's Compensation Clause by forcing him to spend his own funds to defend himself against the investigation undertaken under authority of the statute.

Two separate courts of appeals—the United States Court of Appeals for the Eleventh Circuit and the United States Court of Appeals for the District of Columbia Circuit—reviewed and ultimately rejected (or declined to rule on) each of Hastings's various constitutional claims regarding the Act.[29] In so doing, those courts made several noteworthy observations that bear on the relationship of the Act to judicial independence.

For example, with respect to Hastings's claim that the complaint and investigatory procedures authorized by the Act impermissibly impinged his independence as a federal judge, the Eleventh Circuit concluded that they did not, in part because "the fact that it places the investigation, and determination of what actions to take, entirely within the hands of judicial colleagues makes it likely that the rightful independence of the complained-against judge, especially in the area of decision-making, will be accorded maximum respect."[30] However, the Eleventh Circuit also noted that "court management powers exercised by a judge's colleagues could be unconstitutional if they amounted to an undue burden upon the independence of an individual judge."[31] This statement is significant not only because it acknowledges that, in theory, the Act could be applied in a way that rendered it unconstitutional but also because it accepts the idea that judicial independence has both "individual and institutional aspects," as discussed earlier.

The Eleventh Circuit also evaluated some of the "possible" sanctions specifically mentioned in the Act. Not surprisingly, the Court appeared most concerned with the prospect that a judge could be stripped of case assignments, observing, "this sanction presents a difficult constitutional issue." Yet the Court concluded that it would not decide that question, because Hastings had not been the subject of such a sanction, and "proper adjudication" of its legitimacy must await its "actual imposition."[32]

Regarding Hastings's argument that the Act violates the Compensation Clause by failing to provide for reimbursement of costs incurred by a judge defending against complaints initiated under the Act, the Court of Appeals for the District of Columbia Circuit did not reject the argument out of hand. Instead, it determined the legal issue presented was not ready for consideration, because Hastings had failed to exhaust all of his options in seeking reimbursement—thereby leaving for another day consideration of whether the Act might actually violate the Compensation Clause.[33]

As for McBryde, after the Judicial Council of the United States Court of Appeals for the Fifth Circuit ordered that no new cases be assigned to him for one year and disqualified him from participating in cases involving certain attorneys for three years, he filed a lawsuit in federal court challenging the constitutionality of the Act on numerous grounds. McBryde's contentions included that the Act violated separation of powers principles as well as the free speech and due process provisions of the Constitution.[34] With one exception, both a federal district court and court of appeals rejected McBryde's constitutional challenges to the Act.[35]

The trial court first addressed McBryde's argument that the Act is unconstitutional on its face, separate and apart from the particular application to him—a "facial" challenge, as such challenges are known. The Court turned back this claim, rejecting his argument that "judge-on-judge discipline is inherently unconstitutional" or is otherwise inconsistent with separation of powers principles. The Court also rejected McBryde's arguments that the Act was being applied to him in an unconstitutional manner, with one exception: the Court agreed that a confidentiality clause in the statute barring the disclosure of all material related to the proceedings against McBryde violated his rights to free speech and expression under the First Amendment.[36]

On appeal of that ruling, the United States Court of Appeals for the District of Columbia also rejected McBryde's arguments that the Act is facially unconstitutional. First, it rejected his contention that the impeachment provisions of the Constitution preclude all other methods for disciplining judges. It then rejected his assertion that principles of judicial independence foreclose disciplining judges for conduct related in any way to their activities on the bench. As for McBryde's other arguments that the Act was being applied to him in an unconstitutional manner, the Court declined to address those, concluding the Act itself precludes judicial review of those claims except through the procedures outlined in the Act itself.[37]

McBryde sought further review by the Supreme Court, and the U.S. Department of Justice filed a brief urging the Court to decline his request. In that brief, the Justice Department argued that the "the Act does not on its face violate constitutional principles of judicial independence." The brief went further, seemingly taking issue with the notion that principles of judicial independence are implicated by judicial oversight of individual judges, claiming, "[t]hat premise is fundamentally at odds with the structure of Article III it-self," while also contending that "[n]othing in the text, history or structure of the Impeachment Clauses [of the Constitution] suggests an intent to immu-nize federal judges from all discipline for misconduct not rising to the level of an impeachable offense."[38]

As it had with Judge Hastings's requests for review, the Supreme Court declined to hear Judge McBryde's constitutional challenges to the Act.[39] But nearly four decades ago, ten years before the passage of the Judicial Conduct and Disability Act, the high court did confront an important case in which a sitting federal judge vigorously challenged the authority of his colleagues to regulate his activities.

Stephen S. Chandler served as a judge on the United States District Court for the Western District of Oklahoma from 1943 to 1989, including as chief judge of that court from 1956 to 1969.[40] In December 1965, after what the Su-preme Court described as a "long history of controversy" between Chandler and the Judicial Council of the United States Court of Appeals for the Tenth Circuit (which covers Oklahoma), the Judicial Council issued an order direct-ing that "until further order of the Judicial Council, [Chandler] take no action whatsoever in any case or proceeding now or hereafter pending in the United States District Court for the Western District of Oklahoma; that all cases and proceedings now assigned to or pending before him shall be reassigned to and among other judges of said court; and that until the further order of the Ju-dicial Council no cases or proceedings filed or instituted in the United States District Court for the Western District of Oklahoma shall be assigned to him for any reason whatsoever."[41] Chandler asked the Supreme Court to intervene. The Court described his petition as essentially challenging "all orders of the Judicial Council relating to assignment of cases in the Western District of Oklahoma as fixing conditions on the exercise of his constitutional powers as a judge."[42]

Chandler's request for Supreme Court intervention was extensively briefed and argued before the Court. As a formal matter, the Court declined to review the case, with a majority of the Justices deciding not to grant him permission to file a petition for review on the merits of his claims. But the case deeply divided the Court, and the opinions of the justices about whether to review the case contain numerous statements relevant to consideration of the con-stitutionality of judicial self-regulation.

For instance, delivering the opinion of the Court, Chief Justice Warren Burger explained that "[w]hether the action taken by the Council with respect to the division of business in Judge Chandler's district falls to one side or the other of the line defining the maximum permissible intervention consistent with the constitutional requirement of judicial independence is the ultimate question on which review is sought in the petition now before us." While not made in the context of issuing a broader ruling, this statement by the Court's majority clearly suggests that some level of interference with the activities of an individual federal judge may render those actions unconstitutional.[43]

The majority's decision declining review triggered two vigorous dissenting opinions—one from Justice William O. Douglas and the other from Justice Hugo Black (each joined the opinion of the other)—which viewed skeptically the idea that the Constitution permits judges to investigate and discipline one another. For instance, Justice Douglas wrote:

> Once a federal judge is confirmed by the Senate and takes his oath, he is independent of every other judge. He commonly works with other federal judges who are likewise sovereign. But neither one alone nor any number banded together can act as censor and place sanctions on him. Under the Constitution the only leverage that can be asserted against him is impeachment, where pursuant to a resolution passed by the House, he is tried by the Senate, sitting as a jury. Art. I, s 2 and s 3. . . . What the Judicial Council did when it ordered [Judge Chandler] to "take no action whatsoever in any case or proceeding now or hereafter pending" in his court was to do what only the Court of Impeachment can do. . . . [T]here is no power under our Constitution for one group of federal judges to censor or discipline any federal judge and no power to declare him inefficient and strip him of his power to act as a judge.
>
> * * *
>
> The mood of some federal judges is opposed to this view and they are active in attempting to make all federal judges walk in some uniform step. What has happened to petitioner is not a rare instance; it has happened to other federal judges who have had perhaps a more libertarian approach to the Bill of Rights than their brethren. The result is that the nonconformist has suffered greatly at the hands of his fellow judges.
>
> * * *
>
> It is time that an end be put to these efforts of federal judges to ride herd on other federal judges. This is a form of "hazing" having no place under the Constitution. Federal judges are entitled, like other people, to the full freedom of the First Amendment. If they break a law, they can be prosecuted.

If they become corrupt or sit in cases in which they have a personal or family stake, they can be impeached by Congress. But I search the Constitution in vain for any power of surveillance that other federal judges have over those aberrations. Some of the idiosyncrasies may be displeasing to those who walk in more measured, conservative steps. But those idiosyncrasies can be of no possible constitutional concern to other federal judges.[44]

In addition to joining Justice Douglas's opinion, Justice Black observed: "Judge Chandler, duly appointed, duly confirmed, and never impeached by the Congress, has been barred from doing his work. . . . This case must be viewed for what it is—a long history of harassment of Judge Chandler by other judges who somehow feel he is 'unfit' to hold office."[45] Contending that "Judge Chandler, like every other federal judge" is "subject to removal from office only by the constitutionally prescribed mode of impeachment," Black concluded by observing:

> The wise authors of our Constitution provided for judicial independence because they were familiar with history; they knew that judges of the past—good, patriotic judges—had occasionally lost not only their offices but had also sometimes lost their freedom and their heads because of the actions and decrees of other judges. They were determined that no such things should happen here. But it appears that the language they used and the protections they thought they had created are not sufficient to protect our judges from the contrived intricacies used by the judges of the Tenth Circuit and this Court to uphold what has happened to Judge Chandler in this case. I fear that unless the actions taken by the Judicial Council in this case are in some way repudiated, the hope for an independent judiciary will prove to have been no more than an evanescent dream.[46]

While expressed in the context of dissenting opinions, the views of Justices Douglas and Black demonstrate the gravity of constitutional questions raised by at least some forms of judicial self-regulation.[47] To be sure, the actions taken against Judge Chandler are as severe as any sanction imposed against a fellow judge during the three decades since the Act has been in effect. But the Act permits precisely the kinds of limitations on the independence of a single federal judge that Chandler challenged, and Justices Douglas and Black found impermissible.[48]

When one considers the Supreme Court's observations in the Chandler case as well as the court rulings on the constitutional challenges to the Act

brought by Judge Hastings and Judge McBryde, it appears exceedingly unlikely that any court will find the Act facially unconstitutional.[49] While there
remains the prospect that the Act could be applied in an unconstitutional
manner (and threaten the independence of an individual judge) in the context of a specific proceeding, there is little reason to think that the self-regulatory framework established by Congress is susceptible to dismantling on the
ground that it violates the Constitution.[50]

Implications of Judicial Self-Regulation for Judicial Independence

Before the Judicial Conduct and Disability Act of 1980, the only formal
mechanism for investigating and addressing judicial misconduct was the congressional impeachment process.[51] Those procedures were rarely used, however. In the nearly two centuries preceding the Act, only ten federal judges
were impeached by the U.S. House of Representatives, and none after 1936.
Of those ten federal judges impeached by the House, four were subsequently
acquitted by the Senate. Of the six others, four were convicted and thereby
removed from office, one resigned, and one had the impeachment proceedings dismissed.[52]

While the federal judiciary is generally filled with extraordinarily talented
and hardworking judges, it is difficult to deny that some mechanism for investigating and addressing the infrequent instances of judicial misconduct is
needed. Perhaps more significant, however, is that we live in an age and political culture that favors tangible systems of accountability—reflected in the
proliferation of inspectors general, commissions, and other permanent and
ad hoc mechanisms for investigating shortcomings in the performance of government officials. It is unrealistic to expect we could move from the system
laid out in the Act to one in which the federal judiciary would be left entirely
to itself to address (or ignore) as it sees fit improper conduct by judges.

In view of these observations, our current system of judicial self-regulation,
although imposed by Congress, should be viewed as promoting, not threatening, judicial independence. As one commentator aptly observed, "[a]lthough
the Act creates a risk that particular chief judges and judicial councils might
impermissibly use their discretionary powers to chill the decisional independence of individual judges . . . the risk is not great."[53] At the same time, the
independence of the federal judiciary as a whole is considerably advanced by

a system in which judges are solely responsible for investigating and punishing misconduct from within their ranks, even under a framework imposed upon the judiciary by Congress.

While I offer no view here about the judiciary's performance policing itself, some critics charge it has weakly enforced judicial misconduct standards.[54] Of course, this view matters most when it is held by members of Congress. In fact, it was criticism from Congress about the way in which the Act was being implemented, and the suggestion that Congress might reassess "whether the judiciary should continue to enjoy delegated authority to investigate and discipline itself," that led Chief Justice William Rehnquist in 2004 to appoint an ad hoc committee to examine the statute's implementation.[55]

The Judicial Conduct and Disability Act Study Committee assembled by Rehnquist issued a report in 2006.[56] As the Committee described its task, "[t]he basic question presented is whether the judiciary, in implementing the Act, has failed to apply the Act strictly as Congress intended, thereby engaging in institutional favoritism." To answer that question, among other things, the Committee reviewed a sample of complaints filed and sought to reach its own conclusions about whether the complaints had been handled properly. Having carried out its study, the Committee identified a number of "problematic dispositions," where complaints were terminated without an adequate investigation. While the Committee observed that overall, 2 to 3 percent of terminations were "problematic," it found the rate to be nearly 30 percent when examining high-visibility complaints.[57]

Perhaps mindful of these findings as well as of the congressional criticism that contributed to the Committee's formation, the Judicial Conference responded to some of the Report's recommendations by enacting a comprehensive set of guidelines for investigations and proceedings under the Act.[58] And, while time will tell, there is anecdotal evidence of more vigorous investigation and enforcement under the Act during the past several years. The judiciary's responses to congressional dissatisfaction with its enforcement efforts can be viewed as a kind of dialogue in which the legislature pressures the judiciary to more actively police itself—or risk that Congress will strip judges of some of their autonomy, as some have suggested through proposals for the appointment of an inspector general for the federal courts.[59]

As one would expect, the judiciary understands the relationship between effective self-policing and the preservation of judicial independence. To see this, one need look no further than Canon 1 of the Code of Conduct for United

States Judges,[60] which provides: "An independent and honorable judiciary is indispensable to justice in our society. A judge should maintain and enforce high standards of conduct and should personally observe those standards, *so that* the integrity and *independence of the judiciary may be preserved*. The provisions of this Code should be construed and applied to further that objective."[61]

Of course, the current system of judicial self-regulation has political benefits for the political branches—particularly for Congress. By leaving the investigation and punishment of judicial misconduct short of impeachable offenses in the hands of judges, political actors liberated themselves from such responsibilities. Under the existing system, members of Congress are free to complain about the conduct of judges without much risk they will be expected to do anything about it, except in extreme cases possibly warranting impeachment and removal from office. In fact, members of Congress can avail themselves (and have) of the Act's procedures, by filing a complaint against a sitting federal judge. For example, two members of Congress filed a complaint in May 2002 alleging that a judge had revealed to the press, on the eve of Vice President Gore's nomination for the president in 2000, that the Whitewater Independent Counsel had impaneled a grand jury to investigate President Clinton.[62] In another instance, fifteen members of Congress filed a complaint against a federal judge for comments during a legal society meeting, at which the judge "compared the means by which President Bush attained the presidency in 2000 to how Mussolini and Hitler had assumed power, and stated that American democracy should reassert itself by defeating President Bush in 2004."[63]

Self-regulation of the judiciary also serves an important mutual need of the judiciary and Congress: avoiding interbranch conflict. Were Congress or some congressionally created agency charged with investigating judges and authorized to impose sanctions for perceived misconduct, this would give rise to serious separation of powers concerns and risk generating considerable tension between those branches of government. With the Act, Congress has largely (and wisely) removed itself from the business of disciplining federal judges, while retaining for itself the power to take the ultimate step of removing a judge from office. Those interested in preserving an independent judiciary should hope that Congress maintains its view that this is a desirable arrangement and that both Congress and the judiciary act to ensure its continued political viability.

chapter 10

Judicial Credibility

Louis Fisher

Several chapters in this book have concluded that many of today's challenges to courts represent unsurprising and even healthy outgrowths of our democratic and separation of powers systems. While agreeing, Louis Fisher also argues that our current debates about the judiciary, and the U.S. Supreme Court in particular, are largely misguided and overly deferential to the Court's purported position as our supreme expositor of constitutional law. Instead, we need reinvigorated and better criticism of the judiciary, focusing on the ways in which U.S. courts justify (or fail to justify) their rulings, the extent to which the judges take on policy questions better left to lawmakers, and the degree to which the Court's rulings are based on constitutional text and history or simply its own invented doctrines. This chapter serves as a guide to citizens and legislators, providing them with a rationale and focus in challenging judicial decisions, but also to judges, offering a set of reflections on how courts can improve the credibility of their decisions and, consequently, their role in securing the rule of law.

Critiques of the Supreme Court have typically focused on questions of legitimacy—how the Court's decisions threaten the democratic character of the American polity. Objections are periodically leveled at unelected justices making national policy or blocking the lawmaking efforts of presidents and members of Congress. That should not be the central issue. The Court was created by the Constitution and, as several chapters in this volume have argued, it is an essential part of the system of limited government and checks and balances. The fundamental issue is not democratic legitimacy but how well the Court performs its constitutional task. When the Court gets into trouble, it does so not because it invalidates a congressional or presidential action but because its arguments lack credibility.

The Court justifies its existence and institutional independence largely through its reasoning process. Its decisions must build from acceptable premises to reach plausible conclusions. Decisions that are mere edicts or assertions anchored in vague suppositions are not credible. Brief per curiam decisions, shorn of legal reasoning, also do institutional damage to the Court, as with the Nazi Saboteur Case of 1942.[1] These decisions offend and undermine judicial authority. When the Court fails to make a persuasive case to elected officials and the public, it is seen as acting in an arbitrary and capricious manner. When it did so in the past, it was only a matter of time before the elected branches would prevail, as they did with the decades-long fight over child labor legislation from 1916 to 1941, as we shall see.

The issue of judicial credibility today is complicated and deepened by several new factors. First, presidents and lawmakers have gotten in the habit of regarding judicial rulings as somehow final on the meaning of the Constitution, unless the Court itself decides to change its mind. This claim of judicial finality had been asserted in the past but was never ingrained or broadly accepted until recently. It is increasingly the practice, unfortunately, because of a second development. Law professors, political scientists, and historians have had a pattern of teaching their students that the Court is the final word on the meaning of the Constitution. What is taught is not the Constitution or core American values but hundreds and hundreds of court cases, many of them having scant connection either to constitutional text or the framers' intent. Little is said in these classes about courts being reversed by the political branches or courts being but one participant in a national, ongoing dialogue about constitutional meaning and the place of the Constitution in our lives. We have reached the point where presidents and lawmakers might initially express objections to a ruling but will then immediately bless the doctrine that the Constitution is what judges say it is. This is a new and disturbing development not only for the democratic process but for constitutional government as well. It eliminates the national dialogue that keeps courts in check while also making them a credible part of government. Justices of the Supreme Court are increasingly in the habit of not interpreting a constitutional provision directly but in interpreting what the Court itself said at some earlier date. The legal dispute is not over constitutional values but over highly complex and abstract judicially created "rules" and "standards." Some of these judicial substitutes will be examined later in the chapter.

This increasingly hypertechnical conversation between judges and attorneys, with few observers quite sure what is being said or meant, alienates the public and elected officials. Judges are seen as no longer functioning within a system of three branches but spinning off on their own, presuming to be somehow independent of and superior to government. As will be explained in this chapter, the Court has done that before and has paid a price, eventually brought back to earth as one of many participants helping to form and protect constitutional values. If judges now have their own vocabulary, including such words as "congruence" and "proportionality,"[2] they lose touch with the public and cannot be a credible or respected source of authority.

Judicial Deference to Elected Officials

To what extent should federal courts defer to the constitutional judgments of Congress and presidents? No institution of government is permitted to act in an arbitrary or unconstitutional manner. Each official of the three branches takes an oath to support and defend the Constitution. If a bill passes through both houses of Congress and becomes law, there is a presumption that elected officials have acted within their assigned powers. What burden should apply to federal judges to overcome that presumption and invalidate a statutory provision?

For our first few years under the Constitution, Justices of the Supreme Court were uncertain whether they had any authority to invalidate a constitutional statute. No such authority appears in the Constitution. In *Hylton v. United States* (1796), the Court upheld the constitutionality of a congressional statute that imposed a tax on carriages. If the Court could sustain the constitutionality of a statute, presumably it could strike one down. Yet the Justices proceeded cautiously. Justice Samuel Chase said it was unnecessary "*at this time,* for me to determine, whether this court, *constitutionally* possesses the power to declare an act of Congress void . . . but if the court have such power, I am free to declare, that I will never exercise it, *but in a very clear case.*"[3] A "very clear case" would support judicial invalidation of congressional statutes that transgress textual provisions in the Constitution. Holding to such limits would promote both judicial legitimacy and credibility.

Not until *Marbury v. Madison* (1803) did the Court invalidate statutory language enacted by Congress, and even here the Court was relatively restrained in its claims. This case continues to be woefully misread by professors and judges to assert final judicial authority in declaring the meaning of the Constitution. The author of the decision, Chief Justice John Marshall, never advanced the doctrine of judicial supremacy. It would have been political suicide to make such a claim in 1803, when Jeffersonians controlled Congress and the White House and were itching to impeach and remove Federalist judges. Jeffersonians had already impeached and removed District Judge John Pickering and had begun impeachment proceedings against Justice Chase. Had they been successful with that effort, they might have next turned to Marshall.

It was in this tenuous period that Marshall wrote to Chase on January 23, 1805, stating that if Congress disagreed with decisions by federal courts, it was not necessary to resort to the extreme sanction of impeachment. It was sufficient to pass legislation overriding a judicial ruling. Marshall was trying to avoid a political confrontation he knew he could not win. He told Chase: "I think the modern doctrine of impeachment should yield to an appellate jurisdiction in the legislature. A reversal of those legal opinions deemed unsound by the legislature would certainly better comport with the mildness of our character than [would] a removal of the Judge who has rendered them unknowing of his fault."[4] Less than two years after writing the *Marbury* decision, Marshall in this private letter implicitly acknowledged the significant role of the legislature in shaping constitutional law.

Marshall's modest position in *Marbury* and in subsequent writings has been replaced today by the claim that the Court speaks the final word on constitutional meaning and that the other branches and the public must accept judicial primacy. No such doctrine can be found in Marshall's decisions as a whole or even in the threadbare sentence so often cited: "It is emphatically the province and duty of the judicial department to say what the law is."[5] Read that as often as you like and you will find no basis for judiciary supremacy. Trimmed to its essentials, Marshall announced that courts decide cases, which is a truism. He did not say that courts necessarily have the final say on issues of public policy or constitutional meaning. One can easily rewrite the sentence to produce another truism: "It is emphatically the province and duty of the legislative department to say what the law is." Obviously the president also has a good deal to say on what the law is.[6]

In his long history on the Court, from 1801 to 1835, Marshall only on this single occasion struck down a congressional statute, and he did so to sidestep political and institutional embarrassment. He knew that if he issued a writ of mandamus, as authorized by statute, requiring the Jefferson administration to deliver the judicial commission to Mr. Marbury, neither President Jefferson nor Secretary of State James Madison would comply. To protect his branch and create some breathing room, Marshall held that section of the statute unconstitutional, circumventing the threat of noncompliance.[7] His next three decades as Chief Justice were devoted to two principal themes:

sustaining congressional control over the national economy (through the Commerce Clause and the creation of the U.S. Bank) and asserting federal judicial authority over the states.[8]

The dispute over the U.S. Bank underscores how the meaning of the Constitution depended not only on judicial rulings but on independent assessments by presidents and members of Congress. With regard to the Bank, President Andrew Jackson made it clear that he was not limited by constitutional interpretations issued by the judiciary or by legislative decisions reached by Congress. He could, and did, assert his own independent judgment. Congress had created a national bank in 1791. Over the years, other presidents and Congresses would reaffirm the validity of the Bank. In *McCulloch v. Maryland* (1819), the Court upheld its constitutionality.[9] When a bill reauthorizing the Bank was presented to President Jackson, he was under pressure to sign it because Congress, previous presidents, and the Court had found it to be constitutional.

In his memorable veto message, Jackson insisted that each branch of government was entitled to decide for itself what was authorized by the Constitution: "The Congress, the Executive, and the Court must each for itself be guided by its own opinion of the Constitution. Each public officer who takes an oath to support the Constitution swears that he will support it as he understands it, and not as it is understood by others." Opinions by justices of the Supreme Court are entitled "to have only such influence as the force of their reasoning may deserve."[10] Elected officials did not automatically salute federal courts when they issued decisions. Just as courts were at liberty to assess the constitutional quality of executive and legislative actions, so did presidents and lawmakers independently assess the constitutional quality of judicial rulings.

Some Lessons about Judicial Finality

Having embraced the theory of judicial review and the capacity of courts to strike down executive and legislative actions, judges regularly learned that their decisions could also be reversed and modified by elected officials. An example comes from two revealing decisions issued in the 1850s. In the first, the Court held that the height of the Wheeling bridge over the Ohio River, constructed under state law, constituted a "nuisance" because it was too low to permit navigation by many vessels.[11] Congress, determined to support the state, passed legislation a few months later and declared that bridge and one other bridge to be "lawful structures."[12] Part of the issues during the legislative debate was the meaning of the title "Supreme Court." Lawmakers decided it meant the Court's supremacy over the judiciary, including in some cases state actions, but not supremacy over Congress and the president. The height and obstructive nature of a state bridge was not solely a legal and judicial matter. Most lawmakers argued that the ultimate authority over the bridge lay with Congress under its power to regulate commerce and preserve the intercourse between the states. Other lawmakers (very much in the minority) upheld the authority of the Court to resolve such matters.[13] This debate within Congress highlights the willingness of lawmakers at that time to review the merits of a Court decision and reject it if the reasoning appeared to lack credibility and persuasive force.

A few years later, the dispute returned to the Court, which decided to defer to the legislative judgment, despite its own prior ruling. In dissent, Justices John McLean, Robert Grier, and James Wayne were dismayed that a Court judgment could be so easily set aside and reversed by Congress. The Court had decided the bridge to be obstructive. How could Congress possibly re-open the issue and reach a contrary opinion? The Court had taken the case, investigated the facts, and reached a decision on a judicial question. Congress could not, Justice Grier wrote, "annul or vacate any decree of this court."[14]

But Congress did precisely that and would do so again in the future, with the Court's acquiescence. As the Court noted in 1946: "Whenever Congress' judgment has been uttered affirmatively to contradict the Court's previously expressed view . . . this body has accommodated its previous judgment to Congress' expressed approval."[15] In 1995, Justices Anthony Kennedy and Sandra Day O'Connor wrote a concurrence in which they conceded that "if we invalidate a state law, Congress can in effect overturn our judgment."[16] The Court was entitled to decide a case, as Marshall had said in *Marbury*, but deciding a case did not necessarily dispose of the underlying legal issues for all time. The elected branches were entitled to enter the picture and offer their independent judgments to reopen the matter and decide it differently.

This process of give and take is conspicuous in the efforts of states and the national government to regulate the sale of intoxicating liquors. In 1890, the Court decided that Iowa lacked authority to place restrictions on intoxicating liquors arriving from other states. The state's "police powers" did not override the power of Congress over interstate commerce. By the Court's reasoning, a state's effort to prohibit incoming liquor could not be applied to original packages or kegs. Only after the original package had been broken into smaller packages could the state regulate sale and distribution. In deciding the case, the Court wisely added this qualification: states could not exclude incoming articles "without congressional permission."[17]

Scarcely a month elapsed before Congress began consideration of a bill to reverse the Court and extend to states full authority to regulate incoming liquor. Members of Congress displayed confidence in their capacity to debate and decide the constitutional issue. To Senator George Gray, lawmakers were not entitled to abdicate their duty to the Constitution and defer to other political bodies, "even if the Supreme Court decides otherwise." Senator George Edmunds heartily concurred with that sentiment. He regarded the Court as "an independent and co-ordinate branch of the Government," with authority to decide cases. "But, as it regards the Congress of the United States, its opinions are of no more value to us than ours are to it. We are just as independent of the Supreme Court of the United States as it is of us, and every judge will admit it." He pointed to the pattern of the Court in deciding an issue one way and then, with a different composition, reversing course to correct what now seemed to be a judicial error.[18]

The Court decided its case on April 28, 1890. Less than four months later Congress passed legislation to override the Court. The statute provided that "all fermented, distilled, or other intoxicating liquors or liquids transported into any State or Territory or remaining therein for use, consumption, sale or storage therein, shall upon arrival in such State or Territory be subject to the operation and effect of the laws of such State or Territory enacted in the exercise of its police powers to the same extent and in the same manner as though such liquids or liquors had been produced in such State or Territory, and shall not be exempt therefrom by reason of being introduced therein in original packages or otherwise."[19]

The second half of the nineteenth century illustrates how common it was for the Court to place restrictions on the state exercise of the commerce power, before Congress acted, but then reverse itself after Congress entered the field and passed legislation supporting what the state had done. The Court initially disposed of a case but recognized that whatever the merits or credibility of its reasoning, Congress could change the outcome and scope of state power by passing a new statute. All three branches had a legitimate right to participate in this constitutional dialogue. The Court did not announce, in so many words, "We have decided the matter. The other branches must subordinate themselves to our considered judgment, whether they like it or not." That attitude of judicial supremacy would indeed surface and inflict substantial damage on the Court's credibility and institutional power.

From Marshall to "Self-Inflicted Wounds"

After the 1850s bridge cases, the Supreme Court would soon provoke what Chief Justice Charles Evans Hughes called several "self-inflicted wounds" on the Court: *Dred Scott*, the Legal Tender cases, and the invalidation of the federal income tax.[20] The Dred Scott case of 1857 struck down congressional legislation prohibiting slavery in the territories. The Court also held that blacks as a class were not citizens protected by the Constitution.[21] Newly elected president James Buchanan encouraged judicial supremacy by stating in his inaugural message of March 4, 1857, that the Dred Scott case was "a judicial question, which legitimately belongs to the Supreme Court of the United States, before whom it is now pending, and will, it is understood, be speedily and finally settled."[22]

The judicial supremacy that developed in this case was not purely a power grab by the courts. Congress had tried to legislate on the slavery issue without success, and clearly Buchanan refused to exert presidential authority. Instead, he unrealistically hoped that the Supreme Court would resolve the matter without knowing exactly what it would do. Had the Court decided the issue narrowly, forcing most of the controversy back to the political branches, it might have worked. It was not in the interest of the Court, or the country, to believe its final judgment would have either credibility or finality. No court, particularly one headed by Chief Justice Roger Taney, could resolve the explosive issue of slavery. The Court's decision, issued a few days after Buchanan's address, helped fan the fires of civil war.

Few citizens or newspapers regarded the Court as the final word on slavery or the rights of blacks. To *The New York Tribune*, Taney's decision, "we need hardly say, is entitled to just as much moral weight as would be the judgment of a majority of those congregated in any Washington bar-room."[23] Newspapers in the South, of course, were quite satisfied with the decision. During the campaign of 1858, Senator Stephen Douglas defended Taney's decision without reservation. Abraham Lincoln, in those debates, accepted the decision only to the extent that it affected the particular parties. The larger policy issue for the nation, he said, could not be left to the Court. The elected branches and the general public had to decide national policy.[24]

When Lincoln entered the White House on March 4, 1861, he stated that he had no intention to use federal power to interfere with state policies over slavery. But his inaugural address also indicated that he would not permit slavery policy to be dictated by the Court, drawing a clear distinction between the impact of a Court ruling on particular litigants and the larger issue of national policy. In the first realm the Court was final; in the second it was not. Without mentioning *Dred Scott,* Lincoln told the nation: "The candid citizen must confess that if the policy of the Government upon vital questions affecting the whole people is to be irrevocably fixed by decisions of the Supreme Court, the instant they are made in ordinary litigation between parties in personal actions the people will have ceased to be their own rulers, having to that extent practically resigned their Government into the hands of that eminent tribunal."[25]

Attorney General Edward Bates and Congress made short work of *Dred Scott.* On November 29, 1862, Bates issued a legal opinion that rejected the Court's reasoning about blacks and U.S. citizenship. He concluded that free men of color, if born in the United States, are citizens of the United States.[26] Also in 1862, Congress passed legislation that prohibited slavery in the territories, precisely what the Court in *Dred Scott* maintained Congress had no authority to do.[27] During debate on this bill, no member of Congress even referred to the Court's decision. Neither Bates nor Congress found the Court's decision of such credibility or persuasive value that the matter was closed to further debate and consideration. Lawmakers never doubted their authority to prohibit slavery in the territories, with or without the Court. The Civil War Amendments formally nullified *Dred Scott.*

In 1870, in *Hepburn v. Griswold,* the Supreme Court divided 4 to 3 in declaring unconstitutional a congressional statute that treated paper money as legal tender for discharging debts.[28] Initially it appeared that the Court was equally divided, 4 to 4.[29] Justice Robert Grier switched, giving the Court a 5 to 3 majority to invalidate the statute. The Court planned to release the opinion on January 31, 1870, one day before Grier's retirement. But Justice Samuel Miller asked for an additional week to complete his dissenting opinion. By the time of the Court's decision on February 7, Grier had retired and the majority slipped to 4 to 3. There was little reason to expect judiciary finality on this issue. Grier would have to be replaced and Congress had created a new position on the Court. Fifteen months later, after the addition of two new Justices, the Court reversed itself, 5 to 4.[30] This rapid turnaround highlighted that the meaning of the Constitution did not emerge from a mysterious process of interpreting text and intent but flowed from new appointments. Whatever might be final with one Court could be reversed by the next, underscoring the importance of political judgments and the process of presidential nomination and Senate consent.

The Court was widely condemned for its 5 to 4 decision in 1895 striking down the federal income tax.[31] Neither the Constitution's text nor the Court's precedents obviously paved the way for this ruling. The Constitution provided that "No Capitation, or other direct, Tax shall be laid, unless in Proportion to the Census or Enumeration herein before directed to be taken." In other words, "direct" taxes had to be based on the population of a state rather than its wealth or contribution to the nation's tax base. The Constitution further empowered Congress to lay and collect taxes, duties, imposts, and excises, "but all Duties, Imposts and Excises shall be uniform throughout the United States."

The distinction between "direct" taxes and other kinds of taxes, however, was not clear. In 1796, the Court held that a carriage tax imposed by Congress was not a direct tax and need not be apportioned among the states on the basis of population. It was an indirect tax.[32] Over time, direct taxes seemed to be limited to two categories: a capitation or poll tax, imposed without regard to property, and a tax on land.

In 1861, Congress enacted an income tax of 3 percent for those with an annual income exceeding $800.[33] The tax was not apportioned among the states. In 1869, the Court held that a federal tax on circulation of bank notes was not considered a direct tax. It noted that when delegates at the Philadelphia Convention debated the taxing power and Rufus King asked his colleagues for the precise meaning of direct taxation, "no one answered."[34] A unanimous Court in 1881 limited the meaning of direct taxes to capitation taxes and taxes on real estate. It interpreted the federal income tax of 1864, as amended in 1865, as an indirect tax. If the taxes created "any wrong or unnecessary harshness, it was for Congress, or for the people who makes congresses, to see that the evil was corrected. The remedy does not lie with the judicial branch of the Government."[35]

This tone of judicial modesty on the taxing power would not last. In 1894, Congress enacted an income tax and applied it to both individuals and corporations, to be effective January 1, 1895. In two 5 to 4 decisions in the *Pollock* case, the Court invalidated the income tax. The first decision held that the tax on rents or income of real estate was a direct tax and violated the Constitution by not following the apportionment rule. In the second decision, the Court struck down the income tax, in part because the Court reasoned that invalidation of the other taxes left a tax scheme that Congress could not have intended.

A new political factor, wholly unrelated to the Constitution or the framers' intent, emerged to help shape the Court's decision. During oral argument, attorney Joseph H. Choate warned the justices that the income tax was "communistic in its purposes and tendencies." Justice Stephen Field picked up the same theme: "The present assault upon capital is but the beginning. It will be but the stepping-stone to others, larger and more sweeping, till our political contests will become a war of the poor against the rich; a war constantly growing in intensity and bitterness."[36] Clearly the justices were drawing not from eighteenth-century legal principles but from contemporary fears of socialism and communism. In addition, some vote-switching damaged the Court's credibility.

The Court initially split 4 to 4 on the constitutionality of the income tax. Upon rehearing, the tax was struck down 5 to 4. The justice missing from the first vote was Howell Jackson, but in the second case he voted to *sustain* the tax. The vote should have been 5 to 4 in support of the income tax. Obviously, some other Justice switched sides. Who he was, and why he changed votes, was never revealed. Due to the altered vote and razor-thin majority, the decision was widely condemned. The effort to amend the Constitution did not spark interest until President Theodore Roosevelt recommended that course in 1907 and legislative action began two years later. By 1913, a sufficient number of states had ratified the Sixteenth Amendment: "The Congress shall have power to lay and collect taxes on incomes, from whatever source derived, without apportionment among the several States, and without regard to any census or enumeration." For the second time (following the effective repudiation of *Dred Scott* with the Thirteenth and Fourteenth Amendments), Congress and the states used the constitutional amendment process to invalidate a Supreme Court decision and put the Court on a different legal trajectory.

Also during this period, federal judges drew on prevailing social and political doctrines to nullify legislative efforts to regulate economic conditions, including maximum hours of work and minimum wages. Lawyers from the corporate sector helped translate the philosophy of laissez-faire economics into constitutional doctrine, in part to support "liberty of contract" and to validate the struggle of "survival of the fittest" associated with the nineteenth-century social philosopher Herbert Spencer. Elected officials are accustomed to accepting and rejecting different economic and political theories. For judges to engage in this practice left them far afield from "interpreting the Constitution" and helped weaken the credibility of their decisions.

Previous state legislative efforts, sanctioned in the past under the police power, were now regularly invalidated by the Court. In his dissent in the *Lochner* case, Justice Oliver Wendell Holmes objected that his colleagues had struck down a New York law that limited bakery workers to sixty hours a week or ten hours a day not because of constitutional principles but because of the economic theory of laissez-faire.[37] By the late 1930s, the Court would begin to rethink and jettison this form of judicial obstruction. Instead of the nation deferring to the judiciary, the judiciary would defer to the elected branches and popular support. At times this dialogue would take decades to complete, as with the judicial-congressional struggle over child labor legislation.

The Battle over Child Labor

In 1918 and 1922, the Court would twice invalidate congressional efforts to regulate child labor. Congress turned to a constitutional amendment in 1924 to override the Court, but there were not enough states to ratify the amendment. Throughout that period, Congress never accepted the finality of rulings by the Supreme Court. It returned to child labor legislation in 1938, and this time the Supreme Court in 1941 not only upheld the law but did so unanimously. The story tells a lot about the determination of the public and elected leaders to prevail against judicial opposition. No one treated the Court as infallible or of some transcendent quality. It was one branch of government and quite capable, as with the others, of winning some and losing some, even if the outcome took decades to resolve.

The first child labor bill in 1916 was reported from a House committee with careful attention to constitutional analysis.[38] Two years later a 5 to 4 Court decision struck down the bill as unconstitutional with regard to the power of Congress under the Commerce Clause and under principles of federalism.[39] Within a matter of days Congress was at work on a new version of legislation to regulate child labor. Legislative debate makes it clear that members of Congress regarded themselves, not the Court, as the superior policymaking body on national issues. In Senate debate, Robert Owen noted that some people re-garded judges as "much more learned and wiser than Congress in construing the Constitution." He did not concede this "whimsical notion." Judges were not more learned, he said, nor more wise or patriotic. If they made errors, how would their mistakes be corrected? If Congress erred in making consti-tutional judgments, "the people have an immediate redress; they can change the House of Representatives almost immediately and can change two-thirds of the Senate within four years, while the judges are appointed for life and are removable only by impeachment."[40]

The bill that cleared Congress in 1919 relied not on the commerce power but on the power to tax. This legislation was challenged and ended up before the Supreme Court. In defending the bill, Solicitor General James Beck took note of the prevalence of judicial supremacy but advised the Court to respect the judgment of the people and their elected representatives. To nullify such laws, he argued, would weaken what he called the "constitutional conscience" of the people. It would undermine public respect for and understanding of the Constitution. There was a general impression, which he believed to be a "mischievous one," that the judiciary has "an unlimited power to nullify a law if its incidental effect is in excess of the governmental sphere of the enacting body." Nothing in the history of the country, he told the Court, supported such a theory. Judicial actions in invalidating legislation "so lowers the sense of constitutional morality among the people that neither in the legislative branch of the Government nor among the people is there as strong a purpose as formerly to maintain their constitutional form of Government."[41]

This time the Court, perhaps attempting to send a clear message to Con-gress and the country, mounted a majority of 8 to 1 in striking down the new child-labor statute.[42] If the purpose was to underscore judicial finality in constitutional interpretation, the effort would fall short. In 1924, both houses of Congress passed a constitutional amendment to give Congress the power to "limit, regulate and prohibit the labor of persons under 18 years of age." By 1937, only twenty-eight of the required thirty-six states had ratified the amendment. The years went by, building to the confrontation in 1937 over President Franklin D. Roosevelt's court-packing plan. Congress rebuffed his ill-considered scheme, but by then the Court appeared to recognize that its decades-long resistance to economic regulation had run its course.

Several years before Roosevelt offered his plan, the Court had begun to recognize that its steadfast opposition to legislation had backfired on the judiciary. It needed public support and credibility and was losing both. In a 5 to 4 decision in 1934, the Court upheld a New York price-setting statute, and in 1936 the Court seemed prepared to sustain minimum-wage legislation but delayed its ruling because of Justice Harlan Fiske Stone's illness.[43]

The composition of the Court was about to change dramatically. On June 2, 1937, Justice Willis Van Devanter, one of the conservatives who had steadfastly opposed economic regulation, retired. Roosevelt nominated Hugo Black as his replacement. By 1941 Stone had replaced Charles Evans Hughes as Chief Justice, and Roosevelt was able to nominate six more Justices: Felix Frankfurter, James Byrnes, William O. Douglas, Frank Murphy, Stanley Reed, and Robert Jackson. It was during this period that Congress decided to revive the child-labor bill, including it as part of the Fair Labor Standards Act of 1938. Its constitutionality was challenged, but in 1941 the Court unanimously upheld it.[44]

By the early 1940s, the three branches had forged a more stable relationship in sharing political power. Elected officials developed and enacted public policy without fear that the courts would routinely invalidate statutes on the basis of laissez-faire economic theory. The courts continued to receive and decide cases but had broken free from some of the abstract doctrines that weakened the credibility and public acceptability of their opinions. It would not be long before the Court would again overturn legislation on the basis of principles that had few, if any, roots in the Constitution.

Contemporary Court-Congress Clashes

In 1976, marking the first time in four decades that the Court invalidated a statute passed by Congress pursuant to the Commerce Clause, a 5 to 4 Court held that federal minimum-wage and maximum-hour provisions could not displace state powers in such "traditional government functions" as fire prevention, police protection, sanitation, public health, and parks and recreation.[45] Lower courts had to divine the difference between "traditional" and "non-traditional." There was so little credibility to this new judicial doctrine, and so little understanding on how to ever implement it, that nine years later, Justice Harry Blackmun decided to jump ship and join four Justices in overturning the 1976 ruling.[46]

Some have criticized the Supreme Court's effort to define "commerce" and "economic," concluding that the "inanity of these arguments is only matched by the justices' sanctimony." In these cases, the Court "often operates according to arcane principles of interpretation and intimations of infallibility."[47] The Court acknowledges that previous judicial tests and standards (such as efforts to distinguish between "manufacturing" and "commerce" or between "direct" and "indirect" effects on interstate commerce) "artificially" limited congressional authority and deserved to be discarded.[48]

In exercising its power of judicial review, the Court frequently claims that the federal government is one of enumerated powers. That is not credible. All federal powers are not enumerated in the Constitution. The power of judicial review is not enumerated in the Constitution, nor is the power of Congress to investigate, the power of the president to remove certain executive officers, and many other implied (but not specified) powers. In an effort to use this doctrine to limit the powers of Congress, the Court apparently does not recognize that the same doctrine would radically limit the power of the judiciary, including judicial review.

In 1995, in striking down a congressional effort to regulate guns in the schoolyard, the Court asserted: "We start with first principles. The Constitution creates a Federal Government of enumerated powers."[49] Two years later, in invalidating the Religious Freedom Restoration Act, the Court announced: "Under our Constitution, the Federal Government is one of enumerated powers."[50] In 2000, in deciding that Congress lacked authority to pass the Violence Against Women Act, the Court said it was compelled to so decide "if we are to maintain the Constitution's enumeration of powers."[51] If the Court could not persuasively defend such a fundamental element of jurisprudence as whether powers are enumerated, of what credibility would its decisions have with Congress, scholars, and the public?

The Court has presented several arguments to justify this doctrine of enumerated powers. In one line of attack, it quoted from James Madison: "The powers delegated by the proposed Constitution to the federal government are few and defined. Those which are to remain in the State governments are numerous and indefinite."[52] Madison argues here for limited, not enumerated, federal powers. During debate on the Tenth Amendment, when it was proposed that the states retain all powers except those "expressly delegated" to the national government, he objected to the word *expressly* because the functions and responsibilities of the federal government could not be delineated with such precision. It was impossible to confine a government to the exercise of express or enumerated powers, for there "must necessarily be admitted powers by implication, unless the Constitution descended to recount every minutiae."[53] The word *expressly* was removed from the Tenth Amendment.

The Court has offered a second argument to defend the doctrine of enumerated powers. In concluding that Congress's authority "is limited to those powers enumerated in the Constitution," it reached for support to the hallowed decision of *McCulloch v. Maryland* (1819) to reinforce the principle that the federal government "is acknowledged by all to be one of enumerated powers."[54] There is no credibility to this argument. *McCulloch* plainly made the case for implied, not enumerated, powers. After all, the decision upheld the U.S. Bank, an entity that is not mentioned in the Constitution.

The Court's third argument for enumerated powers has relied on *Marbury v. Madison*: "The judicial authority to determine the constitutionality of laws, in cases and controversies, is based on the premise that the 'powers of the legislature are defined and limited; and that those limits may not be mistaken, or forgotten, the constitution is written.'"[55] The language from *Marbury* supports *limited,* not enumerated, powers. If *Marbury* recognized only enumerated powers, there would be no judicial authority to invalidate congressional statutes. Judicial review is an implied, not an enumerated, power.

In writing for the majority in *City of Boerne v. Flores,* Justice Kennedy stated that when a conflict exists between a Court ruling and a subsequent congressional statute, the Court's decision is superior under the Constitution. After the Court had decided *Employment Division v. Smith* in 1990, Congress passed the Religious Freedom Restoration Act (RFRA) to adopt a standard more protective of religious liberty. To Kennedy, because the provisions of the statute "are beyond congressional authority, it is this Court's precedent, not the RFRA, which must control." Similarly, Justice O'Connor, in a dissent, argued that congressional statutes must conform to decisions reached by the Supreme Court: "Congress, no less than this Court, is called upon to consider the requirements of the Constitution and to act in accordance with its dictates. But when it enacts legislation in furtherance of its delegated powers, Congress must make its judgments consistent with this Court's exposition of the Constitution and with the limits placed on its legislative authority by provisions such as the Fourteenth Amendment."[56]

The positions by Kennedy and O'Connor are legally and politically weak. Instead of lawmakers taking an oath to the Constitution, they would be taking an oath to the Court. There is little in more than two centuries of constitutional development to support such an understanding. Under the interpretation offered by Kennedy and O'Connor, Congress should have accepted the Court's first child-labor decision in 1918 rather than enact subsequent legislation in 1919 and 1938. As we shall see, O'Connor subsequently denied that decisions by the Court fixed the meaning of the Constitution. In her 2003 book, *The Majesty of the Law*, O'Connor offered a more thoughtful and credible model of constitutional interpretation that invites a mix of judicial and nonjudicial forces.

In *Boerne*, Kennedy objected to the RFRA on the grounds that it impermissibly allowed Congress to change the meaning of the Constitution. Citing language from *Marbury*, he wrote: "If Congress could define its own powers by altering the Fourteenth Amendment's meaning, no longer would the Constitution be 'superior paramount law, unchangeable by ordinary means.' It would be 'on a level with ordinary legislative acts, and, like other acts . . . alterable when the legislature shall please to do it.' " He further noted: "Shifting legislative majorities could change the Constitution and effectively circumvent the difficult and detailed amendment process contained in Article V."[57]

His argument is not persuasive. As noted by Michael McConnell, Congress "was not seeking to change the Free Exercise Clause. It was attempting to correct what it considered to be the Supreme Court's misinterpretation, which is not the same thing."[58] The meaning of the Constitution is regularly altered by judicial decisions without recourse to the formal amendment process. The meaning of the Constitution was one thing when the Court twice struck down the child-labor bill and another thing when it upheld it. Indeed, the record of the last two centuries is one of shifting judicial majorities altering the meaning of the Constitution. Two days before the Court invalidated RFRA, it overruled a decision from 1985 that had limited federal assistance to parochial schools.[59] A change in the meaning of the Constitution? Maybe. Accomplished by formal amendment? No.

Kennedy suggested that constitutional interpretation is a judicial monopoly: "Our national experience teaches that the Constitution is preserved best when each part of the Government respects both the Constitution and the proper actions and determinations of the other branches. When the Court has interpreted the Constitution, it has acted within the province of the Judicial Branch, which embraces the duty to say what the law is." What controls "is this Court's precedent, not RFRA."[60] Referring to Marshall's language in *Marbury* about the power of the courts to decide what the law is does not justify this claim of judicial supremacy. Nothing in constitutional history or "national experience" supports Kennedy's assertion.

On what credible grounds does a court decide that a judicial interpretation is superior to what Congress has decided by statute? To Justice Frankfurter, "the ultimate touchstone of constitutionality is the Constitution itself and not what we have said about it."[61] Before joining the Court, Frankfurter offered the following advice to President Franklin D. Roosevelt: "People have been taught to believe that when the Supreme Court speaks it is not they who speak but the Constitution, whereas, of course, in so many vital cases, it is *they* who speak and not the Constitution."[62]

Justice Antonin Scalia has explained the basic difference between judges who interpret the Constitution and those who interpret the Constitution based on what courts have said about it. Anyone who takes a class in constitutional law, reads a constitutional law textbook, or examines a brief filed in a constitutional law case "will rarely find the discussion addressed to the text of the constitutional provision that is at issue, or to the question of what was the originally understood or even the originally intended meaning of the text." Instead, the analysis will begin with Supreme Court cases, "and the new issue will presumably be decided according to the logic that those cases expressed, with no regard for how far that logic, thus extended, has distanced us from the original text and understanding."[63]

Constitutional scholars at times defend the federal judiciary when it decides cases of constitutional law with little, if any, reference to the Constitution. As noted in a recent study by Daniel Farber and Suzanna Sherry, scholars find it unnecessary to "talk much about the text of the Constitution, because . . . it usually does not offer much in the way of guidance or constraint."[64] That is a frank if remarkable argument. The text of the Constitution does not matter. Gone is the notion of a written constitution. What counts is what the Court says about the Constitution, if indeed it even refers to it. Why should such a posture have any credibility? Constitutional analysis is replaced by ipse dixit. The creation of judicial tests and standards has become a routine if not dominant part of constitutional interpretation. What is cited is not constitutional text but "clear and present danger," "rational basis," "substantial effect," "prurient interest," "good faith," "undue burden," and "evolving standards of decency." When Justice Kennedy asks Congress to accept the Court's judgment on the Constitution, it is not the Constitution that is being interpreted but intermediate, subordinate, and ever-changing judicial tests and standards.

Where We Are Today

During the confirmation hearing in September 2005 on the nomination of John G. Roberts Jr. to be Chief Justice, Senator Arlen Specter raised objections to prevalent judicial attitudes: "I am concerned about what I bluntly say is the denigration by the Court of Congressional authority." In striking down legislation to protect women against violence, the Court "did so because of our 'method of reasoning.'" He told Roberts: "We do our homework . . . and we do not like being treated as schoolchildren, requiring, as Justice Scalia says, a task master." Referring to the religious liberty case of *Boerne*, Specter said that the Court "came up with a standard of what is congruent and proportionate. . . . Now, they plucked congruence and proportionality right of thin air."[65]

The vague standard of "congruence and proportionality" was also discussed during the January 2006 hearing on the confirmation of Samuel A. Alito to be Associate Justice. Senator Specter repeated his objection to this standard because it was "denigrating" to the role of Congress in constitutional interpretation, and "no one can figure out" the meaning of these judicial standards.[66] Specter's important line of inquiry was not pursued by other senators. Neither Roberts nor Alito offered reasoned or credible responses to justify such standards as congruence or to demonstrate any respect for the independent capacity of elected branches to interpret the Constitution.

Instead, Roberts in his prepared testimony offered this explanation for the manner in which federal courts discharge their duties: "Judges are like umpires. Umpires don't make the rules, they apply them. The role of an umpire and a judge is critical. They make sure everybody plays by the rules, but it is a limited role. Nobody ever went to a ball game to see the umpire." Some senators responded favorably to this presentation. Senator Sam Brownback remarked: "You had a second point that was very apt, I thought, when you talked about the courts and baseball. The analogy you draw, I found very appealing." Yet Brownback cautioned: "The umpire should call the ball fair or foul, it is in or it is out, but not become actively involved as a player on the field. Unfortunately, we have reached a point where, in many respects, the judiciary is the most active policy player on the field."[67]

Senator Joseph Biden pointed out the differences between baseball and judging. In baseball, the strike zone is defined as the width of the plate and from the shoulders to the knees.[68] The Constitution has a few well-defined strike zones, including minimum ages for representatives, senators, and presidents. Those areas are so well defined that they are never litigated. But there is no unambiguous strike zone for the types of issues that do come to the courts: questions about free speech, religious liberty, due process, equal protection, cruel and unusual punishment, and other contentious matters. Roberts told the committee that umpires "don't make the rules, they apply them." With that remark he conceded, perhaps unintentionally, that the analogy between umpires and judges is far-fetched. No one can doubt that judges make the rules and standards they use to decide cases. Lengthy law review articles analyze the origin, application, and credibility of these rules and standards.[69]

Over the last few decades there is a regrettable pattern of members of Congress and political figures accepting the Supreme Court as final on constitutional interpretation, even when disagreeing with an opinion. On December 12, 2000, the Supreme Court in *Bush v. Gore* ruled against a recount of Florida votes and propelled George W. Bush into the White House.[70] The following day, Al Gore explained why he decided to withdraw from the race: "Now the U.S. Supreme Court has spoken. Let there be no doubt, while I strongly disagree with the court's decision, I accept it. I accept the finality of this outcome, which will be ratified next Monday in the Electoral College. And tonight, for the sake of our unity of the people and the strength of our democracy, I offer my concession."[71]

It may have been good political judgment for Gore to withdraw from the race, but there was no need to automatically endorse a ruling he disagreed with and that others found largely incomprehensible. No one—conservative, liberal, Democrat, Republican, Independent, and so on—can regard the ruling's reasoning as credible or persuasive. Many people supported the decision and its results, but even they concede that the Court issued a ruling that was unprincipled and purely ad hoc.[72]

In 2001, following a federalism decision, Senator Patrick Leahy announced: "As an American, I accept any of [the Court's] decisions as the ultimate interpretation of our Constitution, whether I agree or disagree."[73] In 2008, after the Court decided the habeas corpus case of *Boumediene v. Bush*, Senator Orrin Hatch expressed his disagreement with the opinion, calling it a "lousy" decision, but said "I uphold the Supreme Court, even though it was a 5-to-4 decision. Nevertheless, it is a decision by one-third of the separated powers of this country, and must be recognized as such."[74] Why this deference to opinions that seem poorly reasoned and wrongly decided? Lawmakers in the past never hesitated to criticize judicial rulings on child labor, economic regulation, the commerce power, and other disputes. Through such confrontations they were often able to force courts to change their legal doctrines.

During his confirmation hearing to be Chief Justice, John Roberts gave conflicting views on the propriety of criticizing decisions of the Supreme Court. At first he said that criticizing judicial decisions "comes with the territory. It's a healthy thing. That type of criticism and analysis, saying the judge got it wrong, the court got it wrong, is healthy and good." Yet a few sentences later he backed away from this type of open public debate: "Attacks on judicial independence are not appropriate because judges—and certainly even judges with whom I disagree on the results or particular merits, they should not be attacked for their decisions." He seemed to indicate that when the Court decides a matter, the country should accept the result: "Over time, the legitimacy of the Supreme Court has been established, and it's generally recognized across the political spectrum that it is the obligation of the Court to say what the law is and that the other branches have the obligation to obey what the Supreme Court says the law is."[75]

It should be obvious that Roberts's formulation is much too broad. If the Court decides the meaning of a statute, clearly Congress has every right and authority to pass another statute to reverse the Court. This type of "statutory reversal" happens all the time, as with the recent statute passed by Congress and signed by President Barack Obama reversing the Court's ruling in the case of *Ledbetter v. Goodyear Tire and Rubber Co.* In 2007, the Court held that Lilly Ledbetter's claim of past salary discrimination was "untimely" because she failed to bring a Title VII lawsuit within the statutory period of 180 days, even though evidence of pay disparities between Ledbetter and her male colleagues was entirely concealed from her during the period in which (according to the Court) she was required to file the suit. Congress enacted legislation on January 29, 2009, to overturn the Court's statutory interpretation.[76]

As to cases where the Court decides the meaning of the Constitution, the door is also open for the elected branches to act against the decision. For example, in 1986 the Court decided that Captain Simcha Goldman did not have a constitutional right to wear his yarmulke indoors while on duty. He had to comply with the existing military regulation. Within a year Congress passed legislation telling the Defense Department to change the regulation to permit soldiers to wear religious apparel if it does not interfere with military duties.[77]

In her 2003 book *The Majesty of the Law,* Justice O'Connor offered a healthy understanding about the limits of judicial finality: "If one looks at the history of the Court, the country, and the Constitution over a very long period, the relationship appears to be more of a dialogue than a series of commands." She recognized that just as courts shape the work of the elected branches, so do elected branches (and the public) shape the work of the courts. A "dynamic dialogue" functions between the Supreme Court and the American public. No one, she said, should have assumed that the Court's 1973 decision in *Roe v. Wade* would have settled the abortion issue "for all time." The deeply emotional debate that followed the Court's ruling was "as it should be." A nation that "docilely and unthinkingly approved every Supreme Court decision as infallible and immutable would, I believe, have severely disappointed our founders." The U.S. Constitution "is not—and could never be—defended only by a group of judges." She recalled the words of Judge Learned Hand: "Liberty lies in the hearts of men and women; when it dies there, no constitution, no law, no court can save it; no constitution, no court, no law can even do much to help it. While it lies there it needs no constitution, no law, no court to save it."[78]

A healthy dialogue over constitutional meaning cannot exist if members of Congress, presidents, academics, and citizens bow obediently to judicial rulings, swallowing whatever misgivings or doubts that might surface about the reasoning and credibility of a decision. That type of deferential spirit undermines self-government and the system of checks and balances. William Howard Taft, who served as a federal appellate judge before becoming president (and was Chief Justice of the Supreme Court after serving as president), understood why judicial decisions must be exposed to rigorous and unsparing public critiques. Nothing made judges more "careful in their decisions and anxiously solicitous to do exact justice than the consciousness that every act of theirs is to be subjected to the intelligent scrutiny of their fellow men, and to their candid criticism." Some evaluations would come from practitioners and the legal community, but Taft also saw the value of judgments from the general public: "If the law is but the essence of common sense, the protest of many average men may evidence a defect in a judicial conclusion though based on the nicest legal reasoning and profoundest learning."[79]

Conclusion

Bruce Peabody

What is the status of judicial independence as we enter the second decade of the twenty-first century? Answering this question requires a clear sense of both the core elements of independence and a set of scales for measuring the dangers posed by the criticisms and attacks chronicled in this volume. The preceding chapters have emphasized that normal, healthful court independence does not, and can not, entail removal from the rest of the political and constitutional system. To take just one example, the possibility of judicial impeachment (and removal) reminds us that our political system places weight on other values besides judicial autonomy and that courts must answer to the other institutions of government.

Powers, Autonomy, and Subjective Independence

That said, judicial independence requires institutional powers and autonomy as well as a subjective sense of independence among those comprising the courts. Judges need formal legal and constitutional authority to review cases and settle disputes as well as some level of institutional and subjective remove from legislative and executive powers—and the public. These three dimensions of independence—power to complete institutional roles, actual autonomy from other branches and political vectors, and an individual sense of subjective or psychological independence—may come under attack simultaneously or separately.[1] Citing the example from above, the prospect of judicial impeachment does not, on its own, formally change the powers of the judiciary, but under some circumstances this instrument for disciplining the judiciary could damage the court's ability to complete its work, raise the specter of legislative encroachment, and intimidate sitting judges.[2]

Understanding Attacks

Assessing judicial independence requires not just considering these three dimensions of judicial independence but also appreciating different characteristics of attacks on courts that help determine their seriousness. First, we need to recognize that the significance of court-curbing efforts is often a function of their political status and impact. Obviously a "jurisdiction-stripping" bill that becomes a law constrains the judiciary more than a similar bill that languishes in a congressional subcommittee. Moreover, a proposed constitutional amendment to eliminate judicial review entirely might well represent a lesser threat to judicial independence than a proposal to curtail habeas corpus jurisdiction—provided the latter has a better chance of passing.[3]

This said, the overwhelming number of court-curbing proposals and other reforms never become policy. But courts are not immune to considering the broader implications of criticisms of the judiciary and specific court-curbing initiatives, including those that never see the political light of day. The judicial appointment processes at both the state and federal level and the lengthy terms served by both appointed and elected judges furnish sitting judges with some political experience and judgment. We can anticipate, therefore, that many of these jurists will have some (admittedly inexpert) capacity for (and considerable interest in) evaluating the political seriousness of different critiques and court-curbing initiatives—not just to ascertain the immediate likelihood of seeing a new policy put into place but also to get a feel for the contemporary zeitgeist with respect to court critiques.

Moreover, as suggested in several chapters in this volume, we should not measure the impact of court-curbing proposals by looking only at their immediate policy implications; such initiatives may both signal and contribute to eroding confidence in courts, creating an overall environment in which judicial rulings are more likely to be contested. If politics is indeed the "art of the possible," then actions that help to shift public and elite expectations about sanctioning the judiciary are among the most powerful.

A second point to keep in mind in understanding today's attacks is that to the extent that different threats to judicial independence carry the promise of altering the behavior or powers of courts or judges, we must assess their degree of prospective change. Some actions (such as rebuking a judge in a floor speech) serve as relatively minor "shots across the bow" that leave the basic political universe unchanged, while others (calls to eliminate judicial review) might well destabilize institutional norms and relations and represent more dramatic alterations to our constitutional order.[4]

In this regard, it is useful to assess proposed critiques of courts by applying Sanford Levinson's continuum of legal change and by identifying the differences between "interpretations" and "amendments" in our political order. A proposed change to a prevailing understanding of judicial independence (or the specific powers of the judiciary) might not be regarded as illegitimate or inconsistent with our political traditions if it represents a mere "interpretation," a proposed change that is "already immanent" within our legal and political structures and constitutional traditions. On the other hand, attacks on the courts that pose the prospect of an "extraordinary development" or an "outright mutation [of judicial role] generated by exogenous causes" should be taken more seriously, as these represent more fundamental amendments to our preexisting legal and political "reality."[5]

Finally, in evaluating critiques of courts, we might note that courts' autonomy and powers (and the conditions under which they are objectively and subjectively threatened) are dynamic and historic. A measure that clearly challenges or constrains the judiciary at one moment may come to serve as a vital source of authority in another. The Constitution's Fourteenth Amendment, for example, repealed both the *Dred Scott* decision and, more generally, brought the Supreme Court into greater conformity with the Republican reconstruction agenda of the nineteenth century. But over time, the amendment became the legal touchstone for a revolution in civil rights and civil liberties, expanding the Court's powers and influence enormously. When assessing attacks against the courts, then, we should be conscious that our powers as prognosticators are limited. Today's check of the court may well end up being tomorrow's grant of power—and vice versa.[6]

The criticisms of courts that are the focus of this book, therefore, can be thought of as existing along a continuum of greater and lesser threats to judicial independence. Placing specific critiques on this spectrum is complex, since it involves evaluations of threats across three dimensions (autonomy, power, and subjective impact) as well as an assessment of a measure's likely political seriousness, the degree of change it portends, and, finally, an appreciation for how a threat's full implications are likely to evolve. This entails the recognition that the true impact of a measure may not be fully known for many years.

Assessing Today's Challenges to Independence

With these observations in mind, should we be disturbed by the trends and observations depicted in this book? There is certainly a good deal of evidence in this volume suggesting that contemporary fretting about judicial independence is exaggerated and that the attacks over the past four decades may have less political import than initially meets the eye. While a number of proposed reforms of courts and rhetorical criticisms could induce real alterations in our political system (and can be thought of as genuine "amendments," using the framework of Levinson), few of these proposals are likely to become law in the foreseeable future. Thus, while proposals to do away with "life tenure" and provide, instead, a limited term of service for Supreme Court justices would seem to represent a dramatic change to our prevailing historical practices, these measures are not likely to be approved by Congress.

Of the court-curbing measures that actually have become law in recent years, few obviously compromise the independence of the courts or their operations. Serious judicial impeachment proceedings, for example, have typically targeted judges accused of corruption or criminal activity and will not, therefore, transform most judges' behavior very much.[7] More generally, the formal powers of state and federal judicial systems have not obviously been curtailed over the past few decades; indeed, as some authors in this volume have contended, some changes to the laws and the judicial process (such as the rise of legislation with "expedited review" provisions allowing courts to evaluate new legislation rapidly) have actually expanded courts' jurisdiction, discretion, and institutional powers. In sum, a number of the threatened moves against courts have not come to pass, and most of those that have gone forward are not terribly threatening.

Watching the Future

While many of today's criticisms of courts represent a fairly normal working out of our system of separated powers, there are good reasons for continuing to keep watch over the state of judicial independence. First, the frequent public concerns expressed by judges themselves about the current political climate and the criticisms leveled against them suggest that we need to pay continued heed to the subjective aspect of judicial independence. Even if few of the criticisms of elected officials and other groups actually result in important policy changes, they may well create a climate that constrains how judges view their role and exercise their powers. We need a more informed sense, therefore, of whether the recent anxiety expressed by sitting and retired judges reflects widespread fears on the bench that may actually affect judicial functions.

Second, our continuing examination of threats to judicial independence must take into account not just legislation, reforms, and impeachments that are successful but also the potential effects of political stasis on how the judiciary conducts its business and maintains its autonomy. The most obvious example in this regard concerns judicial budgets and the pay of judges. Judicial leaders have long decried the potential impact of stagnant wages on the quality of the judiciary and the ability of court systems to recruit and retain talented personnel. While Congress's refusal to increase the pay scale of federal judges is surely not the same kind of attack as, say, a proposal to take away a court's jurisdiction over abortion cases, "passive aggression" in this context could hinder the judiciary's ability to complete its work. At the state level, budget constraints have led to restricted judicial staffing and limitations on the core services and operations of courts. To take just one example, as a budget-saving measure, in 2008 the state of New Hampshire suspended jury trials in civil and criminal matters for a month in most of its county courts.[8] Citing this development, the chief justice of the Massachusetts Supreme Court declared that our country's "state courts are in crisis," at "the tipping point of dysfunction."[9]

A third cautionary note about judicial independence in the twenty-first century concerns the historic deference the American judiciary has enjoyed from elected officials and the public. Fifty years ago, Robert McCloskey observed that the Supreme Court of the United States (and the American judiciary generally) developed its prestige and power in substantial part because the populace was willing to embrace simultaneously "popular sovereignty" and "the rule of law"—and that it unproblematically associated the latter with courts. If, however, the American people lose their confidence in courts as the bulwarks of our commitment to legal order, the perceived need to protect judges from popular control is likely to fade as well. While this development may not be imminent, the increasing salience of courts in today's politics suggests that the public's historic political-legal delineations, as identified by McCloskey, are already in some jeopardy.

Finally, the observations in this chapter should highlight the importance of taking a long-range view on today's criticisms of the courts. At the moment, many of these attacks seem to generate more rhetoric than politically palatable policy. But if, in the proximate future, a significant reform, alteration, or restriction of the judiciary comes to pass, we might need to reassess this context as instead providing a fertile medium for substantial change. Many of the underlying issues that have propelled contemporary attacks on the courts remain unresolved—including disappointment by both parties with the capacity of courts to deliver social changes or protect cherished policies and social "values," ongoing battles over the staffing of the judiciary, and continuing uncertainty among the public and elites about the court's proper role in the policy process. In this environment, the swirl of angry words and threatened responses by politicians, leaders, and private citizens could either be a weakening wind or a gathering storm.

Indeed, there is considerable evidence—in this book, in the burgeoning scholarship examining criticisms of courts, and in the words and deeds of our political leaders—indicating that we are entering a time when the judiciary's status in our system of separated powers is up for adjustment, as the familiar political landscape supporting judicial independence continues to rift. As President Obama recently observed, in the 1960s and 1970s liberal judges were accused by conservatives of ignoring "the will of Congress . . . [and] democratic processes" as well as of trying "to impose judicial solutions on problems instead of letting the process work itself through politically." But today, these same warnings are also being sounded by the left, including complaints about "conservative jurisprudence" and judges with "an awful lot of power."[10] If these criticisms from both major parties persist, the equilibrium of our political life suggests that courts will either substantially reduce their profile in public affairs or elected officials will try to do it for them—forcing the issue with the vast array of infrequently used but not forgotten court-curbing tools at their disposal.

Appendix

Timeline of Important Events, 1968–2010

1968   Presidential candidate Richard Nixon's "law and order" campaign targets judges who are "weakening the peace forces against the criminal forces."

1973   *Roe v. Wade* extends the right to privacy to some abortion procedures.

1980   Ronald Reagan elected president in part on promises "to appoint only those opposed to abortion and the 'judicial activism' of the Warren and Burger Courts." During his two terms, Reagan appoints three new Supreme Court justices and elevates William Rehnquist to Chief Justice, replacing Warren Burger.

1982   The Federalist Society for Law and Public Policy Studies is founded. The organization is a self-described "group of conservatives and libertarians dedicated to reforming the current legal order."

1986   Chief Justice Rose Bird is impeached and removed from Supreme Court of California by voters.

1987   Reagan's Supreme Court nominee Robert Bork is voted down by the U.S. Senate, 58 to 42.

1989   *Texas v. Johnson* generates criticism after the Supreme Court rules that flag burning is symbolic speech protected under the First Amendment. Congress introduces a constitutional amendment to reverse the decision, but the measure fails to receive the two-thirds vote needed to be sent to the states for ratification.

1992   *Planned Parenthood v. Casey* upholds aspects of *Roe v. Wade* while limiting the decision's application and approving some state restrictions on abortion access. In dissent, Justice Antonin Scalia criticizes the plurality opinion and warns that, in the wake of the decision, "the Imperial Judiciary lives."

1995   *U.S. v Lopez* strikes down a federal law passed under the authority of the "Commerce Clause," the first such invalidation since the 1930s. From 1995 to 2002, the Court strikes down federal legislation more frequently than at any time since the New Deal.

1997   *City of Boerne v. Flores* strikes down the Religious Freedom Restoration Act, a federal law that placed limits on statues "substantially burdening" religious practices. The *Boerne* decision is criticized by a range of religious groups as well as ideological liberals and conservatives.

2000   *Bush v. Gore* holds that the Florida Supreme Court's standards for re-counting ballots in the disputed presidential election violate the Fourteenth Amendment's equal protection clause. The decision allows George W. Bush to win the state of Florida and defeat Al Gore in the general election.

2002   United States Court of Appeals for the Ninth Circuit rules that the words "under God" in the Pledge of Allegiance violate the establishment clause of the First Amendment.

2003   *Lawrence v. Texas* overturns a Texas law criminalizing sodomy and thirteen similar statutes in other states.

2003   In *Goodridge v. Dept. of Public Health,* the Massachusetts Supreme Judicial Court finds that the state may not "deny the protections, benefits and obligations conferred by civil marriage to two individuals of the same sex who wish to marry."

2005   After seven years of contentious litigation, a Florida judge orders the "removal of nutrition and hydration" from Terri Schiavo, who had been diagnosed by physicians as being in a persistent vegetative state. The ruling is opposed by Florida lawmakers and members of Congress, who attempt, unsuccessfully, to bypass this and other decisions through several strategies, including the passage of a federal bill allowing the Schiavo case to be heard by a federal court.

2005   Family Research Council and Focus on the Family organize the first "Justice Sunday" event criticizing Senate filibusters of conservative court nominees as well as sitting judges.

2005   Gallup reports a twenty-point drop, from June 2001 to June 2005, in those reporting that they "approve" of the "way the Supreme Court is handling its job." Some scholars speculate the dip in approval reflects *Kelo v. City of New London,* a controversial case involving the government's power to take private property for public use. By September 2006, the Supreme Court's approval ratings have returned to their original high levels.

2006   Sandra Day O'Connor retires as Associate Justice. She begins making speeches criticizing attacks on courts and judicial elections.

2008   California Proposition 8 limits marriage to opposite sex partners, overturning a California supreme court decision.

2008   *Boumediene v. Bush* is criticized by Republican presidential candidate John McCain as "one of the worst decisions in the history of this country."

2009   By the end of George W. Bush's presidency, Republican-appointed federal judges outnumber Democratic appointees, 614 to 246.

2009   According to Gallup, 59 percent of Americans approve the job the Supreme Court is doing, a significant increase from comparable figures in 2007 and 2008. Democrats view the Court much more positively than Republicans, perhaps reflecting the new administration of Democratic president Barack Obama and his Supreme Court appointee, Sonia Sotomayor.

2010   In his State of the Union address, with six justices in attendance, President Obama criticizes a Supreme Court decision striking down portions of a campaign finance reform bill. Several weeks later, Chief Justice John Roberts calls the president's comments on the case "very troubling."

Contributors

Tom S. Clark is an assistant professor of political science at Emory University. His areas of research expertise include judicial politics and American political institutions, and he is the author of several articles that examine judicial decision making and the separation of powers.

Neal Devins is the Goodrich Professor of Law at William and Mary Law School as well as the director of the Institute of Bill of Rights Law. He is the author or editor of ten books and has written dozens of scholarly articles on law and politics.

Stephen M. Engel is an assistant professor of political science at Marquette University. He obtained his Ph.D. from Yale University and has served as a research fellow at the American Bar Foundation. He is the author of a number of articles examining American politics and history.

Louis Fisher is a scholar in residence at the Constitution Project. He is the author of over twenty books on the Constitution, law, and politics.

Scott E. Gant is a partner in the Washington, D.C., office of Boies, Schiller & Flexner and an adjunct professor of law at Georgetown Law School. He is the author of numerous scholarly articles as well as the recent book We're All Journalists Now: The Transformation of the Press and Reshaping of the Law in the Internet Age.

Charles Geyh is the John F. Kimberling Professor of Law at the Indiana University School of Law. He is the author of When Courts and Congress Collide: The Struggle for Control of America's Judicial System as well as numerous articles on judicial independence and the relationship between state and federal courts and other branches of government.

Bruce Peabody is an associate professor of political science at Fairleigh Dickinson University in Madison, New Jersey. He has published widely on the separation of powers and constitutional interpretation outside of courts.

J. Mitchell Pickerill is an associate professor of political science at Washington State University. He is the author of books and articles on law and the courts, including Constitutional Deliberation in Congress: The Impact of Judicial Review in a Separated System.

Jason Pierce is an associate professor of political science at the University of Dayton. He is the author of Inside the Mason Court Revolution, a book that examines recent controversies involving the highest court in Australia.

Maya Sabatello is an adjunct assistant professor at the Center for Global Affairs, New York University. She earned her doctorate in Political Science at the University of Southern California. She holds an LL.B. from the Hebrew University of Jerusalem and is a member of the Israeli Bar Association. Her research interests include international law, comparative human rights, politics of identity, culture and law, and bioethics.

Matthew J. Streb is an associate professor of political science at Northern Illinois University. He is the author of books and articles on law, elections, and American politics, including Running for Judge: The Rising Political, Financial, and Legal Stakes of Judicial Elections.

Notes

CHAPTER ONE: The Choreography of Courts-Congress Conflicts

1. For further discussion of the issues addressed in this opening section, see Charles Gardner Geyh, *When Courts and Congress Collide: The Struggle for Control of America's Judicial System* (Ann Arbor: University of Michigan Press, 2006), 51–111.

2. Don Van Natta Jr., "Under Pressure, Federal Judge Reverses Decision in Drug Case," *New York Times*, April 2, 1996, A1.

3. Gebe Martinez, "DeLay Amplifies Knocks on Judges; International Law and Web Shouldn't Sway Kennedy's Decisions, He Says," *Houston Chronicle*, April 20, 2005, A5.

4. American Bar Association, *An Independent Judiciary: Report of the ABA Commission on Judicial Independence and Separation of Powers* (1997), 47. "Robust criticism of judicial decisions is fully protected by the First Amendment to the United States Constitution and is indispensable to the well-being of democracy." Nevertheless: "There is a difference between intemperate criticism of a judge for making a wrong-headed decision, and a threat by a member of Congress or the President to seek the judge's removal for that decision. . . . Public officials should refrain from threatening to initiate impeachment proceedings on the basis of judges' interpretation or misinterpretation of the law in particular decisions." Ibid., 48–49.

5. William N. Eskridge Jr., "Overriding Supreme Court Statutory Interpretation Decisions," 101 *Yale Law Journal* 331 (1991), 334–36, 338–40, 344–45, 397. Congress overrode 121 Supreme Court statutory interpretations from 1967 to 1990, about five to six per year. Ibid., 337–38. This figure does not include congressional codification and approval of the Court's statutory decisions, responses to common law or constitutional decisions, or legislation that inexplicitly overrode a Court decision. Ibid., 336n7. Including these categories, Court decisions were affected by legislation about eight to ten times per year. Ibid. During this period, the Supreme Court issued about eighty statutory interpretation decisions per year. Ibid., 339n15. Lower court decisions were overridden about seven times per year from 1967 to 1974 and an average of seventeen times per year from 1975 to 1990. Ibid., 338

6. *Chisholm v. Georgia*, 2 U.S. 419 (1793) (subsequently overturned by the adoption of the Eleventh Amendment); *Dred Scott v. Sanford*, 60 U.S. 393 (1856) (subsequently overturned by the Fourteenth Amendment); *Pollock v. Farmers' Loan and Trust Co.*, 157 U.S. 429 (1895), 158 U.S. 601 (1895) (subsequently overturned by the Sixteenth

Amendment); *Oregon v. Mitchell,* 400 U.S. 112 (1970) (subsequently overturned by the Twenty-Sixth Amendment).

7. See, for example, John Conyers Jr., "Is the United States Constitution a 'Rough Draft'? An Open Letter to the 105th Congress," 6 *Widener Journal of Public Law* 323 (1997), 325 ("The Constitution has provided us with the most enduring and successful democracy in history, and unless you are absolutely convinced of the need for change, you should give our current political system the benefit of the doubt"). Congressman Conyers's (D-Mich.) warning against unneeded amendments came in the wake of seven constitutional amendments that were "seriously considered" during the 104th Congress: amendments on the budget, taxes, term limits, flag burning, crime victims' rights, school prayer, and birthright citizenship. Ibid., 323–24.

8. Richard B. Bernstein with Jerome Agel, *Amending America: If We Love the Constitution So Much, Why Do We Keep Trying to Change It?* (Lawrence: University Press of Kansas, 1993), 169, 349n2.

9. Geyh, *When Courts and Congress Collide,* 171–222.

10. Nancy Scherer, *Scoring Points: Politicians, Activists, and the Lower Federal Court Appointment Process* (Stanford, CA: Stanford University Press, 2005), 133.

11. 28 U.S.C. § 331 (2008).

12. Deborah J. Barrow, Gary Zuk, and Gerard S. Gryski, *The Federal Judiciary and Institutional Change* (Ann Arbor: University of Michigan Press, 1996), 93–94 (describing the Judicial Conference as the "initiator or agenda setter for enlargement of the third branch").

13. John M. De Figueiredo and Emerson H. Tiller, "Congressional Control of the Courts: A Theoretical and Empirical Analysis of Expansion of the Federal Judiciary," 39 *Journal of Law and Economics* 435 (1996), 459–60.

14. Stephen Reinhardt, "Whose Federal Judiciary Is It Anyway," in *Judges on Judging: Views from the Bench,* ed. David M. O'Brien (Washington, DC: Congressional Quarterly Press, 1997), 77.

15. Impeaching Manuel L. Real, a Judge of the United States District Court for the Central District of California, for High Crimes and Misdemeanors: Hearing on H.R. 916 Before the Subcommittee on Courts, the Internet, and Intellectual Property of the H. Comm. On the Judiciary, 109th Cong. (2006), 2–4. Judge Real intervened in the bankruptcy proceeding of a woman whose parole he was supervising. Chairman Lamar Smith noted that the Ninth Circuit's improper handling of the investigation lent "greater need for our Subcommittee to conduct this hearing."

16. Geyh, *When Courts and Congress Collide,* 223–52.

17. Judicial Transparency and Ethics Enhancement Act of 2006: Hearing on H.R. 5219 Before the Subcommittee on Crime Terrorism, and Homeland Security of the H. Comm. On the Judiciary, 109th Congress (2006) (proposing the creation of an Inspector General for the judiciary to investigate judicial misconduct).

18. 1 Stat. 73 (1789). Section 11 established federal jurisdiction over all civil suits "between a citizen of the State where the suit is brought, and a citizen of another State" so long as the amount in controversy was over five hundred dollars.

19. Removal Act of 1875, ch. 137, 18 Stat. 470.

20. Albert Alschuler, "Mediation with a Mugger: The Shortage of Adjudicative Services and the Need for a Two-Tier System in Civil Cases," 99 *Harvard Law Review* 1808 (1986), 1817–18n39 (arguing that there has been a substantive law explosion, rather than a litigation explosion, in the last half-century).

21. 28 U.S.C. § 1332(a) (2006) (requiring the amount in controversy to exceed $75,000). See Pub.L. 104–317, § 205(a)(1) (1996) (raising the amount in controversy from $50,000 to $75,000); see also Pub.L. 100-702, §§ 201(a), 203(a) (1988) (increasing amount in controversy from $10,000 to $50,000).

22. "End May Be Coming for Diversity Jurisdiction," *American Bar Association Journal* 63 (1977): 477 (reporting on a pending House bill—supported by the Judicial Conference—to end diversity jurisdiction).

23. Judicial Conference of the United States, "Long Range Plan for the Federal Courts" (1995): 22 ("As Congress continues to 'federalize' crimes previously prosecuted in the state courts and to create civil causes of action over matters previously resolved in the state courts, the viability of judicial federalism is unquestionably at risk").

24. 28 U.S.C. § 1332(d), 1453, 1711–15 (2006).

25. Relief of the Parents of Theresa Marie Schiavo, 119 Stat. 15 (2005).

26. P.L. 104-227, 110 Stat. 3034 § 104.

27. Benjamin J. Keele, "Ganging Up against the Courts: Congressional Curtailment of Judicial Review 1988–2004," 7 *Pi Sigma Alpha Undergraduate Journal of Politics* 174 (2007). "Congress regularly enacts at least a half-dozen or more denials of jurisdiction in a two-year period. While controversial and unpopular court decisions may spark a wave of jurisdiction-stripping proposals, a stream of jurisdictional denials constantly flows out of Congress without much publicity or prominent debate." Ibid., 189. This study does not suggest an overall shrinkage in federal jurisdiction: the number of jurisdictional grants exceeds the number of denials. Ibid., 193.

28. "As Workload and Resources Head in Opposite Directions, Crisis Looms for Federal Courts," *The Third Branch* (March 2004).

29. For example: In his capacity as chairman of the Budget Committee of the Judicial Conference, Judge Richard Arnold has described cordial relationships between the Congress and the judiciary. He has noted that "overall, the system of separation and interdependence among the three branches of government works extremely well in the case of the Federal Judiciary budget. It works primarily because of Congress." Richard S. Arnold, "Money, or the Relations of the Judicial Branch with the Other Two Branches, Legislative and Executive," 40 *St. Louis University Law Journal* 19 (1996), 28; see also Richard S. Arnold, "The Federal Courts: Causes of Discontent," 56 *Southern Methodist University Law Review* 767 (2003), 772, 774–75 (2003) ("It was my job to go to Congress and sufficiently humble myself so that they would give us the money, and they did. They are very good about funding the courts."). Similarly, Judge Carolyn Dineen King acknowledged that "appropriations committees in both the Senate and the House understand our unique plight and have been uncommonly

sympathetic. . . . But, in the end, understanding and sympathy will not be enough to carry the day. . . . As long as [the federal deficit] continues, our situation will be at the least very difficult, and if we are forced to make more layoffs, it could be disastrous." Carolyn Dineen King, "Current Challenges to the Federal Judiciary," 66 *Los Angeles Law Review* 661 (2006), 664–65.

30. Oversight of the Courthouse Construction Program: Hearing Before the Subcommittee on Oversight of Government Management, and the District of Columbia, of the S. Comm. On Governmental Affairs, 104th Cong. (1995) (investigating excesses in the federal courthouse construction program); Glen Johnson, "Supreme Court Nominee's Role in Expensive Courthouse Project Questioned," Associated Press, July 12, 1994 (detailing criticism of Justice Breyer's role in the design of a proposed $218 million courthouse in Boston); Subcommittee on Administrative Oversight and the Courts of the S. Comm. On the Judiciary, 104th Cong., Report on the January 1996 Judicial Survey (Comm. Print 1996). Senator Grassley, then chairman of the subcommittee, sent questionnaires to all Article III judges (excluding Supreme Court Justices). He requested a variety of information but generally focused on time management, court administration, and workload.

31. Eugenia F. Toma, "A Contractual Model of the Voting Behavior of the Supreme Court: The Role of the Chief Justice," 16 *International Review of Law and Economics* 433 (1996), 442 ("The larger the difference between the Court [ideological] output rating and the preferred output of Congress . . . the smaller the budget"). Toma also makes a larger claim, suggesting that "Congress penalizes the Court in budgetary terms as a means of inducing outcomes in the direction it desires," Ibid.; see also Frank B. Cross and Blake J. Nelson, "Strategic Institutional Effects on Supreme Court Decisionmaking," 95 *Northwestern University Law Review* 1437 (2001), 1485–69 (discussing Toma's results and assuming the existence of "Congressional resource punishment"). This conclusion does not necessarily follow from the data. Toma's correlations may simply reflect that key members of Congress are more responsive to the needs of judiciary when the two branches are on good terms.

32. *Lindh v. Murphy,* 521 U.S. 320, 336 (1997).

33. *Lowery v. Alabama Power Co.,* 483 F.3d 1184, 1198 (2007).

34. *U.S. v. Detwiler,* 338 F. Supp. 2d 1166, 1179 (D. Or. 2004).

35. David Rubenstein, "Rosenbaum Inquisition," *The Nation,* December 29, 2003.

36. Robert A. Katzmann, *Courts and Congress* (Washington, DC: Brookings Institution Press, 1997), 69–81.

37. 28 U.S.C. § 331 (2008).

38. Charles Gardner Geyh, "Paradise Lost, Paradigm Found: Redefining the Judiciary's Imperiled Role in Congress," 71 *New York University Law Review* 1165 (1996), 1174–76.

39. "109th Congress and Pending Legislation Wrap Up," *The Third Branch* (December 2006).

40. "Judicial Conference Asks Congress to Address Areas of Concern in Bankruptcy Reform Bill," *The Third Branch* (March 2001).

41. "Judicial Conference Opposes Sweeping Restrictions on Educational Programs," *The Third Branch* (October 2000).

42. William H. Rehnquist, "2003 Year-End Report on the Federal Judiciary," *The Third Branch* (January 2004) (criticizing criminal sentencing amendments of the PROTECT Act of 2003, 18 U.S.C. 3553, 3742); William H. Rehnquist, "1997 Year-End Report on the Federal Judiciary," *The Third Branch* (January 1998) (criticizing the Senate for delaying the judicial nominee process).

43. *Roe v. Wade*, 410 U.S. 113 (1973).

44. *City of Boerne v. Flores*, 521 U.S. 507 (1997).

45. Alexander M. Bickel, "The Supreme Court, 1960 Term—Foreword: The Passive Virtues," 75 *Harvard Law Review* 40 (1961).

46. Jeffrey A. Segal, "Supreme Court Deference to Congress: An Examination of the Marksist Model," in *Supreme Court Decision-Making: New Institutionalist Approaches*, ed. Cornell Clayton and Howard Gillman (Chicago: University of Chicago Press, 1999), 255.

47. American Bar Association, "An Independent Judiciary: Report of the Commission on the Separation of Powers and Judicial Independence" (1997), 15–17.

48. *The Federalist*, no. 81 (Alexander Hamilton), ed. Clinton Rossiter, 1961, 484–85.

49. Geyh, *When Courts and Congress Collide*, 118–24, table 1 (Impeachment Inquiries and Outcomes, Federal Judges), 161–64.

50. Emily Field Van Tassel, "Resignations and Removals: A History of Federal Judicial Service—and Disservice—1789–1992," 142 *University of Pennsylvania Law Review* 333 (1993), 370.

51. See, for example, Don Van Natta Jr., "A Publicized Drug Courier Pleads Guilty to 3 Felonies," *New York Times*, June 22, 1996 (describing Judge Baer's self-reversal and recusal amid political controversy); Bennett Roth, "Dole Takes Shot at Clinton's Judicial Selections," *Houston Chronicle*, April 20, 1996, A1 (reporting that Judge Baer was singled out as a part of "Bill Clinton's judicial Hall of Shame" by Senator Bob Dole, then running for president).

52. Cf. Stephen O. Kline, "Revisiting FDR's Court-Packing Plan: Are the Current Attacks on Judicial Independence So Bad?" 30 *McGeorge Law Review* 863 (1999), 940n421. Years later, Justice Owen Roberts released a memorandum justifying his decision to switch sides on the New Deal legislation. In it, he claimed that the Court reached its critical decision at a conference before Roosevelt announced the Court-packing plan. Thus, he stated, "no action taken by the President . . . had any causal relationship to my action." Kline still considers the Court's change as "its most significant capitulation to external pressure." Ibid., 951.

53. Charles Babington, "GOP Is Fracturing over Power of Judiciary," *Washington Post*, April 7, 2005; Carl Hulse and David Kirkpatrick, "Even Death Does Not Quiet Harsh Political Fight," *New York Times*, April 1, 2005, A1.

54. Geyh, *When Courts and Congress Collide*, 266–68. To these, one might add more recent legislation, enacted at the behest of the George W. Bush administration,

denying enemy combatants in the "war on terror" recourse to the federal courts and providing for their trials in military tribunals—legislation that the Supreme Court subsequently invalidated. *Boumediene v. Bush*, 128 S. Ct. 2229 (2008) (striking down the Military Commissions Act of 2006). While this legislation reflected political branch distrust of the federal courts and was enacted during a cycle of anti-court sentiment, congressional acquiescence to the president's initiative may have had more to do with acute anxiety over the war than with a desire to "score points" in its ongoing dispute with the judiciary.

55. *Boumediene v. Bush*.

56. Stephen Dinan, "House Targets Judicial 'Errors' with a New Strategy; Votes to Stop Enforcement of Rulings on Pledge, Posting," *Washington Times*, July 29, 2003, 1. See also Bruce Peabody, "Congress, the Court, and the 'Service Constitution': Article III Jurisdiction Controls as a Case Study of the Separation of Powers," 2 *Michigan State Law Review* 269 (2006).

57. Arthur D. Hellman, "Justice O'Connor and 'The Threat to Judicial Independence': The Cowgirl Who Cried Wolf?" 39 *Arizona State Law Journal* 845 (2007), 853–57.

58. Geyh, *When Courts and Congress Collide*, 267–68.

59. Jeffrey Segal and Harold Spaeth, *The Supreme Court and the Attitudinal Model* (Cambridge, MA: Cambridge University Press, 1993).

60. *United States v. Lopez*, 514 U.S. 549 (1995) (invalidating 18 U.S.C. sec. 922(q) under the Commerce Clause). Congress later amended the statute, applying it only to activity with a firearm that "has moved in or that otherwise affects interstate or foreign commerce." 18 U.S.C. 922(q)(3)(A) (Supp. 2007).

61. *United States v. Morrison*, 529 U.S. 598 (2000) (invalidating 42 U.S.C. sec. 13981 under the Commerce Clause).

62. News Release of the Administrative Office of the U.S. Courts, September 19, 2000, available at www.uscourts.gov/Press_Releases/press09192000.html.

63. Emily Field Van Tassel and Paul Finkelman, *Impeachable Offenses: A Documentary History from 1787 to the Present* (Washington, DC: Congressional Quarterly Press, 1999), 93–95 (reproducing the text of the articles of impeachment against Pickering).

64. Geyh, *When Courts and Congress Collide*, 125–54, 304n86. Pickering was removed in 1804. Supreme Court Justice Samuel Chase was impeached by the House in 1805 but was acquitted by the Senate, with as many as 19 senators voting to remove him and 15 voting against (falling barely short of the two-thirds majority needed). James Peck was impeached in 1830 but was acquitted in the Senate, with 21 voting guilty and 22 voting not guilty. Finally, Judge Charles Swayne was impeached in 1904 and, on the articles that concerned his decision-making, was acquitted by the Senate by votes of 31 to convict and 51 to acquit, and 35 to convict and 47 to acquit.

65. Findings and Conclusions of Robert W. Kastenmeier on Citizen Petitions to Impeach Three Federal Judges 8 (September 25, 1986) (on file with author).

66. Geyh, *When Courts and Congress Collide*, 84–85.

67. Jennifer E. Spreng, "Three Divisions in One Circuit? A Critique of the Recommendations from the Commission on Structural Alternatives for the Federal Courts of Appeals," 35 *Idaho Law Review* 553 (1999); Joseph N. Akrotirianakis et al., "Jerry-Building the Road to the Future: An Evaluation of the White Commission Report on Structural Alternatives for the Federal Courts of Appeals," 36 *San Diego Law Review* 355 (1999).

68. Arthur D. Hellman, "Jumboism and Jurisprudence: The Theory and Practice of Precedent in the Large Appellate Court," 56 *University of Chicago Law Review* 541 (1989).

69. Geyh, *When Courts and Congress Collide,* 68.

70. American Bar Association, "Justice in Jeopardy: Report of the Commission on the 21st Century Judiciary," (2003): 31–33. "There have been a number of instances reported by Commission witnesses, consultants, and in the press, in which the [state] judiciary's budget was threatened in retaliation for unpopular decisions." Ibid. For example, a survey of state court administrators and legislative budget officers found that over 36% of court administrators and 28.9% of budget officers believed that the legislature had threatened to reduce the judiciary's budget to influence or protest court decisions. Over 66% of those respondents also reported that the legislature actually had reduced the court's budget. Ibid. (quoting James W. Douglas and Roger E. Hartley, "The Politics of Court Budgeting in the States: Is Judicial Independence Threatened by the Budgetary Process?" *Public Administration Review* 63 (July/August 2003), 441, table 7).

71. Babington, "GOP Is Fracturing over Power of Judiciary"; and Hulse and Kirkpatrick, "Even Death Does Not Quiet Harsh Political Fight."

72. As Representative John Boehner wrote: "Putting terrorists like these on trial in a civilian court would provide them with access to classified information. Such information—if it fell into the wrong hands—could be exploited on the battlefield to harm American troops." "Military Tribunals Bring Terrorists to Justice, Protect American Troops," *U.S. Federal News* (September 16, 2006).

73. *Boumediene v. Bush*; *Hamdan v. Rumsfeld,* 548 U.S. 557 (2006). See Neal Devins, "Congress, the Supreme Court, and Enemy Combatants: How Lawmakers Buoyed Judicial Supremacy by Placing Limits on Federal Court Jurisdiction," 91 *Minnesota Law Review* 1562 (2007), 1589; and Neal Devins, "Should the Supreme Court Fear Congress?" 90 *Minnesota Law Review* 1337 (2006), 1361–62.

74. See Larry D. Kramer, "The Supreme Court v. Balance of Powers," *New York Times,* March 3, 2001, A13 (arguing that the conservative Supreme Court "must be resisted," adding that that "Presidents and Congresses in the past never hesitated to reprimand an overreaching court," one example being that "Andrew Jackson and Abraham Lincoln ignored what they regarded as unsupportable decisions").

75. Leonard Baker, *John Marshall: A Life in Law* (New York: Macmillan, 1974), 745. But see also Charles Warren, *The Supreme Court in United States History,* vol. 1 (Beard Books, rev. ed., 1926), 758–69 (suggesting that Andrew Jackson never made such a statement).

76. James P. George, "Jurisdictional Implications in the Reduced Funding of Lower Federal Courts," 25 *Review of Litigation* 1 (2006), 23 ("Critics of Congress's short funding have proposed remedies in the form of the courts exercising an inherent power either to bill Congress or raise revenue. Without critiquing them here, they are constitutionally doubtful at best. A more basic solution exists in the Fifth Amendment's Due Process Clause which, along with other doctrines, requires the government to furnish access to courts for justiciable disputes.").

77. Saikrishna Prakash and Steven D. Smith, "How to Remove a Federal Judge," 116 *Yale Law Journal* 72 (2006); Raoul Berger, *Impeachment: The Constitutional Problems* (Cambridge, MA: Harvard University Press, 1973).

78. Peter M. Shane, "Who May Discipline or Remove Federal Judges? A Constitutional Analysis," 142 *University of Pennsylvania Law Review* 209 (1993), 235 (characterizing Berger's argument as based on "the thinnest of reeds"); see also James Pfander, "Removing Federal Judges," 74 *University of Chicago Law Review* 1227 (2007).

79. Pfander, "Removing Federal Judges," 1228 ("Article II and Article III similarly envision a role for the Supreme Court in appointing "inferior" officers and removing them from office. But it would be controversial, to say the least, to conclude that the Court's supervisory power extends to the appointment and removal of the judges of inferior courts. . . . That presidential appointment and Senate confirmation of all federal judges has the sanction of two hundred years of experience surely counts for something.").

80. See polling data cited in Charles Gardner Geyh, "The State of the Onion: Peeling Back the Layers of America's Ambivalence toward Judicial Independence," 82 *Indiana Law Journal* 1215 (2007).

CHAPTER TWO: Congress and Judicial Supremacy

1. Portions of this chapter are drawn from Neal Devins, "Should The Supreme Court Fear Congress?" 90 *Minnesota Law Review* 1337 (2006); and Neal Devins "Congress, the Supreme Court, and Enemy Combatants," 91 *Minnesota Law Review* 1562 (2007). See also Joseph L. Smith, "Judicial Procedures as Instruments of Political Control: Congress's Strategic Use of Citizen Suits," 21 *Legislative Studies Quarterly* 283 (2006).

2. Thomas W. Merrill, "The Making of the Second Rehnquist Court," 47 *St. Louis University Law Journal* 569 (2003), 591; and Jeffrey A. Segal and Harold J. Spaeth, *The Supreme Court and the Attitudinal Model Revisited* (Cambridge, MA: Cambridge University Press, 2002).

3. Lee Epstein and Jack Knight, *The Choices Justices Make* (Washington, DC: CQ Press, 1998); and William Mishler and Reginald S. Sheehan, "Public Opinion, the Attitudinal Model, and Supreme Court Decision Making," 58 *Journal Of Politics* 169 (1996).

4. Lee Epstein, Jack Knight, and Andre W. Martin, "The Political (Science) Context of Judging," 47 *St. Louis University Law Journal* 783 (2003).

5. Howard Gillman, "The Court as an Idea," *Supreme Court Decision-Making*, ed.

Cornell W. Clayton and Howard Gillman (Lawrence: University Press of Kansas, 1999), 69.

6. Cornell W. Clayton, "The Supreme Court and Political Jurisprudence: New and Old Institutionalism," *Supreme Court Decision-Making*, ed. Clayton and Gillman, 32.

7. *Frontiero v. Richardson*, 411 U.S. 677, 678–88 (1973); *Craig v. Boren*, 429 U.S. 190 (1976).

8. Owen Roberts Jr., *The Court and the Constitution* (Cambridge, MA: Harvard University Press, 1951), 61.

9. Gerald N. Rosenberg, "Judicial Independence and the Reality of Political Power," 54 *Review of Politics* 369 (1992).

10. Earl Warren, *The Memoirs of Earl Warren* (Garden City, NY: Doubleday, 1977), 313.

11. Walter F. Murphy, *Congress and the Court* (Chicago: University of Chicago Press, 1962), 245.

12. 102 *Congressional Record* 415–16 (1956).

13. Bruce G. Peabody, "Congressional Attitudes towards Constitutional Interpretation," in *Congress and the Constitution*, ed. Neal Devins and Keith Whittington (Durham, NC: Duke University Press, 2005), 48; and Donald G. Morgan, *Congress and the Constitution* (Cambridge: Belknap Press of Harvard University Press, 1966), 365–83.

14. Bruce G. Peabody, "Congress, the Court, and the 'Service Constitution': Article III Jurisdiction Controls as a Case Study of the Separation of Powers," 2006 *Michigan State Law Review* 269 (2006), 291.

15. Charles G. Geyh, "Judicial Independence, Judicial Accountability, and the Role of Constitutional Norms in Congressional Regulation of the Courts," 78 *Indiana Law Journal* 153 (2003), 209.

16. Murphy, *Congress and the Court*, 238, 246.

17. Phillip P. Frickey, "Getting From Joe to Gene (McCarthy): The Avoidance Canon, Legal Process Theory, and Narrowing Statutory Interpretation in the Early Warren Court," 93 *California Law Review* 397 (2005).

18. Michael Belknap, *The Supreme Court under Earl Warren* (Columbia: University of South Carolina Press, 2005), 308.

19. Stefanie Lindquist and Frank Cross, *Measuring Judicial Activism* (Oxford: Oxford University Press, 2009) (finding Felix Frankfurter to be one of the least "activist" judges, while Douglas, Black, and Brennan are among the most activist).

20. Lucas A Powe Jr., *The Warren Court and American Politics* (Cambridge, MA: Belknap Press of Harvard University Press, 2000), 394–95.

21. *Miranda v Arizona*, 384 U.S. 436, 473 (1966).

22. Yale Kamisar, "The Warren Court and Criminal Justice," in *The Warren Court: A Retrospective*, ed. Bernard Schwartz (New York: Oxford University Press, 1996), 116–17.

23. Louis Fisher and Neal Devins, *Political Dynamics of Constitutional Law*, 4th ed. (St. Paul, MN: Thomson/West, 2006).

24. Neal Devins and Louis Fisher, *The Democratic Constitution* (New York: Oxford University Press, 2004), 132–34, 159–61.

25. J. Mitchell Pickerill, *Constitutional Deliberation in Congress* (Durham, NC: Duke University Press, 2004).

26. Devins, "Should The Supreme Court Fear Congress?"

27. Devins, "Congress, the Supreme Court, and Enemy Combatants."

28. Public Law 109–13, 119 Statute 15, 2005.

29. William H. Rehnquist, "2004 Year End Report on the Federal Judiciary" (2005) 8.

30. Tim Russert, "Constitutional Conversation with Justices Breyer, O'Connor, and Scalia," 2005, available at www.constitutioncenter.org.

31. 18th House ranking Order (August 23, 2005) http://voteview.com/hou108.htm; 108th Senate Rank Ordering (October 24, 2004), http://voteview.com/sen108.htm.

32. Laurie Goodstein and William Yardley, "President Benefits from Efforts to Build a Coalition of Religious Voters," *New York Times*, November 5, 2004, sec. A22.

33. Samuel Issacharoff, "Collateral Damage: The Endangered Center in American Politics," 46 *William and Mary Law Review* 415 (2004), 427–28.

34. C. Lawrence Evans, "Committees, Leaders, and Message Politics," in *Congress Reconsidered*, 7th ed., ed. Lawrence C. Dodd and Bruce I. Oppenheimer (Washington, DC: CQ Press, 2001).

35. Adam Nagourney, "Partisan Tenor of Alito Hearings Reflects a Quick Change in Washington," *New York Times*, January 10, 2006, A17; Robert Toner and David Kirkpatrick, "Liberals and Conservatives Remain Worlds Apart on Roberts Suitability," *New York Times*, September 16, 2005, A22.

36. Keith E. Whittington, "Taking What They Give Us: Explaining the Court's Federalism Offensive," 51 *Duke Law Journal* 477 (2001), 477, 512–515.

37. David R. Mayhew, *Congress: The Electoral Connection*, 2d ed. (New Haven: Yale University Press, 2004), 62.

38. Keith E. Whittington, Neal Devins, and Hutch Hicken, "The Constitution and Congressional Committees: 1971–2000," in *The Least Examined Branch*, ed. Richard W. Bauman and Tsvi Kahana (New York: Cambridge University Press, 2006), 95–105.

39. Neal Devins, "The Academic Expert before Congress," 54 *Duke Law Journal* 1525 (2005), 1542–44.

40. Roger H. Davidson and Walter J. Oleszek, *Congress and its Members*, 10th ed. (2006), 217.

41. Devins, "Academic before Congress," 1543.

42. Morgan, *Congress and the Constitution*, 365–83; and Peabody, "Congressional Attitudes towards Constitutional Interpretation."

43. Peabody, "Congressional Attitudes towards Constitutional Interpretation," 48.

44. Whittington, "Taking What They Give Us," 513.

45. Neal Devins, "The Majoritarian Rehnquist Court," 67 *Law and Contemporary Problems* 63 (Summer 2004); and Barry Friedman and Anna L. Harvey, "Electing the Supreme Court," 78 *Indiana Law Journal* 123 (2003).

46. Devins, "Should The Supreme Court Fear Congress?" 1349.

47. Ibid., 1354–55.

48. Bill Frist, "Frist Comments on Schiavo Bill Enrollment," Press Release, March 21, 2005.

49. Carl Hulse and Adam Nagourney, "Briefly Back in the Spotlight, Delay Now Steps Aside," *New York Times*, March 26, 2005, A9.

50. Sam Rosenfeld, "Disorder in the Court," *American Prospect*, July 2005.

51. H.R. 3799, 108th Congress, (2004).

52. 150 Congressional Record, H7079, September 14, 2004 (statement to Rep. Pence).

53. Gregory A. Caldeira and James L. Gibson, "The Etiology of Public Support for the Supreme Court," 36 *American Journal of Political Science* 635 (1992); and Charles Gardner Geyh, *When Courts and Congress Collide* (Ann Arbor: University of Michigan Press, 2006).

54. Neal Devins, "The Federalism-Rights Nexus: Explaining Why Senate Democrats Can Tolerate Rehnquist Court Decision Making but Not the Rehnquist Court," 73 *University of Colorado Law Review* 1307 (2002).

55. Devins, "Congress, the Supreme Court, and Enemy Combatants," 1563–80.

56. Public Law 109-148, Sec. 1001–1006; 119 Stat. 2739.

57. Public Law 109-366; 120 Stat. 2600.

58. Devins, "Congress, the Supreme Court, and Enemy Combatants," 1572.

59. Ibid., 1573.

60. Jim Inhofe, "Inhofe Statement on Terrorist-Detainee-Treatment Bill," *Congressional Quarterly*, September 15, 2006.

61. 152 Congressional Record H7537, September 27, 2006.

62. David E. Sanger and Scott Shane, "Court's Ruling Is Likely to Force Negotiations over Presidential Powers," *New York Times*, June 30, 2006, A1.

63. Neil A. Lewis and Kate Zerinke, "Measures Seek to Restrict Detainees' Access to Courts," *New York Times*, September 21, 2006, A22.

64. Devins, "Congress, the Supreme Court, and Enemy Combatants," 1577–78.

65. *Boumediene v. Bush*, 553 U.S. 723 (2008).

66. Sam Rosenfeld, "Disorder in the Court," *American Prospect*, vol. 16, July 2005, 24, 26.

67. Devins, "Should the Supreme Court Fear Congress?" 1337.

68. Caldeira and Gibson, "Etiology of Public Support," 635; and Geyh, *When Courts and Congress Collide*.

69. Maura Reynolds, "DeLay Tempers His Statements," *Los Angeles Times*, April 14, 2005, A11.

70. William M. Landers and Richard A. Posner, "The Independent Judiciary in an Interest-Group Perspective," 18 *Journal of Law and Economics* 875 (1975), 885.

71. Devins, "The Federalism-Rights Nexus," 1307.

72. Caldeira and Gibson, "Etiology of Public Support," 636–38.

73. Martha Neil, "Half of U.S. Sees Judicial Activism Crisis," *ABA J. E-Report*, September 20, 2005.

CHAPTER THREE: Presidential Manipulations of Judicial Power

1. Research for this chapter was funded by the National Science Foundation's Doctoral Improvement Grant in Law and Social Sciences (SES-0719031) and an American Bar Foundation Doctoral Research Fellowship in 2007–2008. Earlier drafts were presented at Yale University, Wesleyan University, Marquette University, the University of Tulsa, the City University of New York/John Jay College of Criminal Justice, Grinnell College, Williams College, the American Bar Foundation, and the Midwest Political Science Association 2008 Annual Meeting. The author thanks Bruce Peabody, Stephen Skowronek, Bruce Ackerman, Gregory Huber, David Mayhew, Mark Graber, Daniel Galvin, Bonnie Honig, Robert Nelson, Traci Burch, Laura Beth Nielsen, Stephen Daniels, Julia Azari, Stephen Kaplan, Abbey Steele, and Alex Kirshner for their helpful critiques.

2. For other commentary about today's critiques of courts, see Roger K. Warren and Bert Brandenburg, *Speak to American Values: A Handbook for Winning the Debate for Fair and Impartial Courts* (Washington, DC: Justice at Stake, 2006); and Citizens for Independent Courts, *Uncertain Justice: Politics and America's Courts* (New York: Century Foundation Press, 2000). On academic and journalistic downplaying of the threat, see John Ferejohn, "Independent Judges, Dependent Judiciary: Explaining Judicial Independence," 72 *Southern California Law Review* 353 (1999); and Sam Rosenfeld, "Disorder in the Court," *American Prospect,* June 19, 2005. See Bruce Peabody's review of anti-court rhetoric in Republican national party platforms since the 1980s in this volume's introduction. For a similar analysis of party platforms, see Stephen Engel, "Attacking the Court: A Theory of Political Contingency and Initial Findings Drawn from National Party Platforms," presented at the 2007 Midwest Political Science Association Meeting, April 14, 2007, accessible at www.allacademic .com//meta/p_mla_apa_research_citation/1/9/6/8/o/pages196808/p196808-1.php. On patterns of congressional court-curbing proposals, which follow a similar pattern of recently increasing intensity, see Tom Clark's contribution to this volume.

3. For a discussion of departmentalism versus judicial supremacy, see Susan Burgess, *Contest for Constitutional Authority* (Lawrence: University Press of Kansas, 1992); and Neal Devins and Louis Fisher, *The Democratic Constitution* (New York: Oxford University Press, 2004).

4. Abraham Lincoln, First Inaugural Address, March 4, 1861, available at http:// avalon.law.yale.edu/19th_century/lincoln1.asp.

5. Thomas Jefferson to Thomas Ritchie, December 25, 1820, *The Writings of Thomas Jefferson,* Paul Leicester Ford, ed. (New York: Knickerbocker Press of G. P. Putnam's Sons, 1899).

6. Bruce Ackerman, *We the People: Foundations* (Cambridge, MA: Belknap Press of Harvard University Press, 1991); and Bruce Ackerman, *We the People: Transformations* (Cambridge, MA: Belknap Press of Harvard University Press, 1998). See also Charles Geyh's contribution to this volume, similarly positing that congressional reprisals of courts occur most vigorously in the aftermath of a "critical" or "realigning" election.

7. Stephen Skowronek offers a theory of presidential regimes in *The Politics Presidents Make: Leadership from John Adams to Bill Clinton* (Cambridge, MA: Harvard University Press, 1997). Keith Whittington applies this model to investigate variation in presidential relations with the judiciary in his *Political Foundations of Judicial Supremacy* (Princeton: Princeton University Press, 2007).

8. The underlying assumption, which leads to criticism of unelected judges, is that elections confer legitimacy because they are associated with majoritarian outcomes. See George Lovell, *Legislative Deferrals: Statutory Ambiguity, Judicial Power, and American Democracy* (New York: Cambridge University Press, 2003), 4–39.

9. The phrase "countermajoritarian difficulty" was coined by Alexander Bickel in his book *The Least Dangerous Branch* (New Haven: Yale University Press, 1986), 16. Bickel's characterization of the countermajoritarian judiciary assumes the Constitution to be democratic and that federal judges' unelected status to mark them as an anomaly. However, see Sanford Levinson, *Our Undemocratic Constitution* (New York: Oxford University Press, 2006); and Robert Dahl, *How Democratic Is Our Constitution?* 2nd ed. (New Haven: Yale University Press, 2001).

10. Robert H. Bork, *The Tempting of America* (New York: Free Press, 1993), 199, emphasis added.

11. On Jeffersonian hostilities toward the judiciary, see Bruce Ackerman, *The Failure of the Founding Fathers* (Cambridge, MA: Belknap Press of Harvard University Press, 2005). On Lincoln's confrontations with judicial power on *Dred Scott* and on decisions about executive war-making authority, see, for example, *Ex parte Merryman*, 17 Fed. Cas. 144 (1861) and *The Prize Cases*, 67 U.S. 635 (1863), see Brian McGinty, *Lincoln and the Court* (Cambridge, MA: Harvard University Press, 2008).

12. For a recent retelling of the collapse of Roosevelt's judicial reform proposal, see Burt Solomon, *FDR v. The Constitution* (New York: Walker, 2009).

13. When Carter signed the Omnibus Judgeship Act of 1978, he authorized the largest expansion of federal judgeships in American history; the law created 152 judgeships. The Reagan administration was unable to increase the judiciary's size on a similar scale. Due to the retirement of judges, over two terms Reagan was able to appoint 384 judges to Carter's 262 appointed during his single term. See www.uscourts.gov/ttb/2009-02/article07.cfm?WT.cg_n=TTB_Feb09_article07_newsroom, accessed September 9, 2009. But limited opportunities to appoint new judges, particularly during Reagan's first term, compelled lawyers in that administration to seek out new ways to exert influence on the judiciary.

14. A distinction should be made between the legitimacy of dissent within the bounds of legislative debate and the legitimacy of opposition "out of doors" once the statute is passed and is thus outside of legislative debate. The Founders accepted the former as indicated by the protections afforded by the Constitution's speech and debate clause. Whether or not such freedom extended beyond the legislature is open to historical interpretation. See James P. Martin, "When Repression is Democratic and Constitutional: The Federalist Theory of Representation and the Sedition Act of 1798," 66 *University of Chicago Law Review* 117 (1999), 117, 182.

15. On antijudiciary sentiment in the early republic, see Richard Ellis, *The Jeffersonian Crisis: Courts and Politics in the Young Republic* (New York: Oxford University Press, 1971); and Gordon Wood, "The Origins of Judicial Review Revisited, or How the Marshall Court Made More Out of Less," *Washington and Lee Law Review* 56 (1999). Stephen Skowronek characterized the nineteenth-century United States as a state of "courts and parties" in his *Building a New American State* (New York: Cambridge University Press, 1982).

16. Quoted in *Emory Law Journal* 50 (2001), 569–70.

17. Keith Whittington, "Interpose Your Friendly Hand: Political Supports and the Exercise of Judicial Review by the United States Supreme Court," 99 *American Political Science Review* 583 (November 2005); Mark A. Graber, "The Nonmajoritarian Difficulty: Legislative Deference to the Judiciary," 7 *Studies in American Political Development* 35 (Spring 1993); Howard Gillman, "How Political Parties Can Use the Courts to Advance Their Agendas: Federal Courts in the United States, 1875–1891," 96 *American Political Science Review* 511 (2002); and Barry Weingast, "The Political Foundations of Democracy and the Rule of Law," 91 *American Political Science Review* 245 (June 1997).

18. Prominent work in this vein includes "The Countermajoritarian Difficulty," Barry Friedman's five-part series. See Friedman, "The History of the Countermajoritarian Difficulty, Part One: The Road to Judicial Supremacy," *New York University Law Review* 73 (1998); Friedman, "The History of the Countermajoritarian Difficulty, Part II: Reconstruction's Political Court," *Georgetown Law Review* 91 (2002); Friedman, "The History of the Countermajoritarian Difficulty, Part III: The Lesson of Lochner," *New York University Law Review* 76 (2001); Friedman, "The History of the Countermajoritarian Difficulty, Part IV: Law's Politics," *University of Pennsylvania Law Review* 148 (2000); and Friedman, "The Birth of an Academic Obsession: The History of the Countermajoritarian Difficulty, Part Five," *Yale Law Journal* 112 (2002). See also Charles Geyh's *When Congress and the Court Collide* (Ann Arbor: University of Michigan Press, 2006).

19. While normative judicial supremacy is assumed across a range of legal literature, existing data fails to confirm public endorsement of judicial supremacy. See Brian Feldman, "Evaluating Public Endorsement of the Weak and Strong Forms of Judicial Supremacy," 89 *Virginia Law Review* 979 (September 2003). For discussion of judicial supremacy as a contemporary norm, see Louis Fisher, *Constitutional Dialogues: Interpretation as Political Process* (Princeton: Princeton University Press, 1988); and Kevin Yingling, "Note: Justifying the Judiciary: A Majoritarian Response to the Countermajoritarian Problem," 15 *Journal of Law and Politics* 81 (1999).

20. A distinction must be made between elite-level norms, that is, norms held by members of Congress or the executive that may be particular artifacts of institutional structure or history, and popular-level norms among the American people in their relationship to and understanding of the judiciary. A judicial supremacy norm may be evident in one, both, or neither of these groups.

21. On the likelihood of passage of Roosevelt's court-packing plan, see William

Leuchtenberg, *The Supreme Court Reborn: The Constitutional Revolution in the Age of Roosevelt* (New York: Oxford University Press, 1995), 132–62.

22. On near passage of court-curbing legislation in the late 1950s, see Walter F. Murphy, *Congress and the Court: A Case Study in the American Political Process* (Chicago: University of Chicago Press, 1962); and Lucas Powe Jr., *The Warren Court and American Politics* (Cambridge, MA: Belknap Press of Harvard University Press, 2000), 60–62, 99–102, 127–42. On court-curbing during the 1970s, see Gary Orfield, "Congress, the President, and Anti-Busing Legislation, 1966–1974," 4 *Journal of Law and Education* 108 (January 1975). Jurisdiction was stripped by the United States Military Commissions Act of 2006, Pub. L. No. 109-366 (2006) and Detainee Treatment Act of 2005, Pub. L. No. 109-148 (2005). That statute was later invalidated by the Supreme Court in *Boumediene v. Bush,* 553 U.S. 723 (2008).

23. See Bernard Bailyn, *The Pamphlets of the American Revolution, 1750–1776* (Cambridge, MA: Harvard University Press, 1965); and Bernard Bailyn, *The Ideological Origins of the American Revolution* (Cambridge, MA: Harvard University Press, 1967).

24. Sometimes politicians can be overt about their harnessing strategy. During the conflict over school busing in the 1970s and 1980s, members of Congress were explicit that their jurisdiction-stripping strategy was not meant to undermine judicial legitimacy but to guide judges toward particular policy outcomes. Examples of such harnessing include Senator Gordon's (R-WA) comment, "we are not attempting to directly reverse Supreme Court decisions, but, to put it more delicately, simply to guide the Supreme Court into a slightly different channel"; see House Judiciary Committee, *Busing Hearings,* part 1 (1972), 502; and Senate Judiciary Committee, Subcommittee on Separation of Powers, *Busing Hearings* (1981), 9.

25. In particular, see Lovell, *Legislative Deferrals.*

26. In this chapter, I assume that "actors' understanding of their own interests is apt to evolve as the ideological setting of politics changes." Robert C. Lieberman, "Ideas, Institutions, and Political Order: Explaining Political Change," 96 *American Political Science Review* 689 (December 2002). Rationality is therefore understood as situated in a context that changes over time; what is rational at Time 1 may no longer be so at Time 2.

27. Presidential rhetoric is conceptualized here as an indicator of political circumstance or as a president's response to new exigencies that impel him or her to challenge traditional meanings. For example, Gordon Wood illustrates how Federalists reconceptualized sovereignty to bolster their idea of a government further removed from the people than the Articles of Confederation. See Wood, *The Creation of the American Republic, 1776–1787* (Chapel Hill: University of North Carolina Press, 1998), 519–64. See also Stephen Skowronek, "The Reassociation of Ideas and Purposes: Racism, Liberalism, and the American Tradition," 100 *American Political Science Review* 385 (August 2006).

28. On anti-court and anti-judge sentiment as drawing on colonial experiences with judges and on protestant agency, see Ellis, *Jeffersonian Crisis.* On anti-Federalist concerns about an unelected judiciary, see, for example, "Centinel," no. 1 (October 5,

1787), in *The Anti-Federalist Papers and the Constitutional Convention Debates*, ed. Ralph Ketchum (New York: Signet Classics, 1986).

29. Jefferson to Madison, March 15, 1789, in *Papers of Thomas Jefferson*, vol. 14, J. Boyd, ed. (Princeton: Princeton University Press, 1958), 659.

30. On the anti-Federalist base of Jefferson's supporters, see Saul Cornell, *The Other Founders: Anti-Federalism and the Dissenting Tradition in America, 1788–1828* (Chapel Hill: University of North Carolina Press, 1999), 191.

31. On eighteenth-century ideas regarding opposition politics, parties, and civic instability, see Ralph Ketcham, *Presidents above Party* (Chapel Hill: University of North Carolina Press, 1987), 50–70, 76–85; James Ceaser, *Presidential Selection* (Princeton: Princeton University Press, 1979), 41–104; Stanley Elkins and Erick McKitrick, *The Age of Federalism* (New York: Oxford University Press, 1993); and Marshal Smelsner, "The Federalist Period as an Age of Passion," 10 *American Quarterly* 391 (Winter 1958).

32. On early American political assumption of unity among federal branches, see G. Edward White, "Recovering Coterminous Power Theory: The Lost Dimension of Marshall Sovereignty Cases," in *Origins of the Federal Judiciary: Essays on the Judiciary Act of 1789*, ed. Maeva Marcus (New York: Oxford University Press, 1992), 66–105. On the idea of the written Constitution as providing fixed and immutable principles, see Phillip A. Hamburger, "The Constitution's Accommodation of Social Change," 88 *Michigan Law Review* 241 (1989).

33. Andrew A. Lipscomb, ed., *Writings of Thomas Jefferson* (Washington, DC: Thomas Jefferson Memorial Association, 1903), 11:50–51.

34. Washington *Federalist*, September 5, 1803; see also *Trial of Judge Chase*, appendix, Massachusetts Historical Society. Box L1804.

35. Thomas Jefferson to Joseph H. Nicholson, May 13, 1803, Thomas Jefferson Papers, Library of Congress.

36. Callender's pamphlet, *The Prospect before Us*, written in 1799, condemned Federalists for endangering liberty, among other charges. See *The Prospect before Us* (Richmond, VA: M. Jones, S. Pheasants, and J. Lyon, 1800). Callender was later tried and imprisoned for sedition in a trial presided over by Samuel Chase, prompting one of Chase's articles of impeachment.

37. *Marbury v. Madison*, 5 U.S. 137 (1803).

38. On the connection between loyal opposition and exit costs, see Ian Shapiro, *The State of Democratic Theory* (Princeton: Princeton University Press, 2003), 43–45, 90–91.

39. John Quincy Adams, "Reply to the Appeal of the Massachusetts Federalists," in *Documents relating to New England Federalism, 1800–1815*, ed. Henry Adams (Boston: B. Franklin, 1877), 149.

40. Stephen Higginson to Pickering, March 17, 1804. Discussion of northern secession following Jefferson's election is a theme in numerous letters. See Tapping Reeve to Uriah Tracy, February 7, 1804, Washington, D.C.; Cabot to Pickering, February 14, 1804; Theodore Lyman to Pickering, February 29, 1804, Boston; Pickering

to Rufus King, Washington, D.C., March 4, 1804; Roger Griswold to Oliver Wolcott, March 11, 1804, Washington, D.C. See *Documents relating to New England Federalism, 1800–1815,* ed. Adams (1877), 331–66.

41. *Stuart v. Laird,* 5 U.S. (1 Cranch) 299 (1803).

42. See Ellis, *Jeffersonian Crisis,* 69–82; Ackerman, *Failure of the Founding Fathers,* 199–223; Keith E. Whittington, *Constitutional Construction* (Cambridge, MA: Harvard University Press, 1999), 20–71.

43. Carl Prince notes that of the thirty lower federal judgeships established by the 1801 act, three judges were removed for political reasons and fifteen were removed by the Repeal Act, reducing Federalist judges to twelve. Prince, "The Passing of the Aristocracy: Jefferson's Removal of the Federalists, 1801–1805," 57 *Journal of American History* 568 (December 1970). On the impeachment of federal district judge Pickering, see Lynn W. Turner, "The Impeachment of John Pickering," 54 *American Historical Review* 485 (April 1949).

44. Whittington, *Constitutional Construction,* 60.

45. The vote on the Chase impeachments suggested an emerging consensus that judges should not be directly involved in politics. According to Whittington, the Eighth Article did not condemn Chase's views per se but rather his airing of those views in the context of his judicial capacity: "The Republicans did not denounce Chase's politics as illegitimate, but rather insisted that his office precluded his acting on those political views." Oppositional views were thereby beginning to receive legitimacy in the sense that they were unavoidable, but they could be expressed only in certain institutional settings. Whittington, *Constitutional Construction,* 50.

46. It is too much to claim that the Jeffersonians intended this possibility. All that can be claimed is that a consequence of the Chase impeachment was to set the potential for making the Court into a weapon of political gain: a partisan tool ironically swathed in its promotion as a nonpartisan neutral branch. Alleged judicial neutrality allowed for the elected branches to use the Court more readily than any overt expression of the judiciary as part of a ruling Federalist elite ever could.

47. Robert Remini claims that Jackson never made the defiant statement. Robert V. Remini, *Andrew Jackson and the Course of American Freedom, 1822–1832,* vol. 2 (New York: Harper and Row, 1981), 276–77.

48. Richard P. Longaker, "Andrew Jackson and the Judiciary," 71 *Political Science Quarterly* 341 (September 1956).

49. According to Longaker, if Jackson enforced Marshall's ruling in *Worcester v. Georgia,* 31 U.S. 515 (1832), by using federal power to overturn state law, he would have potentially jeopardized support in states with large native populations like Georgia, Tennessee, Alabama, and Mississippi. He might have also compelled politicians in these states to back South Carolina's nullification doctrine. Stephen Skowronek also views Jackson's policy moderation—going "out of his way to emphasize gradualism and mutual accommodation"—as a way to hold together his disparate coalition. See Skowronek, *Politics Presidents Make,* 130–37.

50. Andrew Jackson to Andrew Jackson Donelson, July 5, 1822, *The Correspon-*

dence of Andrew Jackson, vol. 3 (Washington, DC, 1926–1935), 167. The immediate case in contention was *McCulloch v, Maryland,* 17 U.S. 316 (1819).

51. Remini, 361. See *Register of Debates,* February 24, 1832, p. 1855–56, available at http://memory.loc.gov/cgi-bin/ampage?collId=llrd&fileName=012/llrd012.db&recNum=219.

52. 1 U.S. Stat. 73, 85–86 (1789). Repealing Section 25 would have severely undermined the federal government's ability to maintain any uniformity among the states and to assert the supremacy of the federal constitution over the individual states, particularly because many antebellum suits against federal law began in state courts. If Section 25 had been repealed, the Supremacy Clause would have been a dead letter. See Maeva Marcus and Natalie Wexler, "The Judiciary Act of 1789: Political Compromise of Constitutional Interpretation?" *Origins of the Federal Judiciary: Essays on the Judiciary Act of 1789,* ed. Maeva Marcus (New York: Oxford University Press, 1992).

53. Robert Remini, *Andrew Jackson and the Bank War* (New York: W.W. Norton, 1967); Gerald Magliocca, *Andrew Jackson and the Constitution* (Lawrence: University Press of Kansas, 2007); Richard Ellis, *The Union at Risk: Jacksonian Democracy, State's Rights, and the Nullification Crisis* (New York: Oxford University Press, 1989).

54. Joel H. Silbey, *Martin Van Buren and the Emergence of American Popular Politics* (New York: Rowman and Littlefield, 2002), xii–xiii.

55. Ceaser, 123. See also Richard Hofstadter, *The Idea of a Party System* (Berkeley: University of California Press, 1969), 213.

56. Martin Van Buren, *An Inquiry into the Origin and Course of Political Parties in the United States* (New York: Augustus M. Kelly, 1967), 7; and Martin Van Buren, "Substance of Mr. Van Buren's Observations in the Senate of the United States on Mr. Foot's amendment to the Rules of the Senate, by which it was proposed to give the Vice President the right to call to order for words spoken in debate," Papers of Martin Van Buren, Library of Congress, series 2, box 7, microfilm 7, page 8.

57. Thomas Jefferson to David Denniston and James Cheethan, June 6, 1801, Jefferson Papers, Library of Congress, series 10, box 3.

58. Van Buren, "Substance," 15.

59. Van Buren, *Inquiry,* 271, 234, 353.

60. See John Aldrich, *Why Parties?* (Chicago: University of Chicago Press, 1995). For a critique of functionalism in the party literature, see Daniel Galvin, "Parties as Political Institutions in American Political Development," paper delivered at the American Political Science Association meeting, Toronto, Canada, September 6, 2009.

61. Gerald Leonard, *The Invention of Party Politics: Federalism, Popular Sovereignty, and Constitutional Development in Jacksonian Illinois* (Chapel Hill: University of North Carolina Press, 2002), 232.

62. On parties' role in constitutional interpretation, see Larry Kramer, *The People Themselves: Popular Constitutionalism and Judicial Review* (New York: Oxford University Press, 2004); and Keith Whittington, "Give 'The People' What They Want?" 81 *Chicago-Kent Law Review* 911 (2006).

63. According to Gerald Leonard, one of Van Buren's "central purposes and justifications," as leader of the new Democratic Party in 1836, was "the effective amend-

ment of the Constitution to prevent elections by the House of Representatives." See Leonard, "Party as a 'Political Safeguard of Federalism': Martin Van Buren and the Constitutional Theory of Party Politics," 54 *Rutgers Law Review* 223 (Fall 2001), 247–49.

64. Van Buren, *Inquiry*, 316, 317, 329, 336.

65. As such, if Federalist or Whig opposition won an election, it was only through democracy's lack of organization—Van Buren's explanation for the electoral crisis of 1824—or by the beguilement of the voting public—his explanation for his own loss in 1840. See *Inquiry*, 349.

66. Ibid., 370–71.

67. "Lincoln at Chicago, July 10, 1858," in *The Complete Lincoln-Douglas Debates of 1858*, ed. Paul M. Angle (Chicago: University of Chicago Press, 1991), 36–37.

68. "First Inaugural Address of Abraham Lincoln," March 4, 1861, emphasis added.

69. *Louisville Democrat*, quoted in Stanley Kutler, *Judicial Power and Reconstruction Politics* (Chicago: University of Chicago Press, 1968), 11.

70. Lincoln at Springfield, July 17, 1858. *The Complete Lincoln-Douglas Debates of 1858*, ed. Paul M. Angle (Chicago: University of Chicago Press, 1991), 77.

71. Abraham Lincoln, *Abraham Lincoln: Speeches and Writings*, 2 vols. (New York: Literary Classics of the United States, 1989), 302–3.

72. "Fifth Joint Debate, at Galesburgh, October 7, 1858," *Political Debates between Abraham Lincoln and Stephen Douglas* (Cleveland, OH: The Burrows Brothers Company, 1894), 218–19.

73. "Speech of Hon. Abraham Lincoln, Delivered in Springfield, Saturday Evening, July 17, 1858," *Political Debates between Abraham Lincoln and Stephen Douglas*, 77.

74. See, for example, James Madison's speech to the House of Representatives in 1791 against the Bank. See also Attorney General Edmund Randolph's opinion on the Bank, Thomas Jefferson's critique of the Bank, and Secretary of the Treasury Alexander Hamilton's support for the Bank, all of which were presented to Washington for his consideration before he signed the law authorizing the First National Bank of the United States. Excerpts of these documents can be found in Paul Brest et al., *Processes of Constitutional Decisionmaking*, 5th ed. (New York: Aspen Publishers, 2006), 28–36.

75. Lincoln, as an orthodox Whig, before he became a Republican, consistently upheld judicial authority and, on that basis, upheld the constitutionality of the National Bank. See Mark Graber, "Popular Constitutionalism, Judicial Supremacy, and the Complete Lincoln-Douglas Debates," *Chicago-Kent Law Review* 81 (2006), 924.

76. "Speech of Hon. Abraham Lincoln, Delivered in Springfield, Saturday Evening, July 17, 1858," 77.

77. First Inaugural Address of Abraham Lincoln, March 4, 1861, available at www .yale.edu/lawweb/avalon/presiden/inaug/lincoln1.htm, emphasis added.

78. Indeed, Lincoln went so far as to mention, in his inaugural, the possibility of a thirteenth amendment that would secure slavery-property interests in the southern states.

79. First Inaugural Address of Abraham Lincoln.

80. Republican Party Platform of 1860, May 17, 1860. John T. Woolley and Gerhard Peters, *The American Presidency Project* (online). Santa Barbara, CA: University of California (hosted), Gerhard Peters (database), available at www.presidency.ucsb.edu/ws/?pid=29620, accessed September 8, 2009.

81. Mark Graber, *Dred Scott and the Problem of Constitutional Evil* (New York: Cambridge University Press, 2006), 185–99.

82. Abraham Lincoln, February 12, 1861, "Fragment of Speech Intended for Kentuckians," in *The Collected Works of Abraham Lincoln,* vol. 4, ed. Roy P. Basler (New Brunswick, NJ: Rutgers University Press, 1953), 200.

83. Abraham Lincoln, February 14, 1861, "Speech at Steubenville, Ohio," in ibid., 207.

84. I use the term *anti-constitutional* to distinguish it from the contemporary sense of *unconstitutional.* The traditional understanding of *unconstitutional* is something that is not permitted by the legal strictures of our constitution. By contrast, by *anti-constitutional* I mean to invoke this concept of illegitimate versus legitimate opposition, that is, an "anti-constitutional" view would be an alternate constitutional vision or interpretation that is out of political favor, is advocated by a faction viewed as holding an intent to undermine national stability, and is thus inconsistent with the politically regnant constitutional paradigm.

85. Howard K. Beale, ed., *The Diary of Edward Bates, 1859–1866* (Washington, DC: American Historical Association, 1933), 553.

86. Lincoln, *Collected Works,* vol. 4, 268, 401.

87. Reagan's attorney general, Edwin Meese III, has been credited with the development of originalism as a jurisprudential philosophy, which aimed to discredit rulings disagreeable to conservatives as judicially activist. See Mark Kozlowski, *The Myth of the Imperial Judiciary* (New York: New York University Press, 2003), 30–49.

88. Reva Siegel and Robert Post have argued that originalism is not the opposite of legal realism or living constitutionalism but is essentially a type of living constitutionalism to the extent that any judicial philosophy is, at base, a tool to promote political interest. See Post and Siegel, "Originalism as a Political Practice: The Right's Living Constitutionalism," 75 *Fordham Law Review* 545 (2006).

89. See Steven M. Teles, *The Rise of the Conservative Legal Movement: The Battle for Control of the Law* (Princeton: Princeton University Press, 2008).

90. Quoted in David O'Brien, "Judicial Legacies: The Clinton Presidency and the Courts," in *The Clinton Legacy,* ed. Colin Campbell and Bert Rochman (New York: Chatham House, 2000), 76.

91. See Steven M. Teles, "Transformative Bureaucracy: Reagan's Lawyers and the Dynamics of Political Investment," 23 *Studies in American Political Development* 61 (Spring 2009).

92. While Reagan could not immediately counter judicial expansion under Carter with a similar bill, Reagan left a profound legacy on the federal judiciary through appointments, staffing of the Judiciary Department, and extensive recruiting of judicial candidates to fill vacancies produced by retirement. See David M. O'Brien, "Why

Many Think That Ronald Reagan's Court Appointments May Have Been His Chief Legacy," in *The Reagan Presidency: Pragmatic Conservatism and Its Legacies*, ed. W. Elliot Brownlee and Hugh Davis Graham (Lawrence: University Press of Kansas, 2003).

93. Charlie Savage, *Takeover: The Return of the Imperial Presidency and the Subversion of American Democracy* (New York: Little, Brown, 2007), 70–84, 229–49.

94. Steve Calabresi and John Harrison, Memo for the Attorney General on Presidential Signing Statements. August 23, 1985, available at www.archives.gov/news/samuel-alito/accessuib-060-89-269/Acco60-89-269-box3-SGChronologicalFile.pdf.

95. Ibid. The characterization of the Litigation Strategy Working Group is from Savage, *Takeover*, 233.

96. Samuel A. Alito Jr., deputy assistant attorney general, Office of Legal Counsel to the Litigation Strategy Working Group, February 5, 1986, available at www.archives.gov/news/samuel-alito/accession-060-89-269/Acco60-89-269-box6-SG-LSWG-AlitotoLSWG-Feb1986.pdf.

97. See David S. Birdsell, "George W. Bush's Signing Statements: The Assault on Deliberation," 10 *Rhetoric and Public Affairs* 335 (2007); Christopher Kelley, "The Law: Contextualizing the Signing Statement," 37 *Presidential Studies Quarterly* 737 (December 2007); and Phillip J. Cooper, "George W. Bush, Edgar Allan Poe, and the Use and Abuse of Presidential Signing Statements," 35 *Presidential Studies Quarterly* 515 (September 2005).

98. See Charles Cameron and Nolan McCarty, "Models of Vetoes and Veto Bargaining," 7 *Annual Review of Political Science* 409 (May 2004).

99. See Andy Sullivan, "Specter to Grill Officials on Bush Ignoring Laws," Reuters, June 21, 2006, available at www.washingtonpost.com/wp-dyn/content/article/2006/06/21/AR2006062101594.html; see also Statement of Senator Patrick Leahy, Ranking Member, Judiciary Committee Hearing on Presidential Signing Statements, June 27, 2006, at http://judiciary.senate.gov/member_statement.cfm?id=1969&wit_id=2629. On withholding funds, see H.R. 264, 110th Congress, 1st Sess. (2007), in particular §§ 3(a) and 3(b). On banning their use by judges, see S. 1747, 110th Congress, 1st Session (2007), § 4 and H.R. 3045, 110th Congress, 1st Sess. (2007), § 4. President Obama has vowed to use signing statements far more sparingly than his immediate predecessors. See "Obama Reins in Signing Statements," *Boston Globe*, March 10, 2009, available at www.boston.com/news/nation/washington/articles/2009/03/10/obama_reins_in_signing_statements/.

100. As the American Bar Association noted, "For individual plaintiffs, a signing statement might well elude the case or controversy requirement because the immediate injury is to the lawmaking powers of Congress. The President thus becomes the final judge of his own constitutional power, and he invariably rules in favor himself." Report of the Task Force on Presidential Signing Statements and the Separation of Powers Doctrine, 25.

101. *Hamdan v. Rumsfeld*, 548 U.S. 557 (2006). Scalia dissenting. For further discussion of the Detainee Treatment Act (DTA), see Neal Devins's contribution to this volume.

102. Phillip J. Cooper, *By Order of the President: The Use and Abuse of Executive Direct Action* (Lawrence: University Press of Kansas, 2002), 520.

103. Richard Hofstadter, *The Paranoid Style of American Politics and Other Essays* (Cambridge: Harvard University Press, 1964).

104. Elisabeth Bumiller, "McCain Draws Line on Attacks as Crowds Cry 'Fight Back,'" *New York Times*, October 10, 2008.

105. Representative Joe Wilson's September 2009 outburst in Congress accusing President Obama of lying during a speech on healthcare reform may appear, at first glance, to be an exception to this assessment; however, note the Republican leadership's reaction. Senate Minority Leader Mitch McConnell (R-KY) said, "I think we ought to treat the president with respect, and anything other than that is not appropriate." House Republican Whip, Eric Cantor (R-VA), similarly stated, "Obviously, the president of the United States is always welcome on Capitol Hill. He deserves respect and decorum." He also called Wilson's apology "the appropriate thing to do." In short, responsible and loyal opposition is supported, but accusations of lying, which imply that Obama's policy aims are destructive to the essence of constitutional government, are simply over the line. See Carl Hulse, "In Lawmaker's Outburst, A Rare Break of Protocol," *New York Times*, September 10, 2009.

106. Mark R. Levin, *Men In Black: How the Supreme Court is Destroying America* (Washington, DC: Regnery, 2005), 22.

107. Sheryl Gay Stolberg, "In Court Pick, Obama Seeks Experience of Real World," *New York Times*, May 23, 2009, available at www.nytimes.com/2009/05/24/us/politics/24web-obama.html?sq=obama%20empathy%20federal%20judges&st=cse&adxnnl=1&scp=7&adxnnlx=1252436639-X3ZgueS9EZH8ez5azSDHNw.

108. David Savage, "Roberts Sees Role as Judicial 'Umpire.'" *Los Angeles Times*, September 13, 2005, available at http://articles.latimes.com/2005/sep/13/nation/na-roberts13. Senator John Cornyn's reaction to the empathy standard was emblematic of the Republican response and of its reliance on the concept of a judge as a neutral umpire: "The problem is you've got to call balls and strikes as a judge and the ethnicity focus—the focus on sex and on race and saying that there may be different outcomes depending who the judge is—is antithetical to the whole idea of the rule of law objective and neutral justice. And that's the reason why this deserves some questions." Cornyn quoted in Janie Lorber, "The Sunday Word: Confirmations and Torture Investigations," *The Caucus: The Politics and Government Blog of the New York Times*, July 12, 2009, available at http://thecaucus.blogs.nytimes.com/2009/07/12/the-sunday-word-confirmations-and-torture-investigations/?scp=37&sq=republican%20reaction%20to%20empathy%20standard%20for%20judges&st=cse.

CHAPTER FOUR: Institutional Interdependence and the Separation of Powers

1. The principle of judicial independence demands that in theory, judges and courts should be free from influence or interference by other political actors or institutions, whereas norms of independence may exist in forms such as what Charles

Geyh refers to as "customary independence," or the zone of independence that Congress respects as a matter of custom when exercising its constitutional powers over courts and judges.

2. In reality, some of these proposals and rhetorical flourishes may better be characterized as expressions of the interests of influential minorities.

3. *Schiavo ex rel. Schindler v. Schiavo* 404 F.3d 1270 2005.

4. See Bruce G. Peabody, "Congress, the Court, and the 'Service Constitution': Article III Jurisdiction Controls as a Case Study of the Separation of Powers," 2006 *Michigan State Law Review* 269 (2006), 291.

5. Bert Brandenberg and Amy Kay, "Crusading against the Courts: The New Mission to Weaken the Role of the Courts in Protecting our Religious Liberties" (Justice at Stake Campaign 2007), 7, available at www.gavelgrab.org/wp-content/resources/CrusadingAgainstCourts.pdf, accessed June 29, 2009.

6. See for example, Mark C. Miller, *The View of the Courts from the Hill: Interactions between Congress and the Federal Judiciary* (Charlottesville: University of Virginia Press, 2009).

7. Brandenburg and Kay, "Crusading against the Courts," 16.

8. Ross K. Baker, *Strangers on a Hill: Congress and the Court* (New York: W.W. Norton, 2007), 116.

9. Miller, *View of the Courts from the Hill,* 17, 18, 210.

10. See www.law.georgetown.edu/judiciary, accessed June 29, 2009.

11. See www.law.georgetown.edu/news/events/conference_story.html, accessed June 29, 2009.

12. For an overview of priority placed on judicial independence by the incoming president, see www.abajournal.com/magazine/advocate_for_the_courts/, accessed November 30, 2009. See also foreword to this book.

13. For a discussion on the mission and purposes of the center, see www.ajs.org/cji/cji_threats.asp, accessed November 30, 2009.

14. Frank Cross, "Judicial Independence," in *The Oxford Handbook of Law and Politics,* ed. Keith E. Whittington, R. Daniel Kelemen, and Gregory Caldeira (Oxford: Oxford University Press, 2008), 557, 562.

15. Richard Neustadt, *Presidential Power: The Politics of Leadership from FDR to Carter* (New York: Macmillan, 1980), 29, emphasis in original.

16. See Charles O. Jones, *The Presidency in a Separated System* (Washington, DC: Brookings Institution, 1994).

17. Quoted in Neustadt, *Presidential Power,* 29.

18. Charles Cameron, *Veto Bargaining: Presidents and the Politics of Negative Power* (Cambridge: Cambridge University Press, 2000).

19. The concept could be extended to federal-state, inter-state or intra-state relations as well, but those relationships fall outside the scope of this chapter.

20. Jeffrey A. Segal and Harold J. Spaeth, *The Supreme Court and the Attitudinal Model Revisited* (New York: Cambridge University Press, 2002).

21. Cross, "Judicial Independence," 562.

22. Jones, *Presidency in a Separated System*.

23. Miller, *View of the Courts from the Hill*, 9, emphasis in original.

24. For a discussion of SOP games, see Jeffrey A. Segal, "Separation of Powers Games in the Positive Theory of Congress and Courts," 91 *American Political Science Review* 28 (1997).

25. William Eskridge, "Overriding Supreme Court Statutory Interpretations," 101 *Yale Law Journal* 331 (1991); and William Eskridge, "The Judicial Review Game," 88 *Northwestern University Law Review* 382 (1993).

26. See, for example, Walter Murphy, *Elements of Judicial Strategy* (Chicago: University of Chicago Press, 1964); Lee Epstein and Jack Knight, *The Choices Justices Make* (Washington, DC: CQ Press, 1998); Lee Epstein, Jack Knight, and Andrew Martin, "Constitutional Interpretation from a Strategic Perspective," in *Making Policy, Making Law*, ed. Mark C. Miller and Jeb Barnes (Washington, DC: Georgetown University Press, 2004); and Andrew Martin, "Statutory Battles and Constitutional Wars: Congress and the Supreme Court," *Institutional Games and the U.S. Supreme Court*, ed. James Rogers, Roy Flemming, and Jon R. Bond (Charlottesville: University of Virginia Press, 2006).

27. Kevin R. den Dulk and J. Mitchell Pickerill, "Bridging the Lawmaking Process: The Effects of Organized Interests on Court-Congress Interaction," 35 *Polity* 419 (2003), 420.

28. James R. Rogers, "Information and Judicial Review: A Signaling Game of Legislative-Judicial Interaction," 45 *American Journal of Political Science* 84 (2001).

29. Walter Murphy, "Who Shall Interpret? The Quest for the Ultimate Constitutional Interpreter," 48 *Review of Politics* 401 (1986).

30. Louis Fisher, *Constitutional Dialogues: Interpretation as Political Process* (Princeton: Princeton University Press, 1988). See also Barry Friedman, "Dialogue and Judicial Review," 91 *Michigan Law Review* 577 (1993).

31. Keith E. Whittington, *Constitutional Construction: Divided Powers and Constitutional Powers and Constitutional Meaning* (Cambridge, MA: Harvard University Press, 1999).

32. Neal Devins, *Shaping Constitutional Values: Elected Government, the Supreme Court, and the Abortion Debate* (Baltimore: Johns Hopkins University Press, 1996).

33. Jeb Barnes and Mark C. Miller, "Governance as Dialogue," in *Making Policy, Making Law*, ed. Mark C. Miller and Jeb Barnes (Washington, DC: Georgetown University Press, 2004), 202.

34. Cameron, *Veto Bargaining*, 9.

35. Ibid., 176.

36. J. Mitchell Pickerill, *Constitutional Deliberation in Congress: The Impact of Judicial Review in a Separated System* (Durham, NC: Duke University Press, 2004), ch. 2.

37. Ibid., 75–81, 85–92, 123–25.

38. See, for example, J. Mitchell Pickerill, "(Judicial) Veto Bargaining between the Supreme Court and Congress," *Extensions* (Fall 2008).

39. 540 U.S. 93; 558 U.S. 50.

40. Robert Dahl, "Decision-Making in a Democracy: The Supreme Court as a National Policymaker," 6 *Journal of Public Law* 279 (1957).

41. Mark A. Graber, "The Nonmajoritarian Difficulty: Legislative Deference to the Judiciary," 7 *Studies in American Political Development* 35 (1993).

42. George I. Lovell, *Legislative Deferrals: Statutory Ambiguity, Judicial Power, and American Democracy* (Cambridge: Cambridge University Press, 2003), 45.

43. Keith Whittington, "Interpose Your Friendly Hand: Political Supports and the Exercise of Judicial Review by the United States Supreme Court," 99 *American Political Science Review* 583 (November 2005), 587; see also Michael J. Klarman, "Rethinking the Civil Rights and Civil Liberties Revolutions," 82 *Virginia Law Review* 1 (1996); and Lucas A. Powe Jr., *The Warren Court and American Politics* (Cambridge, MA: Belknap Press of Harvard University Press, 2000).

44. Whittington, "Interpose Your Friendly Hand," 587–89.

45. Klarman, "Rethinking the Civil Rights and Civil Liberties Revolutions."

46. Kevin McMahon, *Reconsidering Roosevelt on Race: How the Presidency Paved the Road to Brown* (Chicago: University of Chicago Press, 2004).

47. Howard Gillman, "How Parties Can Use the Courts to Advance their Agendas," 96 *American Political Science Review* 511 (2002); Howard Gillman, "Courts and the Politics of Partisan Coalitions," in *The Oxford Handbook of Law and Politics*, ed. Keith E. Whittington, R. Daniel Kelemen, and Gregory Caldeira (Oxford: Oxford University Press, 2008), 644–62; J. Mitchell Pickerill and Cornell W. Clayton, "The Rehnquist Court and the Political Dynamics of Federalism," 2 *Perspectives on Politics* 233 (2004); and Cornell W. Clayton and J. Mitchell Pickerill, "Guess What Happened on the Way to the Revolution? Precursors to the Supreme Court's Federalism Revolution." 34 *Publius* 85 (2004).

48. See, for example, Tom Ginsburg, *Judicial Review in New Democracies: Constitutional Courts in Asian Cases* (Cambridge, U.K.: Cambridge University Press, 2003); Ran Hirschl, *Toward Juristocracy: The Origins and Consequences of the New Constitutionalism* (Cambridge, MA: Harvard University Press, 2004).

49. See, for example, Pickerill and Clayton "Rehnquist Court and the Political Dynamics of Federalism"; see also Robert G. McCloskey, *The American Supreme Court* (Chicago: Chicago University Press, 1960).

50. See, for example, Greg D. Adams, "Abortion: Evidence of an Issue Evolution," 41 *American Journal of Political Science* 718 (1997); J. Mitchell Pickerill and Cornell W. Clayton, "The New Right Regime and Religious Freedom," paper presented at the annual meeting of the American Political Science Association, 2006.

51. For a discussion of the focus on the countermajoritarian problem, see Barry Friedman, "The Countermajoritarian Problem and the Pathology of Constitutional Scholarship," 95 *Northwestern University Law Review* 933 (2001); and Barry Friedman, "The History of the Countermajoritarian Difficulty, Part II: Reconstruction's Political Court," *Georgetown Law Journal* (2002) 91:1–66.

52. Keith E. Whittington, *Political Foundations of Judicial Supremacy: The Presidency, the Supreme Court, and Constitutional Leadership in U.S. History* (Princeton: Princeton University Press, 2007).

53. For an elaboration on this point, see Lovell, *Legislative Deferrals*.

54. Cross, "Judicial Independence," 558.

55. See, for example, Carlo Guarnieri and Patrizia Pederzoli, *The Power of Judges: A Comparative Study of Courts and Democracy* (Oxford: Oxford University Press, 2002), 152.

56. See, for example, Gerhard Casper, "An Essay in the Separation of Powers: Some Early Versions and Practices," 30 *William and Mary Law Review* 211 (1989); Lee R. West, "Judicial Independence: Our Fragile Fortress against Elective Tyranny," 34 *Oklahoma City University Law Review* 59 (2009); and Myron T. Steele, "Judicial Independence," 18 *Widener Law Journal* 299 (2009).

57. See, for example, Stephen Breyer, "Judicial Independence: Remarks by Justice Breyer," 95 *Georgetown Law Journal* 903 (2007).

58. See, for example, Segal and Spaeth, *Supreme Court and the Attitudinal Model.*

59. Terri J. Peretti, "Does Judicial Independence Exist?" in *Judicial Independence at the Crossroads,* ed. Stephen R. Burbank and Barry Friedman (Thousand Oaks, CA: Sage Publications, 2002), 103–33. See also Louis Fisher, *Religious Liberty in America: Political Safeguards* (Lawrence: University Press of Kansas, 2002); and Louis Fisher, "Constitutional Interpretation by Members of Congress," 63 *North Carolina Law Review* 707 (1986).

60. Richard A. Posner, *The Problems of Jurisprudence* (Cambridge, MA: Harvard University Press, 1990), 6.

61. Cross, "Judicial Independence," 565.

62. Miller, *View From the Hill,* 208.

63. See Stephen B. Burbank and Barry Friedman, "Reconsidering Judicial Independence," in *Judicial Independence at the Crossroads,* ed. Burbank and Friedman, 9–42; and Stephen Burbank, "Judicial Independence, Judicial Accountability, and Interbranch Relations," *Georgetown Law Journal* (2006) 95:909.

64. See, for example, J. Mark Ramseyer and Eric Rasmussen, "Why are Japanese Judges So Conservative in Politically Charged Cases?" 95 *American Political Science Review* 331 (2001).

65. See, for example, Thomas Keck, "Party, Policy, or Duty: Why Does the Supreme Court Invalidate Federal Statutes?" 101 *American Political Science Review* 321 (2007); Pickerill and Clayton, "Rehnquist Court and the Political Dynamics of Federalism"; Graber, "Political Construction of Judicial Review"; Pickerill, *Constitutional Deliberation in Congress*; and Whittington, *Political Foundations of Judicial Supremacy.*

66. Charles G. Geyh, "Customary Independence," in *Judicial Independence at a Crossroads,* ed. Burbank and Friedman, 160–90; and Charles G. Geyh, *When Courts and Congress Collide: The Struggle for Control of America's Judicial System* (Ann Arbor: University of Michigan Press, 2006).

67. For a discussion of diffused responsibility and accountability in a separated system, see Jones, *Presidency in a Separated System.*

68. See Neal Devins, "Should the Supreme Court Fear Congress?" 90 *Minnesota Law Review* 1337 (2006).

69. Arthur Hellman, "Justice O'Connor and 'The Threat to Judicial Independence': The Cowgirl Who Cried Wolf?" 39 *Arizona State Law Journal* 845 (2007).

70. In his 2010 State of the Union address, President Obama criticized the Court's decision in *Citizen's United v. Federal Election Commission* (2010). While some thought this public criticism impolitic, it does not appear to be part of a broader systematic attack on the judiciary by Obama or Democrats in Congress. In fact, his criticism of the case was somewhat legalistic in nature and would seem to fit into the pattern of rhetorical jabs at the court described earlier in the chapter.

CHAPTER FIVE: The Public and Judicial Independence

1. Stuart S. Nagel, "Court-Curbing Periods in American History," 18 *Vanderbilt Law Review* 925 (1965); Gerald N. Rosenberg, "Judicial Independence and the Reality of Political Power," 54 *Review of Politics* 369 (1992); and Tom S. Clark, "The Politics of Judicial Independence: Court-curbing and the Separation of Powers," Ph.D. dissertation, Princeton University (2008); see also C. Herman Pritchett, *Congress Versus the Supreme Court, 1957–1960* (Minneapolis: University of Minnesota Press, 1961); and Walter F. Murphy, *Congress and the Court* (Chicago: University of Chicago Press, 1962).

2. David E. Mayhew, *Congress: The Electoral Connection* (New Haven: Yale University Press, 1974). Fenno makes this interpretation of position-taking and credit-claiming clear. He argues that members can easily introduce legislation with no chance of enactment and nevertheless use the bill to shore up support with their constituents. Richard F. Fenno, *Congressmen in Committees* (Boston: Little, Brown, 1973).

3. James L. Gibson, Gregory A. Caldeira, and Lester Kenyatta Spence, "Measuring Attitudes toward the United States Supreme Court," 47 *American Journal of Political Science* 354 (2003), 356.

4. Gregory Casey, "The Supreme Court and Myth: An Empirical Investigation," 8 *Law and Society Review* 385 (1974).

5. David Easton, *A Systems Analysis of Political Life* (New York: Wiley, 1965).

6. Michael W. Giles and Thomas Lancaster, "Political Transition, Social Development, and Legal Mobilization in Spain," 83 *American Political Science Review* 817 (1989); James L Gibson, Gregory A. Caldeira, and Vanessa Baird, "On the Legitimacy of National High Courts," 92 *American Political Science Review* 343 (1998); and Clifford J. Carrubba, "A Model of the Endogenous Development of Judicial Institutions in Federal and International Systems," 71 *Journal of Politics* 55 (2009).

7. Of course, the connection between specific and diffuse support has been questioned, and the extent to which diffuse support is simply a function of specific support has been the subject of scholarly debate.

8. Robert H. Durr, Andrew D. Martin, and Christina Wolbrech, "Ideological Divergence and Public Support for the Supreme Court," 44 *American Journal of Political Science* 768 (2000); Valerie J. Hoekstra, "The Supreme Court and Local Public Opinion," 94 *American Political Science Review* 89 (2000); Anke Grosskopf and Jeffery J. Mondak, "Do Attitudes toward Specific Supreme Court Decisions Matter? The Impact of Webster and Texas v. Johnson on Public Confidence in the Supreme

Court," 51 *Political Research Quarterly* 633 (1998); Gregory A. Caldeira and James L. Gibson, "The Legitimacy of the Court of Justice in the European Union: Models of Institutional Support," 89 *American Political Science Review* 356 (1995); and Gregory A. Caldeira, "Neither the Purse Nor the Sword: Dynamics of Public Confidence in the Supreme Court," 80 *American Political Science Review* 1209 (1986).

9. Gregory A. Caldeira and James L. Gibson, "The Etiology of Public Support for the Supreme Court," 36 *American Journal of Political Science* 635 (1992), 638.

10. Rosenberg, "Judicial Independence and the Reality of Political Power."

11. Mayhew, *Congress: The Electoral Connection.*

12. Fenno, *Congressmen in Committees.*

13. Mayhew, *Congress: The Electoral Connection.*

14. Glenn R. Parker and Roger Davidson, "Why Do Americans Love Their Congressmen So Much More Than Their Congress?" 4 *Legislative Studies Quarterly* 53 (February 1979).

15. Fenno, *Congressmen in Committees.*

16. Clark, "Politics of Judicial Independence"; and Bruce G. Peabody, "Congress, the Court, and the 'Service Constitution': Article III Jurisdiction Controls as a Case Study of the Separation of Powers," 2006 *Michigan State Law Review* 269 (2006), 313–15.

17. Clark, "Politics of Judicial Independence."

18. In order to achieve the greatest degree of candor possible, though, I have promised each of them anonymity.

19. For example, one bill that was introduced several times during the late 1960s and early 1970s would have provided for a method to remove justices without impeaching them. This bill was generally introduced not as a constitutional amendment but rather as an ordinary statute, despite the constitutional rule that Justices may only be removed through impeachment. See, for example, S. 4153, 93rd Congress, 2nd Session.

20. H.R. 3073, 109th Congress, 1st Session.

21. I have deleted the first issue from this quotation because it is too idiosyncratic and would likely identify Congressman B.

22. In her biography of Harry Blackmun, Linda Greenhouse describes the extent to which Blackmun read and kept correspondence, both negative and positive. Moreover, an examination of other former justices' personal papers reveals that the practice of reading and keeping such correspondence is not unusual. Linda Greenhouse, *Becoming Justice Blackmun: Harry Blackmun's Supreme Court Journey* (New York: Times Books, 2005).

23. See, for example, Edward Keynes and Randall K. Miller, *The Court vs. Congress: Prayer, Busing, and Abortion* (Durham, NC: Duke University Press, 1989).

24. Letter from Carroll Hubbard to Harry A. Blackmun, dated October 20, 1975, Papers of Harry A. Blackmun, U.S. Library of Congress, Manuscript Division, box 1375, folder 6, Congressional Matters, 1970–1978.

25. Of course, it remains an open question entirely whether members of Con-

gress only respond to constituent opinion or whether they sometimes try to lead public opinion. It is most likely the case that a little of both goes on. It seems implausible, however, that if a link between Court-curbing and public opinion exists that it would *only* exist through congressional leadership of public opinion. Court-curbing is a particularly attractive way in which members of Congress can position-take in response to their constituents' views. For a similar argument, see Peabody, "Congress, the Court, and the 'Service Constitution,'" 313–15.

26. Laurence Baum, *Judges and Their Audiences* (Princeton: Princeton University Press, 2006).

27. William Lasser, *The Limits of Judicial Power: The Supreme Court in American Politics* (Chapel Hill: University of North Carolina Press, 1988).

28. I have dealt with this question extensively elsewhere. See Tom S. Clark, *The Limits of Judicial Independence* (New York: Cambridge University Press, forthcoming, 2011).

29. Of course, the 1937 conflict is a relatively extreme example. However, it is in many ways exemplary of the general pattern of conflict that has occurred repeatedly throughout history. I focus here on this example as an illustration of the general patterns described here because of its salience in scholarship on Court-curbing.

30. To identify polls, I searched Roper's iPoll for all surveys containing the phrase "Supreme Court." I include all surveys that ask respondents "how much confidence" they have in "the Supreme Court" and allow four responses: a great deal, some, hardly any, or none at all. Only surveys with individual-level responses and demographics were included, as this information is needed to estimate state-level opinion. This procedure resulted in six polls total—four during the 109th Congress and two during the 108th Congress—and 6,504 individual responses.

31. I estimate state-level opinion using the MRP method developed by Lax and Phillips. See Jeffry R. Lax and Justin H. Phillips, "How Should We Estimate Public Opinion in the States?" 53 *American Journal of Political Science* 107 (2009). This process involves pooling all respondents together and modeling the probability of the respondents' responses as a function of demographic variables, including gender, race, educational level, and age. The estimates from that equation are then used to estimate the predicted response for each demographic type (a given age, education level, race, and gender). Using data from the 2000 Census, the predicted responses are then poststratified by the actual distribution of each demographic block in the state. This procedure yields a state-level estimate of confidence in the Supreme Court.

32. The t-statistic for the difference is t=4.7, df=489.

33. The line in this figure is a nonlinear scatterplot smoother (lowess) line.

34. To account for the nonindependence of individual members' sponsorship decisions, I estimate the model with random intercepts for the individual member (allowing each member to have a given proclivity to sponsor Court-curbing) and for the Congress (allowing an underlying difference between the 108th and 109th Congresses).

35. Ideological distance is measured as the absolute distance from the member to the median justice on the Supreme Court. Members are assigned their Poole NOMI-

NATE Common Space score and the Supreme Court is assigned its median's Judicial Common Space score. Keith T. Poole, "Estimating a Basic Space from a Set of Issue Scales," 42 *American Journal of Political Science* 954 (1998); and Lee Epstein, Andrew D. Martin, Jeffrey A. Segal, and Chad Westerland, "The Judicial Common Space," 23 *Journal of Law, Economics, and Organization* 303 (2007).

36. Specifically, I assume an increase of 1 in Common Space distance. The estimate coefficient associated with ideological distance is $\hat{\beta}=9.04$ (se=0.62).

37. The estimated coefficient associated with confidence in the Court is negative and strong ($\hat{\beta}=-0.31$, se=0.10).

38. These data come from an original data collection I have conducted for other research. Clark, "Politics of Judicial Independence."

39. I measure public liberalism with Stimson's measure of "public mood," which is an index created from public opinion surveys on a variety of policy issues. James A. Stimson, *Public Opinion in America: Moods, Cycles, and Swings,* 2nd ed. (Boulder, CO: Westview Press, 1999). I measure the Court's liberalism by aggregating all Supreme Court decisions by year and identifying what proportion of the outcomes is coded as "liberal" in the United States Supreme Court Judicial Database. Harold J. Spaeth, "The Original U.S. Supreme Court Judicial Database," September 9, 2008 update.

40. Poole, "Estimating a Basic Space from a Set of Issue Scales."

41. The R^2 statistic for the model with public liberalism alone is 0.14. While the correlation between judicial liberalism and Court-curbing conservatism is negative, it is not statistically distinguishable from no correlation at all, t=0.95.

42. Donald Grier Stephenson Jr., *Campaigns and the Court* (New York: Columbia University Press, 1999), 146.

43. William E. Leuchtenburg, *The Supreme Court Reborn: The Constitutional Revolution in the Age of Roosevelt* (New York: Oxford University Press, 1995), 116.

44. A Gallup poll taken in November 1936 revealed that 59% of Americans thought the Supreme Court should "be more liberal in reviewing New Deal measures." Survey by Gallup Organization, November 15–20, 1936. Retrieved December 19, 2008, from the iPOLL Databank, Roper Center for Public Opinion Research, University of Connecticut, all polls cited available at www.ropercenter.uconn.edu/ipoll.html.

45. Forty-one percent of respondents said they favored "as a general principle . . . limiting the power of the Supreme Court to declare acts of Congress unconstitutional." Survey by Gallup Organization, November 15–20, 1936. Retrieved December 19, 2008, from the iPOLL Databank, Roper Center for Public Opinion Research, University of Connecticut.

46. Stephenson, *Campaigns and the Court,* 152. Roosevelt's salience on the Court matter was more likely a practical response to charges he was seeking to establish a dictatorship. Ibid., 149–53.

47. The legislation would have limited the number of additional justices to six.

48. Survey by Gallup Organization, July 4–11, 1938. Retrieved December 19, 2008, from the iPOLL Databank, Roper Center for Public Opinion Research, University of Connecticut.

49. See, for example, Bruce Ackerman, *We The People: Transformations* (Cambridge, MA: Belknap Press of Harvard University Press, 1998).

50. Gerald N. Rosenberg, *The Hollow Hope: Can Courts Bring about Social Change?* (Chicago: University of Chicago Press, 1991).

51. Matthew C. Stephenson, "Court of Public Opinion: Government Accountability and Judicial Independence," 20 *Journal of Law, Economics, and Organization* 379 (2004); Georg Vanberg, *The Politics of Constitutional Review in Germany* (New York: Cambridge University Press, 2005); Jeffrey K. Staton, "Constitutional Review and the Selective Promotion of Case Results," 50 *American Journal of Political Science* 98 (2006); Clark, "Politics of Judicial Independence"; and Carrubba, "Model of the Endogenous Development."

52. Vanberg, *The Politics of Constitutional Review in Germany*; Staton, "Constitutional Review and the Selective Promotion of Case Results"; Carrubba, "Model of the Endogenous Development"; and Clark, *Limits of Judicial Independence*.

53. Rosenberg, *Hollow Hope*.

54. Survey by Gallup Organization, September 8–11, 2008. Retrieved December 19, 2008, from the iPoll Databank, Roper Center for Public Opinion Research, University of Connecticut.

55. Survey by Quinnipiac University Rolling Institute, July 8–13, 2008. Retrieved December 19, 2008, from the iPoll Databank, Roper Center for Public Opinion Research, University of Connecticut.

56. Survey by Gallup Organization, July 7–9, 2003. Retrieved December 19, 2008, from the iPOLL Databank, Roper Center for Public Opinion Research, University of Connecticut.

57. Survey by Gallup Organization, August 29–September 5, 2000. Retrieved December 19, 2008, from the iPOLL Databank, Roper Center for Public Opinion Research, University of Connecticut.

58. Survey by Harris Interactive, February 5–11, 2008. Retrieved December 19, 2008, from the iPoll Databank, Roper Center for Public Opinion Research, University of Connecticut.

59. Survey by Harris Interactive, January 6–10, 2000. Retrieved December 19, 2008, from the iPOLL Databank, Roper Center for Public Opinion Research, University of Connecticut.

60. For example, the proportion of respondents in the General Social Survey self-identifying as conservative decreased from 17.5% to 16.1% between 2004 and 2006. Similarly, the proportion self-identifying as liberal increased from 9.1% to 11.5% during the same period.

61. Clark, "Politics of Judicial Independence."

CHAPTER SIX: Judicial Elections and Public Perception of the Courts

1. Deborah Goldberg, Craig Holman, and Samantha Sanchez, *The New Politics of Judicial Elections: How 2000 Was a Watershed Year for Big Money, Special Interest Pres-*

sure, and TV Advertising in State Supreme Court Campaigns (Washington, DC: Justice at Stake, 2002).

2. Marie Hojnacki and Lawrence Baum, "'New Style' Judicial Campaigns and the Voters: Economic Issues and Union Members in Ohio," 45 The Western Political Quarterly 921 (1992).

3. William C. Bayne, "Lynchard's Candidacy, Ads Putting Spice into Justice Race," 29 Commercial Appeal (October 2000), DS1.

4. On the other hand, Hall finds that judicial elections are just as contested and competitive as elections to the U.S. House. Melinda Gann Hall, "State Supreme Courts in American Democracy: Probing the Myths of Judicial Reform," 95 American Political Science Review 315 (2001).

5. The reports were entitled The New Politics of Judicial Elections 2002: How the Threat to Fair and Impartial Courts Spread to More States in 2002; The New Politics of Judicial Elections 2004: How Special Interest Pressure on Courts Has Reached a "Tipping Point"—and How to Keep Our Courts Fair and Impartial; and The New Politics of Judicial Elections 2006: How 2006 Was the Most Threatening Year Yet to the Fairness and Impartiality of Our Courts—and How Americans Are Fighting Back.

6. Blankenship only contributed $1,000 directly to Benjamin's campaign.

7. West Virginia law gave individual justices discretion over whether they should recuse themselves from a case.

8. Quoted in Adam Liptak, "U.S. Supreme Court Is Asked to Fix Troubled West Virginia Justice System," New York Times, October 12, 2008.

9. Caperton, et al., v. A. T. Massey Coal Co., 129 S. Ct. 2252 (2009).

10. The Federalist, no. 78 (Alexander Hamilton), Clinton Rossiter ed., 1961, 396.

11. See the quotation from Texas Supreme Court Chief Justice Thomas R. Phillips in Jesse Rutledge, "Texas Chief Justice Urges Reform of N.C. Judicial Election System," July 3, 2002. www.ncjudges.org/media/news_releases/7_3_02.html (accessed April 10, 2009).

12. For example, California uses retention elections for its appellate court justices but nonpartisan elections for superior court judges.

13. Of course, concerns about judicial independence predated Marbury, as, for example, Letters of Brutus.

14. For more on the history of judicial elections, see Matthew J. Streb, "The Study of Judicial Elections," in Running for Judge: The Rising Political, Financial, and Legal Stakes of Judicial Elections, ed. Matthew J. Streb (New York: New York University Press, 2007), 8–11.

15. Charles Gardner Geyh, "Why Judicial Elections Stink," 64 Ohio State Law Journal 43 (2003).

16. James Sample, Lauren Jones, and Rachel Weiss, The New Politics of Judicial Elections, 2006: How 2006 Was the Most Threatening Year Yet to the Fairness and Impartiality to Our Courts—and How Americans Are Fighting Back (Washington, DC: Justice at Stake, 2007), 15.

17. Chris W. Bonneau, "The Dynamics of Campaign Spending in State Supreme

Court Elections," in *Running for Judge,* ed. Streb, 64. Note, however, that Frederick and Streb found that spending has not risen substantially at the intermediate appellate court level. Brian Frederick and Matthew J. Streb, "Paying the Price for a Seat on the Bench: Campaign Spending in Contested State Intermediate Appellate Court Elections," 8 *State Politics and Policy Quarterly* 410 (2008).

18. Sample, Jones, and Weiss, *New Politics of Judicial Elections, 2006,* 17.

19. Florida Department of State Division of Elections. August 6, 2003, available at www.election.dos.state.fl.us, accessed January 26, 2009.

20. Bill Rankin, "Bernes Wins Judicial Election; Appeals Court Race Long, Costly," *Atlanta Journal-Constitution,* July 21, 2004, D1.

21. Sample, Jones, and Weiss, *New Politics of Judicial Elections, 2006,* 24.

22. Ibid., 18.

23. Madison McClellan, "Merit Appointment versus Popular Election: A Reformer's Guide to Judicial Selection Methods in Florida," 43 *Florida Law Review* 529 (1991).

24. Emily Heller, "Judicial Races Get Meaner," *National Law Journal,* October 25, 2004, available at www.law.com/jsp/article.jsp?id=1098217051328, accessed August 6, 2007.

25. Sample, Jones, and Weiss, *New Politics of Judicial Elections, 2006,* 20.

26. See, for example, Damon M. Cann, "Campaign Contributions and Judicial Behavior," *American Review of Politics* 23 (2002): 261–74; Damon M. Cann, "Justice for Sale? Campaign Contributions and Judicial Decisionmaking," *State Politics and Policy Quarterly* 7 (2007): 281–97; Madhavi McCall, "Buying Justice in Texas: The Influence of Campaign Contributions on the Voting Behavior of Texas Supreme Court Justices," *American Review of Politics* 22 (2001): 349–73; Chris W. Bonneau and Damon M. Cann, "The Effect of Campaign Contributions on Judicial Decisionmaking," unpublished manuscript, available at http://ssrn.com/abstract=1337668.

27. Justice at Stake Campaign, "Poll of American Voters," conducted by Greenberg, Quinlan, Rosner Research, Inc. October 30–November 7, 2001, available at www.justiceatstake.org, accessed July 12, 2006.

28. Sandra Day O'Connor, "Justice for Sale: How Special Interest Money Threatens the Integrity of Our Courts," *Wall Street Journal,* November 15, 2007, available at www.opinionjournal.com/editorial/feature.html?id=110010864, accessed November 15, 2007.

29. Marcia Coyle, "It Won't Be Long: Supreme Court Took a Narrow View in Ruling on Judicial Candidates Talking on Issues, So Lawsuits Are Expected Soon," *Broward Daily Business Review,* July 17, 2002, A8.

30. *Republican Party of Minnesota v. White,* 536 U.S. 765 (2002) (Scalia, opinion), 713, 782.

31. Geyh, "Why Judicial Elections Stink," 64.

32. Rachel P. Caufield, "The Changing Tone of Judicial Election Campaigns as a Result of *White,*" in *Running for Judge,* ed. Streb.

33. Sample, Jones, and Weiss, *New Politics of Judicial Elections, 2006,* 30–31.

34. Quoted in ibid.

35. Quoted in ibid., 33.

36. Ibid., vi.

37. Justice at Stake Campaign, "Buying Time—Spending Rockets Before Elections," November 13, 2008, available at www.brennancenter.org/content/resource/buying_time_spending_rockets_before_elections/, accessed January 26, 2009.

38. Goldberg, Holman, and Sanchez, *The New Politics of Judicial Elections*, 17.

39. Sample, Jones, and Weiss, *New Politics of Judicial Elections, 2006*, 8.

40. Anthony Champagne, "Television Ads in Judicial Campaigns," 35 *Indiana Law Review* 669 (2001–2002), 670.

41. Justice for All PAC, "Buy a Seat for Karmeier"; and Illinois Republican Party, "Maag Bad Judgment," emphasis added.

42. Committee to Reelect Harold See, "Anderson Misleading"; and Committee to Elect James Anderson, "See Disqualified," emphasis added.

43. Alabama Civil Justice Reform, "Trial Lawyer Money," emphasis added.

44. And for the Sake of the Kids, "McGraw Clear Differences."

45. Will T. Scott for Supreme Court, "Stumbo Sides with Criminals."

46. For example, see Jeff Goodell, *Big Coal: The Dirty Secret Behind America's Energy Future* (Boston, MA: Houghton Mifflin Harcourt, 2007), 44–45.

47. Steven Walters, "Another Wisconsin Supreme Court Race Heats Up," *Milwaukee Journal Sentinel*, January 24, 2009.

48. Citizens for Truth in Government, "Dickinson Bars."

49. For this project, I read through the transcripts of numerous television ads in judicial elections from 2000 to 2006. Although I did not perform a systematic analysis, the themes that I mention here were quite common. One would not have difficulty replacing the ads highlighted here with dozens of other examples.

50. Whether ads in judicial elections are more or less accurate than ads in other kinds of elections is unclear.

51. Viveca Novak, "Judicial Campaigns: Beginning to Look a Lot Like Congress: Would-Be Judges Employ Big Bucks, TV Ads, and Questionable Attacks," November 20, 2006, available at www.factcheck.org/judicial-campaigns/judicial_campaigns_beginning_to_look_a_lot.html, accessed February 2, 2009.

52. Barbara A. Bardes and Robert W. Oldendick, *Public Opinion: Measuring the Public Mind*, 3rd ed. (Belmont, CA: Thomson Wadsworth, 2007), 124.

53. James L. Gibson, Gregory A. Caldeira, and Lester Kenyatta Spence, "The Supreme Court and the U.S. Presidential Election of 2000: Wounds, Self-inflicted or Otherwise?" 33 *British Journal of Political Science* 535 (2003).

54. Christine Barbour and Gerald C. Wright (with Matthew J. Streb and Michael R. Wolf), *Keeping the Republic: Power and Citizenship in American Politics*, 3rd ed. (Washington, DC: CQ Press, 2006), 270.

55. Damon M. Cann and Jeff Yates, "Homegrown Institutional Legitimacy: Assessing Citizens' Diffuse Support for State Courts," *American Politics Research* 36 (2008): 297–329, 305.

56. James L. Gibson, Gregory A. Caldeira, and Vanessa A. Baird, "On the Legiti-

macy of National High Courts," 92 *American Political Science Review* 343 (1998); James L. Gibson, Gregory A. Caldeira, and Lester Kenyatta Spence, "Measuring Attitudes toward the United States Supreme Court," 47 *American Journal of Political Science* 354 (2003); Anke Grosskopf and Jeffrey J. Mondak, "Do Attitudes toward Specific Supreme Court Decisions Matter? The Impact of Webster and *Texas v. Johnson* on Public Confidence in the Supreme Court," 51 *Political Research Quarterly* 633 (1998).

57. Cann and Yates, "Homegrown Institutional Legitimacy."

58. Sara C. Benesh, "Understanding Public Confidence in American Courts," 68 *American Journal of Political Science* 697 (2006).

59. James P. Wenzel, Shaun Bowler, and David J. Lanoue, "The Sources of Public Confidence in State Courts: Experience and Institutions," 31 *American Politics Research* 191 (2003).

60. Justice at Stake Campaign, "Poll of American Voters"; and Geyh, "Why Judicial Elections Stink."

61. Benesh, "Understanding Public Confidence in American Courts," 704.

62. Wenzel, Bowler, and Lanoue, "Sources of Public Confidence in State Courts," 200.

63. Cann and Yates, "Homegrown Institutional Legitimacy," 313.

64. Christine A. Kelleher and Jennifer Wolak, "Explaining Public Confidence in the Branches of State Government," *Political Research Quarterly* 60 (2007): 707–21.

65. Kathleen Hall Jamieson and Bruce W. Hardy, "Will Ignorance and Partisan Election of Judges Undermine Public Trust in the Judiciary?" *Daedalus* (Fall 2008), 15.

66. James L. Gibson, "Challenges to the Impartiality of State Supreme Courts: Legitimacy Theory and 'New-Style' Judicial Campaigns," 102 *American Political Science Review* 59 (2008). See also James L. Gibson, "Campaigning for the Bench: The Corrosive Effects of Campaign Speech?" *Law and Society Review* 42 (2008): 899–927; and James L. Gibson, "'New Style' Judicial Campaigns and the Legitimacy of State High Courts," *Journal of Politics* 71 (2009): 1285–1304.

67. Gibson, "'New Style' Judicial Elections," 1294.

68. Gibson, "Challenges to the Impartiality of State Supreme Courts," 72.

69. Gibson, "'New Style' Judicial Elections."

70. See, for example, Justice at Stake Campaign, "Poll of American Voters"; Geyh, "Why Judicial Elections Stink"; and Chris W. Bonneau and Melinda Gann Hall, *In Defense of Judicial Elections* (New York: Routledge, 2009).

71. Matthew J. Streb, "Partisan Involvement in Partisan and Nonpartisan Trial Court Elections," in *Running for Judge*, ed. Streb.

72. Melinda Gann Hall, "Voting in State Supreme Court Elections: Competition and Context as Democratic Incentives," 69 *Journal of Politics* 1147 (2007); and Matthew J. Streb, Brian Frederick, and Casey LaFrance, "Voter Roll-Off in a Low-Information Context: Evidence from Intermediate Appellate Court Elections," 37 *American Politics Research* 644 (2009).

73. Streb, Frederick, and LaFrance, "Voter Roll-Off." For the argument that voter

information guides may not be useful to voters, see Matthew Streb, *Rethinking American Electoral Democracy* (New York: Routledge, 2008), 31–32.

74. See, for example, Melinda Gann Hall and Paul Brace, "Toward an Integrated Model of Judicial Voting Behavior," *American Politics Quarterly* 20 (1992): 147–68; and Paul Brace and Melinda Gann Hall, "Integrated Models of Judicial Dissent," *Journal of Politics* 54 (1993): 914–35.

75. North Carolina State Board of Elections. "NC Public Funding Programs," available at www.sboe.state.nc.us/content.aspx?id=21, accessed January 28, 2009.

76. Matthew J. Streb and Brian Frederick, "Judicial Reform and the Future of Judicial Elections," in *Running for Judge,* ed. Streb, 208.

77. Bonneau and Hall, *In Defense of Judicial Elections.*

78. Owen G. Abbe and Paul S. Herrnson, "Public Financing for Judicial Elections? A Judicious Perspective on the ABA's Proposal for Campaign Finance Reform," 35 *Polity* 535 (2003), 547.

79. Brian F. Schaffner and Jennifer Segal Disacro, "Judicial Elections in the News," in *Running for Judge,* ed. Streb.

80. Candidates must still do some fundraising to qualify for public funding.

81. For an argument that the constitutionality of many judicial canons is threatened, see Richard L. Hasen, "First Amendment Limits on Regulating Judicial Campaigns," in *Running for Judge,* ed. Streb.

82. William G. Mayer, "In Defense of Negative Campaigning," 111 *Political Science Quarterly* 437 (1996), 442. See also Geer, *In Defense of Negativity.*

83. David B. Rottman, "Community Courts: Prospects and Limits." 231 *National Institute of Journal Justice,* 46 (August 1996), available at www.ncsconline.org/wc/publications/Res_CtComm_Prospects&LimitsPub.pdf, accessed February 2, 2009. See also Jamieson and Hardy, "Will Ignorance and Partisan Election."

CHAPTER SEVEN: Conflicts with Courts in Common Law Nations

1. For an introduction to the juridification literature, including its application to legal reforms in Great Britain and elsewhere, see Lars Blichner and Anders Molander, "Mapping Juridification," *European Law Journal* 14, no. 1 (2008): 36–54; Mark Bevir, "The Westminster Model, Governance, and Judicial Reform," *Parliamentary Affairs* 61, no. 4 (2008): 559–77; Michael Delli Carpini, "Adversarial Legalism and Parliamentary Democracy: Attitudes towards the Juridification of Politics in Germany and the U.S.," *Conference Papers: Law and Society* (2007) 1; Aileen McHarg, "Reforming the United Kingdom Constitution: Law, Convention, Soft Law," *Modern Law Review* 71, no. 6 (2008): 853–77; Jiri Přiban, "The Juridification of European Identity: Its Limitations and the Search of EU Democratic Politics," *Constellations* 16, no. 1 (2009): 44–58; and Gordon Silverstein, "Juridification in America: How the Equilibrium between Law and Politics Changed, and Why It Matters," *Conference Papers: American Political Science Association* (2008): 1–22.

2. It also bears mentioning that some argue that recent attacks against the U.S.

courts pale in historical comparison as well. See William Pryor Jr., "Not-So-Serious Threats to Judicial Independence," *Virginia Law Review* 93, no. 7 (2007): 1759–83.

3. See Human Rights Watch, *World Report 2009* (2009).

4. Roger Atwood, "Media Crackdown: Chavez and Censorship," *Georgetown Journal of International Affairs* 7 (2006): 25–32.

5. "Middle East and Africa—Zimbabwe's Judges—Cuffed Justice," *The Economist*, September 27, 2002, 63.

6. Salman Masood, "Ousted Judge in Pakistan Defends Independence of Courts," *International Herald Tribune*, March 30, 2007, 3.

7. "Pakistan's Chief Justice Returns to Work," *New York Times*, March 22, 2009, A8.

8. John E. Finn, "The Rule of Law and Judicial Independence in Newly Democratic Regimes," *Good Society Journal* 13 (2004): 12–16.

9. See, for example, Peter H. Russell and David M. O'Brien, *Judicial Independence in the Age of Democracy: Critical Perspectives from around the World* (Charlottesville: University Press of Virginia, 2001).

10. Bevir, "Westminster Model."

11. The aggrandizement of judicial power does not necessarily come at the expense of democratic processes or democratic will. See chapter 4 in this volume for the relevant literature.

12. Blichner and Molander, "Mapping Juridification," 42.

13. See Donald Jackson, *The United Kingdom Confronts the European Convention on Human Rights* (Tampa: University Press of Florida, 1997).

14. Secretary of State for the Home Department, *Rights Brought Home: The Human Rights Bill* (Cm 3782) (October 1997).

15. Lord McCluskey saw the HRA as "a field day for crackpots, a pain in the neck for judges and legislators, and a goldmine for lawyers." *Scotland on Sunday*, February 6, 2000. See also Anthony V. Baker, "So Extraordinary, So Unprecedented an Authority: A Conceptual Reconsideration of the Singular Doctrine of Judicial Review," *Duquesne Law Review* 39 (2001): 729–85; and Tom Campbell, "Human Rights: A Culture of Controversy," *Journal of Law and Society* 26 (1999): 6–26.

16. Department of Constitutional Affairs, Ministry of Justice, *Review of the Implementation of the Human Rights Act* (2006): 10.

17. Stephen Sedley, "The Rocks or the Open Sea: Where Is the Human Rights Act Heading?" *Journal of Law and Society* 32, no. 1 (2005): 3–17.

18. Ruth Costigan and Philip Thomas, "The Human Rights Act: A View from Below," *Journal of Law and Society* 32, no. 1 (2005): 51–67.

19. Lord Chancellor and Secretary of State for Justice, *Responding to Human Rights Judgments: Government Response to the Joint Committee on Human Rights' Thirty-First Report of Session 2007–08* (January 2009), 41–58.

20. C. A. Gearty, *Can Human Rights Survive?* (Cambridge: Cambridge University Press, 2006), 174.

21. Christine Sypnowich, "Taking Britain's Human Rights Act Seriously," *University of Toronto Law Journal* 58, no. 1 (2008): 105–17.

298   Notes to Pages 175–182

22. Gearty, *Can Human Rights Survive?*

23. See Lieve Gies, "*Celebrity Big Brother,* Human Rights, and Popular Culture," *Entertainment, Sports, and Law Journal* 7, no. 1 (April 2009): 1–15.

24. *Douglas v. Hello!* [2003] EWHC 786 (Ch); and *Campbell v. MGN Limited* [2004] UKHL 22.

25. *R. v. Sec. of State for the Home Department,* November 25, 2002, [2002] UKHL 46.

26. Mathew Hickley, "31 Killers Have Sentences Cut after Human Rights Challenges," *Mail Online,* March 6, 2009.

27. *The Queen on Application of S; S; M; A; S; K; & G v. Secretary of State for the Home Department* [2006] EWHC 1111.

28. Antonella Lazzeri and Kathryn Lister, "Soft Judges in the Dock," *The Sun,* February 12, 2007.

29. David Charter, "Cameron Answers Critics over Plan to Scrap Human Rights Act," *Times Online,* June 26, 2006.

30. "Jack Straw Backs Overhaul of Human Rights Act," *Times Online,* December 8, 2008.

31. Lord Chancellor and Secretary of State for Justice, *Rights and Responsibilities: Developing Our Constitutional Framework* (March 2009).

32. Lord Chancellor and Secretary of State for Justice, *The Governance of Britain: Constitutional Renewal* (2008).

33. Judicial Appointments Commission, *Annual Report, 2007–2008: Selecting on Merit and Encouraging Diversity* (2008).

34. Diana Woodhouse, "The Constitutional and Political Implications of a United Kingdom Supreme Court," *Legal Studies* 24 (2004): 134–55.

35. See Constitutional Reform Act 2005, s. 23–31.

36. E. Thompson. "The Washminster Mutation," in *Responsible Government in Australia* (Richmond, Australia: Drummond for the Australasian Political Studies Association, 1980), 32–40.

37. Michael Coper and George Williams, eds., *How Many Cheers for Engineers?* (Sydney, Australia: Federation Press, 1997). For the relevant case law, see Chief Justice Latham in *South Australia v. Commonwealth* (the *First Uniform Tax* case) (1942) 65 CLR 373, 409; *Bank of New South Wales v. Commonwealth* (the "Bank Nationalisation" case) (1948) 76 CLR 1, 151–152; and Chief Justice Barwick in *Attorney-General (Cth); Ex rel McKinley v Commonwealth* (1975) 135 CLR 1, 17.

38. See *Buck v. Bavone* (1976); and *Miller v. TCN Channel Nine* (1986).

39. See *Australian Capital Television v. Commonwealth* (1992) 177 CLR 106; and *Nationwide News v. Wills* (1992) 177 CLR 1.

40. *Theophanous v. Herald and Weekly Times Ltd.* (1994) 182 CLR 104.

41. *Langer v. Commonwealth* (1996) 186 CLR 302.

42. *McGinty v. State of Western Australia* (1996) 186 CLR 140.

43. For more on the "stolen generation," see Justin Healey, *The Stolen Generation* (Balmain, Australia: Spinney Press, 2001); and Human Rights and Equal Opportunity Commission, *Bringing Them Home* (1997).

44. See *Coleman v. Power* (2004) 220 CLR 1; *Mulholland v. Australian Electoral Commission* (2004) 209 ALR 582; and *McKinnon v Secretary, Department of Treasury* (2006) HCA 45.

45. *Mabo and Others v. Queensland* (No. 2) (1992) 107 ALR 1. For additional information, see Nonie Sharp, *No Ordinary Judgment: Mabo, The Murray Islanders' Land Case* (Canberra, Australia: Aboriginal Studies Press, 1996).

46. To follow the treatment of *terra nullius* and Aboriginal sovereignty within Australian constitutional law before *Mabo*, see *Blankard v. Galdy* 2 Salkeld 411; *Cooper v. Stuart* (1889) 14 A.C. 286; *Milirrpum v. Nabalco Pty Ltd.* (1971) 17 FLR 141; *Koowarta v. Bjelke-Peterson* (1982) 153 CLR 168; and *Commonwealth v. Tasmania* (1983) 158 CLR 1.

47. G. Hughes, "High Court Failed Nation with Mabo, Says Mining Chief," *The Australian*, July 1, 1993, 1–2.

48. *The Wik Peoples v. The State of Queensland* (1996) 141 ALR 129.

49. Native Title Amendment Act 1998.

50. See, for example, *Western Australia v. Ward* (2002) 76 ALJR 1098; *Wilson v. Anderson* (2002) 76 ALJR 1306; and *Members of the Yorta Yorta Aboriginal Community v. Victoria* (2002) 77 ALJR 356.

51. For more recent statistics, see the National Native Title Tribunal website at www.nntt.gov.au, accessed December 2, 2009.

52. See, for example, Lisa Strelein, *Compromised Jurisprudence: Native Title Cases since Mabo* (Canberra, Australia: Aboriginal Studies Press, 2009).

53. Jason Pierce, *Inside the Mason Court Revolution: The High Court of Australia Transformed* (Durham, NC: Carolina Academic Press, 2006).

54. Hon. Michael Kirby, "Attack on Judges: A Universal Phenomenon," American Bar Association, January 5, 1998.

55. Pierce, *Inside the Mason Court Revolution*, 3.

56. "Heffernan/Kirby Debate Dominates Friday Forum," *Lateline*, March 15, 2002.

57. Greg Jennet, "Heffernan Sacked and Ordered to Apologise," *Lateline*, March 3, 2002.

58. George Williams, *A Charter of Rights for Australia*, 3d ed. (Sydney, Australia: UNSW Press, 2007).

59. Legislative Council Standing Committee on Law and Justice, New South Wales Parliament, *A NSW Bill of Rights*, October 2001.

60. See, for example, Gareth Griffith, *A NSW Charter of Rights? The Continuing Debate*, New South Wales Parliamentary Library Briefing Paper 5/06.

61. H. Charlesworth, "Australia's First Bill of Rights: The Australian Capital Territory's Human Rights Act," in *Protecting Rights without a Bill of Rights: Institutional Performance and Reform*, ed. T. Campbell, J. Goldsworthy, and A. Stone (Aldershot, U.K.: Ashgate, 2006), 289–304.

62. Simon Evans and Carolyn Evans, "Legal Redress under the Victorian Charter of Human Rights and Responsibilities," 17 *Public Law Review* 264 (2006).

63. See *ALP National Party Platform and Constitution 2004*, available at www.alp.org.au/platform/index.php, accessed March 15, 2007.

64. See *Federal Platform: The Liberal Party of Australia,* available at www.liberal .org.au/documents/federalplatform.pdf, accessed March 15, 2007.

65. "Carr Urges Action against Charter," *Sydney Morning Herald,* April 20, 2009.

66. Frank Brennan et al., *National Human Rights Consultation Committee Report,* September 2009. See also Michael Pelly, "Rights Push Finally Put out of Misery," *The Australian,* April 23, 2010.

CHAPTER EIGHT: The Siege on the Israeli Supreme Court

1. Israel's Declaration of Independence (1948) does not explicitly mention the word *democracy* but stipulates obligations associated with a democratic regime, for example equality of social and political rights, freedom of religion, and commitment to the principles of the UN Charter. In 1985, "the Basic Law: the Knesset" was amended to officially express the existence of the State of Israel as "Jewish and democratic state," Article 7A(1). Similar wording was adopted in the two 1992 Basic Laws concerning human rights.

2. Yoav Dotan, "Do the 'Haves' Still Come Out Ahead? Resource Inequalities in Ideological Courts: The Case of the Israeli High Court of Justice," 33 *Law and Society Review* 1059 (1999), 1062.

3. The Court's acceptance of petitions filed by Palestinians was by default: although normally citizens of a warring party do not have access to the national courts of its enemy during the battle, when such a petition was first filed in 1972, the government did not object, hence allowing the Court to rule on the merits. The governmental policy hasn't changed since. David Kretzmer, *The Occupation of Justice: The Supreme Court of Israel and the Occupied Territories* (Albany: State University of New York Press, 2002), 19–20.

4. Jonathan Adiri, "Terror in the Court: Counter-Terrorism and Judicial Power in the Israeli Case Study," 1 *Northwestern Interdisciplinary Law Review* 55 (2008), 82; Anne-Marie Slaughter, "A Typology of Transjudicial Communication," 29 *University Richmond Law Review* 99 (1994); Eyal Benvenisti, "Reclaiming Democracy: The Strategic Uses of Foreign and International Law by National Courts," 102 *American Journal of International Law* 241 (2008), 251–52 (discussing the emerging judicial dialogue in courts in Canada, Great Britain, France, Germany, Hong Kong, India, and New Zealand).

5. Daphne Barak-Erez, "The International Law of Human Rights and Constitutional Law: A Case Study of an Expanding Dialogue," 2 *International Journal of Constitutional Law* 611 (2004), 613.

6. Yoram Rabin and Arnon Gutfeld, "Marbury v. Madison and Its Impact on Israeli Constitutional Law," 15 *University of Miami International and Comparative Law Review* 303 (2007–2008), 328.

7. The majority of immigrants arrived from East European states, the Soviet republics, and Middle East countries. Gad Barzilai, "Between the Rule of Law and the Laws of the Ruler: The Supreme Court in Israeli Legal Culture," 152 *International Social Science Journal* 193 (1997), 194.

8. Yair Zalmanovitch, "Israel in Transition: Transitions in Israel's Policymaking Network," 555 *Annals* 193 (1998), 205; and Menachem Mautner, "The Decline of the Formalism and the Rise of the Values in the Israeli Law," 17 *Iunei Mishpat* 503 (1993), 584 (in Hebrew).

9. In the sixty-two years since its establishment, Israel has had thirty-two governments (the latest one took power in March 2009). Adiri, "Terror in the Court," 61; see also Gideon Doron, "Judges in a Borderless State: Politics versus the Law in the State of Israel," 14 *Israel Affairs* 587 (2008), 587.

10. James W. Torke, "The English Religious Establishment," 12 *Journal of Law and Religion* 399 (1995–96), 400.

11. Amnon Straschnov, "The Judicial System in Israel," 34 *Tulsa Law Journal* (1999), 527.

12. Other reasons are security justifications, a "democratic" concern of waiting for the Jewish population to arrive in Israel from the Diaspora, and, arguably, also the impact of the Common Law concept that emphasizes parliamentary supremacy. See Barzilai, "Between the Rule of Law," 194; and Ran Hirschl, "The Political Origins of Judicial Empowerment through Constitutionalization: Lessons from Four Constitutional Revolutions," 25 *Law and Social Inquiry* 91 (2000), 110–11.

13. Barzilai, "Between the Rule of Law," 194.

14. For a list and text of the Basic Laws, see the website of the Knesset, available at www.knesset.gov.il/description/eng/eng_mimshal_yesod.htm.

15. Articles 15(c) and 15(d) of Basic Law: The Judiciary, 1984, S.H. 78, available at www.knesset.gov.il/laws/special/eng/basic8_eng.htm. Note that although in 2000 the Administrative Courts were established as separate chambers of the District Courts, with the jurisdiction to hear some of these petitions, in practice many of the administrative issues are still at the original jurisdiction of the Supreme Court. Guy E. Carmi, "A Constitutional Court in the Absence of a Formal Constitution? On the Ramifications of Appointing the Israeli Supreme Court as the Only Tribunal for Judicial Review," 21 *Connecticut Journal of International Law* 67 (2005–2006), 73.

16. Martin Edelman, *Courts, Politics, and Culture in Israel* (Charlottesville; University of Virginia Press, 1994), 34–35; Michael Birnhak and David Gosersky, "Specialized Seats, Minority Opinions, and Judicial Pluralism," 22 *Tel Aviv University Law Review* 499 (1999), 504–5.

17. Israeli Justices are forbidden from engaging in politics, actively or passively. Shimon Shetreet, *Justice in Israel: A Study of the Israeli Judiciary* (London: Martinus Nijhoff, 1994), 318.

18. Some have argued, however, that in practice, the justices dominate the process. Issachar Rozen-Zvi, "Constructing Professionalism: The Professional Project of the Israeli Judiciary," 31 *Seton Hall Law Review* 760 (2001), 797; and Birnhak and Gosersky, "Specialized Seats," 502.

19. The minister of justice is the political head of Israel's Ministry of Justice, holding primary responsibilities in the fortification and creation of the rule of law in Israel.

20. The process of selecting Justices in Israel is set out in the Basic Law: Adjudi-

cation 1984 (38 L.S.I. 101 (1983–84)), the Courts Law [Consolidated Version] 1984 (38, L.S.I. 271 (1983–84)); and the Rules of the Judiciary (Procedures for the Judicial Selections Committee) 1984 (K.T. 4689, 2370).

21. Birnhak and Gosersky, "Specialized Seats," 504–5; and Hirschl, "The Political Origins of Judicial Empowerment," 118. The custom of the "religious seat" was established in the first composition of the Court; the first Sephardi Justice was nominated in 1962, the first woman justice appointee was nominated in 1977, and the first Israeli-Arab justice was nominated in March 1999.

22. Rabin and Gutfeld, "Marbury v. Madison and Its Impact on Israeli Constitutional Law," 329.

23. Only under its power as HCJ, 2,149 petitions were opened and 2,368 were closed in the year of 2008, with the average time that it takes the Court to issue a decision at about ten months. For statistics on Israel's judicial system, see http://elyon1.court.gov.il/heb/haba/7-12_2008.pdf. Overall, the judicial activity of Israel's court system relative to the size of the population was rated as first in a group of seventeen developed democratic states, among them Australia, Denmark, Britain, Norway, Italy, Germany, New Zealand, and France. See Raanan Marziano-Kinan et al., "The Workload of Judiciaries: Comparative Analysis of 17 States," available at http://elyon1.court.gov.il/heb/haba/Courts_burden_Final_report_5.07.pdf.

24. The number of Justices at the Court is determined by a Knesset resolution.

25. Procedural Regulations (the Supreme Court of Israel) 1984.

26. Article 26 of the Court's Law [Consolidated Version] 1984 (38, L.S.I. 271 (1983–84)). The option for "further hearing" applies to both decisions of the Court as court of appeals and as High Court of Justice.

27. Ariel L. Bendor, "Investigating the Executive Branch in Israel and in the United States: Politics as Law, the Politics of Law," 54 *University of Miami Law Review* 193 (2000), 196.

28. Kretzmer, *Occupation of Justice*, 13.

29. Basic Law: Human Rights and Dignity (1992) and Basic Law: Freedom of Occupation (1992).

30. CA 1908/94 *United Mizrahi Bank v. Migdal* (1995) P.D. 49(4) 221.

31. For a comparison between Israeli and U.S. decisions regarding judicial review, see Rabin and Gutfeld, "Marbury v. Madison and Its Impact on Israeli Constitutional Law."

32. HCJ 212/03 *Herut v. Elections Committee* (2003) P.D. 57(1) 750; Rabin and Gutfeld, "Marbury v. Madison and Its Impact on Israeli Constitutional Law," 321.

33. Ibid., 327.

34. Ibid., 325.

35. The General Limitation Clause in Article 8 of Basic Law: Human Rights and Dignity requires that infringement on the rights stipulated would be by law, and only if it is befitting the values of the State of Israel, enacted for a proper purpose, and to an extent no greater than is required. Article 4 of Basic Law: Freedom of Occupation stipulates similarly.

36. Carmi, "A Constitutional Court in the Absence of a Formal Constitution?" 75.

37. Rabin and Gutfeld, "Marbury v. Madison and Its Impact on Israeli Constitutional Law," 323–24.

38. Basic Law: Human Rights and Dignity was adopted by a vote of 32 to 31 (and one abstention); Basic Law: Freedom of Occupation was adopted by a simple majority vote of 23 to 0. Ibid., 325.

39. Carmi, "A Constitutional Court in the Absence of a Formal Constitution?" 74.

40. Ran Hirschl, "The New Constitutionalism and the Judicialization of Pure Politics Worldwide," 75 *Fordham Law Review* 721 (2006–2007), 723, 727.

41. For example, finding illegal the exemption of Yeshiva students from military service. HCJ 3267/97 *Amnon Rubinstein v. Minister of Defense*, available at http://elyon1.court.gov.il/files_eng/97/670/032/A11/97032670.a11.htm.

42. For example, requiring registration as Jews for non-Orthodox conversions carried out abroad. HCJ 1031/93 *Pessaro (Goldstein) et al. v. Minister of the Interior* (1995), P.D. 49(4) 661; HCJ 5070/95 *Na'amat v. Minister of the Interior* (2002) P.D. 56(2) 721; HCJ 2597/99 *Toshbeim v. Minister of the Interior* (2004) P.D. 58(5) 412; HCJ 2579/99 *Toshbeim v. Minister of the Interior* (2005) (unpublished).

43. For example, registration of same-sex marriage. HCJ 3045/05 *Ben-Ari v. The Director of the Population Administration in the Ministry of the Interior,* available at http://elyon1.court.gov.il/files/05/450/030/A09/05030450.a09.htm.

44. For example, reversal of decisions of the Central Elections Committee to bar Arab Israeli political leaders from participation in parliamentary elections in light of statements they made in support of the Palestinian fighting against the occupation or their accusation of incitement, support of terrorist groups and refusal to recognize Israel's right to exist. See El. Ap. 11280/02 *General Elections Committee for the Sixteenth Knesset v. MK Tibi et al.* (2002) PD 57(4) 1; Ha'aretz Service, Supreme Court overturns ban on Arab parties from national elections, *Ha'aretz* (Israel), January 26, 2009, available at http://haaretz.com/hasen/spages/1057497.html. Muslim and Christian Arabs make up about 20% of Israel's 7.4 million citizens.

45. For example, the Court's holding that an Arab family should not be denied access and membership in a Jewish settlement established as cooperative society (H.C. 6698/95, Kaadan v. Israel Lands Administration, P.D. 54(1), 258), although legally (and also ideologically) the land in Israel belongs *only* to the Jewish people as a collective and cannot be owned by individuals; the Court held that public signs placed in municipalities populated by both Jews and Arabs must also be in Arabic, although the use of Hebrew as the unified national language of the state is considered one of the main characteristics of Israel as "Jewish and democratic." HCJ 4112/99 *Adallah et al v. Municipality of Tel-Aviv-Jaffa* (2002), available at http://elyon1.court.gov .il/files/99/120/041/A10/99041120.a10.htm, See also Doron, "Judges in a Borderless State," 595–96; Hirschl, "New Constitutionalism," 738–40; Gideon Sapir, "How Should a Court Deal with a Primary Question That the Legislature Seeks to Avoid? The Israeli Controversy over Who Is Jew as an Illustration," 39 *Vanderbilt Journal of Transnational Law* 1233 (2006).

46. For example, prohibition of torture during interrogation of terrorist suspects (the torture case); invalidation of "Early Warning" military procedures by which Israeli soldiers used local Palestinian residents to arrest Palestinians suspected of terrorist activity. H.C. 5100/94, *Public Committee against Torture in Israel et al. v. the State of Israel and the General Security Service* (1999) P.D. 53(4) 817; HCJ 3799/02 *Adallah, The Legal Center for Arab Minority Rights in Israel et al v. GOC Central Command, IDF* (June 2005), available at http://elyon1.court.gov.il/files/02/990/037/A32/02037990.a32.pdf.

47. Benvenisti, "Reclaiming Democracy," 255.

48. Mark A. Graber, "A Non-Majoritarian Difficulty: Legislative Deference to the Judiciary," 7 *Studies in American Political Development* 35 (1993), 36–37; and Barzilai, "Between the Rule of Law and the Laws of the Ruler," 196.

49. Hirschl, "New Constitutionalism," 746; and Sapir, "How Should a Court Deal with a Primary Question That the Legislature Seeks to Avoid?" 1281.

50. Ruth Gavison, "The Role of Courts in Rifted Democracies," 33 *Israel Law Review* 216 (1999).

51. Only two parliaments completed full tenure years, and 62% of the governments served less than two years. Gavison, "The Role of Courts in Rifted Democracies," 246; and Adiri, "Terror in the Court," 61.

52. Aharon Barak, "Human Rights in Israel," 39 *Israel Law Review* 12 (2006), 16.

53. Aharon Barak, "A Judge on Judging: The Role of a Supreme Court in a Democracy," 116 *Harvard Law Review* 19 (2002), 28.

54. Barak, "Human Rights in Israel," 21. The Court anchored these other rights in the right to dignity, stipulated in both Basic Laws.

55. Amos N. Guiora and Erin M. Page, "Going Toe to Toe: President Barak's and Chief Justice Rehnquist's Theories of Judicial Activism," 29 *Hastings International and Comparative Law Review* 51 (2005–2006), 55 (discussing the U.S. "hands-off" approach as reflected during Chief Justice Rehnquist's tenure, also in some of the more recent and controversial cases such as *Hamdi v. Rumsfeld,* 524 U.S. 507, 2004 and *Rasul v. Bush,* 124 S. Ct. at 2686).

56. Adiri, "Terror in the Court," 91–92, 109–10. In comparison, in 1980, only 2% of the petitions to the Court were submitted by NGOs or public officials. By 1991, such petitions had risen to 13%. By 2008, the share of petitions submitted by Knesset members or human rights NGOs was 43%.

57. Jonathan Adiri, "Counter Terror Warfare: The Judicial Front," 24–25, available at www.ict.org.il/Portals/0/Articles/39793-Jonathan_Adiri.pdf.

58. HCJ Administrative Detention Appeal 10/94 *Anonymous v. Minister of Defense,* P.D. 53(1) 97 (13 November 1997); HCJ 7048/97, *Anonymous v. Minister of Defense,* P.D. 54(1) 721 (April 2000).

59. Barak, "A Judge on Judging," 29.

60. Alon Harel, "Skeptical Reflection on Justice Aharon Barak's Optimism," 39 *Israel Law Review* 261 (2006), 265, 269; and Joshua Segev, "The Changing Role of the Israeli Supreme Court and the Question of Legitimacy," 20 *Temple International and Comparative Law Review* 1 (2006), 9.

61. Assaf Meydani, "Judicial Behaviour: A Socio-Cultural Strategic Approach—Conceptual Framework and Analysis of Case Studies in Israel," 14 *Israel Affairs* 704 (2008), 717. This is the case despite the customary rule of selecting sectarian justices. Note also that although the older generation of the Court's justices were all educated in central Europe, since the mid-1970s they have all "received their education in pre-independence Palestine or post-Israel's independence" (that is, not in Europe). Kretzmer, *Occupation of Justice*, 9–10.

62. Gavison, "Role of Courts in Rifted Democracies," 236–46.

63. Doron, "Judges in a Borderless State," 588. See also Kretzmer, *Occupation of Justice*, 14–15.

64. Hirschl, "New Constitutionalism," 738.

65. Adiri, "Terror in the Court," 82; and Slaughter, "Typology of Transjudicial Communication," 99–137.

66. The Court has done so by adopting the "presumption of accord," by which it would interpret domestic legislation as conforming to Israel's international obligations (both under customary and treaty-based international law) as much as possible. Kretzmer, *Occupation of Justice*, 35; Bargaining chips case, paragraph 20; Barak-Erez, "International Law of Human Rights and Constitutional Law," 615.

67. Convention Relative to the Protection of Civilian Persons in Time of War, 1949 (hereafter: the Fourth Geneva Convention). For an historical explanation of this governmental position see Kretzmer, *Occupation of Justice*, 32–35.

68. The Court's willingness to examine the applicability of the Fourth Geneva Convention to the Occupied Territories took place only after the Oslo Agreements in 1993, when the Palestinian Authority gained full or partial control over parts of these areas. Kretzmer, *Occupation of Justice*, 40.

69. Barak-Erez, "International Law of Human Rights and Constitutional Law," 629. See for example, Paragraph 12 of the "Assigned residence" case, where the Court stipulated the questions dealing with the legality of a military order requiring Palestinian residents of the West Bank to move to the Gaza Strip for a period of two years in terms of their compatibility with international law. HCJ 7015/02 *Adjuri v. IDF Commander in West Bank* (2002) P.D. 56(6) 352.

70. The policy of targeted killing refers to the fatal shooting of subjects suspected of involvement in terrorism. It has been used by Israel, the United States, and others in the fight against terrorism and has been criticized for the derogation from one's right to a fair trial and for the extensive harm it causes, including the lives of civilians who did not participate in hostilities. Other national courts have not addressed the legality of this policy. HCJ 769/02 *Public Committee Against Torture in Israel v. Government of Israel*, available at http://elyon1.court.gov.il/files/02/690/007/A34/02007690.a34.pdf (hereafter "Targeted killing" case).

71. Barak-Erez, "International Law of Human Rights and Constitutional Law," 629.

72. Benvenisti, 242, 248, 272.

73. Since its inception, Israel has been the object of more investigation committees than any other state in the UN, and generally it has been argued that the Arab-

Israeli conflict has attracted within the UN machinery excessive amounts of time and energy while disregarding other major trouble spots around the world. Jason S. Greenberg, "Torture of Terrorists in Israel: The United Nations and the Supreme Court of Israel Pave the Way for Human Rights to Trump Communitarianism," *ILSA Journal of International and Comparative Law* 7 (2001): 539, 545; and Yehuda Z. Blum, "Israel and the United Nations: A Retrospective Overview," in *Israel Among the Nations*, ed. A. E. Kellerman et al. (Cambridge, MA: Kluwer, 1998), 69, 75.

74. Survey by NGO Monitor, "Measuring Attitudes of Israelis toward Human Rights Issues and Organizations," December 2008.

75. Targeted killing case, paragraph 17.

76. Amnon Reichman, "When We Sit to Judge We Are Being Judged: The Israeli GSS Case *Ex Parte* Pinochet and Domestic/Global Deliberation," 9 *Cardozo Journal of International and Comparative Law* 41 (2001), 64, 69–70; and Benvenisti, "Reclaiming Democracy," 244, 247, 270.

77. Reichman, "When We Sit to Judge We Are Being Judged," 73.

78. Ronen Shamir, " 'Landmark Cases' and the Reproduction of Legitimacy: The Case of Israel's High Court of Justice," 24 *Law and Society Review* 781 (1990), 795.

79. H.C. 5100/94, *Public Committee against Torture in Israel et al. v. the State of Israel and the General Security Service* (1999) P.D. 53(4) 817. See, for example, statements following the Torture case, Dan Izenburg, "Ten-Year Battle against Brutality Ends in Victory," *Jerusalem Post*, September 10, 1999, 1B, quoting Andre Rosenthal, one of the leading attorneys: "Had I dreamt of what I wanted the judges to do, I couldn't have come up with anything better." Note that the Torture case is relevant to both Palestinians in the Occupied Territories and many Arab Israelis who were interrogated by the GSS.

80. Shamir, " 'Landmark Cases,' " 796.

81. The public trust in the Court is second only to the military. Whereas a decade ago the public trust in the Court was 90%, between 2004 and 2007 it declined from 79% to 61%; the trust in the prime minister remained relatively stable (45%/43%); the trust in the Knesset is the lowest, declining in these years from 46% to 33%. Yoav Dotan, "Judicial Rhetoric, Government Lawyers, and Human Rights: The Case of the Israel High Court of Justice during the *Intifada*," 33 *Law and Society Review* 319 (1999), 325 and note 11. See also Nahum Barnea and Tova Zimuki, "With Them Again," *Yedioth Ahronoth*, Holiday Magazine, 3; and Yael Hadar, Israel Democracy Institute, "Safeguarding Democracy in Israel," April 2008, update available at www.idi.org.il/sites/english/TheGuttmanCenterSurveys/Pages/GuttmanSurvey4.aspx.

82. See cases in note 42.

83. That the Arab Israeli minority has not responded with such attacks on the Court can be explained on similar (although opposite) grounds. Unlike the Orthodox Jewish group, Arab Israelis do not enjoy any higher political and legal power; if anything, they are often more marginalized and discriminated against. Uri Misgav, "No Respect to the Sector," *Yedioth Ahronoth*, February 20, 2009, Shabbat Supplement, 12–13. Successful petitions thus grant them equal rights and civil liberties as they are

entitled to, hence strengthening, in the eyes of some, the Court's reputation as the protector of the "small citizen."

84. HCJ 5016/96 *Horev v. Minister of Transport* (1997) P.D. 51(4) 1.

85. See "Fourteenth Knesset," at the Knesset's website, available at www.knesset .gov.il/review/PrintPage.aspx?kns=14&lng=3; and Deborah Sontag, "250,000 Israeli Orthodox Hold Protest Rally, Peaceably," *New York Times*, February 15, 1999.

86. Barak, "Human Rights in Israel," 34. Deborah Sontag also describes the armed security forces surrounding the Court's building during the ultra-Orthodox demonstrations and the personal bodyguards required. Sontag, "250,000 Israeli Orthodox Hold Protest Rally, Peaceably," *New York Times*, February 15, 1999, available at www .nytimes.com/1999/02/15/world/250000-israeli-orthodox-hold-protest-rally-peace ably.html.

87. Shetreet, *Justice in Israel*, 397.

88. See note 42.

89. See Sontag, "250,000 Israeli Orthodox Hold Protest Rally, Peaceably."

90. Evelyn Gordon, "The Creeping Delegitimization Of Peaceful Protest," available at www.daat.ac.il/daat/ezrachut/english/gordon2.htm.

91. Doron, "Judges in a Borderless State," 599.

92. In 2003–2004, the public support of the military stood at 84–86%. Adiri, "Counter Terror Warfare," 35. Although this level of trust has reduced by 2008, it remains high; in a survey by NGOs Monitor from December 2008, 58% of Jewish Israelis believe the arguments raised by the IDF.

93. Doron, "Judges in a Borderless State," 596.

94. Ilan Saban, "After the Storm? The Israeli Supreme Court and the Arab-Palestinian Minority in the Aftermath of October 2000," 14 *Israel Affairs* 623 (2008), 626.

95. In a public survey carried out in August 2003 by the Mellman Group for New Israel Fund, 66% of Jewish respondents preferred protecting national security, in comparison to 46% who saw strengthening democratic values and 48% who saw promoting human rights in Israel as most important.

96. See note 46.

97. Aryeh Dayan, "A Ticking Time Bomb in the Knesset: Some 64 MKs Have Signed a Bill Specifically Authorizing the Shin Bet to Use Torture Under Certain Conditions—Despite the Fact That Israel Has Signed an International Treaty Prohibiting It," *Ha'aretz* (Israel), November 1, 1999; Uzi Mahnaimi, "Sharon to Push for Torture Law," *Sunday Times* (London), March 11, 2001; and "Overseas News; Sheetrit vs. Shin Bet Torture and 'Deri' Law," *Ha'aretz* (Israel), March 20, 2001.

98. See, for example, HCJ 6427/02, *The Movement for Quality Government in Israel v. The Knesset* (dismissing challenge to bypass law about drafting Yeshiva students to the military service), available at http://elyon1.court.gov.il/files/02/270/064/ A22/02064270.a22.pdf; dismissal of challenge to by-pass law on the Bargaining chips case. CA 6659/06 *A and B v. the State of Israel* (June 11, 2008), available at http://www.hamoked.org. See also B'Tselem's position paper on the Proposed Law:

Imprisonment of Illegal Combatants, available at www.btselem.org/Download/2000 _Hostages_Law_Position_Paper_Eng.rtf.

99. For example, shortly after the Court's 2000 ruling allowing feminist women to pray at the Western Wall, in contrast to previously held Orthodox regulation, Shas, an ultra-Orthodox party, submitted several bills to override the decision. The bills did not pass, yet following a "further hearing" in April 2003, the Court reversed itself (by a vote of 5 to 4) on the grounds that continued meetings represented a threat to public safety and order (due to the aggression of other Orthodox prayers in the area). The Court required the government to provide an alternate site, the Robinson's Arch, which was completed by October 2003. HCJ 3358/95 *Anat Hoffman et al v. Director General of the Prime Minister's Office et al.*, available at http://elyon1.court.gov.il/ files/95/580/033/F10/95033580.f10.pdf; HCJ 257/89 *Hoffman v. Western Wall Commissioner*, 48(2) PD (1994), 265; Sarah Szymkowicz, "Women of the Wall," *Jewish Virtual Library*, available at www.jewishvirtuallibrary.org/jsource/Judaism/WOW.html.

100. Carmi, "A Constitutional Court in the Absence of a Formal Constitution?" 69 and note 7; Kretzmer, *Occupation of Justice*, 187–89.

101. See, for example, the test adopted in the Targeted killing case and its critique in Michelle Lesh, "Case Notes: The Public Committee against Torture in Israel v. the Government of Israel—The Israeli High Court of Justice Targeted Killing Decision," 8 *Melbourne Journal of International Law* 373 (2007), 395.

102. Kretzmer, *Occupation of Justice*, 187–89; Orna Ben-Naftali and Keren Michaeli, "Legality of Preventing Killing," 101 *American Journal of International Law* 459 (2007), 463. See also Assigned residence case (note 74) for the Court's decision that article 49 of the Fourth Geneva Convention does not apply.

103. Kretzmer, *Occupation of Justice*, 55–56, 188. Kretzmer analyses the Court's jurisprudence in cases relating to the occupied territories from the 1967 Six-Day War to 2000. Ibid., ix.

104. HCJ 2056/04 *Beit Sourik Village Council v. Government of Israel* (2004) P.D. 58(5) 807. The governmental decision to construct the separation barrier was made after a wave of terrorist attacks against Israeli citizens and communities in 2002. It has raised significant international and national controversy, as its route is planned to be almost entirely (80%) within the West Bank itself and considering the human rights implications it has on the lives of the Palestinian residents.

105. B'Tselem, The Separation Barrier, Judgment of the High Court of Justice regarding Beit Sourik, available at www.btselem.org/english/Separation_Barrier/ Beit_Surik_Ruling.asp.

106. See note 19.

107. The estimation is that the new minister of justice, Yaakov Neeman, appointed following the change of government in February 2009, would continue Friedman's efforts for a reform. Sima Kadmon, "More Friedman Than Friedman," *Yedioth Ahronoth*, Sabbath Supplement, March 13, 2009, 4–5.

108. Saban, "After the Storm?" 625. Such attacks are not unique to Israel's Su-

preme Court. For a comprehensive discussion, see Hirschl, "New Constitutionalism," 747–51.

109. Barak, "Human Rights in Israel," 20.

110. While historically the justices often dominated the process, the selection committee's vote now requires a 7 to 2 majority, hence taking away from the judicial power.

111. Carmi, "A Constitutional Court in the Absence of a Formal Constitution?" 69; and Ron Dror, "Looking Back without Missing It," *The Lawyer* 65 (February 2007), 48.

112. Hirschl, "New Constitutionalism," 747. See, for example, after the Court's May 2009 ruling that the state fund all conversion facilities equally, whether they be Orthodox, Reform, or Conservative, Moshe Gafni, Knesset Finance Committee chairman from United Torah Judaism (an ultra-Orthodox party) was quoted as saying, "MKs are not a bunch of marionettes who will do whatever the Supreme Court tells them to do"; he added that he would "block" the implementation of the decision. Matthew Wagner, "Gafni: No Funds for Reform Conversions," *Jerusalem Post*, May 21, 2009. For a comparative perspective, see also chapter 1 in this book, discussing the many ways in which the U.S. Congress can register its displeasure with the U.S. Supreme Court.

113. Gavison, "Role of Courts in Rifted Democracies," 217.

114. See note 93.

115. Lee Epstein and Jack Knight, "Toward a Strategic Revolution in Judicial Politics: A Look Back, a Look Ahead," 53 *Political Research Quarterly* 625 (2000), 752; and Jeffrey A. Segal, "Separation-of-Powers Games in the Positive Theory of Congress and Courts," 91 *American Political Science Review* 28 (1997), 30–31.

116. Aharon Barak, *A Judge in a Democratic Society* (Jerusalem: Keter Books, 2004), 379, cited in Adiri, "Terror in the Court," 64.

117. Barak, "A Judge on Judging," 28.

118. See Justice Barak's response to questions about the ultra-Orthodox uproar against the Court: "What sense of deprivation? They are a minority in society and want to be the majority in the Court? I don't understand what sort of political theory brings that to pass." Dror, "Looking Back," 48. Translation by the author of this chapter.

119. Hirschl, "New Constitutionalism," 752.

120. Barnea and Zimuki, "With Them Again," 3.

121. The Israeli Court's ability to pressure the authorities to resolve conflicts outside of the Court (particularly in the context of the Occupied Territories) has been one of the influential effects of the Court. Whereas the overwhelming majority of the petitions that reach the Court's final decision support the government, the likelihood of a Palestinian petitioner winning an out-of-court settlement is substantially higher. Dotan, "Judicial Rhetoric," 319–63; Kretzmer, *Occupation of Justice*, 189–190; and Adiri, "Counter Terror Warfare," 35 (estimates the success rate of counter-terror petitions at 30%).

122. Benvenisti, "Reclaiming Democracy," 242.

123. Yuval Shany, "How Supreme Is the Supreme Law of the Land? Comparative

Analysis of the Influence of International Human Rights Treaties upon the Interpretation of Constitutional Texts by Domestic Court," 31 *Brooklyn Journal of International Law* 341 (2005–2006), 381.

CHAPTER NINE: Self-Regulation and an Independent Judiciary

1. Sandra Day O'Connor, "Judicial Accountability Must Safeguard, Not Threaten, Judicial Independence: An Introduction," 86 *Denver University Law Review* 1 (2008), 2. It would seem peculiar to disregard the independence of individual judges when examining judicial independence, given that judicial decisions are made by individual judges, either acting alone (as with trial court judges) or as part of panels or courts in which multiple judges render decisions in a given matter and decisions are reached by counting the individual votes of the members of the panel or court. See Irving R. Kaufman, "Chilling Judicial Independence," 88 *Yale Law Journal* 681, 713 (1979) ("The heart of judicial independence . . . is judicial individualism").

2. This chapter will focus on the federal judiciary. A survey of judicial self-regulation in fifty states is beyond the scope of this book. However, many of the same conceptual and normative issues raised by self-regulation of the federal judiciary are presented by the process of self-regulation in the states. Yet one important distinction between the federal system and some states is the election of state judges. The election of judges presents unique issues regarding judicial independence, and self-regulation procedures and dynamics are also likely to differ from the federal system in a jurisdiction where judges regulating the conduct of colleagues are themselves subject to the electoral process. One further distinction between the federal system and some states is that in certain jurisdictions both judges and nonjudges play a role in the oversight of judicial conduct. Whether this should be considered *self*-regulation is open to debate, but this marks a notable departure from the current federal system. See Edwin L. Felter Jr., "Accountability in the Administrative Law Judiciary: The Right and the Wrong Kind," 86 *Denver University Law Review* 157 (2008), 181 (discussing discipline in state judicial branches, including states where sanctions can be imposed by bodies composed of nonjudges and sometimes nonlawyers); see also James J. Alfini, Shailey Gupta-Brietzke, and James F. McMartin IV, "Dealing with Judicial Independence in the States: Judicial Independence, Accountability and Reform," 48 *South Texas Law Review* 889 (2007).

3. Prior to the Judicial Conduct and Disability Act of 1980, self-regulation of the federal judiciary operated without a statutory framework and largely rested in the hands of the Judicial Councils, which had been created decades earlier to coordinate and manage the work of the courts. For some of the history leading to enactment of the Judicial Conduct and Disability Act of 1980, see David E. Kyvig, *The Age of Impeachment: American Constitutional Culture since 1960* (Lawrence: University Press of Kansas, 2008), 196–202. The statute was amended in 1990 to make minor revisions. P.L. 101-650, Judicial Improvements Act of 1990. In 2002 the statute was again

revised and also recodified as a separate chapter in the United States Code. P.L. 107-273. The 2002 version of the law retained most of the provisions of the original stat-ute. See Arthur D. Hellman, "When Judges Are Accused: An Initial Look at the New Federal Judicial Misconduct Rules," 22 *Notre Dame Journal of Law, Ethics, and Public Policy* 325 (2008), 327. The statute currently appears in the United States Code at 28 U.S.C. § 351 *et seq.*

4. 28 U.S.C. §§ 351(a), (d).

5. 28 U.S.C. §§ 352, 353; 28 U.S.C. § 332 (composition of judicial councils). For an overview of initial review of complaints, see *Implementation of the Judicial Conduct and Disability Act of 1980*, 33–37.

6. See 28 U.S.C. § 352(b)(1)(A)(ii) (complaint may be dismissed if "directly re-lated to the merits of a decision or procedural ruling").

7. See 28 U.S.C. § 352(b)(2).

8. The Judicial Conference was created by Congress to make policy with regard to the administration of the United States courts and is comprised of the chief judge of each circuit, the chief judge of the Court of International Trade, and a district judge from each judicial circuit chosen by appeals court and district judges from that circuit, with the Chief Justice of the United States as its presiding officer. See 28 U.S.C. § 331.

9. 28 U.S.C. §§ 354(a), 355(a).

10. 28 U.S.C. § 354(a)(3).

11. The Administrative Office of the United States Courts produces an annual re-port, which includes statistics about complaints filed and action taken under the Act during the preceding year. For example, see Administrative Office of the United States Courts, *2009 Annual Report of the Director: Judicial Business of the United States Courts* (Washington, DC: U.S. Government Printing Office, 2010), Tables S-22A and 22B. In the most recent version of this report, the table reporting on complaints filed identifies categories of complainants—almost all of whom were prison inmates or litigants.

12. *Hastings v. Judicial Conference of the United States*, 829 F.2d 91, 95 (D.C. Cir. 1987).

13. *In the Matter of Certain Complaints Under Investigation by an Investigating Com-mittee of the Judicial Conference of the Eleventh Circuit*, 783 F.2d 1488, 1492 (11th Cir. 1986); *Hastings v. Judicial Conference of the United States*, 829 F.2d 91, 95–96 n.12 (D.C. Cir. 1987).

14. Hastings challenged the constitutionality of his conviction in the Senate on the grounds that a committee of twelve senators heard evidence against him, rather than the full Senate. Although a federal trial court initially ruled in Hastings's favor, and vacated the Senate's conviction, that decision was later reversed in light of a sub-sequent Supreme Court decision, *Nixon v. United States*, 506 U.S. 224 (1993), which held that the Senate's use of its power under the impeachment trial provision of the Constitution was a "political question," not subject to judicial review. *See Hastings v. United States*, 837 F. Supp. 3 (D.D.C. 1993).

15. *In re Complaint of Judicial Misconduct against United States District Judge G. Thomas Porteous, Jr. under the Judicial Conduct and Disability Act of 1980*, Order and Public Reprimand, No. 07-05-351-0085 (September 10, 2008).

16. Judicial Council of the Fifth Circuit, Docket No. 07-05-351-0086 (May 27, 2009).

17. Kent resigned from office on June 30, 2009, before the Senate could begin consideration of whether to convict him.

18. See Judicial Conference of the United States, Committee on Judicial Conduct and Disability, 517 F.3d 563 (January 14, 2008); Lara A. Bazelon, "Putting the Mice in Charge of the Cheese: Why Federal Judges Cannot Always Be Trusted to Police Themselves and What Congress Can Do About It," 97 *Kentucky Law Journal* 439 (2008–2009), 453–68 (critically discussing handling of complaints against Real); and Terry Carter, "Real Trouble: A Federal Judge's Behavior Could Move the Line between Judicial Freedom and Misconduct," *ABA Journal* (September 2008).

19. 28 U.S.C. §§ 354(a), 355(a).

20. See, for example, S. Rep. 96-362 (containing statements from Senators asserting unconstitutionality).

21. *United States v. State of Washington*, 98 F.3d 1159, 1165 (9th Cir. 1996) (Kozinski, J.) (citing concerns by members of Congress); see also Lynn A. Baker, "Unnecessary and Improper: The Judicial Councils Reform and Judicial Conduct and Disability Act of 1980," 94 *Yale Law Journal* 1117 (1985) (arguing the Act is unconstitutional).

22. U.S. Constitution, Article III, Section 1.

23. See, for example, *Northern Pipeline Co. v. Marathon Pipe Line Co.*, 458 U.S. 50, 58 (1982) ("The 'good Behaviour' Clause guarantees that Art. III judges shall enjoy life tenure, subject only to removal by impeachment"); Stephen G. Breyer, "Judicial Independence in the United States," 40 *St. Louis University Law Journal* 989 (1996), 992 (describing judges as among federal office holders subject to removal through the impeachment process set out in Article II of the Constitution and observing, "the only power of removal open to Congress is the impeachment process"); Martin H. Redish, "Judicial Discipline, Judicial Independence, and the Constitution: A Textual and Structural Analysis," 72 *Southern California Law Review* 673 (1999), 692 ("the good-behavior language must be construed as nothing more than a cross-reference to the availability of impeachment"). However, some argue that the "good behavior" standard of the Tenure Clause is not coextensive with the standard for removal of "all civil Officers of the United States," set out in Article II or suggest that judges can be removed from office through means other than impeachment. See, for example, Saikrishna Prakash and Steven D. Smith, "How to Remove a Federal Judge," 116 *Yale Law Journal* 72 (2006), 136 ("The impeachment-only argument imagines a connection that is not there because it hastily reaches a conclusion—that impeachment is the sole means of removing judges—and then seeks to read the grant of good-behavior tenure as if that grant confirmed the preconceived conclusion").

24. *McBryde v. Committee to Review Circuit Council Conduct and Disability Order of the Judicial Conference of the United States*, 264 F.3d 52, 67 n.5 (D.C. Cir. 2001) ("we

do not decide whether a long-term disqualification from cases could, by its practical effect, affect an unconstitutional 'removal'")

25. 28 U.S.C. §§ 354(a), 355(a).

26. 28 U.S.C. § 354(a)(3); see also S. Rep. 96-362 ("Although the question has never been finally settled, the Committee has respected the position that removal of federal judges by any means other than impeachment is arguably unconstitutional. Therefore, the proposed legislation is designed to avoid this important issue, and removal of federal judges short of impeachment."). Under the terms of the statute, this limitation does not appear to apply to the actions available to the Judicial Conference itself. See 28 U.S.C. §§ 354(a), 355(a). It appears, however, that the Judicial Conference has viewed itself as operating under this same constraint.

27. This view has been expressed numerous times by the Supreme Court. See, for example, *Republican Party of Minnesota v. White*, 536 U.S. 765, 795 (2002) (Kennedy, J., concurring) ("There is a consensus that the design of the Federal Constitution . . . has preserved the independence of the Federal Judiciary"); *Thomas v. Union Carbide Agr. Products Co.*, 473 U.S. 568, 583 (1984) (noting "the role of the independent judiciary within the constitutional scheme of tripartite government"); and *Northern Pipeline Co. v. Marathon Pipe Line Co.*, 458 U.S. 50, 59 (1982) (observing that the Tenure and Compensation Clauses "were incorporated into the Constitution to ensure the independence of the Judiciary from control of the Executive and Legislative Branches of government").

28. *In the Matter of Certain Complaints Under Investigation by an Investigating Committee of the Judicial Conference of the Eleventh Circuit*, 783 F.2d 1488, 1502 (11th Cir. 1986).

29. Ibid.; *Hastings v. Judicial Conference of the United States*, 829 F.2d 91, 95 (D.C. Cir. 1987).

30. *In the Matter of Certain Complaints Under Investigation by an Investigating Committee of the Judicial Conference of the Eleventh Circuit*, 783 F.2d 1488, 1508 (11th Cir. 1986).

31. Ibid., at 1505 (11th Cir. 1986).

32. Ibid., at 1510 (11th Cir. 1986).

33. *Hastings v. Judicial Conference of the United States*, 829 F.2d 91, 103 (D.C. Cir. 1987). Several years later Judge McBryde sought compensation for some of the legal fees he incurred in responding to proceedings under the Act, on the grounds that failure to reimburse him would be indirect diminution of his compensation, prohibited by the Compensation Clause. A federal court of appeals rejected his argument based on the facts of his case. *McBryde v. United States*, 299 F.3d 1357, 1367–69 (Fed. Cir. 2002). The Act was amended in 2002 to permit reimbursement of expenses incurred by a judge during investigation of a complaint that was eventually dismissed. 28 U.S.C. § 361.

34. *McBryde v. Committee to Review Circuit Council Conduct and Disability Order of the Judicial Conference of the United States*, 83 F. Supp.2d 135 (D.D.C 1999).

35. Ibid.; and *McBryde v. Committee to Review Circuit Council Conduct and Disability Order of the Judicial Conference of the United States*, 264 F.3d 52 (D.C. Cir. 2001).

36. *McBryde v. Committee to Review Circuit Council Conduct and Disability Order of the Judicial Conference of the United States,* 83 F. Supp.2d 135, 151–56, 171–78 (D.D.C 1999).

37. *McBryde v. Committee to Review Circuit Council Conduct and Disability Order of the Judicial Conference of the United States,* 264 F.3d 52, 62–63, 64–68 (D.C. Cir. 2001) (relying on former 28 U.S.C. § 372(c)(10), which provided that Judicial Conference action under the statute "shall be final and conclusive and shall not be judicially reviewable on appeal or otherwise").

38. *McBryde v. Committee to Review Circuit Council Conduct and Disability Orders of the Judicial Conference of the United States,* No. 01-1778, Brief for the United States in Opposition at 13, 14, 16.

39. *See Hastings v. Judicial Conference of the United States,* 657 F. Supp. 672, 674 (D.D.C. 1986) (listing unsuccessful requests for Supreme Court review); *McBryde v. Committee to Review Circuit Council Conduct,* 537 U.S. 821 (2002).

40. In 1975, Chandler assumed "senior status" and a reduced case load.

41. The Council later issued another order allowing Chandler to continue to sit in cases previously assigned to him.

42. *Chandler v. Judicial Council of the Tenth Circuit of the United States,* 398 U.S. 74, 82 (1970); see also Kyvig, *Age of Impeachment,* 197–99 (discussing the *Chandler* case and its aftermath).

43. *Chandler v. Judicial Council of the Tenth Circuit of the United States,* 398 U.S. 74, 84 (1970), emphasis added. At the same time, the majority observed: "There can, of course, be no disagreement among us as to the imperative need for total and absolute independence of judges in deciding cases or in any phase of the decisional function. But it is quite another matter to say that each judge in a complex system shall be the absolute ruler of his manner of conducting judicial business." This statement, however, only forecloses the most extreme view of judicial independence, under which every individual judge would be free from any oversight.

44. *Chandler v. Judicial Council of the Tenth Circuit of the United States,* 398 U.S. 74, 136–37, 140–41 (1970) (Douglas, J., dissenting).

45. Ibid., at 142 (Black, J., dissenting).

46. Ibid., at 142–43 (Black, J., dissenting).

47. As federal appeals court judge Harry Edwards has explained, "[t]he dissenting opinions in *Chandler* are important because they suggest, without apparent challenge from the Court's majority, that judicial independence protects a judge not only from external legislative and executive censors and sanctions, but also from regulation by colleagues on the bench." Harry T. Edwards, "Regulating Judicial Misconduct and Diving "Good Behavior" for Federal Judges," 87 *Michigan Law Review* 765 (1989), 769–70.

48. The *Chandler* case was one of the events that ultimately led to enactment of the Act. See Kyvig, *Age of Impeachment,* 199–200.

49. I take no position here about the details of the constitutional analyses offered

by any of the Justices in *Chandler* or by the judges deciding the *Hastings* and *McBryde* constitutional claims. For our present purposes, the most relevant question is a predictive one, about the vulnerability of the Act to future constitutional attack. My view that a facial attack on the Act is very unlikely to succeed is, of course, informed by those decisions.

50. The constitutional challenges made by Judge Hastings and Judge McBryde do not appear to have directly questioned whether Congress would have the power to itself carry out the kinds of investigations, and impose the kinds of sanctions, authorized by the Act. As a general proposition, Congress may not delegate a power that it does not itself possess. It is conceivable that a credible argument against the constitutionality of the Act could be developed along those lines—but it is beyond the scope of this chapter to develop such an argument or fully assess its viability. See Harry T. Edwards, "Regulating Judicial Misconduct and Diving 'Good Behavior' for Federal Judges," 87 *Michigan Law Review* 765 (1989), 787 ("In my view, the most significant flaw in the Act is Congress' attempt to 'delegate' power it never had.").

51. Separate and apart from the self-regulatory system created by the Judicial Conduct and Disability Act, both before and since the statute was enacted, judges have used informal efforts to resolve problems. Charles Geyh has previously argued that "informal processes serve a critical role in addressing judicial misconduct and disability." Charles Gardner Geyh, "Informal Methods of Judicial Discipline," 142 *University of Pennsylvania Law Review* 243 (1993), 312. The Judicial Conduct and Disability Act Study Committee concluded that such informal efforts mainly seek to address decisional delay, mental and physical disability, and complaints about a judge's temperament. See *Implementation of the Judicial Conduct and Disability Act of 1980*, 99–100 (identifying mechanisms and procedures outside the Act that "seek to remedy judicial misconduct or disability or prevent its occurrence"). Self-imposed standards governing recusal might be viewed as a type of semi-formal self-regulation.

52. See "History of the Federal Judiciary," available at www.fjc.gov/history/home .nsf.

53. Peter M. Shane, "Who May Discipline or Remove Federal Judges? A Constitutional Analysis," 142 *University of Pennsylvania Law Review* 209 (1993), 240.

54. See, for example, Donald E. Campbell, "Should the Rooster Guard the Henhouse: Evaluating the Judicial Conduct and Disability Act of 1980," 28 *Mississippi College Law Review* 381 (2009); Bazelon, "Putting the Mice in Charge of the Cheese"; and Geyh, "Informal Methods of Judicial Discipline," 244 and note 4 (noting argument of some that "judges cannot be trusted to judge judges"). The small number of sanctions imposed compared with the large number of complaints against judges might lead some to doubt whether self-regulation of the judiciary has been effective. But the statistics alone do not warrant such a conclusion. While disciplinary action is rarely taken, that may reflect an absence of merit to most complaints as opposed to some systemic flaw in the process of self-policing by federal judges. Moreover, most complaints are dismissed on the grounds that they relate to the merits of judicial

action taken in a case, which are addressed through the appeals process rather than disciplinary proceedings and are therefore outside the scope of the Act. See 28 U.S.C. § 352(b)(1)(A)(ii).

55. See Hellman, "When Judges Are Accused," 328.

56. See *Implementation of the Judicial Conduct and Disability Act of 1980*. For an earlier study of the Act's implementation, see Jeffrey N. Barr and Thomas E. Willging, "Decentralized Self-Regulation, Accountability, and Judicial Independence under the Federal Judicial Conduct and Disability Act of 1980," 142 *University of Pennsylvania Law Review* 25 (1993); see also Richard L. Marcus, "Who Should Discipline Federal Judges, and How?" 149 F.R.D. 375 (1993) (discussing operation of the Act).

57. *Implementation of the Judicial Conduct and Disability Act of 1980*, 2, 39, 44, 67–68. The Committee's designation of a disposition as "problematic" does not mean the Committee concluded the claim had merit. The Committee did not evaluate, or offers its views, about whether misconduct would have been found in those cases where there were procedural shortcomings in the handling of a complaint. And while the judgment is somewhat subjective, the Committee described as "high-visibility" complaints which brought public and/or legislative attention. Ibid., at 67–68.

58. See Judicial Conference of the United States, Rules for Judicial-Conduct and Judicial-Disability Proceedings, adopted March 11, 2008. For a discussion of the new rules, see Hellman, "When Judges Are Accused."

59. Legislation introduced during the 111th Congress includes S. 220 and H.R. 486, which would create an inspector general for the federal judiciary to "conduct investigations of alleged misconduct in the judicial branch" but would not have the power to punish or discipline any judge. See Mark C. Miller, *The View of the Courts from the Hill: Interactions between Congress and the Federal Judiciary* (Charlottesville: University of Virginia Press, 2009), 170–79 (discussing proposals for an inspector general for the federal judiciary).

60. The Code, enacted by the United States Judicial Conference, was first adopted in 1973.

61. Code of Conduct for United States Judges, Canon 1 (Code effective July 1, 2009), emphasis added. The commentary to Canon 1 observes, "[t]he Code is to be construed so it does not impinge on the essential independence of judges in making judicial decisions." It further observes, the Code "may provide standards of conduct for application in proceedings under . . . the Judicial Conduct and Disability Act of 1980," including "disciplinary action."

62. See *Implementation of the Judicial Conduct and Disability Act of 1980*, 73. The Committee concluded that the complaint was prematurely dismissed. Ibid., 74.

63. See ibid., 73. The Committee concluded that the complaint was prematurely dismissed. Ibid., 93. The judge both publicly apologized and was admonished, and the Committee appears to have concluded that the matter was correctly handled by the judges involved in the process. Ibid., 94–95.

CHAPTER TEN: Judicial Credibility

1. Louis Fisher, *Nazi Saboteurs on Trial: A Military Tribunal and American Law* (Lawrence: University Press of Kansas, 2003), 108–17, 134.

2. For example, *City of Boerne v. Flores*, 521 U.S. 507, 520, 530–34 (1997).

3. 3 Dall. 171, 175 (1796), emphasis in original.

4. Louis Fisher and Katy J. Harriger, *American Constitutional Law*, 8th ed. (Durham, NC: Carolina Academic Press, 2009), 43.

5. *Marbury v. Madison*, 5 U.S. (1 Cr.) 137, 177 (1803).

6. Cass R. Sunstein, "Beyond *Marbury*: The Executive's Power to Say What the Law Is," 115 *Yale Law Journal* 2580 (2006).

7. Fisher and Harriger, *American Constitutional Law*, 41–42.

8. *United States v. Peters*, 9 U.S. (5 Cr.) 115 (1809) (holding that state legislatures lack authority to interfere with the operation of the federal judicial process); *Fletcher v. Peck*, 10 U.S. (6 Cr.) 87 (1810) (holding that state legislation had violated the Impairments Clause); *Martin v. Hunter's Lessee*, 1 Wheat. 304 (1816) (establishing the Court's authority to review state court decisions involving federal questions); and *Cohens v. Virginia*, 6 Wheat. 264 (1821) (upholding the Court's authority to review a criminal case in which the state itself was a party).

9. 17 U.S. (4 Wheat.) 316 (1819).

10. *A Compilation of the Messages and Papers of the Presidents*, ed. James D. Richardson, vol. 3, 1145 (20 vols., New York: Bureau of National Literature, 1897–1925) (hereafter "Richardson").

11. *Pennsylvania v. Wheeling &. Bridge Co.*, 54 U.S. (13 How.) 518 (1852).

12. 10 Stat. 110, 112, sec. 6 (1852).

13. Cong. Globe, 32d Cong., 1st Sess. 2195–96 (1852); ibid., 967, 1038, 1042–44, 1069–70, 2216 (A).

14. *Pennsylvania v. Wheeling v. Belmont Bridge Co.*, 59 U.S. (18 How.) 421, 449 (1856).

15. *Prudential Ins. Co. v. Benjamin*, 326 U.S. 408, 425 (1946).

16. *United States v. Lopez*, 514 U.S. 549, 580 (1995).

17. *Leisy v. Hardin*, 135 U.S. 100, 125 (1890).

18. 21 Cong. Rec. 4958–59, 4964 (1890).

19. 26 Stat. 313, ch. 728 (1890).

20. Charles Evans Hughes, *The Supreme Court of the United States* (New York: Columbia University Press, 1936), 50–54.

21. *Dred Scott v. Sandford*, 60 U.S. (19 How.) 393 (1857).

22. *The Works of James Buchanan*, ed. John Bassett Moore (Philadelphia: J. B. Lippincott, 1910), vol. 10, 106.

23. Stanley I. Kutner, *The Dred Scott Decision: Law or Politics?* (New York: Houghton Mifflin, 1967), 47.

24. *Political Debates between Abraham Lincoln and Stephen A. Douglas* (Cleveland, OH: The Burrows Brothers Co., 1894), 70–71, 76–77, 78–79.

25. Richardson, vol. 7, 3210.

26. 10 Ops. Att'y Gen. 382 (1862).

27. 12 Stat. 432 (1862).

28. 8 Wall. (75 U.S.) 603 (1870).

29. Charles Fairman, *History of the Supreme Court of the United States, vol. 6, Reconstruction and Reunion, 1964–88* (New York: Macmillan, 1971), vol. 1, 716.

30. *Legal Tender Cases,* 12 Wall. (79 U.S.) 457 (1871).

31. *Pollock v. Farmers' Loan & Trust Co.,* 157 U.S. 429 (1895); and *Pollock v. Farmers' Loan & Trust Co.,* 158 U.S. 601 (1895).

32. *Hylton v. United States,* 3 U.S. (3 Dall.) 171, 175 (1796).

33. 12 Stat. 309-11, sec. 49–51 (1861).

34. *Veazie Bank v. Fenno,* 75 U.S. (8 Wall.) 533, 544, 546–47 (1869).

35. *Springer v. United States,* 102 U.S. 586, 594 (1881).

36. *Pollock v. Farmers' Loan and Trust Co.,* 157 U.S. 429, 532, 607 (1895).

37. *Lochner v. New York,* 198 U.S. 45, 75 (1905).

38. H. Rept. No. 46, 64th Cong., 1st Sess. (1916).

39. *Hammer v. Dagenhart,* 247 U.S. 251 (1918).

40. 56 Cong. Rec. 7433 (1918).

41. "Brief on Behalf of Appellants and Plaintiff in Error," *J. W. Bailey and J. W. Bailey, Collector of Internal Revenue for the District of North Carolina v. Drexel Furniture Company,* February 1922, reprinted in Landmark Briefs and Arguments of the Supreme Court of the United States: Constitutional Law (Arlington, VA: University Publications of America, 1975), 47, 54.

42. *Child Labor Tax Case,* 259 U.S. 20 (1922).

43. *Nebbia v. New York,* 291 U.S. 502 (1934). See John W. Chamber, "The Big Switch: Justice Roberts and the Minimum-Wage Cases," 1 *Labor History* 44 (1969), 57.

44. *United States v. Darby,* 312 U.S. 100 (1941).

45. *National League of Cities v. Usery,* 426 U.S. 833 (1976).

46. Fisher and Harriger, *American Constitutional Law,* 342–43.

47. David L. Faigman, *Constitutional Fictions: A Unified Theory of Constitutional Facts* (New York: Oxford University Press, 2008), 2.

48. *United States v. Lopez,* 514 U.S. 549, 554–56 (1995).

49. Ibid., 552.

50. *City of Boerne v. Flores,* 521 U.S. 507, 515 (1997).

51. *United States v. Morrison,* 529 U.S. 598, 615 (2000).

52. *United States v. Lopez,* 514 U.S. at 552 (citing *Federalist,* no. 45).

53. 1 Annals of Cong. 761 (August 18, 1789).

54. *United States v. Lopez,* 514 U.S. at 566 (citing 4 Wheat. 405).

55. *City of Boerne v. Flores,* 521 U.S. at 516 (citing 1 Cr. 176).

56. Ibid., 545–46 (citing 1 Cr. 176).

57. Ibid., 529 (citing 1 Cr. at 177).

58. Michael W. McConnell, "Institutions and Interpretation: A Critique of *City of Boerne v. Flores,*" 111 *Harvard Law Review* 153, 173 (1997).

59. *Agostini v. Felton,* 521 U.S. 203 (1997), reversing Aguilar v. Felton, 473 U.S. 402 (1985).

60. *City of Boerne,* 521 U.S. at 535–36 (citing *Marbury v. Madison*).

61. *Graves v. New York ex rel. O'Keefe,* 306 U.S. 466, 491–92 (1939).

62. Max Freedman, annot., *Roosevelt and Frankfurter: Their Correspondence* (Boston: Little, Brown, 1967), 383, emphasis in original.

63. Antonin Scalia, *A Matter of Interpretation: Federal Courts and the Law* (Princeton: Princeton University Press, 1997), 39.

64. Daniel A. Farber and Suzanna Sherry, *Judgment Calls: Principle and Politics in Constitutional Law* (New York: Oxford University Press, 2008), 5.

65. "Confirmation Hearing on the Nomination of John G. Roberts, Jr. to be Chief Justice of the United States," hearing before the Senate Committee on the Judiciary, 109th Cong., 1st Sess. (2005), 3, 299, 301.

66. "Confirmation Hearing on the Nomination of Samuel A. Alito, Jr. to be an Associate Justice of the Supreme Court of the United States," hearing before the Senate Committee on the Judiciary, 109th Cong., 2d Sess. (2006), 4.

67. "Confirmation Hearing on the Nomination of John G. Roberts, Jr.," 55, 46.

68. Ibid., 185.

69. Kathleen M. Sullivan, "Foreword: The Justices of Rules and Standards," 106 *Harvard Law Review* 22 (1992); Louis Kaplow, "Rules Versus Standards: An Economic Analysis," 42 *Duke Law Journal* 557 (1992); Antonin Scalia, "The Rule of Law as a Law of Rules," 56 *University of Chicago Law Review* 1175 (1989); Margaret Jane Radin, "Reconsidering the Rule of Law," 69 *Boston University Law Review* 781 (1989); and Pierre Schlag, "Rules and Standards," 33 *UCLA Law Review* 379 (1985).

70. 531 U.S. 98 (2000).

71. "Text of Al Gore's Speech," December 13, 2000, available at http://abcnews .go.com/print?id=122220.

72. The literature on *Bush v. Gore* is vast, but the problems with the Court's ruling are ably analyzed in Charles L. Zelden, *Bush v. Gore: Exposing the Hidden Crisis in American Democracy* (Lawrence: University Press of Kansas, 2008).

73. 147 Cong. Rec. 2457 (2001).

74. 154 Cong. Rec. S5575 (June 12, 2008).

75. "Confirmation Hearing on the Nomination of John G. Roberts, Jr.," 257, 256.

76. *Ledbetter v. Goodyear Tire & Rubber Co.,* 550 U.S. 618 (2007); Public Law 111-2, 123 Stat. 5 (2009).

77. Louis Fisher, *Religious Liberty in America: Political Safeguards* (Lawrence: University Press of Kansas, 2002), 114–22. The public law enacted in 1987 (101 Stat. 1086–87, § 508) reversed the Court's opinion in *Goldman v. Weinberger,* 475 U.S. 503 (1986).

78. Sandra Day O'Connor, *The Majesty of the Law: Reflections of a Supreme Court Justice* (New York: Random House, 2003), 44, 45, 47.

79. William Howard Taft, "Criticism of the Federal Judiciary," 29 *American Rev.* 641 (1895), 642–43.

Conclusion

1. Further, as some scholars have noted, one of these aspects of judicial independence may actually be decreased in the course of augmenting the other. Joseph L. Smith, "Judicial Procedures as Instruments of Political Control: Congress' Strategic Use of Citizen Suits," 31 *Legislative Studies Quarterly* 283 (2006) (discussing how Congress employs judicial procedures as instruments of political control).

2. To take a different example, while state judicial elections would seem to reduce the judiciary's autonomy from the public, scholars have suggested that this connection may not have much impact on judges' decisionmaking, underscoring the potential importance of the subjective sense of independence. Melinda Gann Hall and Chris Bonneau, *In Defense of Judicial Elections* (New York: Routledge, 2009).

3. Bruce Peabody, "Congress, the Court, and the "Service Constitution: Article III Jurisdiction Controls as a Case Study of the Separation of Powers," 2006 *Michigan State Law Review* 269 (2006), 291 (discussing how the Jenner-Butler bill was perceived as a significant threat to judicial independence despite, ultimately, its somewhat modest substance).

4. See chapter 1 in this volume for a discussion of different "tiers" of threats to the judiciary.

5. Sanford Levinson, "How Many Times Has the United States Constitution Been Amended? (A) < 26; (B) 26; (C) 27; (D) > 27: Accounting for Constitutional Change," in *Responding to Imperfection: The Theory and Practice of Constitutional Amendment*, ed. Sanford Levinson (Princeton: Princeton University Press, 1995).

6. Joseph L. Smith, "Congress Opens the Courthouse Doors: Statutory Changes to Judicial Review under the Clean Air Act," *Political Research Quarterly* (March 2005).

7. "House Considers Impeachment of Federal Judge," Associated Press, November 17, 2009.

8. "State Courts at the Tipping Point," editorial, *New York Times*, November 24, 2009.

9. Hon. Margaret H. Marshall, "At the Tipping Point: State Courts and the Balance of Power," The Benjamin N. Cardozo Lecture, New York City Bar Association, November 10, 2009.

10. President Barack Obama, "Remarks by the President to the Travel Pool Aboard Air Force One," April 28, 2010, available at www.whitehouse.gov/the-press-office/remarks-president-travel-pool-aboard-air-force-one.

Index

Abbe, Owen, 164

Aborigines, 182–84. *See also* native title rights cases (Australia)

abortion, 53–54, 56, 103, 115; constitutional meaning and, 111; electoral accountability and, 73; questionnaires and, 153; Republican Party and, 121–22; *Roe v. Wade* and, 5, 111, 154, 248

Abrahamson, Shirley, 157–58

accountability, 4, 73, 160, 224

activist judges. *See* judicial activism

Adair v. United States (1908), 114

Adams, Abigail, 77

Adams, John Quincy, 78, 82, 83

Aderholt, Robert, 103

Administrative Office of the U.S. Courts, 30

advertising, 127, 155–58, 161, 165, 294n49; Australian political, 182

Afghanistan, 121, 176

African Americans, 85, 234–35

Agricultural Adjustment Act (1938), 138

Akin, Todd, 103

Alabama, 90

Alabama Supreme Court, 154, 156–57

Alaska, 150

Alito, Samuel, 11, 56, 96, 146, 245

American Bar Association (ABA), 104–5, 148–49, 167, 184

American Judicature Society, 105

Anderson, James, 156–57

Annenberg Public Policy Center, 160

announce clause, 152–53, 160

Antarctic Science, Tourism, and Conservation Act (1996), 28

Appellate Committee of the House of Lords, 178–79

appointment process. *See* selection of judges

Arkansas, 90, 162

asylum, 176

attacks on courts, 9–10, 58–61, 73, 250, 254; in Australia, 169–72, 180; in democracies, 209; global, 193, 194, 195; in Great Britain, 169–72; impeachment and, 100; in Israel, 205, 208; judges/judiciary and, 20, 21, 42, 119–22; judicial elections and, 154–58; as symbolic, 101, 120

attitudinal model, 47

Australia, 168–69, 179–91; attacks on courts in, 169–72, 180, 190, 191; bill of rights of, 181, 187–88, 189–90; implied rights cases and, 180, 181–86; native title rights cases and, 180, 181, 183–84, 186–91; preferential balloting procedure of, 182

Australian Capital Territory (ACT), 187, 189, 191

Australian Labor Party (ALP), 189

autonomy of judges, 22, 27, 106–7, 249, 251; budgets and, 253; power and, 32, 108

Baer, Harold, 24, 33

ballots (Australia), 182

Barak, Aharon, 192, 194, 201; activism of, 197; Bargaining chips case and, 202; on branches of government, 209; constitutional revolution and, 197, 198–99, 205, 208; on international law, 204

Barak-Erez, Daphne, 204

Bargaining chips case (Israel), 202, 206

Baschab, Pam, 157

Basic Laws (Israel), 192, 196, 198–99, 201, 300n1, 302n35

Bates, Edward, 91, 235

Beit Sourik case, 207
Benesh, Sara, 159, 160
Benjamin, Brent, 148–49, 166
Bickel, Alexander, 31, 69–70, 273n9
Biden, Joseph, 245–46
bill of rights: Australian, 181, 187–88, 189–90; constitutional amendments and, 25; lack of Israeli, 196, 198
Bipartisan Campaign Reform Act (2000), 113
Bird, Rose, 8
Black, Hugo, 52, 222, 223, 240
Blackie, Fergus, 170
Blackmun, Harry, 129, 131, 240, 288n22
Blair, Tony, 172
Blankenship, Don, 148, 292n6
Blichner, Lars, 171, 179, 190
Bonneau, Chris, 151
Borbidge, Bob, 185
Boumediene v. Bush (2008), 246, 265–66n54
Bracks, Steve, 189
branches of government, 1, 68–69, 99, 218, 240; conflict between, 226; constitutional interpretations and, 229, 231; interactions among, 106–8, 116–17; Israeli, 194, 195, 209; judges as independent of, 228; judicial review and, 111; separation of powers and, 14–15; Van Buren and, 84
Brandenburg, Bert, 103
Brennan, William, 52
Brennan Center for Justice, 147–48, 151, 154, 160, 161, 167; public funding and, 163
Breyer, Stephen, 55, 104
bribery, 215
bridge cases, 231–32, 234
British courts, 172–79, 187, 203; Australia and, 181, 191. *See also* Great Britain
Brown, Gordon, 172, 177
Brownback, Sam, 103, 122, 245
Brown v. Board of Education (1954), 5, 7, 50, 53, 115
Brutus, 4, 76
B-2 bomber strategy for Court curbing, 128–29
Buchanan, James, 85, 234–35
Buckley v. Valeo (1976), 113, 163
budgets, 28–29, 30, 118, 267n70; Congress and, 38, 109; court power over own, 39–40; of

Federal Judiciary, 263n29; judicial autonomy and, 253; threats to cut, 33
Burger, Warren, 130, 221–22
Burger Court, 46, 48, 52–54
Bush, George W., 33–34, 39, 56, 60, 226, 246, 265n52; criticisms of court by, 8; enemy combatants and, 61, 121; religious conservatives and, 116; signing statements and, 95
Bush v. Gore (2000), 159, 246
Butler, Pierce, 138
Byrnes, James, 240

Calabresi, Steven, 94–95
California, 37, 167, 292n12
California Supreme Court, 8
Callender, James, 77, 276n36
Cambodia, 169
Cameron, Charles, 107–8, 111
Cameron, David, 176
campaign expenditures, 113, 151–52, 292–93n17; independent, 164; judicial reform groups' concerns about, 154–56; legitimacy and, 161
campaigns, 98. *See also* elections; judicial elections
Campbell, Naomi, 176
Canberra, Australia, 190
Cann, Damon, 160
Caperton v. A. T. Massey Coal Co. (2009), 157
Carr, Bob, 189
Carter, Jimmy, 53, 70, 273n13, 280n92
case assignments, 102–3, 209, 220; rule of four and, 197, 201; suspension of, 218
celebrity trials, 175–76
Center for Judicial Independence, 105
Chandler, Stephen S., 221–23, 314nn40, 41
Charter of Citizenship and Aspirations (Australia), 189
Charter of Human Rights and Responsibilities (Australia), 188
Chase, Samuel, 4, 36, 77–80, 229, 230, 276n36, 277n45
Chaudhry, Iftikhar Muhammad, 170–71
Chavez, Hugo, 169
checks and balances on courts, 117–18, 126; in Israel, 209

Child Labor Act (1916), 113

child labor legislation, 113, 228, 238–40, 247

Choate, Joseph H., 237

Cicero, 201

Citizens United v. Federal Election Commission (2010), 8–9, 11, 113, 287n70

City of Boerne v. Flores (1997), 242–43, 245

civil rights, 56, 168, 251; in Australia, 179

Civil Rights Act (1964), 113

civil war, 234–35

Clark, Tom, 6, 123

Class Action Fairness Act (2005), 28, 29

Clinton, Bill, 108, 226

Code of Conduct for United States Judges, 225–26, 316n61

common law (Israel), 195–96

common law nations and critiques of courts, 168, 169. *See also* Australia; Great Britain

Commonwealth Constitution (Australia), 179–82

communication in courts-Congress disputes, 23–41, 130; tier one, 23, 36–41; tier two, 23, 24–31; tier three, 23, 31–35

Communists, 49, 50–51, 53

compensation clause, 217–18, 219, 220, 313nn27, 33

complaints against judges, 214–17, 225–26, 311n11; disciplinary action and, 215, 218, 222, 315n54, 316n61

confidence in Supreme Court, 132–35, 158–61. *See also* public opinion

confidentiality, 220

Congress, 110, 206, 254; anti-court rhetoric and, 45–46, 122; attacks on Court by, 54–64, 123, 135–38, 142, 240–44; *Brown v. Board* and, 115; child labor legislation and, 238–40; court checking powers of, 4, 45; court-curbing legislation by, 48–54, 103–4; as deferential to courts, 120; delegation of power by, 315n50; elections and, 127–30, 151; Hastings and, 216; healthcare reform and, 282n105; impeachment and, 109, 223, 224; interpretation of Constitution by, 46, 50–51, 58, 261n5; Jeffersonians and, 79; judges' terms and, 252; judicial finality and, 228, 231–34, 246; judicial self-regulation

and, 225; minority interests in, 115; New Deal Democrats in, 140–41; party agendas and, 57; polarization of, 55, 57; power of, 15–16, 22–23, 45; presidents and, 17, 107–8; public opinion and, 131–32, 135–38, 158, 159; Schiavo case and, 102; signing statements and, 94–96; slavery and, 234–35; Supreme Court decision-making and, 46–48, 49; taxes and, 236–37; veto bargaining and, 111–13. *See also* court-curbing legislation; courts-Congress conflicts

Congressional Accountability for Judicial Activism Act (2005), 128–29

conservatives/conservatism, 3, 59, 136, 291n60; attacks on courts by, 9–10; religious, 56, 115–16, 121. *See also* Democratic Party; liberals/liberalism; Republican Party

constitution, lack of in Israel, 193, 196, 198, 210

Constitution, U.S., 209, 262n7, 315n50; First Amendment of, 49, 50–51, 113, 153, 220, 222; Tenth Amendment of, 241–42; Fourteenth Amendment of, 243, 251; Sixteenth Amendment of, 237; amendments to, 25, 112, 237, 243, 279n63; Article III of, 6, 37, 40, 48, 217, 218, 221; congressional interpretations of, 46, 50–51, 58, 261n5; congressional powers outlined in, 45; crisis of 1937 and, 132, 289n29; Jackson and, 81; judicial self-regulation and, 217–24; sanctity of, 74, 80; silences of, 89–90; Van Buren and, 82. *See also* interpretation of U.S. Constitution; statutes

constitutional amendments, 112, 243, 279n63; in Australia, 185, 187; judicial rulings and, 25; taxes and, 237

Constitutional Convention of 1787, 41, 107

Constitutional Deliberation in Congress (Pickerill), 112

Constitutional Reform Act (2005) (Great Britain), 177–78

constitutional reforms (Great Britain), 172, 177–78

constitutional revolution (Israel), 197, 198–99, 205, 208

Constitution Restoration Act (2004), 59, 120

contested elections, 148, 155, 161

Convention for the Protection of Human Rights and Fundamental Freedoms (HRA), 173–77, 179, 297n15; Australia and, 181, 187, 191

Corrigan, Maura, 152

corruption, 83, 148–49, 169

Corwin, Edward, 139

Council of Europe, 173

countermajoritarian problem (Israel), 203

countermajoritarian problem (U.S.), 69–70, 114, 116, 204, 273n9

counterterrorism, 201; in Israel, 203, 206, 207, 211. *See also* terrorists

court-curbing legislation, 5, 6–9, 119, 250, 254; elections and, 127–29; as electoral posturing, 124–25, 136; Jefferson and, 75–80, 97; judges' behavior and, 252; judicial legitimacy and, 142–44; jurisdiction-stripping and, 46, 48–54, 100, 103–4, 105; New Deal Democrats and, 140; periodicity of, 144–45; public opinion and, 126–31, 132–35, 141–42; statutes and, 47, 75

court-packing. *See* Roosevelt's Court-packing plan

court-packing in Venezuela, 169

courts, U.K.: transfer of power from Parliament, 177–178

courts, U.S., 17, 27–28, 168; appeals courts and, 219; child labor legislation and, 238–40; Congress' power to check, 4, 45; disestablishment of, 33, 40, 42; federal, 3, 48, 59; international context of, 191; legitimacy and, 165–67; public opinion of, 161–65; relative independence of, 105–6, 117

courts-Congress conflicts, 19–44; tier one, 23, 24–31; tier two, 23, 31–35; tier three, 23, 36–41

credibility. *See* judicial credibility

credit-claiming, 124, 127, 287n2

Criminal Justice Act (2003), 176

criminal law, 49, 52

critical commentary, 20, 102, 250–51; by Congress, 24–25, 45–46; by courts, 29

Cross, Frank, 106, 118

Dahl, Robert, 72, 113–14

Daily Mirror, The, 176

Daily Show with Jon Stewart, The, 68

death penalty, 58

decisions. *See* judicial rulings

Declaration of Independence (Israel), 300n1

Defense of Marriage Act (1996), 103

DeLay, Tom, 11, 24, 32, 33, 59

democracies, contemporary, 194–95, 209

Democratic Party, 9–10, 122, 278n63; *Brown v. Board* and, 115; in Congress, 60; court-curbing legislation and, 133; Jackson and, 20, 83; New Deal and, 140–41; party platforms of, 5–6; Southern Democrats and, 55–56, 115; Van Buren and, 84–85, 90, 92. *See also* conservatives/conservatism; liberals/liberalism; Republican Party

departmentalism, 69–70, 97, 110

Department of Constitutional Affairs, 174

desegregation, 5, 49

Detainee Treatment Act (DTA) (2005), 61–63

Devins, Neal, 45, 111

Dickinson, Jess, 158

diffuse support for courts, 125, 138, 142, 144, 287n2

disciplinary action against judges, 215, 218, 222, 315n54, 316n61. *See also* good behavior; impeachment; removal of judges

disestablishment of courts, 40, 42

disestablishment of judgeships, 37

diversity jurisdiction, 27–28

Dole, Robert, 32

Douglas, Michael, 175

Douglas, Stephen, 85–86, 234

Douglas, William O., 51–52, 222–23, 240

Dred Scott v. Sanford (1857), 234–35, 251; Lincoln and, 85–87, 91–92; Van Buren and, 85

ECHR (European Convention on Human Rights), 173–75, 187

Edmunds, George, 233

Eisenhower, Dwight, 107

elections, 89, 109, 273n8, 279n63; Australian, 182; Congressional, 127–30, 151; 1824 presidential, 83. *See also* campaign expenditures; judicial elections

electoral politics, 90–91, 116, 121, 123, 146; accountability and, 73; attacks on courts and, 120; loyal opposition and, 98; selection

of judges and, 87–89. *See also* campaign expenditures
emergency powers, 201
Employment Division v. Smith (1990), 242
enemy combatant cases, 54, 61, 121
England. *See* Great Britain
English Civil War, 74
enumerated powers and the Court (U.S.), 241–42
enumerated rights (Australia), 180, 191
Environmental Protection Agency (EPA), 28
Equal Access Act (1984), 53
Equal Rights Amendment (1972), 48
Erdman Act (1898), 114
European Convention on Human Rights (ECHR), 173–75, 187
European Court on Human Rights, 173
European Union, 211
Evans, Gareth, 189
executive branch, 95, 97, 158; in Great Britain, 178; judiciary relations with, 15, 74, 213. *See also* presidential power; presidents

facial challenges, 220, 314–15n49
factions, 82, 85, 280n84; in Israel, 206
Fair Labor Standards Act (1938), 240
Family Research Council, 59
Farber, Daniel, 244
Federal Constitutional Appeals Court (Australia), 185
federal courts. *See* courts, U.S.
Federal Farm Bankruptcy Act (1934), 138
federalism, 57, 115; Australian principles of, 180; judges and, 69–70
Federalist Papers, 12–14, 16, 32, 179
Federalists, 20, 82, 85; impeachment of, 229–30; Jefferson and, 76–79; judges, 37
federal judiciary. *See* judges/judiciary
Feldman, Daniel, 208
Field, Stephen, 237
First Amendment, 49, 50–51, 113, 220, 222; announce clause and, 153. *See also* Constitution, U.S.
Fisher, Keith R., 149
Fisher, Louis, 101, 110, 227
flag burning, 129
Florida, 90, 151, 161

Florida Bar Association, 151
Florida Family Policy Council, 154
Fourteenth Amendment, 243, 251
fragility of courts, 13
Frankfurter, Felix, 51, 52, 139, 240, 244
free speech, 49, 50–51, 113, 220, 222; announce clause and, 153. *See also* First Amendment
Friedman, Barry, 4
Frist, Bill, 59

Gant, Scott, 41, 213
Gavison, Ruth, 203, 208
General Security Service (GSS), 206, 306n79
Geneva Conventions, 203, 305n68
Georgia, 22, 90, 151
Georgia Supreme Court, 152
Geyh, Charles, 19, 143, 153, 282n1, 315n51
Gibson, James, 161
Gingrich, Newt, 32
Goldberg, Arthur, 51–52
Goldman, Simcha, 247
good behavior standard and judicial service, 12–13, 312n23; Article III of Constitution and, 217, 218; Chase and, 79; DeLay's criticism of, 24; Jefferson and, 75; removal of judges and, 215. *See also* disciplinary action against judges; impeachment
Gore, Al, 60, 226, 246
Graber, Mark, 17, 114
Gray, George, 233
Great Britain, 168–69, 172–79, 187, 203; attacks on courts in, 169–72; Australia and, 181, 191; as model for Israel's legal system, 209
Greenhouse, Linda, 288n22
green paper on Human Rights Act (1998), 177
Grier, Robert, 232, 235
Guantanamo Bay, 61
Gun-Free School Zones Act (1990), 35
guns, 35, 241
Gutfeld, Arnon, 198

habeas corpus proceedings, 33, 61–62, 250
Hague Regulations, 203
Hamdan v. Rumsfeld (2006), 61, 96
Hamilton, Alexander, 12–13, 16, 32, 149
Hamiltonians, 82

Hand, Learned, 248

Harlan, John Marshall, 51, 52

Harrison, John, 94–95

Hastings, Alcee, 215–16, 218, 219–20, 221, 224, 311n14; constitutional challenges by, 315n50

Hatch, Orrin, 246

hate crimes legislation, 113

Hawaii, 149

healthcare reform, 98, 282n105

Heffernan, Bill, 186

Hellman, Arthur, 121

Hello! magazine, 175

Helvering v. Davis (1937), 139

Hepburn v. Griswold (1870), 235

Herrnson, Paul, 164

High Court of Justice (HCJ) (Israel), 193, 302n23

Hirschl, Ran, 203

Hitler, Adolf, 226

Holmes, Oliver Wendell, 238

home secretary, 176

Horton, Willie, 157

House Judiciary Committee, 24, 36–37

House of Lords, 172, 174, 178–79

House of Representatives, 39, 41, 56, 279n63; child labor legislation and, 238; court-curbing legislation and, 54; elections in, 83, 127–28; Hastings and, 216; impeachment and, 21–22; Kent and, 217; New Deal Democrats in, 140–41; Pledge Protection Act and, 103

House of Representatives (Australia), 189

Howard, John, 186

Hubbard, Carroll, 129–30

Hughes, Charles Evans, 138, 234, 240

human rights, 193, 198; Israel and, 199, 201, 204–5, 207–8, 211, 300n1

Human Rights Act (1998) (Great Britain), 172

Human Rights Act (2004) (Australia), 187–88

Human Rights Consultative Committee (Australia), 189

Human Rights Watch, 169

Hylton v. United States (1796), 229

Illinois Supreme Court, 151, 152, 156

impeachment, 8, 36–37, 73, 118, 249, 261n4; attacks on courts and, 100; Chase and, 4, 36,

77–80, 229, 230, 276n36, 277n45; Congress and, 109, 223, 224; Douglas on, 222; of Federalists, 229–30; good behavior and, 312n23; Hastings and, 215–16, 218, 219–20, 221, 224, 311n14, 315n50; Jefferson and, 70, 75–80, 97; judges' behavior and, 252, 253; judicial self-regulation and, 226; Kent and, 217; Musharraf and, 170; public opinion on, 43; tenure clause and, 217; threats of, 21–22, 32–33, 103, 119, 122; Warren Court and, 22. *See also* removal of judges

impeachment clause, 221

"Impeach Warren" campaign, 8

implied constitutional powers, 241

implied rights cases (Australia), 180, 181–86, 190, 191

income tax, 163; invalidation of federal, 234, 236–37

independence of individual judges, 214, 219, 310n2, 314n43

independence of judiciary, 214, 218. *See also* judicial independence

interest groups, 10, 59; in Israel, 202; judicial elections and, 151–53; questionnaires and, 153–54

International Covenant on Civil and Political Rights, 187, 188

international law, 54, 197, 203–4, 211–12. *See also* Australia; Great Britain; Israel

interpretation of law (Israel), 206

interpretation of U.S. Constitution, 25, 30, 71–72, 83, 228, 236; branches of government and, 229, 231; child labor legislation and, 238–40; Congressional, 46, 50–51, 58, 261n5; vs. constitutional construction, 110–11; economy and, 238; enumerated powers in, 241–42; Jackson and, 69, 88, 231; Jefferson and, 69, 76–78; judicial finality and, 246; judicial supremacy and, 70, 243–44; Lincoln and, 86–90; Reagan and, 69, 93–96

interstate commerce, 113, 232–33

Iowa, 232–33

Iraq, 60, 121

Ireland, 178

Israel, 301n9, 305n70; branches of government in, 194, 195, 209; human rights and, 199,

201, 204–5, 207–8, 211, 300n1; terrorists and, 200, 206, 308n104. *See also* Supreme Court, Israeli
Israel Bar Association, 196
Israeli Supreme Court. *See* Supreme Court, Israeli

Jackson, Andrew, 22, 39, 80–85, 97, 277n49; constitutional interpretation and, 69, 88, 231; Lincoln and, 86, 87, 88; objectives of, 99; opposition and, 92; political realignment and, 20; presidential vetoes and, 95
Jackson, Howell, 237
Jackson, Robert, 240
Jacksonian Democracy, 150
Jefferson, Thomas, 20, 21, 70, 75–80, 82, 97; Chase and, 4; constitutional interpretation and, 69, 76–78; *Dred Scott* ruling and, 87; judicial review and, 81; Lincoln and, 86, 88; majoritarian politics and, 89; *Marbury* and, 87; Marshall and, 230; objectives of, 99; Van Buren and, 82, 83
Jeffersonians, 79, 80–81
Jenner, William E., 50
Jenner bill, 51
Johnson, Andrew, 37
Jones, Charles O., 109
Judaism, 199–200, 205, 247, 303n45
judgeships, 26–27; elimination of, 79; expansion of, 38, 280n92
judges/judiciary, 11, 30, 79, 84; attacks on, 20, 21, 42, 119–22; attacks on in other nations, 169–72, 176, 180, 205, 208; authority of, 32, 70, 72–75, 92, 108, 120; autonomy of, 22, 27, 32, 106–107, 249, 251, 253; canons of, 152–53, 165; Code of Conduct for U.S., 225–26, 316n61; complaints against, 214–17, 218, 222, 225–26, 311n11, 315n54, 316n61; deference of, 229–31; executive branch and, 37, 69–70; immunity of, 12; independence of individual, 214, 310n2, 314n43; legal rules made by, 16; neutrality and, 80, 92–94, 245–46; public concerns expressed by, 252–53; state, 12, 149–59, 310n2, 320n2; terms of, 10, 12, 21, 75, 150, 252; as umpires, 245–46; unelected, 75, 76; vocabulary of, 229, 245. *See also* judicial credibility; judicial

independence; judicial review; judicial rulings; legitimacy; public opinion; selection of judges
judicial activism, 2, 64, 98–99, 120, 269n19; in Australia, 185; in *Bush v. Gore,* 60; impeachment threats and, 21, 32–33, 68, 185; in Israel, 192, 197, 204, 208–12; O'Connor on, 68
Judicial Appointments Commission, 178
Judicial Committee of the Privy Council, 178–79
Judicial Conduct and Disability Act (1980), 27, 41, 213, 214, 310n3; congressional impeachment and, 224–26; constitutionality of, 217–24; Study Committee of, 225, 315n51
Judicial Conference of the United States, 29, 34, 214, 311n8, 313n26; Kent and, 216–17; policy positions in, 30
Judicial Councils, 27, 215–16, 220, 221, 310n3
judicial credibility, 227–48; child labor laws and, 228, 238–40; contemporary court-congress clashes and, 240–45; deference to elected officials and, 228–31; finality and, 231–34; vs. legitimacy, 227; self-inflicted wounds and, 234–48
judicial elections, 147–67; advertising and, 155–58, 161, 165, 294n49; attacks on courts and, 154–58; campaign expenditures and, 151–52; contested, 148, 155, 161; court legitimacy and, 148–49, 160, 161, 165–67; new politics of, 147, 149, 150–54, 154–58; nonpartisan, 150, 159, 160, 162, 165; partisan, 150, 151, 159, 160, 161, 162, 165; public perception of state courts and, 158–61, 161–65; retention, 150, 159, 161, 292n12; states' process of, 149–50, 158–61, 161–65, 320n2
judicial independence, 42; meaning of, 14–17, 105–6; traditional understanding of, 12–14
judicial review, 16, 30–31, 41, 76, 81; branches of government and, 111; as countermajoritarian, 69–70; vs. court-curbing, 48–49; exploitation of, 34–35; in Great Britain, 174–76; in Israel, 197, 198–99, 208; lesser restrictions on, 28; *Marbury* and, 150, 198–99; New Deal Democrats and, 140; proposals to eliminate, 250; supporters of, 114–15; Van Buren and, 84

judicial rulings, 23–24, 30, 39; constitutional amendments and, 25; enforcement of, 143; finality of, 228, 231–34, 239, 246–47; overturned, 261n6; presidents and, 68. *See also under individual cases*

Judicial Selection Committee (Israel), 196

judicial supremacy, 73, 243–44, 274n20; vs. institutional interdependence, 109–11; Lincoln and, 87; Marshall and, 229–31; presidents and, 69–70, 71, 97; slavery and, 234

Judiciary Act (1789), 27, 78, 81, 84

Judiciary Act (1801), 79

Judiciary Committee, 129

Judiciary Reorganization Bill (1937), 139

juridification, 168; Australia's rights-driven, 180–91; dimensions of, 171–72; through implied rights (Australia), 181–86; through institutional reform, 177–79; of political order, 171; through rights documents, 186–91; through rights protection (Great Britain), 173–77

jurisdiction stripping, 41, 48–54, 250, 263n27, 275n24; manipulation of, 33–34; Republicans and, 59–60. *See also* court-curbing legislation

Justice at Stake Campaign, 103, 154, 161, 167

Kansas-Nebraska Act (1854), 85

Karmeier, Lloyd, 156

Katzmann, Robert, 30

Kay, Amy, 103

Kelleher, Christine, 160

Kennedy, Anthony, 11, 24, 232, 242–44

Kent, Samuel B., 216–17

Kentucky, 154, 157

Kentucky Resolution, 77

King, Carolyn Dineen, 263n29

King, Rufus, 236

King, Steve, 33

Kirby, Michael, 184–85, 186

Klarman, Michael, 115

Knesset (Israeli legislature), 195–96, 300n1; human rights groups and, 207; judicial review of, 208; parliamentary supremacy in, 200; public trust in, 306n81

Koschnick, Randy, 157–58

Kramer, Larry, 4

Kretzmer, David, 207

Kruger, Alec, 182

Kruger v. Commonwealth (1997), 182

Labor Party (Australia), 187, 190

Labour Party (Great Britain), 172, 173

laissez-faire economics, 237–38, 240

Lasser, William, 131, 145

Law Lords, 176, 179

Leahy, Patrick, 246

Least Dangerous Branch, The (Bickel), 273n9

Ledbetter, Lilly, 247

Ledbetter v. Goodyear Tire and Rubber Co. (2007), 247

legal realism, 42–43, 93

Legal Tender cases, 234–35

legislating from the bench, 8–9, 32, 120, 157

legislation: legislative supremacy and, 109; presidential veto and, 112–13; repealing outdated, 116. *See* Congress; Knesset (Israeli legislature)

Legislative Deferrals (Lovell), 114

legitimacy, 142–44, 227; elections as conferring, 273n8; in Israel, 210; judicial elections and, 148–49, 160, 161, 165–67; *White* and, 160–61

legitimacy theory, 125–26, 131, 142, 145–46

Leonard, Gerald, 83

Levinson, Sanford, 251

Lewis, Ron, 128

Liberal Party (Australia), 187, 189

liberals/liberalism, 9–10, 136–38, 141–42, 290n39, 291n60. *See also* conservatives/conservatism; Democratic Party; Republican Party

Liberia, 169

Lincoln, Abraham, 69, 70, 85–92, 97, 234–35; first inaugural address of, 86, 89, 279n78; interpretation of Constitution by, 86–90; objectives of, 99; opposition and, 98

liquor, 232–33

Litigation Strategy Working Group, 95

Lochner v. New York (1905), 238

Louisiana, 90, 161

Louisville Democrat, 86

Lovell, George, 114

loyal opposition, 71, 74, 82, 98

Maag, Gordon, 156
Mabo, Eddie, 183
Mabo v. Queensland (1992), 183–85
Madison, James, 75, 81, 83, 230, 241
Maine, 149
Majesty of the Law, The (O'Connor), 243, 248
majoritarian politics, 89–91, 273n8; judicial
    review and, 115
majorities, dynamic, 92
Marbury, William, 230
Marbury v. Madison (1803), 76, 150, 198–99,
    229–30; enumerated powers and, 242; Jef-
    ferson and, 87; Kennedy and, 243; Marshall
    and, 78–79, 232
Marriage Protection Act, 103, 120
Marshall, John, 4, 39, 76, 277n49; Jackson
    and, 80; judicial supremacy and, 229–31;
    Marbury and, 78–79, 232
Marshall Court, 20, 76, 79
Mason, Anthony, 181
Massachusetts Supreme Court, 253
Massey Coal Company, 148, 157, 164, 166
maximum-hour provisions, 240
Mayer, William, 165
Mayhew, David, 124, 127
McBryde, John, 216, 218, 220, 221, 224, 313n33;
    constitutional challenges by, 315n50
McCain, John, 98
McCarthyism, 98
McCloskey, Robert, 253
McConnell, Michael, 243
McConnell v. Federal Election Commission
    (2003), 113
McCulloch v. Maryland (1819), 83, 87, 231, 242
McGraw, Warren, 148
McLean, John, 232
McReynolds, James, 138
media, 234–35; advertising and, 127, 155–58,
    161, 165, 182, 294n49
media (Australia), 181–82
Meese, Edwin, III, 93, 95, 280n87
merit selection, 160
message politics, 56–57
Michigan, 161
Michigan Supreme Court, 152
military (Israel), 200, 204, 205, 206, 209;
    public opinion of, 306n81, 307n92

military (U.S.), 247
Military Commission Act (MCA) (2009), 61–62
military tribunals, 34, 61, 266n54
Miller, Mark, 104, 109
Miller, Samuel, 235
Miller, Zell, 56
minimum wage, 138, 139, 240
ministry of Australia, 180
minority groups, protection of in Israel, 200
minority interests, 115
Miranda v. Arizona (1966), 51–52
misconduct, judicial, 217, 221, 224–25, 316n57;
    disciplinary action and, 215, 218, 222,
    315n54, 316n61
Mississippi, 90
Mississippi Supreme Court, 158
Missouri, 90
Mizrahi Bank v. Migdal (1995), 198
mobocracy, 77
Molander, Anders, 171, 179, 190
Monroe, James, 83
Moore, Roy, 59, 156
Mugabe, Robert, 170
multiparty politics, 195, 208
Murphy, Frank, 240
Murphy, Walter, 51, 110
Musharraf, Pervez, 170–71
Mussolini, Benito, 226

Nagel, Stuart, 124
National Industrial Recovery Act, 138
National Native Title Tribunal (Australia), 184
National Right to Life Committee, 59
national security (Israel), 193, 200, 202, 206,
    307n86
national security (U.S.), 49
native title rights cases (Australia), 180, 181,
    183–84, 186–91
Nazi Saboteur Case (1942), 228
Neeman, Yaakov, 308n107
Neustadt, Richard, 107, 109
New Deal legislation, 20, 22, 48, 265n52;
    Democrats and, 140–41; judicial authority
    and, 70; public opinion and, 141; during
    Roosevelt's first term, 138–40, 141–42. *See
    also* Roosevelt, Franklin Delano; Roosevelt's
    Court-packing plan

New Hampshire, 149, 253
New Jersey, 149
New South Wales (NSW), Australia, 187
newspapers, 234–35
Nixon, Richard, 52
nonpartisan elections, 150, 159, 162; legitimacy
    and, 160; public opinion and, 165
normalization of court-Congress relations, 20, 21
North Carolina, 90, 154, 162, 163
Northern Territory, Australia, 185

Obama, Barack, 3, 11, 41–42, 163, 254, 287n70;
    criticisms of courts by, 8, 122; healthcare
    reform and, 282n105; loyalty of opposition
    and, 98; selection of judges by, 99; signing
    statements and, 281n99; statutory reversal of
    Court by, 247
obstructions of justice, 216
Occupied Territories, 203, 206, 207, 305n68,
    306n79
O'Connor, Sandra Day, 73, 104, 121, 146, 214,
    242–43; branches of government and,
    68–69, 99; campaign expenditures and, 152;
    judicial finality and, 232, 248; Project on the
    State of the Judiciary and, 104
Office of Legal Council (OLC), 93, 95
Omnibus Judgeship Act (1978), 273n13
opposition, 75, 76, 79, 97–98; loyal, 71, 74, 82,
    98; stable, 78, 80; Van Buren and, 92
originalism, 93, 99, 280n87
Owen, Robert, 239

Pakistan, 169, 170, 171
Palestinians, 201, 207, 300n3, 306n79, 308n104
Panner, Owen, 29
Parker, Tom, 157
Parliament (Australia), 181, 186
Parliament (Great Britain), 172, 174, 175;
    Criminal Justice Act and, 176; transferral of
    power to courts from, 177–78
Parliament (Israel), 195, 198, 200. *See also*
    Knesset (Israeli legislature)
partisan elections, 150, 151, 159, 162; legitimacy
    and, 160, 161; public opinion and, 165. *See
    also* judicial elections
partisan interests, 93
party competition, 74

party platforms, 5–6, 8, 42, 57
passive virtues, 31
Peck, James, 36
perjury, 216
Personal Responsibility and Work Opportunity
    Reconciliation Act (1996), 108
petitions, 221, 302n23; filed by Palestinians,
    300n3
Pickering, John, 230
Pickering, Thomas, 36
Pledge of Allegiance, 10, 34, 54, 56, 59–60, 103;
    public opinion and, 129
Pledge Protection Act (2005), 9–10, 103, 120
political communication (Australia), 182–83
political neutrality, 80
political policy (Israel), 199–203
political realignment, 19–21, 42, 272n6
Pollock v. Farmers' Loan and Trust Company
    (1895) 261n6, 317n31, 318n36
popular sovereignty, 83, 85, 86, 253; Jefferson
    and, 77, 78; Lincoln and, 89–90, 91
Populists, 20, 21, 22
Porteous, G. Thomas, 216
position-taking by members of Congress, 124,
    127, 136, 287n2
Posner, Richard, 117
presidential power, 20, 68–99, 109; Jackson
    and, 69, 80–85; Jefferson and, 69, 70,
    75–80; Lincoln and, 69, 70, 85–92; Reagan
    and, 69, 70, 71–72, 92–96; signing state-
    ments and, 93–96, 99, 281n99, 281n100;
    Van Buren and, 80–85; vetoes and, 95,
    107–8, 111–13
presidents, 83; Congress and, 17, 107–8;
    departmentalist, 97; judicial rulings and, 68,
    228; judicial supremacy and, 69–70, 71, 97.
    See also under individual presidents
private censures, 215, 218
Progressives, 20, 21, 22
Prop 187, 167
public censures of judges, 215, 218
*Public Committee against Torture in Israel et al. v.
    the State of Israel,* and the General Security
    Service (1999), 206
public opinion, 125–46, 289n25, 290n39;
    Congress and, 131–32, 135–38, 158, 159;
    corruption and, 148–49; Court-curbing

legislation and, 126–31, 132–35, 141–42; of courts, improving, 161–65; as determinate of attacks on courts, 145–46; of HRA, 175; impeachment and, 43; of Israeli military, 306n81, 307n92; Israeli Supreme Court and, 205; judges' knowledge of, 214, 219, 310n2; judicial elections and, 158–61, 161–65; judicial politics and, 131–41; of Knesset, 306n81; legitimacy and, 142–44; legitimacy theory and, 125–26; Roosevelt's Court-packing plan and, 138–42; of state courts, 158–61; of Supreme Court, 132–35, 144–45, 158–61; *White* and, 153
public policy (Israel), 197, 199–203, 210

Queensland government (Australia), 183–85
questionnaires, judicial, 153–54

Rabin, Yoram, 198
Radical Republican Congress, 37
rational choice theory, 109–10
Reagan, Ronald, 56, 71–72, 92–96, 280n87, 280n92; constitutional interpretation and, 69, 93–96; Court-curbing and, 53; objectives of, 99; religious conservatives and, 116; selection of judges by, 70
Reagan administration, 273n13
Real, Manuel, 217, 262n15
Reconstruction, 22, 37, 251
Reed, Stanley, 240
regulations, 172; economic, 247
Rehnquist, William, 35, 55, 225
Rehnquist Court, 54, 57, 58–61
religious activists, 103
religious apparel, 247
religious conservatives, 56, 115–116, 121
Religious Freedom Restoration Act (RFRA) (1993), 241, 242–43
removal of judges, 12, 27, 40–41, 218; Bird and, 8; good behavior and, 215; judicial self-regulation and, 226; Real and, 217; without impeachment, 288n19, 313n26. *See also* impeachment
representative government (Australia), 181, 182
Republican Party, 3, 9–10, 55, 82; court-curbing legislation and, 133; disestablishment

of judgeships by, 37; *Dred Scott* and, 87; in House of Representatives, 41; Jefferson and, 20; jurisdiction stripping and, 59–60; party platforms of, 5–6; Reconstruction and, 251; religious conservatives and, 56, 115–16, 121–22. *See also* conservatives/conservatism; Democratic Party; liberals/liberalism
Republican Party of Minnesota v. White (2002), 153, 160–62
rescue provisions, 163
retention elections, 150, 159, 161, 292n12. *See also* judicial elections
rhetoric, hostile, 73–75, 86, 123–25; periodicity of, 145–46
rights of blacks, 234–35
rights protection (Great Britain), 173–77, 191
Roberts, John G., Jr., 11, 80, 99, 104, 245, 246; confirmation hearings of, 56; on criticism, 247
Roberts, Owen, 22, 48, 138, 265n52
Roberts Court, 54, 146
Rockefeller Republicans, 55
Roe v. Wade (1973), 5, 111, 154, 248
Roosevelt, Franklin Delano, 20, 21, 48, 69, 138–40, 142; court composition and, 238–40; Frankfurter and, 244
Roosevelt, Theodore, 237
Roosevelt's Court-packing plan, 21, 22, 37–38, 265n52; court composition and, 238–40; failure of, 70, 73; lessons from, 50; public opinion and, 138–42; as threat, 33. *See also* New Deal legislation
Rosenbaum, James, 29
Rosenberg, Gerald, 124, 142, 143
Rottman, David, 166
Rudd government, 190–91
rule of four, 197, 201
rule of law, 253
Rules Committee (House of Representatives), 129

salaries of judges, 30, 109
same-sex marriage, 54, 56, 59–60, 61, 121, 153; electoral accountability and, 73
same-sex sodomy, 58
Sandra Day O'Connor Project on the State of the Judiciary, 104

Scalia, Antonin, 55, 96, 153, 244
scalpel strategy for court-curbing, 128
Schiavo, Terri, 28, 54, 59, 102, 120
school busing, 53, 129–30, 131, 275n24
school prayer, 53, 115
Scott, Will T., 157
Scrutiny of Legislation Committee (Australia), 187
secession, 78, 90–91
Second Bank of the United States, 83, 84, 88
sectarian seat (Israel), 196, 302n21
Sedition Act (1798), 76–77
See, Harold, 156
selection of judges, 6, 26, 48, 109, 250; in Australia, 187; electoral politics and, 87–89; in Great Britain, 178–79; in Israel, 196; by Obama, 99; presidential power and, 20, 68, 109; public opinion of courts based on, 159–60; by Reagan, 70; Republicans and, 10; states' judicial selection and, 149–50, 310n2, 320n2. See also judicial elections
self-regulation of courts, 27, 41, 213–26, 315n51, 315n54; constitutionality of, 217–24; current system of, 214–17; implications of for judicial independence, 224–26; in states, 310n2
Senate, 140–41, 159, 216; elections and, 127, 128, 151; selection of judges and, 26, 109
Senate Judiciary Committee, 11
Sensenbrenner, James, 27
Sentencing Commission, 55
separation of powers games, 109–10
separation of powers system, 14–15, 100–122, 117; in Great Britain, 178; interconnections in, 106–8; inter-institutional nature of, 108–17; in Israel, 203; judicial self-regulation and, 219, 226; limits within, 119; recent attacks on courts and, 102–6; rethinking judicial independence in, 117–19
September 11th, 2001, 200
sexual minorities, 186, 200
Shamgar, Meir, 201
Shelby, Richard, 103
Sherry, Suzanna, 244
sieges. See attacks on courts
signing statements, 93–96, 99, 281n100; Obama and, 281n99
Sixteenth Amendment, 237

slavery, 234–35, 279n78; electoral accountability and, 73; Lincoln and, 89–90
social issues, 58–61
Social Security Act (1935), 139
Sotomayor, Sonia, 99
Souter, David, 29
South Carolina, 81, 90
South Dakota, 161
Southern Democrats, 55–56, 115
Southern lawmakers, 50, 53
specific support of court rulings, 125, 287n2. See also diffuse support for courts
Specter, Arlen, 245
Spencer, Herbert, 238
Stanhope, Jon, 189
state courts, 11, 40, 231; judges/judiciary in, 12, 149–50, 310n2, 320n2; legitimacy of, 148–49; public opinion of, 158–61; self-regulation of, 310n2. See also under individual state
State of the Union addresses, 8, 11, 287n70
statutes, 110; in Australia, 182–84; Basic Laws and (Israel), 198; congressional interpretation of, 109; Court authority on, 30, 242, 244; court-curbing legislation and, 47, 75; in Great Britain, 177; invalidating, 229–30, 233, 235, 239, 240; judicial self-regulation and, 214–15, 218–20; liquor transportation and, 233; reversal of, 25, 49, 247; signing statements and, 94; veto bargaining and, 108, 112
Steward Machine Co. v. Davis (1937), 139
Stewart, Jon, 68
Stokes, Jerry, 157
Stone, Harlan Fiske, 240
Strasbourg court, 173, 174, 175
strategic model of judicial decision-making, 47. See also attitudinal model
Straw, Jack, 176–77
Stumbo, Janet, 157
subject matter jurisdiction, 33–34, 38–39
Sun, The, 176
Supreme Court, Israeli, 192–212, 306n81; accessibility of, 197; empowerment of/resentments against, 197–204; international law and, 203–4; law-making capacity of, 202; lessons from judicial activism in, 208–12; political and legal context of, 195–97; political and public policy involvement by,

199–203; responses to judicial activism in, 204–8

Supreme Court, U.K., 172, 177–179, 191

Supreme Court, U.S., 124, 268n79; accountability and, 4; appellate jurisdiction of, 15; attacks on by Congress, 54–64, 123, 135–38, 142; case assignments and, 102–3, 197, 201, 209, 218, 220; Congressional preferences and, 46–48, 49; enemy combatants and, 61, 121; Georgia's defiance of, 22; international law and, 211; judges' terms and, 10, 12, 21, 75, 150, 252; judicial finality and, 70, 71, 86, 231–34, 246; legitimacy of state courts and, 148–49; liberal decisions of, 136–38; Lincoln and, 86; military tribunal appeals to, 61; Obama and, 42; party policy agendas and, 57; Pledge Protection Act and, 10; political realignment and, 20; presidential power and, 71; public opinion of, 132–35, 144–45, 158–61; Republican appointments to, 3; self-inflicted wounds by, 234–38; subject matter jurisdiction and, 39. *See also* interpretation of U.S. Constitution; Presidential power; Roosevelt's Court-packing plan; *and under specific cases*

Supreme Court Appointments Commission (Great Britain), 179

Sutherland, George, 138

Swayne, Charles, 36

Taft, William Howard, 248

Tal Law (1998), 207

Taney, Roger B., 70, 234; Lincoln and, 87, 88, 91–92; Van Buren and, 85

Tasmania, 188

Tasmanian Law Reform Institute, 188

taxes, 163, 234, 236–37

Teles, Steven, 10

Ten Commandments, 34, 54, 56, 59, 103

Tennessee, 90

Tenth Amendment, 241–42

tenure clause, 217–18, 312n23, 313n27

Terri Schiavo bill, 120. *See also* Schiavo, Terri

terrorists, 176, 267n72, 304n46, 305n70; counterterrorism and, 201, 203, 206, 207, 211; Israel and, 200, 206, 308n104

Theophanous v. Herald and Weekly Times Ltd. (1994), 182

Thomas, Clarence, 11, 96

threats to judiciary, 20, 102–6; continuum of, 250–51; vs. critical commentary, 25; following through on, 36; of impeachment, 21–22, 32–33, 103, 119, 122; real vs. imagined, 105, 106, 118

Tjoflat, Gerald Bard, 29

transnational judicial dialogue, 194, 203, 211

trial lawyers, 151, 156–57

two-party system, 82

tyranny, 117

Uganda, 169

umpire metaphor, 245–46

United Kingdom, 173, 174

United Kingdom Supreme Court, 172, 177–79, 191

United Nations, 204, 305–6n73

United States, 2, 171, 194, 305n70; international law and, 204

U.S. Bank, 231, 242, 279n74

Van Buren, Martin, 80–85, 81, 278n63; Democratic Party and, 84–85, 90, 92; majoritarian politics and, 89, 90–91; opposition and, 92

Van Devanter, Willis, 138, 139, 141, 240

Venezuela, 169–70, 171. *See also* Chavez, Hugo

vetoes: bargaining with, 108, 111–13; judicial, 111–13; presidential, 95, 107–108, 111–113

Victoria, Australia, 188, 189, 191

violence, 245

Violence Against Women Act (1994), 35, 241

Virginia, 90

vocabulary of judges, 229, 245

voter equality (Australia), 182

Wales, 178

Wallace, George, 52

war on terror, 33–34, 39, 121, 266n54

Warren, Earl, 20, 50, 51–52

Warren Court, 21, 46, 48, 49–54; Congress and, 55; vs. contemporary court, 57; impeachment proposals during, 22

Washington Supreme Court, 152

Watergate scandal, 93

Wayne, James, 232

Webster, Peter D., 154

welfare reform bills, 108
Wells, H. Thomas, Jr., 104–5
Wenzel, James, 159, 160
Wersal, Greg, 153
West Coast Hotel v. Parrish (1937), 139
West Virginia, 150, 166
West Virginia Supreme Court, 148, 157, 164
We the People Act, 103, 120
Wheeling bridge, 231–32
Whig Party, 20, 82
White, Mark, 154
White case. See *Republican Party of Minnesota v. White* (2002)
white paper on Constitutional Reform Act (2005), 177
Whitewater Independent Counsel, 226
Whittington, Keith, 110, 115, 277n45

Wik Peoples v. The State of Queensland, The (1996), 183, 185
Wisconsin Supreme Court, 157
Wolak, Jennifer, 160
women, 35, 241, 245, 308n99
Wood, Gordon, 275n27
Worcester v. Georgia (1832), 80, 81, 87, 277n49
writ of certiorari, 196–97

Yates, Jeff, 160
Yeshiva students, 205, 207
Yosef, Ovadia, 206

Zardari, Asif, 170–71
Zeta-Jones, Catherine, 175
Zimbabwe, 169, 170, 171